Deploying Cisco Unified Contact Center Express

Michael HouTong Luo, CCIE# 6183

Copyrights

ISBN-13: 978-1-329-18462-6

Warning and Disclaimer

This book is designed to provide information about the Cisco Unified Contact Center Express. Every effort has been made to make this book as complete and as accurate as possible, but no warranty or fitness is implied.
The information is provided on an "as is" basis. The author shall have neither liability nor responsibility to any person or entity with respect to any loss or damages arising from the information contained in this book or from the use of the discs or programs that may accompany it.

Trademark Acknowledgments

All terms mentioned in this book that are known to be trademarks or service marks have been appropriately capitalized.
Author cannot attest to the accuracy of this information. Use of a term in this book should not be regarded as affecting the validity of any trademark or service mark.

About the author

Michael HouTong Luo, CCIE No. 6183 (Routing/Switching, Collaboration) has more than 20 years in IT industry across multiple countries. Michael is specialized in large-scale network design and Unified Communications. Michael has achieved many certifications such as VMware, Oracle, Microsoft, Juniper and Avaya. Another book published by Michael was "Deploying Cisco Unified Presence" (ISBN-13: 978-0-557-03953-1).

Author's Contact
houtong@gmail.com
http://htluo.blogspot.com/

Chapter 1 Preface

Why I wrote this book

When I started my job at Cisco TAC in 2006, information on Contact Center Express is very scarce. Training partners do have training classes. But those classes focus on scripting other than system design, installation, integration, or troubleshooting.

Don't we have Cisco documentations? Yes we do. But we all know how product manuals work. They tell you what each piece of the product does. But they don't tell you how to put different pieces together to achieve a specific goal.

I've been wanting to write a book on Contact Center Express since then. But I've been procrastinating due to job, family and other stuff.

Now it's 2015. I'm surprised to see no book has yet been published on this topic. I decided to start writing this book to finish something that I wanted to do many years ago.

This book is not meant to be the bible or encyclopedia of UCCX. It only covers the "core function" of UCCX. What makes this book different from Cisco's configuration guide is – configuration guide is more "menu driven" while this book is more "task driven". Configuration guide tells you what each menu in the software does. This book tells you what you have to do to achieve a specific goal.

This book was written based on CUCM version 10.5.1.11900-13 and UCCX version 10.5.1.10000-24.

Who this book is for?

This book is mainly for system integrators who want to set up UCCX quickly and configure specific functions. I assume the readers have basic knowledge of CUCM and contact center terminologies such as agents, IVR, etc.

I wrote this book with my personal time. Due to limited time and resource, I am pretty sure there will be errors or mistakes in this book. Please kindly send me your feedback to my email at houtong@gmail.com, regardless it was typo, grammar, functional mistakes or suggestions.

A brief history of UCCX

Cisco Unified Contact Center Express (a.k.a. UCCX) has many different names in history:

- IPIVR – Internet Protocol Interactive Voice Responder
- CRA – Customer Response Application
- CRS – Customer Response System
- IPCC Express – Internet Protocol Contact Center Express
- CCX – Contact Center Express
- UCCX – Unified Contact Center Express

Interesting enough, different components of UCCX were developed and supported by different companies. For example, Cisco has been developing the "CCX Engine" while Spanlink (now Calabrio) has been developing the "Desktop Suite" (Cisco Agent Desktop, Cisco Supervisor Desktop, etc.). Cisco TAC front ends all support tickets. But the "Desktop Suite" cases might end up in Spanlink/Calabrio support (behind the scene though).

You will notice some "inconsistencies" on naming conventions, log formats, and DNS requirement, etc. between the "core" components and "desktop" components.

Also, different UC products (such as CUCM and UCCX) are being developed by different teams in parallel, without a unified architect from beginning. Though Cisco was trying to make the installation process and administration interface look similar, but in fact they are very different and sometimes confusing.

Understanding some basic concept will help you understand the dependency between products and guarantee a successful integration.

What is UCCX

What on earth is UCCX? Well, instead of throwing you a definition full of technical jargons or marketing pitches, let's begin with some real life use cases.

When you call into a bank's customer service hotline (usually referred as "800 Numbers"), you usually hear a welcome prompt like *"Thanks for calling ABC Bank. For English, please press 1. For Spanish, please press 2."* After selecting the language, you might be asked to choose the service you want, enter your account number, etc. etc. Then finally, you either get what you want from the automatic response system (e.g. your account balance), or you are transferred to a live person (agent).

This is a common use case of a Contact Center system. Some other vendors may use the term "Call Center" versus "Contact Center" because majority of the functions are voice calls related. But call handling is just part of the function for UCCX. That is why Cisco refers it as "Contact Center" versus "Call Center". We will cover the details in corresponding chapters.

Assumptions

To avoid turning this book into an encyclopedia, we will have to make some assumptions.

1. You have a compatible version of CUCM installed or you know how to install one. Please refer to cisco.com for compatibility information between different versions of UCCX and CUCM.
2. You know the basic operation of CUCM, such as activating services, creating users and devices, , assign roles and permissions, etc.
3. You understand the difference between "Application Users" and "End Users".
4. You have a DNS server and you know how to create A records (forward lookup) and PTR records (reverse lookup).
5. You have some basic scripting knowledge if you were to look into UCCX scripting.

Reference Lab

In this book, we'll use a reference lab as illustrated below.

- CUCM publisher/subscriber, UCCX (Contact Center Express), CUP (IM & Presence) are all in the same LAN
- Two CUCM end users: Agent1 and Agent2
- Three Cisco 7965 IP phones: two of them are being used as agent phones and have two lines configured. First line 1xxx is a regular line. Second line 7xxx is an "ICD line" (dedicated for Call Center). The third phone is to emulate a customer phone and has only one line configured 1003.
- Three computers are running Windows 7. Two of them have Cisco Agent Desktop running. The third computer (SPARE) can be used for any other applications such as Supervisor Desktop, etc.

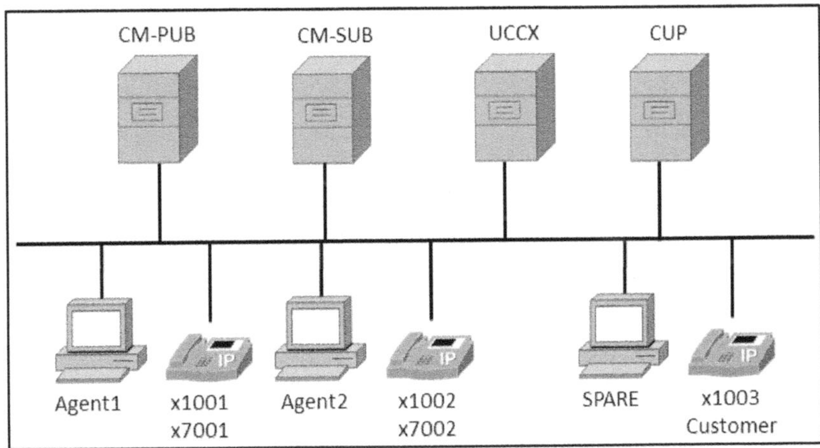

Figure 1-1 Reference Lab

Chapter 2 Installation

Preparation

There is a saying that "Success = 90% preparation + 10% execution". Before you spinning the UCCX installation CD, there is some preparation work need to be done on CUCM, DNS. Some information needs to be collected such as IP addresses, usernames, passwords, etc.

The list below will help you prepare the CUCM, DNS and collect necessary information.

1. DNS Server IP Address	Pre-existing
2. NTP Server IP Address	Pre-existing
3. UCCX Server Name	New
4. UCCX Server IP Address	New
5. UCCX Server Subnet Mask	New
6. UCCX Server Default Gateway	New
7. UCCX Server "Platform" username/password	New
8. UCCX Server "Security" password	New for the first UCCX server
9. UCCX Server "Application" username/password	New
10. CUCM Publisher IP Address	Pre-existing
11. CUCM AXL username	Pre-existing or create new
12. CUCM AXL password	Pre-existing or create new
13. CUCM End User name (UCCX Admin Candidate)	Pre-existing or create new
14. UCCX License File (Optional)	May use the built-in 60-day demo license

DNS Server

UCCX server itself does not require DNS. But the desktop components (Cisco Agent Desktop, Script Editor, etc.) by default resolve UCCX server by hostname. Thus Cisco makes DNS a mandatory requirement during installation.

On DNS server, you should have A and PTR records created for UCCX server. Below are some examples of the A and PTR records.

If you don't have DNS set up properly, you might not be able to use some of the features on the desktop components.

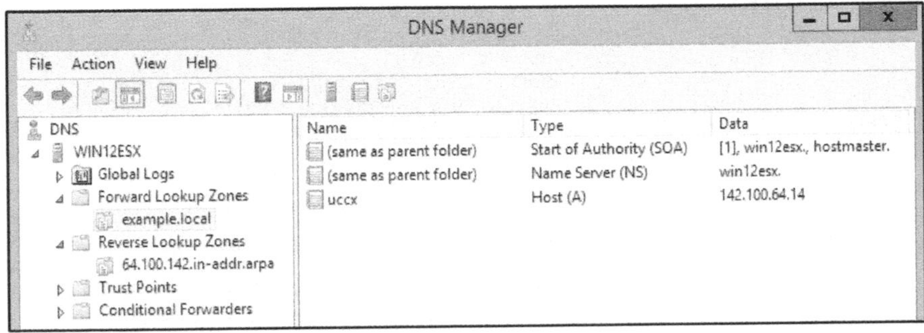

Figure 2-1 DNS Forward Lookup Zone

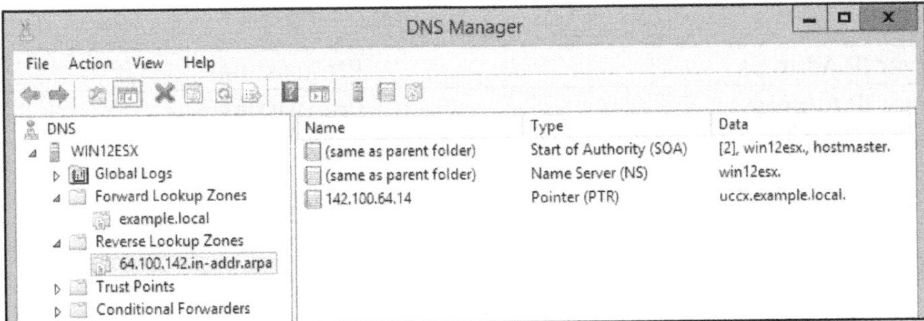

Figure 2-2 DNS Reverse Lookup Zone

NTP Server

NTP Server is usually a router or server in your network. You may use any NTP server that is accessible from UCCX. My personal preference is to use CUCM as the NTP server if possible, because:

1) If you have a CUCM, it can serve as a NTP server. You don't have to find another NTP server.
2) Having UCCX time sync up to CUCM time makes it easy to cross reference logs in troubleshooting

Application, Platform and Security Passwords

During UC application installation (e.g. CUCM, CUPS, UCCX, Unity Connection), you are usually asked for three passwords:

- Application Username and Password
- Platform Username and Password
- Security Password

In a "unified" world, shouldn't we have one single sign on (SSO) password? Well, yes and no. For security and maintenance purpose, Cisco unified communication products usually have three different passwords for different purposes. We'll explain each one of them from the most commonly to the least commonly used.

Application username/password

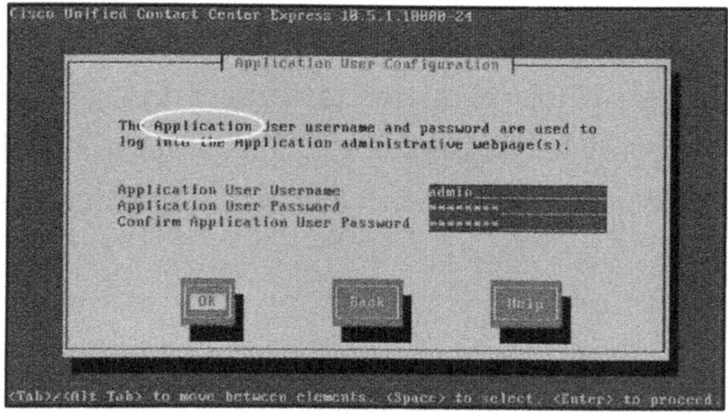

Figure 2-3 Application Administrator

Application credential is the most commonly used credentials. You will use this credential to manage the application, such as modify user capabilities, create triggers, customer service queues, scripts, etc. This credential is stored in the application's database (Informix). It is also referred as "CCX Admin" in web GUI.

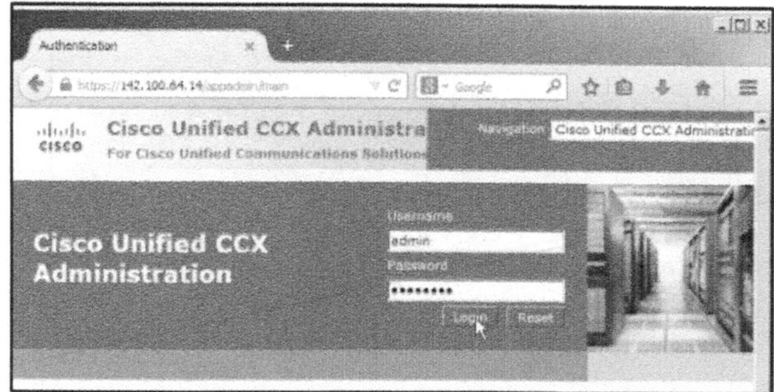

Figure 2-4 Application Administration Login

Platform username/password

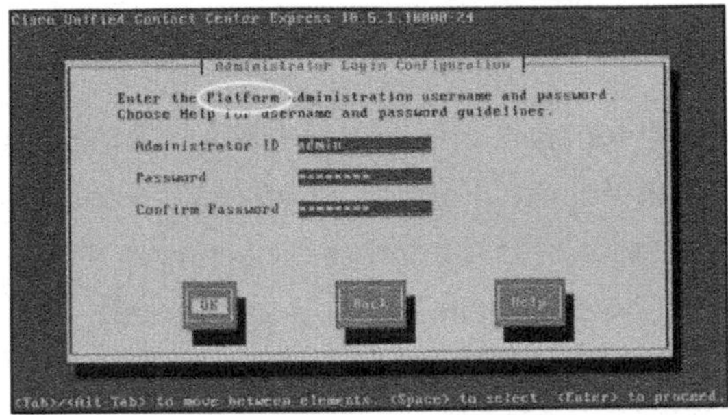

Figure 2-5 Platform Administrator

Platform credential is used for platform related tasks, such as log into command line interface (CLI), disaster recovery backup/restore, change network configuration, change NTP configuration, etc. This credential is stored in Linux user account file (/etc/passwd).

Please note:

1. This credential is also referred to as "OS Admin" or "Operating System Admin" in the web GUI.
2. Platform credential is different from application credential. They are stored in different locations. You may give them the same username and password. But they are still two separate accounts. Changing the password of one account won't change it on the other.

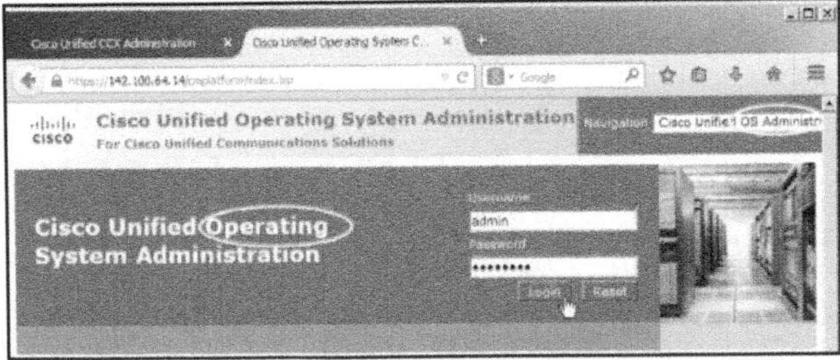

Figure 2-6 Platform (OS) Administration Login

Security password

Security password is used for server-to-server communications within the same product family.

Products in the same family need to have the same security password for backend communication. For example, all CUCM servers should have the same secret password in the same cluster so they can synchronize their configuration.

Products in different families don't use security password to communicate. They use AXL credentials. For example, the secret password on UCCX server doesn't have to be the same as CUCM. However, the primary and secondary UCCX server (in High-Availability model) should have the same secret password.

Please know that some different families have been consolidated into one family. For example, CUP (Cisco Unified Presence) used to be a standalone product. Now CUP has joined the CUCM family, thus required to share the same secret password with other CUCM servers.

During installation, one of the frequently asked questions is – "Is this server the First Node in the cluster"? This is a little bit confusing because the definition of "cluster" is very vague.

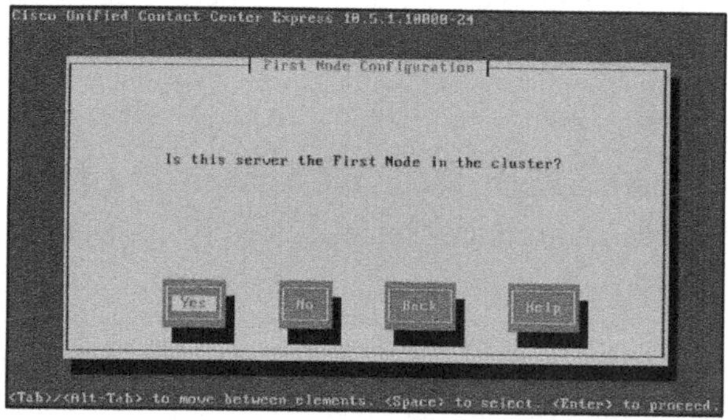

Figure 2-7 First Node in Cluster

This question should be rephrased as "Is this the first UCCX (or CUCM, or Unity) node in the cluster?"

If you answered "Yes", you have the freedom to choose a secret password. You may use any password you like because you are installing the first server of its kind in the cluster.

If you answered "No", you will be asked to enter the pre-existing secret password configured on the "first node".

The chart below should help you understand what secret password to use in what scenario. Please note this chart is based on UC release 10.5.

You are installing …	Secret Password to Use
CUCM Publisher (First node)	New password
CUCM subscriber(s)	Security password previously configured on CUCM Publisher
IM and Presence server (CUP)	Security password previously configured on CUCM Publisher
First UCCX server	New password
Secondary UCCX server	Security password previously configured on first UCCX server
First Unity Connection server	New password
Secondary Unity Connection server	Security password previously configured on first Unity Connection server

AXL Credential

In UC Application integration, you are always asked for the "AXL username/password". What is AXL and why we need that for integration?

AXL stands for **A**dministrative **X**ML **L**ayer. It is an Application Programming Interface (API) provides a mechanism for inserting, retrieving, updating, and removing data from the database by using an eXtensible Markup Language (XML) Simple Object Access Protocol (SOAP) interface. This allows a programmer to access Cisco Unified CallManager data by using XML and receive the data in XML form, instead of using a binary library or DLL.

In English, the AXL credential is a key to access the database of a different product. (To access the database of the same product, "secret password" is used instead of "AXL credential")

With AXL, not only the application can read the foreign database, but also it can write data to the database (i.e. change the configuration). Generally speaking, anything you can do from within the Admin web GUI can be done via AXL by an application.

When integrating UC applications (such as UCCX, CUPS, etc.) with CUCM, some provisioning and synchronization need to be done on CUCM, such as:

- Creating special accounts on CUCM (e.g. jtapi and rmcm users for UCCX)
- Creating devices on CUCM (e.g. CTI ports for UCCX, voice messaging ports for Unity)
- Retrieving user list from CUCM (e.g. UCCX users, CUPS users)

With AXL, all the above can be done from one single place (e.g. UCCX) versus two different places (UCCX and CUCM). This makes integration more streamline and easier.

CUCM AXL account is not a system generated (default) account. You'll have to create it manually. You may share the same CUCM AXL account with multiple UC applications. Or you may create one AXL account for each applications (if security or audit is your concern).

Following are the steps to create AXL account on CUCM. You may skip this part if you already know how to do that.

The best practice is to create an Access Control Group. Then create the account and assign it to the group.

Create a group called "AXL Group"

Go to [**CUCM Admin > User Management > User Settings > Access Control Group**]. Then click on "Add New".

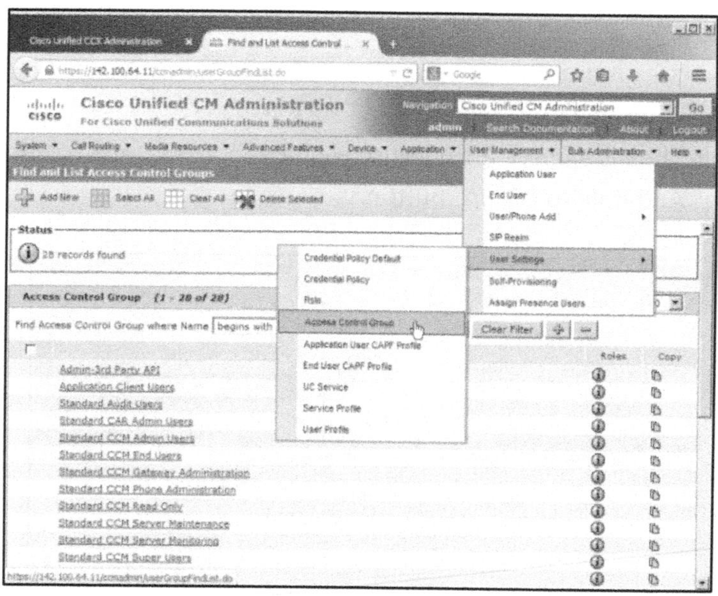

Figure 2-8 CUCM Access Control Group

Enter "AXL Group" (or any name you like) into the text field. The click "Save".

Give permission to the group

On upper right hand corner, from "Related Links", choose "Assign Role to Access Control Group".

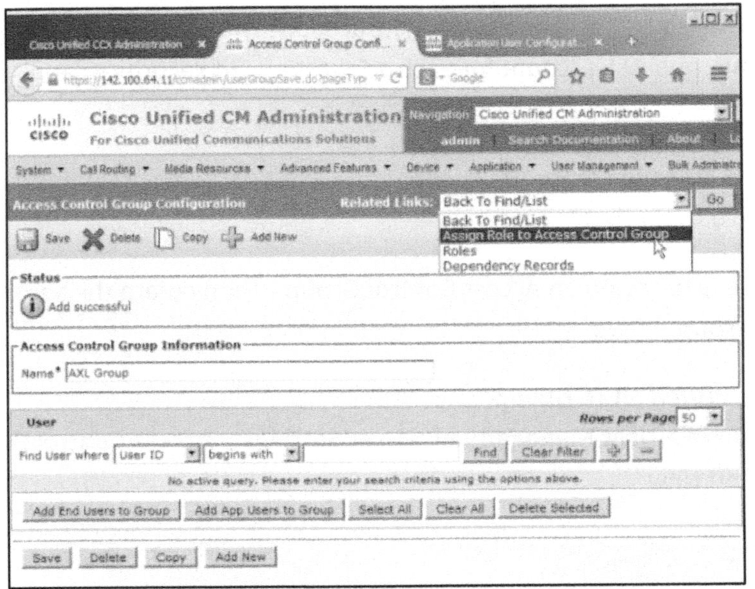

Figure 2-9 Assign Role to Access Control Group

You'll see the "role" box is empty. It's because we haven't assign any role to the group yet. Now click on "Add Role to Group" button.

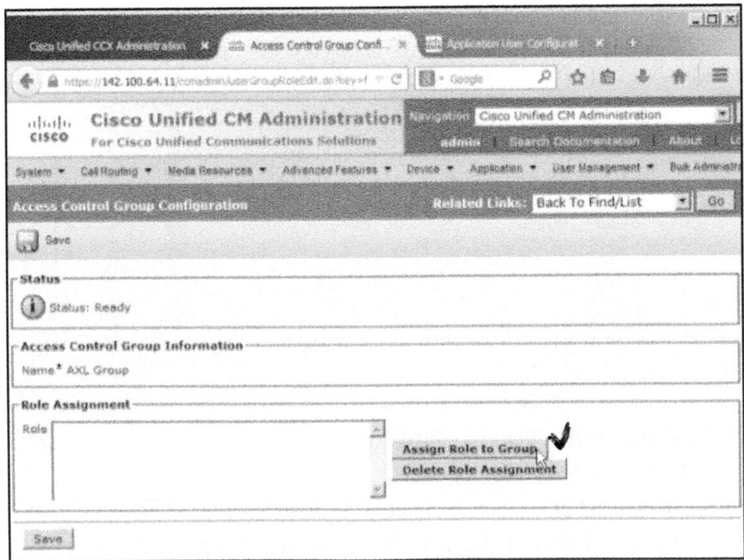

Figure 2-10 Assign Role to Access Control Group (Continued)

Make sure the checkbox next to "Standard AXL API Access" is checked. Then click "Add Selected".

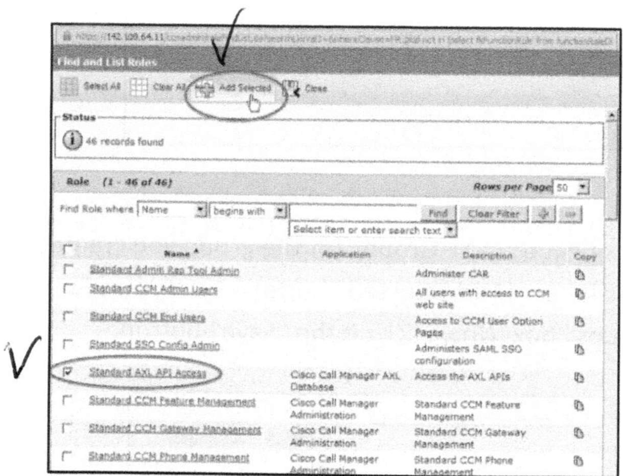

Figure 2-11 Role List

Now you'll see "Standard AXL API Access" showing up in the "Role" box. Click "Save" button. You have created an Access Control Group.

Create an account and put it in "AXL Group"

Go to **[CUCM Admin > User Management > Application User]**. Click "Add New" button. It's recommended to create the account as "Application User" because it will be used by applications. (Though you may also create it as "End User")

Enter "axl" (or any username you like) in the "User ID" field. Enter the password in "Password" field. Enter it again in "Confirm Password" field. It's recommended to use a password different from any of the admin passwords for security reason.

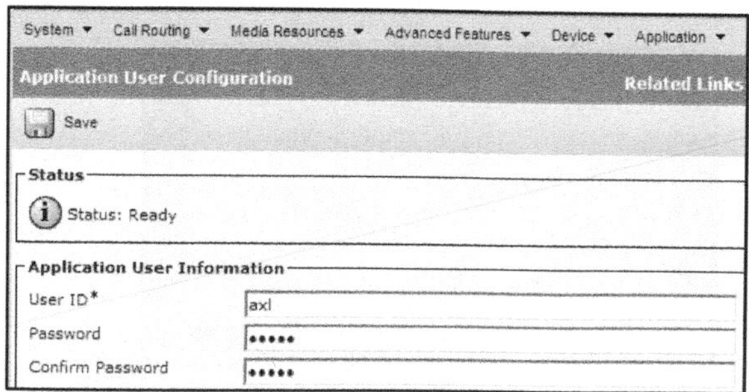

Figure 2-12 Creating AXL User

Scroll down to the bottom of the page. You'll see the "Groups" box is empty. It's because we haven't put the user into any group yet. Click on the "Add to Access Control Group" button.

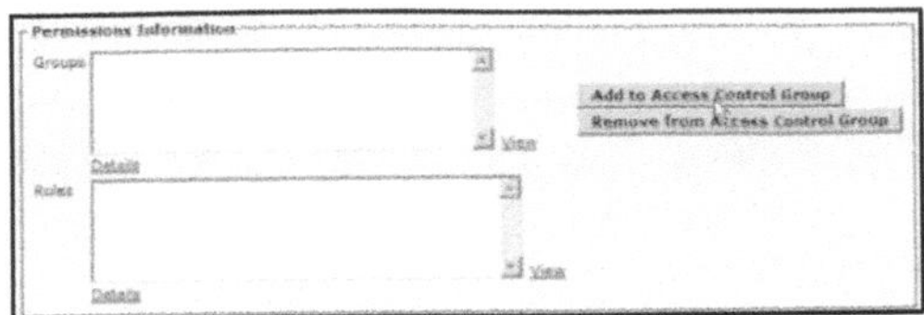

Figure 2-13 Adding AXL User to Group

Make sure the checkbox next to "AXL Group" (or the group you created in the previous step) is checked. Then click on "Add Selected" button. Now you see the "AXL Group" is showing up in the "Groups" box. Now click on the "Save" button.

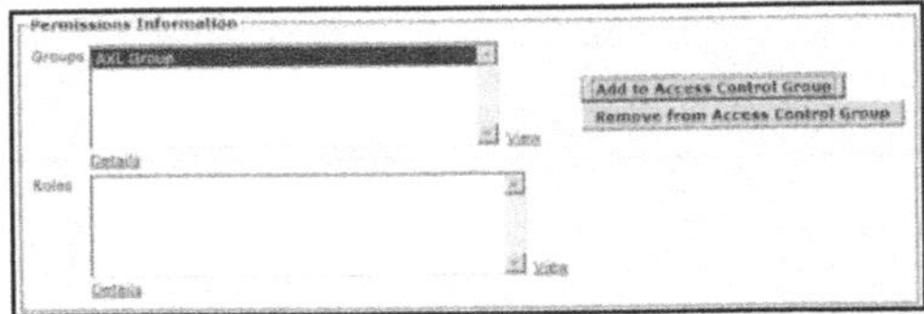

Figure 2-14 After Adding User to Group

At this point, we have successfully created an AXL account. We may use this account for any UC application integration that requires AXL credential.

CUCM End User as UCCX Admin Candidate

Why we need a CUCM end user to be a UCCX admin? Didn't we already create the "Application User" during installation? Why can't we just use that account?

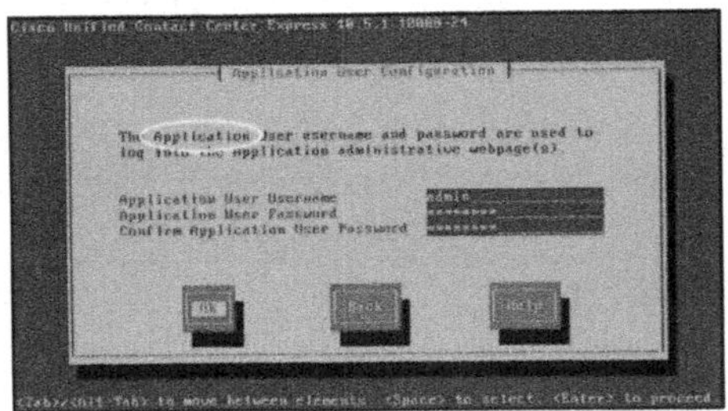

Figure 2-15 Application Administrator

Yes we did. And yes we could use that account (on UCCX version 10 or newer). Here's the reason why a CUCM end user needs to be UCCX admin:

In earlier versions of UCCX, all user authentication (including admin accounts, service accounts, end user accounts) are done by CUCM (via AXL). UCCX itself does not perform any user authentication at all (not even for its own administrator logon).

In pre-10 versions of UCCX, an admin account was created during installation. But that admin account was supposed for temporary use. When logging into the UCCX application admin web page the first time, the temporary admin account will be used. Then the system will force you go through an initialization process. The last step of that process is to synchronize the end users from CUCM and you will have to pick one of them as the UCCX admin. After that, the temporary admin account is disabled. You will have to user the CUCM end user account going forward.

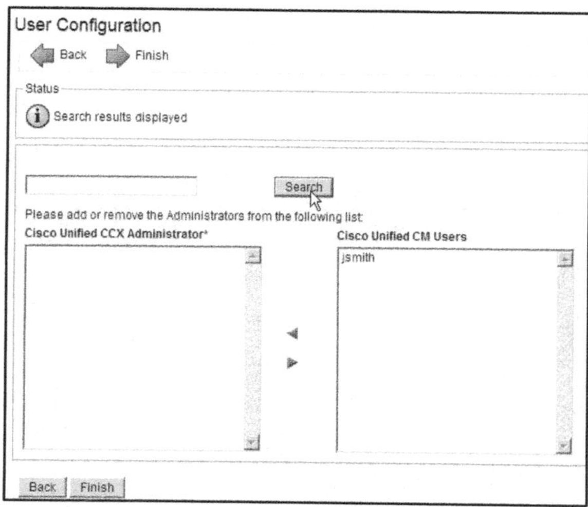

Figure 2-16 CUCM User As UCCX Administrator

Due to the tight integration between UCCX and CUCM (via AXL), user authentication is being handled by CUCM even though the request was initiated from UCCX side (such as admin logon, agent logon, etc.)

But this raises the concern of availability – what if the end user was deleted from CUCM? UCCX will be locked out from admin web page. This is in fact what happened in real life – Cisco TAC received numerous cases on this.

Finally, Cisco made the change ("improvement") on UCCX version 10. The application admin account will remain active after UCCX initialization. However, they still ask you to specify a CUCM end user as UCCX admin user for the sake of centralized management and audit.

The best practice is to use CUCM end user account as much as possible. In case CUCM not able to handle the authentication request, use the UCCX local admin account as a backup.

Please note UCCX can only see the CUCM end users. UCCX cannot see CUCM application users. You cannot assign a CUCM application user as the UCCX admin.

Installation Steps

Once you get the "preparation" part done, installation should be pretty straightforward – just follow the screen prompts and answer the questions. We'll walk through the installation process. You may skip this part if you already know how to do it.

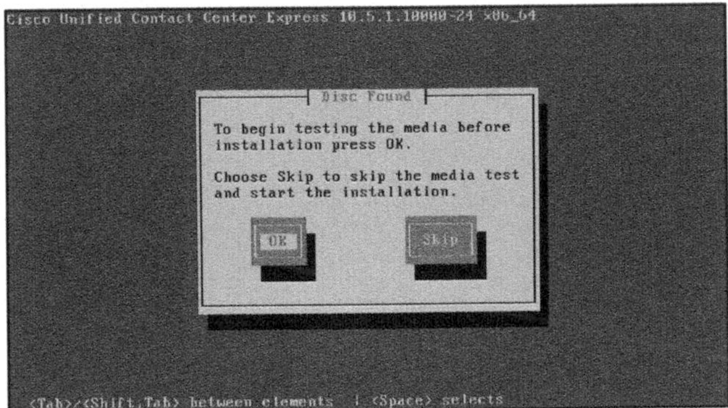

Figure 2-17 Media Test

This is the first screen when you spin the CD. Unless you suspect the CD was bad, you may just skip the media test.

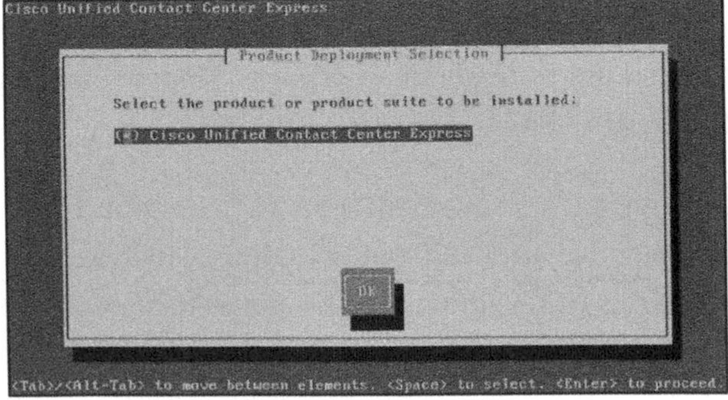

Figure 2-18 Product Selection

Don't have many choices here. So just hit "OK".

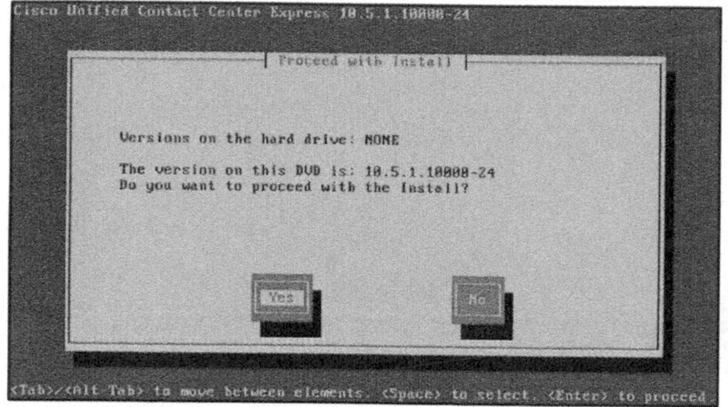

Figure 2-19 Proceed with Install

Same here. Hit "Yes".

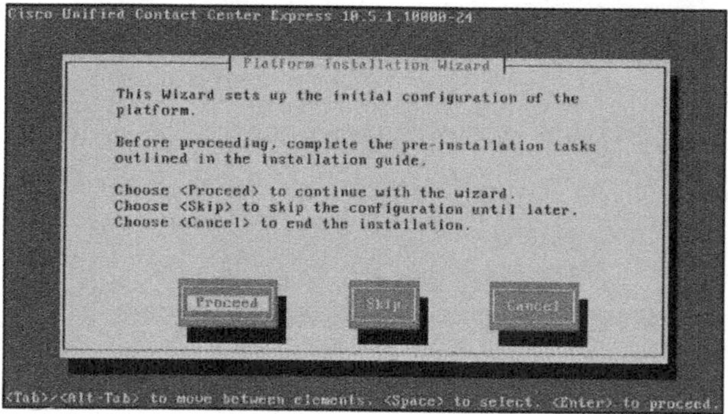

Figure 2-20 Installation Wizard

Hit "Proceed" here, unless you want to enter the information later versus right now.

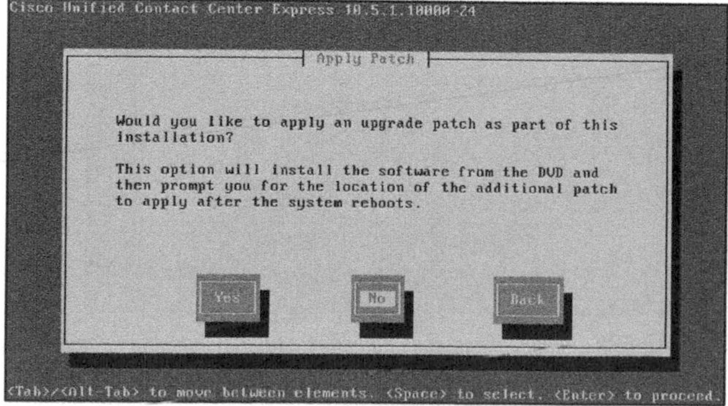

Figure 2-21 Apply Patch

Say "No" unless you plan to apply a patch during upgrade.

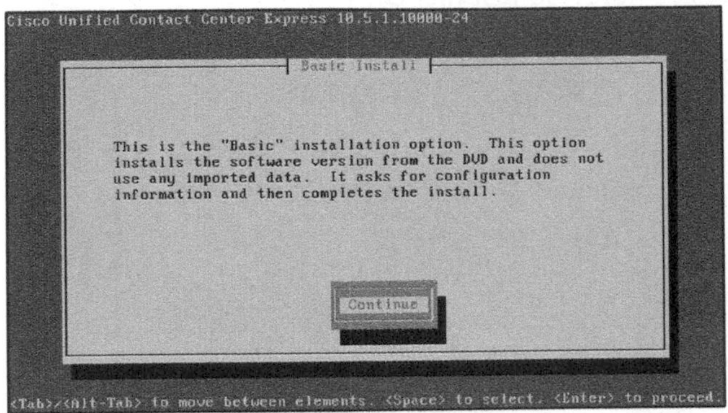

Figure 2-22 Basic Install

Hit "Continue".

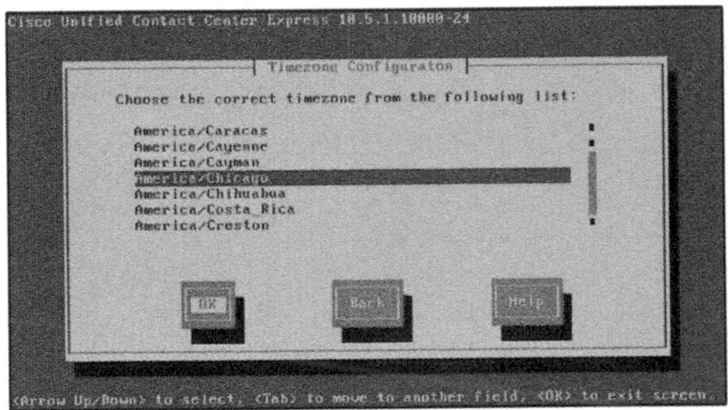

Figure 2-23 Timezone

Choose your time zone.

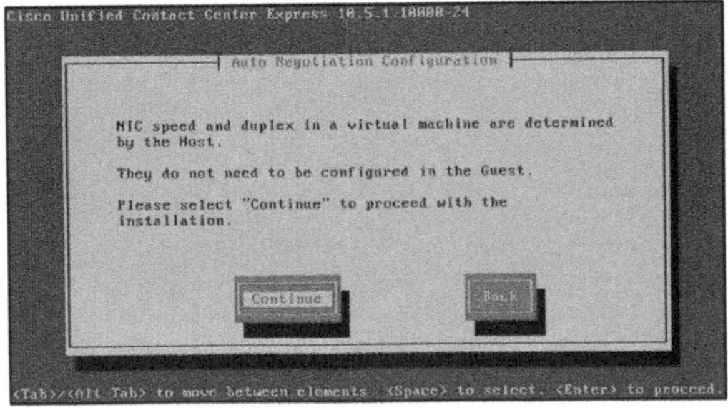

Figure 2-24 Auto Negotiation

Hit "Continue".

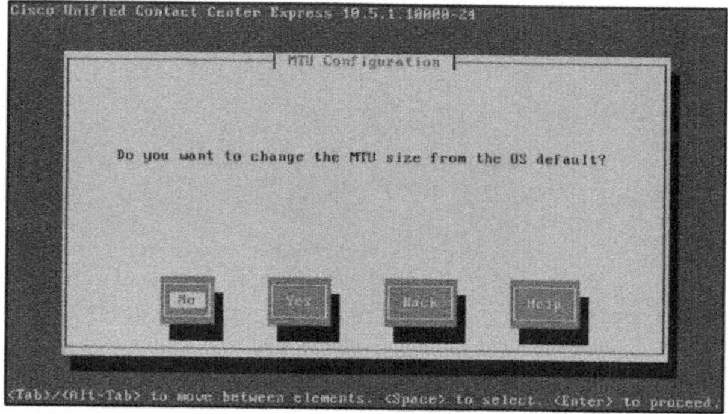

Figure 2-25 MTU

Say "No" unless you want to change the MTU size.

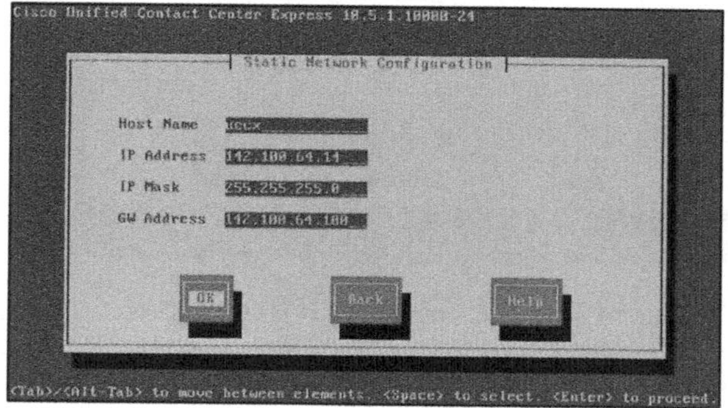

Figure 2-26 Static Network Configuration

Give the server a name, an IP address, mask and gateway address. Please note the server name should match the entries in DNS server. We have covered the DNS before. But for your reference, here are some examples of the DNS entries (forward and reverse lookup zones).

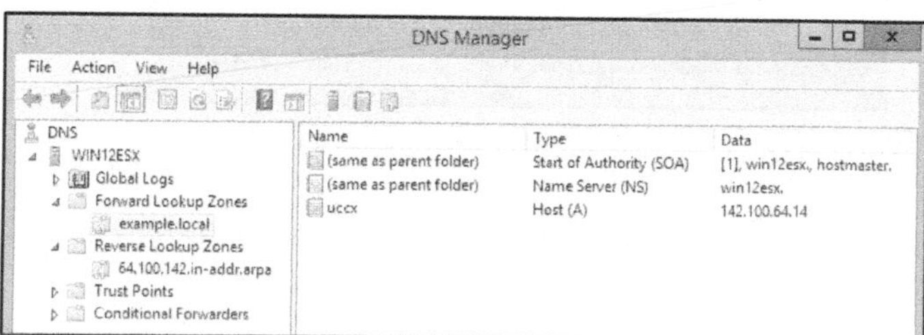

Figure 2-27 DNS Forward Lookup Zone

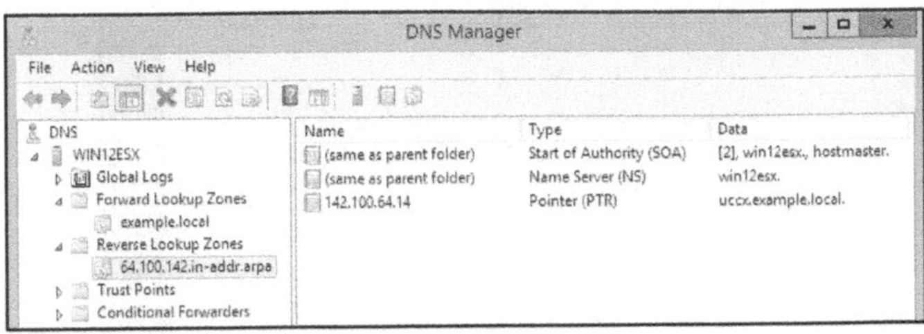

Figure 2-28 DNS Reverse Lookup Zone

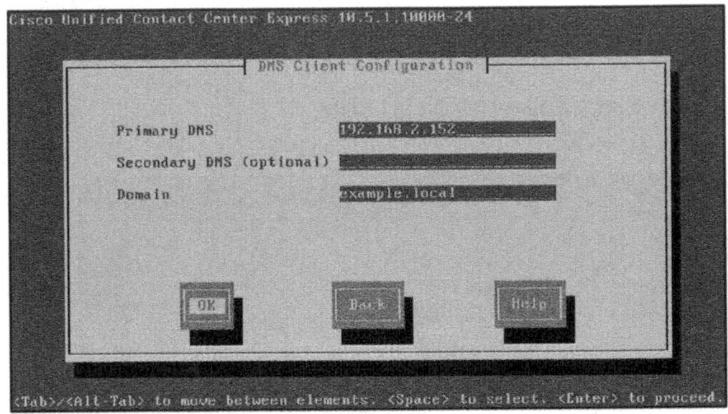

Figure 2-29 DNS Client Configuration

Enter the IP of the DNS server. The domain entered here should match with DNS domain.

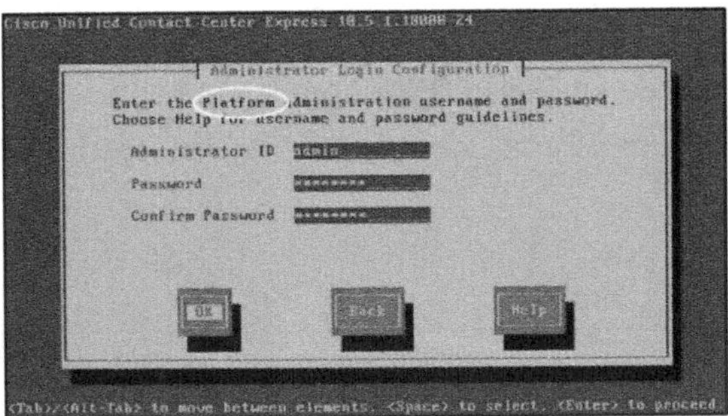

Figure 2-30 Creating Platform Administrator Account

Now we are creating a "Platform Administration" credential. Refer to "Preparation" part for details.

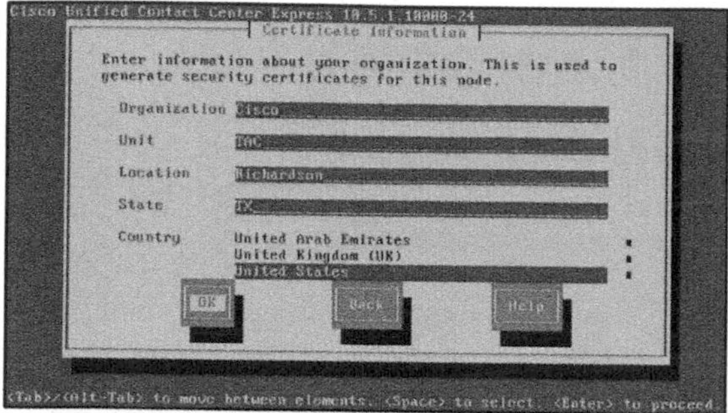

Figure 2-31 Certificate Information

Now enter the information to be used in certificates. The information here doesn't really matter in most cases. So just be free to enter anything.

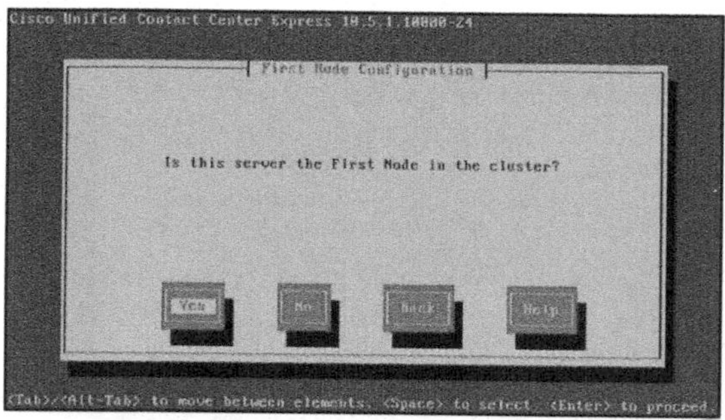

Figure 2-32 First Node in Cluster

Here comes the tricky question of "First Node". You should say "Yes" if you are installing the first UCCX server. Please refer to "Preparation" section for details.

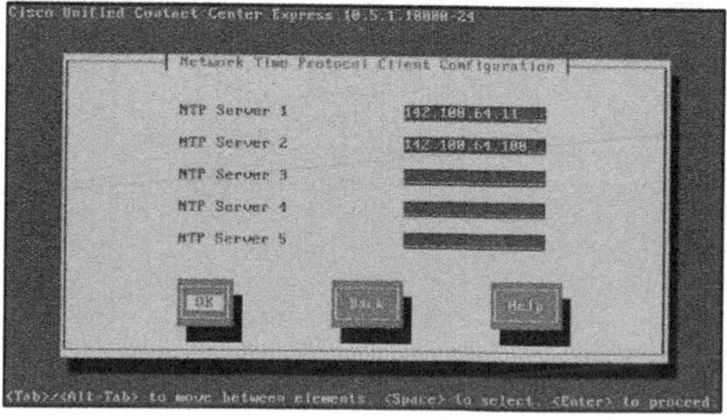

Figure 2-33 NTP Client Configuration

Now Enter NTP server IP address(es). The best practices is to use CUCM as the first NTP server. So the UCCX has the same timestamp as the CUCM. This makes troubleshooting easier.

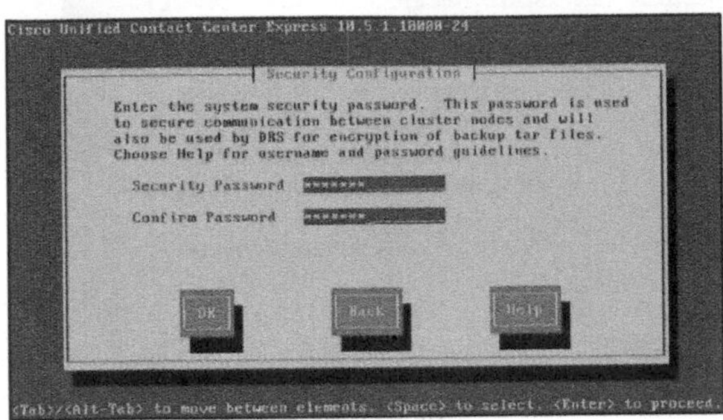

Figure 2-34 Security Password

Since we are installing the first UCCX server, we can create a security password. Keep the password in a safe place. You will need it when installing a second UCCX server.

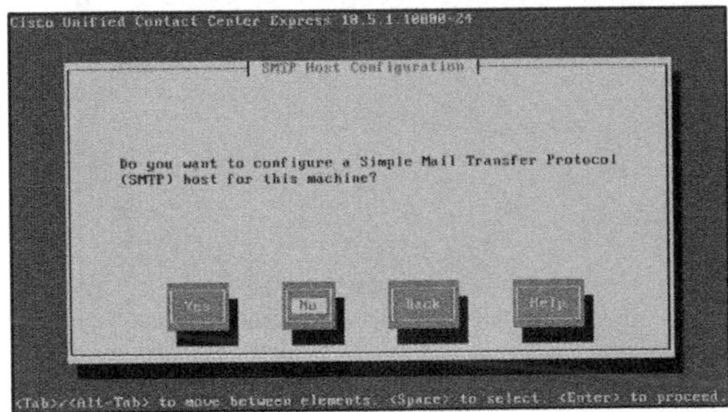

Figure 2-35 SMTP Host Configuration

Say "No" unless you want to configure SMTP host.

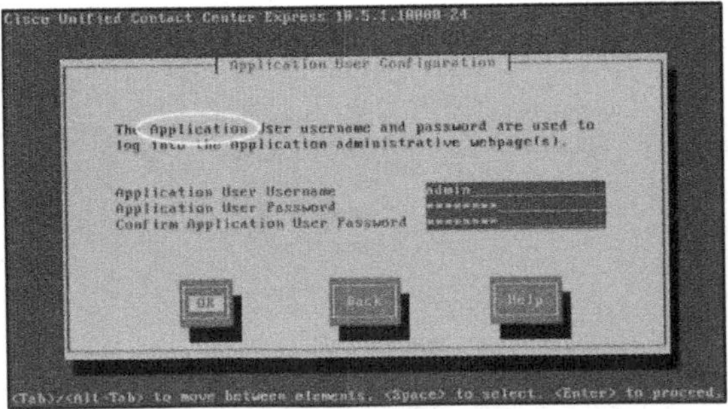

Figure 2-36 Creating Application Administrator Account

Now we are creating an application account. We will use this account to log into UCCX application administration web page. Don't confuse it with "Platform Admin" account. Please refer to "Preparation" part for details.

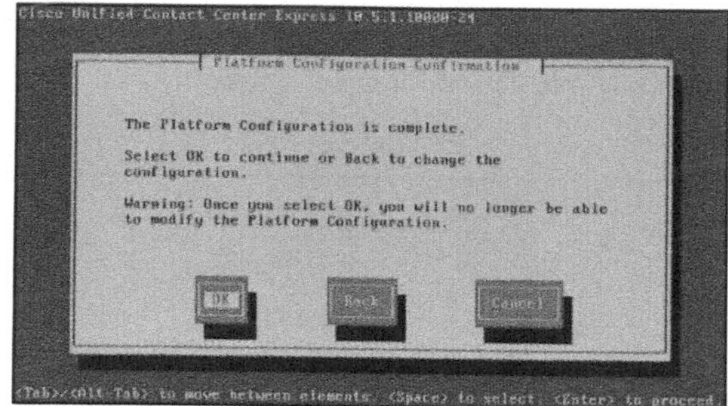

Figure 2-37 Platform Configuration Confirmation

Hit "OK" unless you want to go back and change something.

All questions have been answered at this point. It will take one to two hours to complete the installation depending on the speed of your hard drive.

When the installation is completed, the system will reboot automatically. It takes quite a while for the UCCX to fully come up. Here are some milestones:

1) Server responds to ping
   This means the network card driver has been loaded

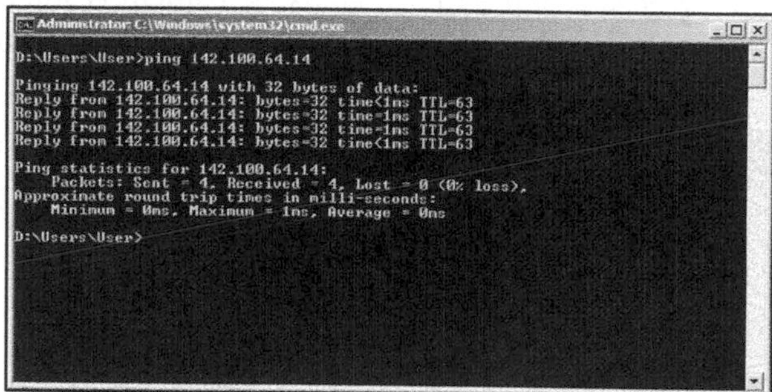

Figure 2-38 Pinging UCCX Server

2) CLI module started
   You may try to access the CLI (Command Line Interface) either from the console or via SSH. Please note the UCCX CLI is not the Linux shell. It is actually an application on top of shell. It will take some time for the CLI to come up.

If CLI module is still coming up, you'll get this:

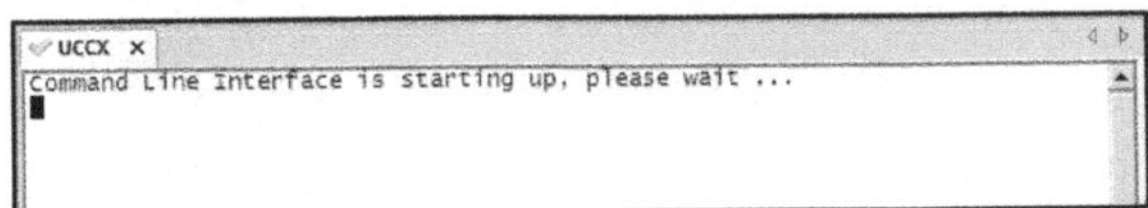

Figure 2-39 Opening CLI Connection to UCCX

If CLI module is fully up, you'll get the command prompt like this:

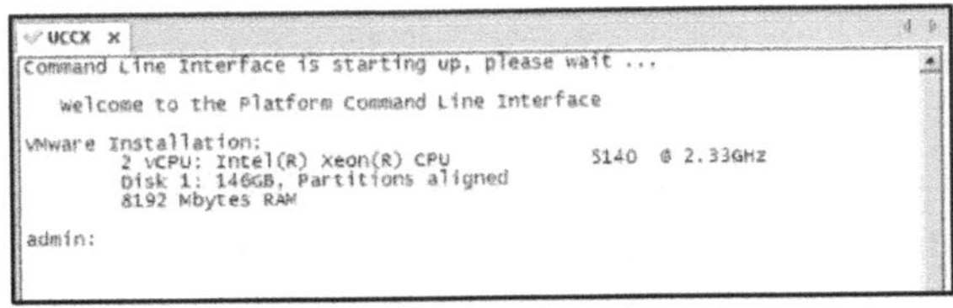

Figure 2-40 CLI Connection Created

3) Tomcat module is up
Tomcat is the web server module in Linux. If Tomcat is still coming up, you won't be able to connect to the server via web browser. You'll get "Connection Timeout" message.

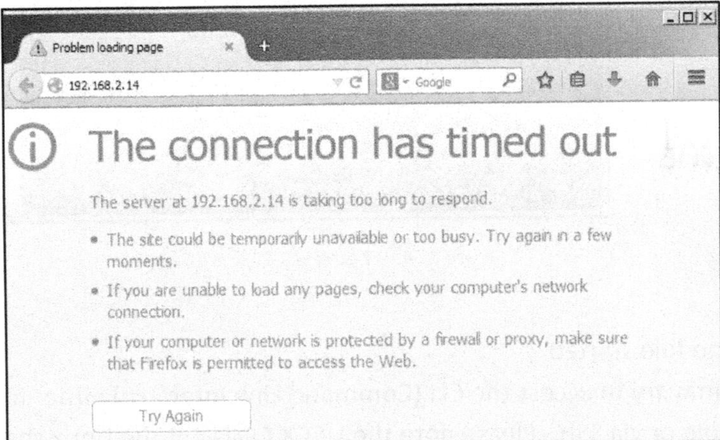

Figure 2-41 Tomcat Not Started

How do we know if Tomcat is still coming up? You may use the "utils service list page" CLI command to see the services status on the server. You will find a service named "Cisco Tomcat" in the list. [Starting] state means the service is still coming up. [Started] state means the service is fully up.

```
UCCX
A Cisco DB Replicator[STARTING]
Cisco AMC Service[STARTING]
Cisco Audit Event Service[STARTING]
Cisco CDP[STARTING]
Cisco CDP Agent[STARTING]
Cisco CallManager Serviceability[STARTING]
Cisco Certificate Change Notification[STARTING]
Cisco Certificate Expiry Monitor[STARTING]
Cisco DRF Local[STARTING]
Cisco DRF Master[STARTING]
Cisco Database Layer Monitor[STARTING]
Cisco Desktop Administrator Service[STARTING]
Cisco Desktop Agent E-Mail Service[STARTING]
Cisco Desktop Browser and IP Phone Agent Service[STARTING]
Cisco Desktop Call/Chat Service[STARTING]
Cisco Desktop Enterprise Service[STARTING]
Cisco Desktop LDAP Monitor Service[STARTING]
Cisco Desktop License and Resource Manager Service[STARTING]
Cisco Desktop Recording and Playback Service[STARTING]
Cisco Desktop Recording and Statistics Service[STARTING]
Cisco Desktop Sync Service[STARTING]
Cisco Desktop VoIP Monitor Service[STARTING]
Cisco Log Partition Monitoring Tool[STARTING]
Cisco RIS Data Collector[STARTING]
Cisco RTMT Reporter Servlet[STARTING]
Cisco Syslog Agent[STARTING]
Cisco Tomcat[STARTING]
Cisco Tomcat Stats Servlet[STARTING]
Cisco Trace Collection Service[STARTING]
Cisco Trace Collection Servlet[STARTING]
Cisco Unified CCX Administration[STARTING]
Cisco Unified CCX CVD Dependent Webapp[STARTING]
:enter for 1 line, space for one page, q to quit
```

Figure 2-42 Services Status

4) CCX Administration is up

CCX Administration is the admin module on top of Tomcat. It comes up after Tomcat is up. If Tomcat is up but CCX Administration is not, you'll get a 404 error when you try to get to the UCCX Administration web page.

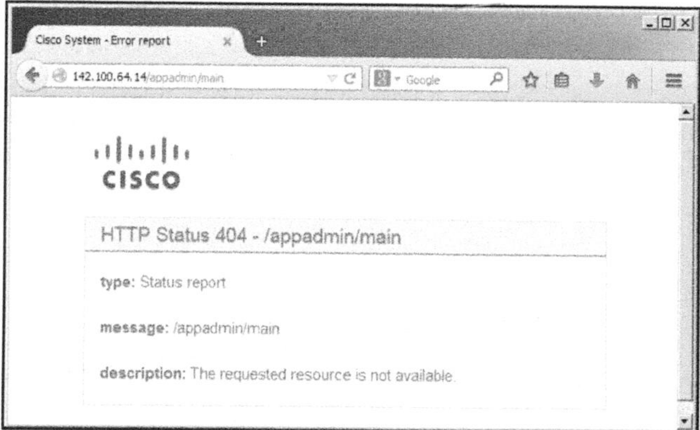

Figure 2-43 Tomcat Started but UCCX Administration is not

You may connect to the UCCX Admin web page if the "Cisco Unified CCX Administration" service state is [Started].

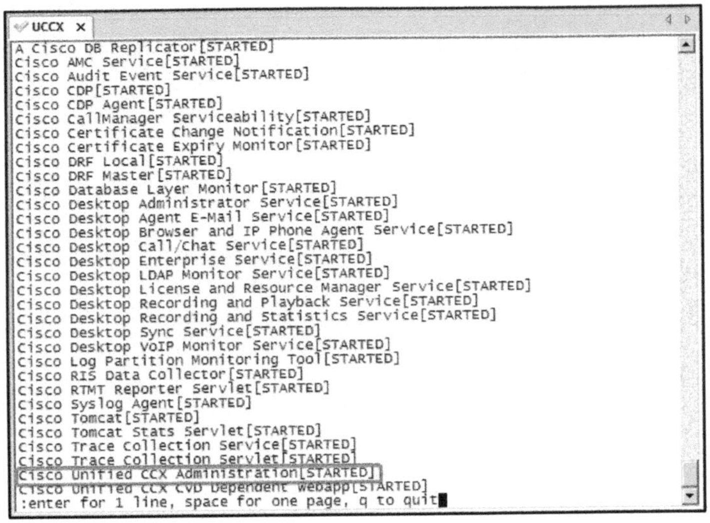

UCCX ×

```
A Cisco DB Replicator[STARTED]
Cisco AMC Service[STARTED]
Cisco Audit Event Service[STARTED]
Cisco CDP[STARTED]
Cisco CDP Agent[STARTED]
Cisco CallManager Serviceability[STARTED]
Cisco Certificate Change Notification[STARTED]
Cisco Certificate Expiry Monitor[STARTED]
Cisco DRF Local[STARTED]
Cisco DRF Master[STARTED]
Cisco Database Layer Monitor[STARTED]
Cisco Desktop Administrator Service[STARTED]
Cisco Desktop Agent E-Mail Service[STARTED]
Cisco Desktop Browser and IP Phone Agent Service[STARTED]
Cisco Desktop Call/Chat Service[STARTED]
Cisco Desktop Enterprise Service[STARTED]
Cisco Desktop LDAP Monitor Service[STARTED]
Cisco Desktop License and Resource Manager Service[STARTED]
Cisco Desktop Recording and Playback Service[STARTED]
Cisco Desktop Recording and Statistics Service[STARTED]
Cisco Desktop Sync Service[STARTED]
Cisco Desktop VoIP Monitor Service[STARTED]
Cisco Log Partition Monitoring Tool[STARTED]
Cisco RIS Data Collector[STARTED]
Cisco RTMT Reporter Servlet[STARTED]
Cisco Syslog Agent[STARTED]
Cisco Tomcat[STARTED]
Cisco Tomcat Stats Servlet[STARTED]
Cisco Trace Collection Service[STARTED]
Cisco Trace Collection Servlet[STARTED]
Cisco Unified CCX Administration[STARTED]
Cisco Unified CCX CVD Dependent Webapp[STARTED]
:enter for 1 line, space for one page, q to quit
```

Figure 2-44 UCCX Administration Service

Chapter 3 Initialization

When you log into UCCX application administration web page the first time, UCCX will guide you through an "initialization" process. This is a one-time process to set the system parameters, activate services and upload license. You may reconfigure those parameters later on. But you cannot skip this one-time initialization process.

Log onto UCCX Admin the first time

To access the UCCX application administration web page ("AppAdmin"), type the IP address of the UCCX server in a web browser and hit enter. Then click on the "Cisco Unified Contact Center Express Administration" link.

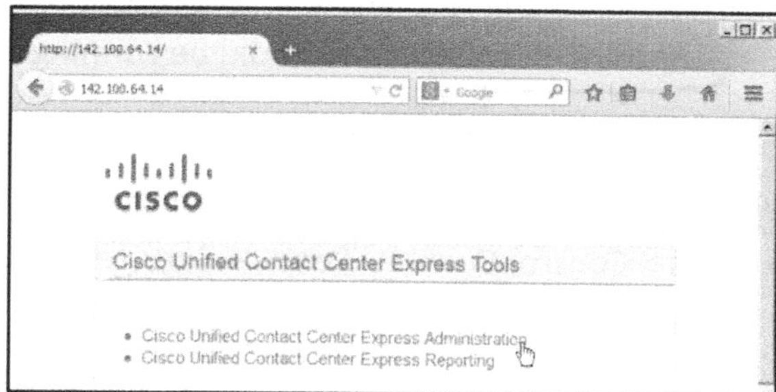

Figure 3-1 UCCX Web Portal

You may also go directly to the AppAdmin web page by adding "/appadmin" to the end of the IP address. For example "http://142.100.64.14/appadmin".

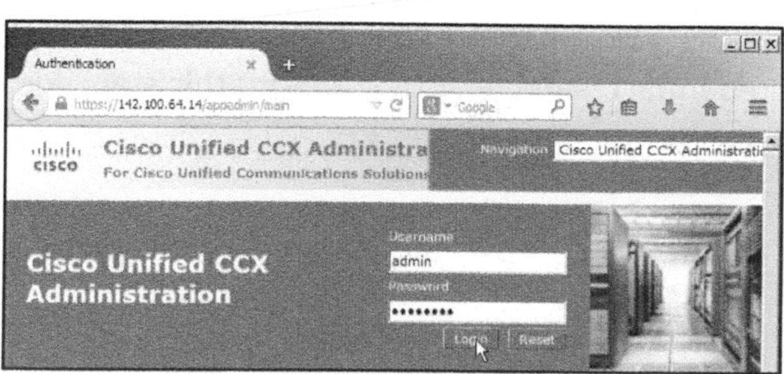

Figure 3-2 UCCX Admin

Enter the application credential created during installation and hit "Login" button.

AXL Credential

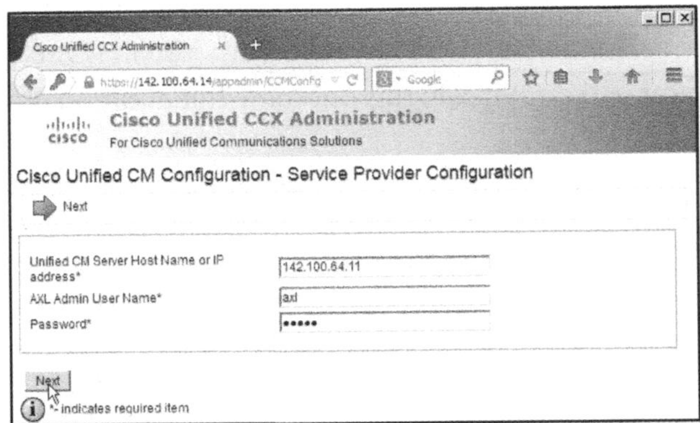

Figure 3-3 AXL Credential

The first screen is to enter the IP address and AXL credential of the CUCM server. What it didn't mention was the "Cisco AXL Web Service" should be running on that CUCM.

On CUCM version 10.5, "Cisco AXL Web Service" is activated by default. But if UCCX not able to pass this step, that's one of the item you should check on **[CUCM > Cisco Unified Serviceability > Tools > Control Center – Feature Services > Cisco AXL Web Service]**.

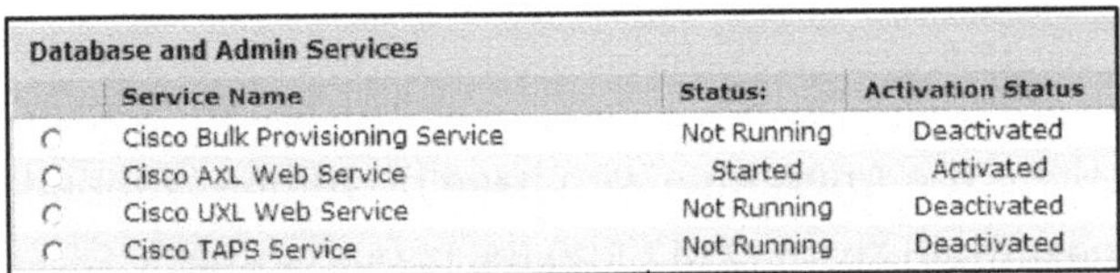

Database and Admin Services

	Service Name	Status:	Activation Status
○	Cisco Bulk Provisioning Service	Not Running	Deactivated
○	Cisco AXL Web Service	Started	Activated
○	Cisco UXL Web Service	Not Running	Deactivated
○	Cisco TAPS Service	Not Running	Deactivated

Figure 3-4 CUCM Services List

You should have AXL credential created on CUCM before this step. Please refer to "Preparation" part for details.

License Upload

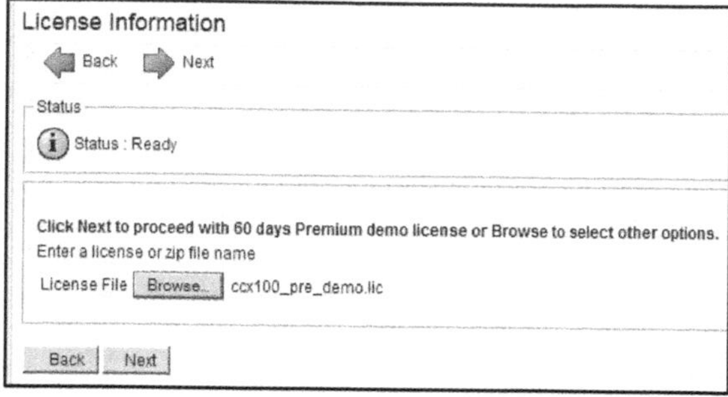

Figure 3-5 Upload UCCX License

This screen is to allow you upload UCCX license file. If you don't have any license file, you may just click "Next" button. UCCX will use the demo license if you didn't upload any.

Component Activation

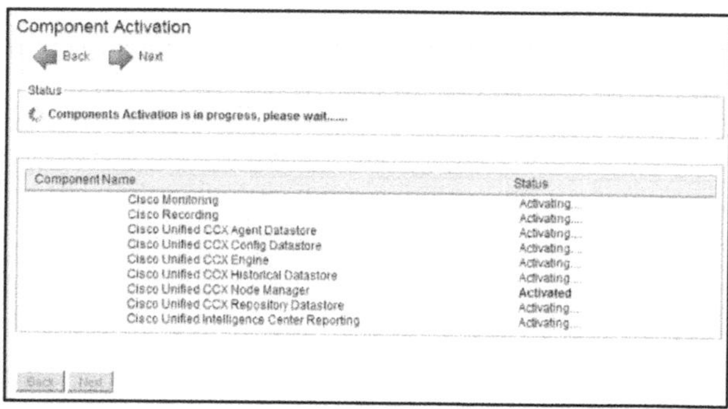

Figure 3-6 UCCX Component Activation

This screen is showing you that UCCX is activating components (services). Once it's done, you'll see a screen like below.

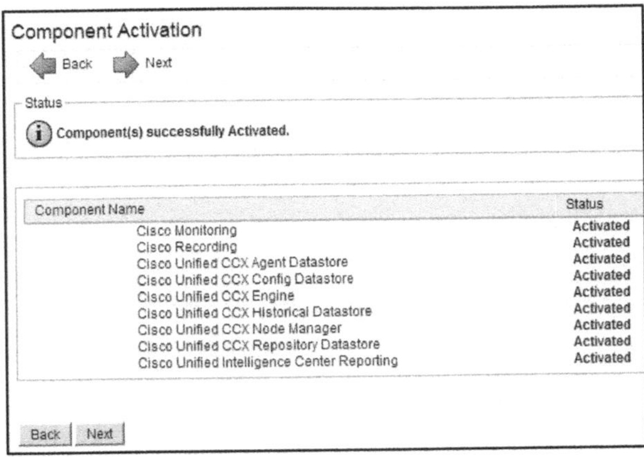

Figure 3-7 UCCX Components Activated

Datastore Activation

The following screen is to activate datastore (database). Since this is the first server, you have to activate all datastore. Thus all checkboxes are checked and you cannot uncheck them.

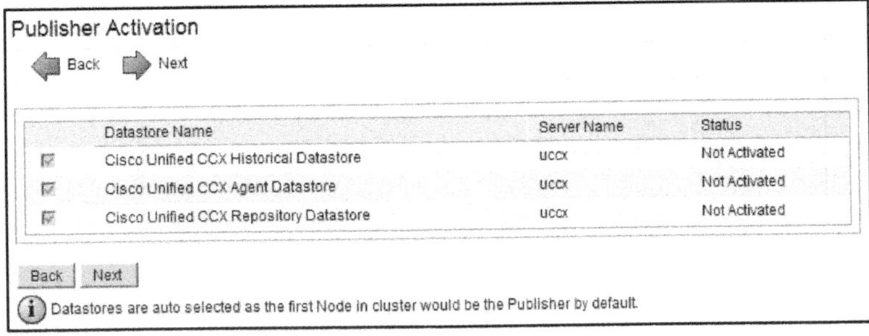

Figure 3-8 UCCX Datastore Activation

Just hit "Next" to continue.

Cisco Unified CM Configuration

The next page is called "Cisco Unified CM Configuration". It consists of three sections:

- AXL
- Telephony (previously known as "JTAPI")
- RmCm

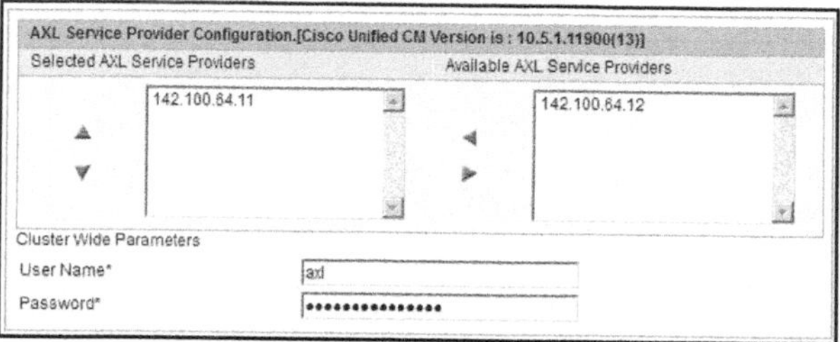

Figure 3-9 AXL Configuration

AXL allows UCCX read/write CUCM database. This section is automatically populated with the information entered in previous steps. If you have AXL service activated on a CUCM subscriber, you may move it from "Available AXL Service Providers" list to the "Select AXL Service Providers" list. This provides some redundancy in case the primary one failed.

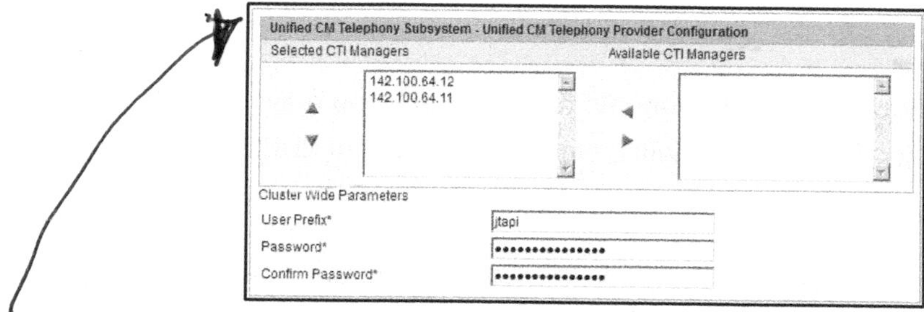

Figure 3-10 CM Telephony (JTAPI) Configuration

"Unified CM Telephony Subsystem" used to be called "JTAPI Subsystem" in earlier version of UCCX. It allows UCCX to control IP phones via "CTIManager service" on CUCM.

Multiple CTI Managers (CUCMs) should be selected for redundancy.

In "User Prefix" field, you define the user prefix and password. What is going to happen is:

1) UCCX will create user account(s) in CUCM Application User database.
2) The user account name will be <user_prefix>_<node_id>. For example, you entered "jtapi" as the user prefix. There's only one UCCX server. The account

created will be "jtapi_1". If there are two UCCX servers, two accounts will be created. The account names will be "jtapi_1" and "jtapi_2" respectively.

3) Password for the newly created accounts will be the password you specify here.

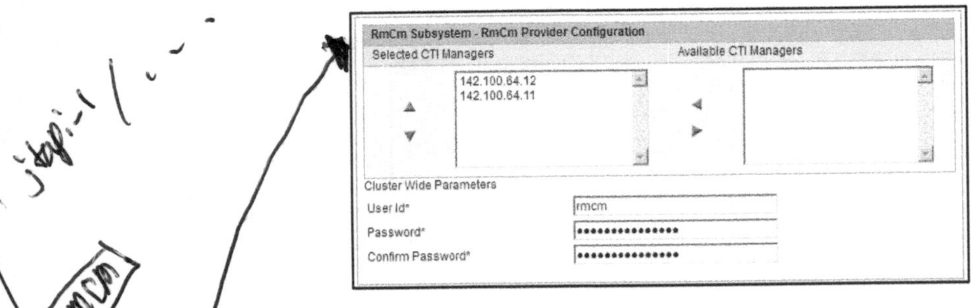

Figure 3-11 RMCM (RM-JTAPI) Configuration

RmCm (Resource Manager Contact Manager) is very similar to "Telephony" (JTAPI), except that it is used to poll the IP phones' status (off-hook, on-hook, talking, etc.) UCCX needs to know the phone status to make routing decisions.

UCCX will create only one RmCm account regardless of the number of UCCX servers. Thus it is called "User ID" versus "User Prefix" here.

After entering the information for "Telephony" and "RmCm", you may click "Next" to continue. Once you click "Next", UCCX will create the accounts in CUCM Application User database.

CUCM Application User list before clicking "Next". Note the "jatpi_1" and "rmcm" users have been created.

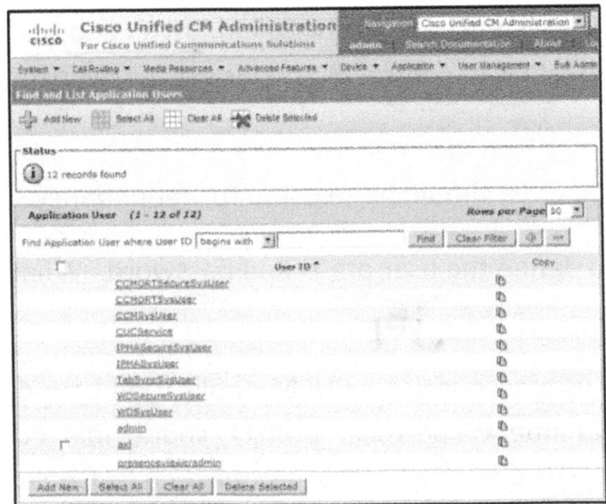

Figure 3-12 CUCM Application User List

CUCM Application User list after clicking "Next":

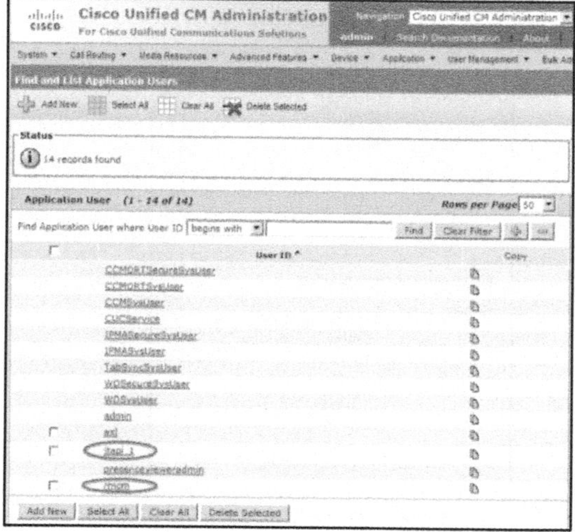

Figure 3-13 jtapi and rmcm users created as CUCM Application Users

Though nothing prevents you from modifying these accounts from CUCM Admin web page, it's recommended to do it from UCCX Admin. So that the information is consistent between UCCX and CUCM.

System Parameter Configuration

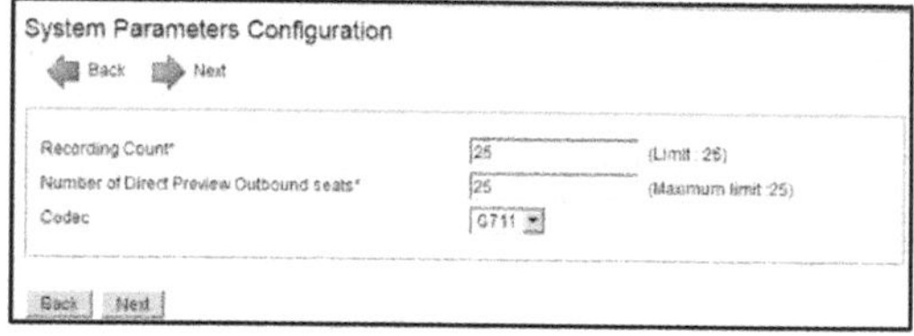

Figure 3-14 UCCX System Parameters

This screen is to specify the recording count, outbound seats and codec. Use maximum counts and G711.

Language Configuration

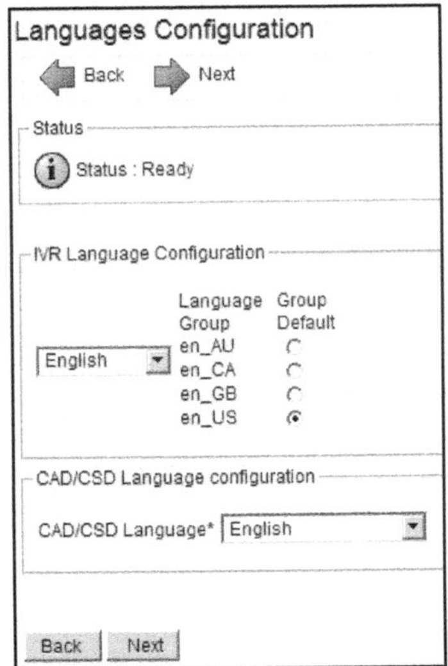

Figure 3-15 UCCX Language Configuration

This screen is to choose the default language.

CUCM user as UCCX Administrator

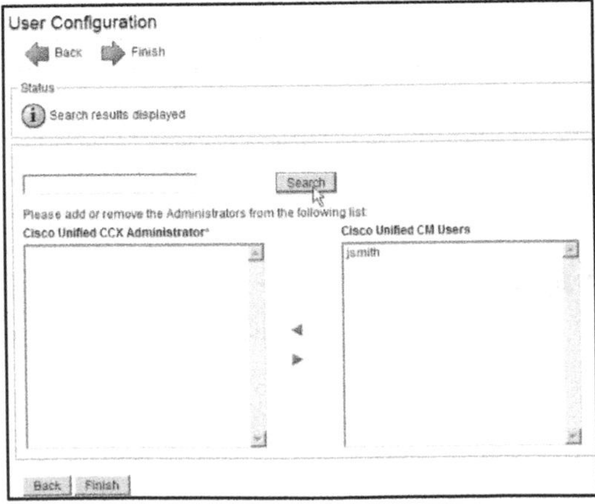

Figure 3-16 Designate CUCM user as UCCX Admin

This screen is to appoint a CUCM end user as UCCX admin. Highlight the user(s) you want from "Cisco Unified CM Users" list and move it to the "Cisco Unified CCX Administrator" list. Then click "Finish" button. Use the search box if the desired user(s) didn't show up on the candidate list.

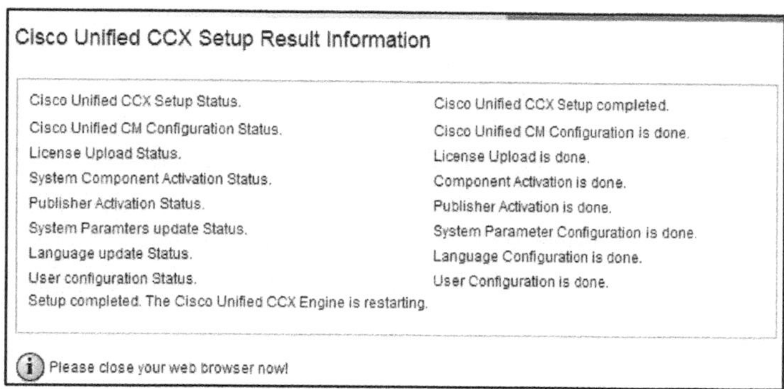

Figure 3-17 UCCX Setup Result

This screen concludes UCCX initialization. We are done with UCCX initialization!

Chapter 4 UCCX Terminologies

Through the years, UCCX has evolved from a simple IVR (Interactive Voice Responder) to a multi-function system. It will be difficult to cover all terminologies in one shot. We will cover the most important terminologies here and cover the others in corresponding function chapters.

Terminologies covered here are:

- Trigger
- Application
- Resource
- Customer Service Queue

Generally speaking, UCCX is a server in "client-server" model. It receives request from clients and responds with information. Who are the clients? It depends on the scenarios. It could be CUCM requesting for call routing decisions, it could be HTTP clients request for database lookup, etc., etc.

Trigger

Trigger is like a "touch point" on UCCX server. When something touches it, it triggers an application so UCCX can produce a response based on pre-defined logic, hence the name "trigger".

For example, if a phone call hits a "Telephony Trigger", it triggers an UCCX application. UCCX produces response based on the predefined logic in the application (such as routing calls to agent).

Application

UCCX application is a container that has scripts, prompts, grammars and documents. In most cases, an application contains at least one script. An application may or may not have prompts, documents or grammars.

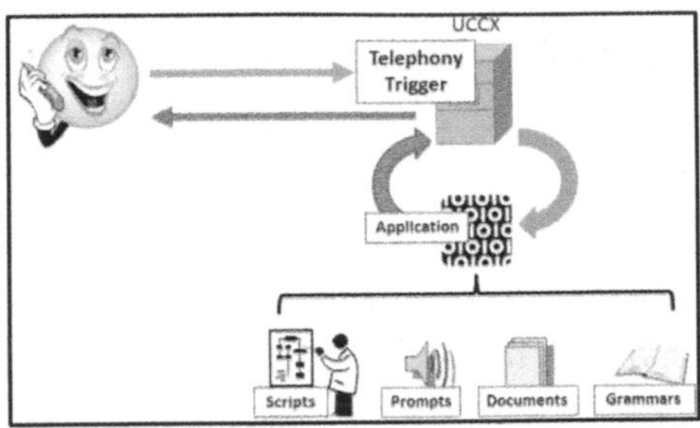

Figure 4-1 UCCX Application and Other Components

Script

Script is where the business logic was built. For example "If the call has been waiting in the queue for more than 5 minutes, play an apology recording".

Resource

Resource is someone (or something) that can handle the incoming request. In UCCX, a resource is usually an agent that can answer the incoming calls.

Contact Service Queue (CSQ)

If every caller can be served by any agent immediately, we don't need a queuing mechanism. In real life, a caller usually has to wait in a queue for some time before he/she can talk to an agent. Also, there might be different queues for different callers (for example, English queue and Spanish queue).

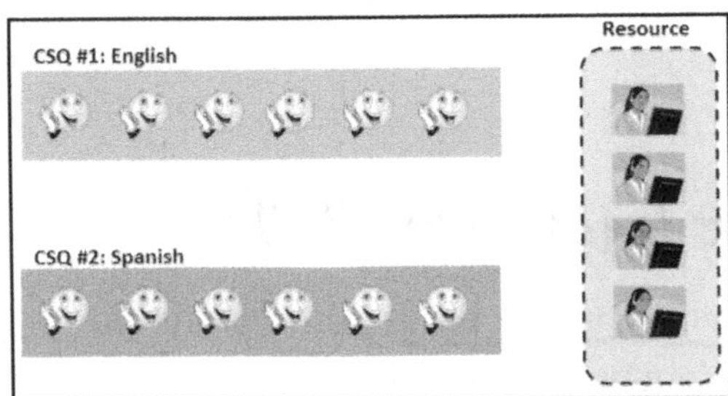

Figure 4-2 UCCX Contact Service Queues

Desktop Suite

Desktop Suite was originally developed by Spanlink (now Calabrio). It is a suite of desktop applications to be used with Cisco Contact Center servers. Desktop Suite consists of the following applications:

- Cisco Agent Desktop (CAD)
- Cisco Supervisor Desktop (CSD)
- Cisco Desktop Administrator (CDA, now known as Cisco Desktop Work Flow Administrator)

For many years, Desktop Suite is the de facto client software for Cisco Contact Center. Though Cisco has introduced the next generation desktop "Finesse", many customers are still using the Desktop Suite. Desktop Suite still dominates the market. We will use Desktop Suite as the primary client software.

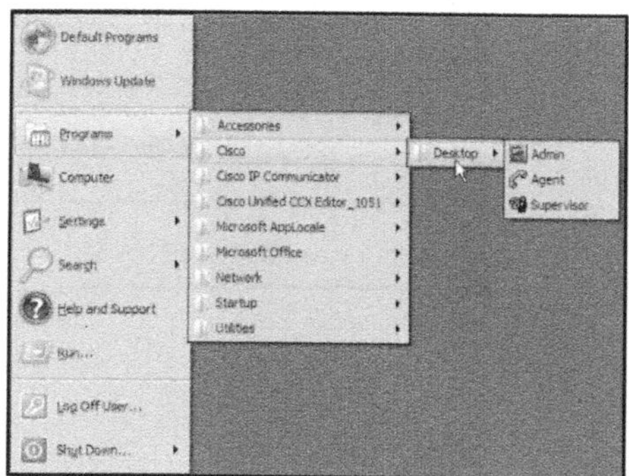

Figure 4-3 Desktop Suite Shortcuts

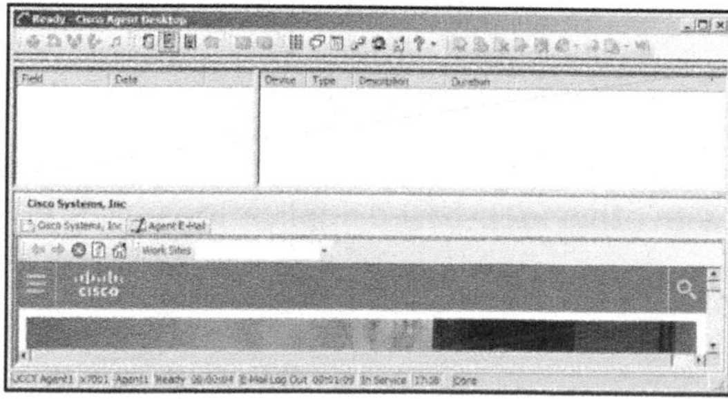

Figure 4-4 Cisco Agent Desktop (CAD)

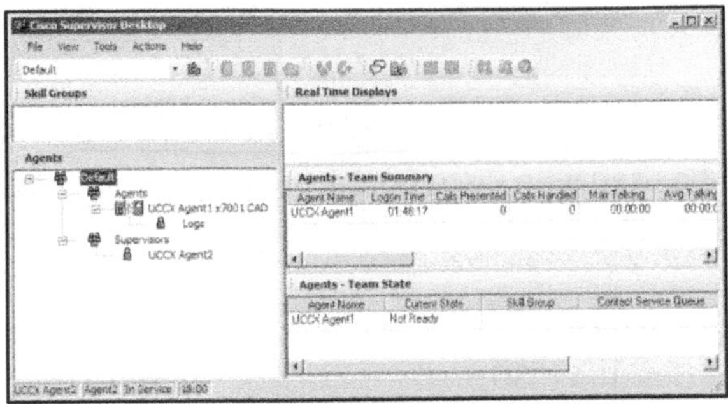

Figure 4-5 Cisco Supervisor Desktop (CSD)

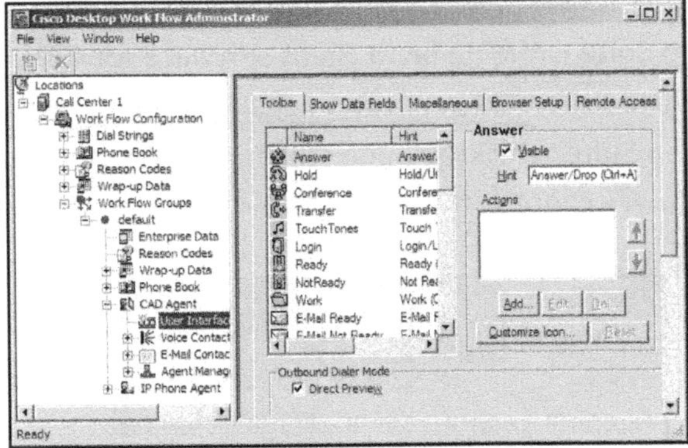

Figure 4-6 Cisco Desktop Administrator (CDA)

Cisco Finesse

Cisco Finesse is the next-generation desktop. Finesse is web-based. The benefits are:

- No client software installation (clientless)
- Use standard HTTP(s) protocol
- Easy integration with other web-based applications
- Easy upgrade/customization because it's clientless

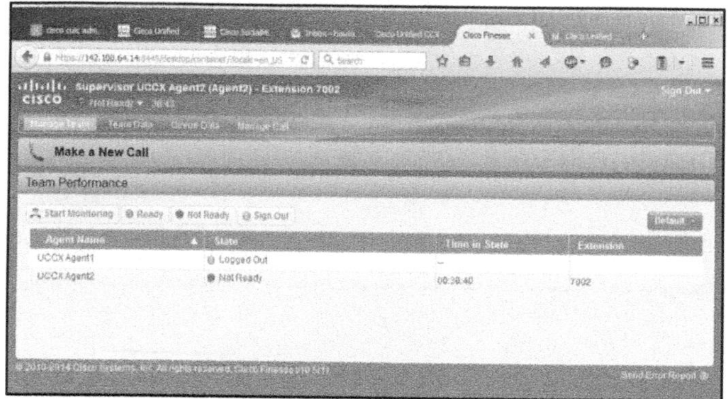

Figure 4-7 Cisco Finesse

Some of the features are only available with Finesse, not available with Desktop Suite, for example, agent-based progressive and predictive outbound dialer.

On UCCX 10.5 or lower versions, you can choose either Desktop Suite or Finesse, but not both. On UCCX 10.6 or above, you may use both at the same time.

Chapter 5 Intelligent Call Distribution

Intelligent Call Distribution (ICD) is probably the most common use case of a call center. Like the example we mentioned before, a typical ICD will be like this:

1. A customer calls into a Bank's customer service hotline.
2. Customer hears welcome prompts.
3. Customer selects the service by using telephone buttons.
4. Customer is connected to a customer service representative (agent).

In this chapter, we are going to discuss how to set up ICD with CUCM and UCCX.

Let's consider a simple setup like the diagram below.

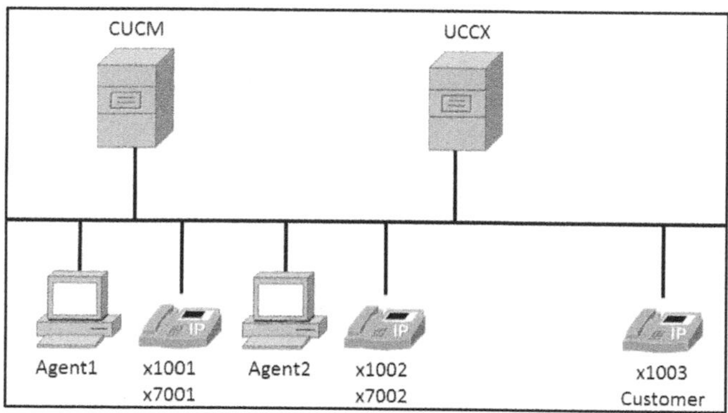

Figure 5-1 Reference Lab

We have two agents named "Agent1" and "Agent2". Each of them has their own computers and IP phones. Each IP phone has two lines:

- A regular line with extension number 1xxx
- An ICD line with extension number 7xxx

Do we always need two lines? Of course not. You may just use one line. But having two lines here will give you better idea how an ICD line work and what's its difference with the regular line.

We use a third IP phone to emulate a customer. The extension number is 1003.

The expected behavior is:

1. Customer (x1003) calls into a hotline number
2. If any agent is available, the call will be routed to the agent.
3. If not, customer will be waiting in a queue (hearing music on hold or prompts)

Call flow illustrated below.

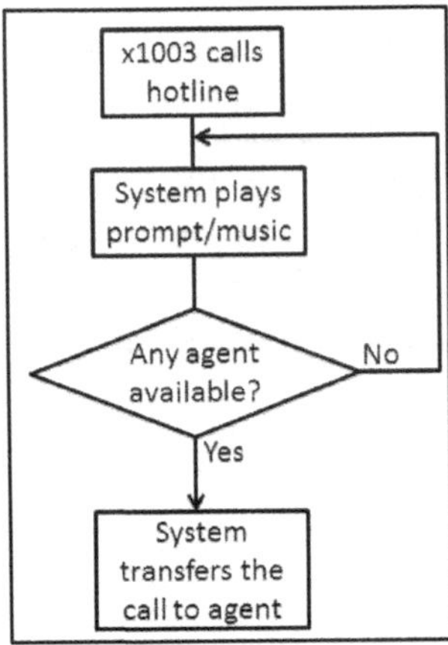

Figure 5-2 Call Center Flow Chart

Task List

CUCM Tasks:

1. Provision phones (agent phones)
2. Provision end users (agents)

UCCX Tasks:

1. Provision "Call Control Group" (CTI Ports)
2. Provision "Resource" (agents)
3. Provision "Contact Service Queue" (CSQ)
4. Provision "Application"
5. Provision "Triggers" (CTI Route Points)

We have talked about some of the terms above, except for "CTI Ports" and "CTI Route Points".

CTI

CTI (Computer Telephony Integration) is a common name for any technology that allows interactions on a telephone and a computer to be integrated or coordinated. For example, an software on your laptop computer can use CTI to control your desk phone (make calls, answer calls, etc.)

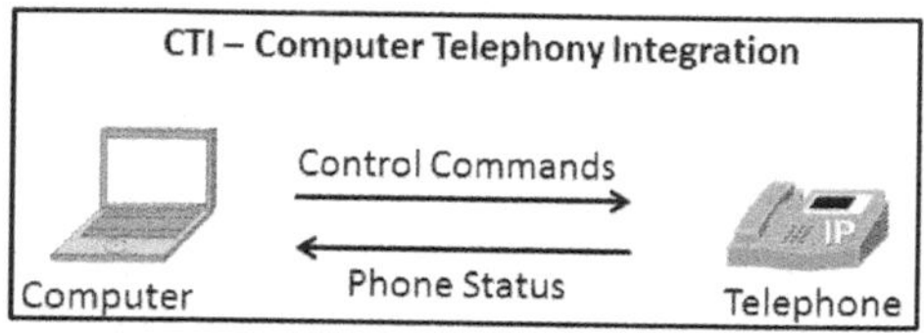

Figure 5-3 Computer Telephony Integration

Well known CTI standards include:

- CSTA – Computer Supported Telecommunications Applications
- JTAPI – Java Telephony API
- TSAPI – Telephony Server Application Programming Interface
- TAPI – Telephony Application Programming Interface

UCCX uses JTAPI. That's why we keep hearing "JTAPI triggers", "JTAPI Subsystem", "JTAPI version", etc. Cisco renamed "JTAPI" to "Unified CM Telephony" in later version of UCCX, which I don't like. I think "JTAPI" is more straightforward and consistent with other components in UCCX. Some engineers still use the term "JTAPI" versus "Unified CM Telephony". We will use these two terms interchangeably in this book.

UCCX and CUCM integration via JTAPI is illustrated below.

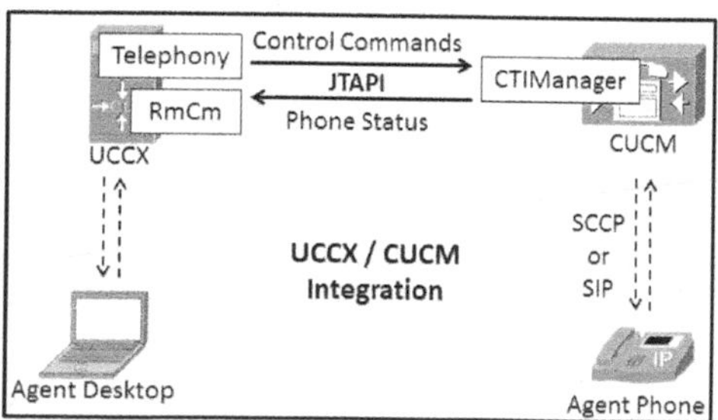

Figure 5-4 UCCX Integrated with CUCM

"Unified CM Telephony Subsystem" (JTAPI) and "RmCm Subsystem" in UCCX Control Center:

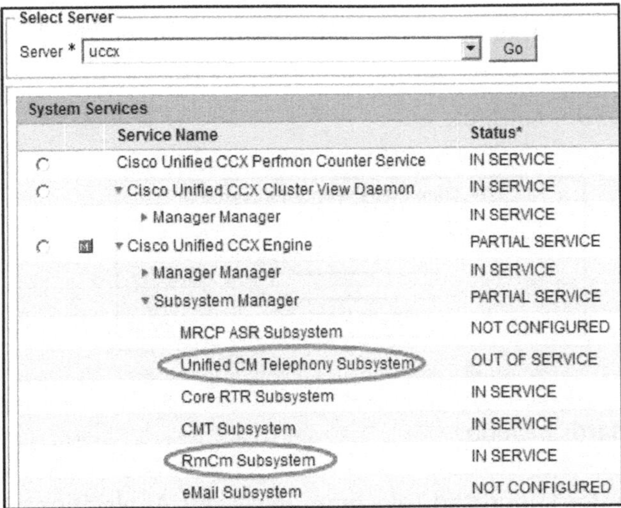

Select Server

Server * uccx Go

System Services

Service Name	Status*
Cisco Unified CCX Perfmon Counter Service	IN SERVICE
Cisco Unified CCX Cluster View Daemon	IN SERVICE
Manager Manager	IN SERVICE
Cisco Unified CCX Engine	PARTIAL SERVICE
Manager Manager	IN SERVICE
Subsystem Manager	PARTIAL SERVICE
MRCP ASR Subsystem	NOT CONFIGURED
Unified CM Telephony Subsystem	OUT OF SERVICE
Core RTR Subsystem	IN SERVICE
CMT Subsystem	IN SERVICE
RmCm Subsystem	IN SERVICE
eMail Subsystem	NOT CONFIGURED

Figure 5-5 UCCX Subsystems

"Cisco CTIManager" in CUCM Control Center:

Select Server

Server* 142.100.64.11--CUCM Voice/Video Go

Performance and Monitoring Services

Service Name	Status:	Activation Status
Cisco Serviceability Reporter	Not Running	Deactivated
Cisco CallManager SNMP Service	Not Running	Deactivated

Directory Services

Service Name	Status:	Activation Status
Cisco DirSync	Not Running	Deactivated

CM Services

Service Name	Status:	Activation Status
Cisco CallManager	Started	Activated
Cisco Unified Mobile Voice Access Service	Not Running	Deactivated
Cisco IP Voice Media Streaming App	Started	Activated
Cisco CTIManager	Started	Activated
Cisco Extension Mobility	Not Running	Deactivated
Cisco DHCP Monitor Service	Started	Activated

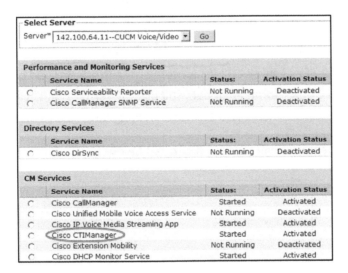

Figure 5-6 CUCM Services

CTI Port

A CTI port is like a phone device in CUCM. As a matter of fact, you go to **[CUCM Admin > Device > Phone]** to find/create/modify the CTI ports. Like phone devices, CTI ports have "registered" and "unregistered" states.

CTI ports, as the name indicates, are used by CTI applications (such as UCCX). Why are CTI ports needed? It is because when a customer call comes in, it has to connect to something before the caller can hear the audio (greetings, prompts, music, etc.) That "something" could be a physical device (phone) or a virtual device (a CTI port, or a voicemail port). Since UCCX needs to do some call screening/processing before passing it to a real person, it doesn't make sense to use a bunch of physical phones just to do the greeting and music. Using virtual device (CTI ports) is a better way.

Each CTI port can handles one call at a time. Thus the number of CTI ports decided the number of concurrent calls the system can handle. UCCX license determines how many CTI ports the system can use. Please note UCCX refers CTI ports as "IVR ports" because UCCX uses those for IVR purpose.

Call Control Group

Call Control Groups are no more than containers of CTI ports. Grouping CTI ports make it easy for capacity planning. For example, you have limited number of CTI ports to serve two hotlines. When all CTI ports are occupied, additional callers will hear busy tone. Say, you would like to give one of the hotlines higher priorities so the calls to that hotline are less likely to get busy signal. You may divide the CTI ports into two Call Control Groups and dedicate the groups to corresponding hotlines. The hotline with more CTI ports is less likely to get busy signal.

CTI Route Point

CTI route point is a pseudo number that redirect calls. "CTI Route Point" on CUCM is corresponding to "Telephony Trigger" on UCCX (which in turn, associated with an UCCX application). A CTI Route Point is somewhat similar to Hunt Pilot or Voicemail Pilot.

In the example diagram below, CUCM has two CTI route points with directory number 6000 and 6010 respectively. UCCX has two triggers corresponding to the two route points. Each trigger is associated with an UCCX application. If customer phone calls 6000, the call will trigger UCCX application #1. If customer phone calls 6010, the call will trigger UCCX application #2.

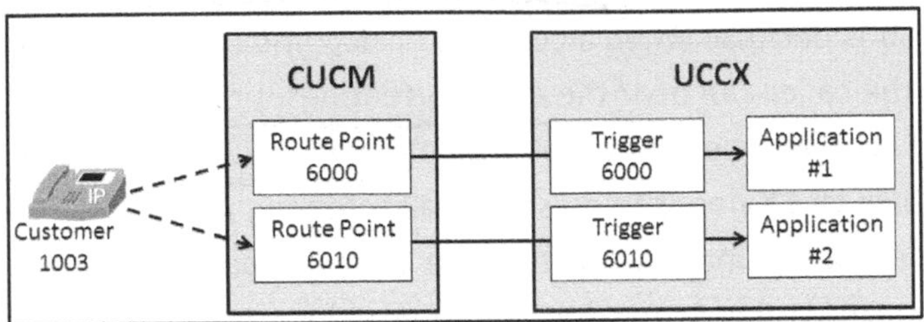

Figure 5-7 Route Point, Trigger and Application

Both CTI ports and CTI route points need to be associated with the UCCX "Telephony User" (JTAPI User) on CUCM (done by UCCX via AXL protocol). UCCX needs to authenticate with CUCM CTIManager with the credential before it can control CTI route points and CTI ports.

CUCM Terminology	Corresponding **UCCX** Terminology
CTI Port	IVR Port
CTI Route Point	Telephony Trigger
	Call Control Group

Device Association

As discussed before, CTI applications (such as UCCX) talk to CTIManager (on CUCM) with CTI/JTAPI protocol. For security, CTIManager needs to validate the request by user credentials. CTIManager needs to know who has permission to control which device(s). This is done by the "Device Association" on CUCM user management page.

UCCX controls CTI Route Points and CTI Ports via "JTAPI user". UCCX controls agent phones via "RMCM" (a.k.a. "RM JTAPI") user.

CUCM Application User	CUCM Devices	Auto Association
JTAPI User (e.g. "jtapi_1", "jtapi_2")	CTI Ports, CTI Route Points	Yes
RMCM User (e.g. "rmcm")	Agent Phones	No

Please note:

1) We create the CTI Ports (Call Control Groups) and Route Points (Triggers) from UCCX. The corresponding CUCM devices are associated to the JTAPI user automatically. You don't have to do it explicitly from CUCM.

2) We create/configure agent phones from CUCM. We will have to associate the agent phones to RMCM user manually from CUCM.

Primary Extension and IPCC Extension

CUCM (and other UC applications) are moving from device-centric to user-centric. On the CUCM End User configuration page, there are two settings called "Primary Extension" and "IPCC Extension". Once you have a phone associated with the user, you may select the extensions from the drop-down list.

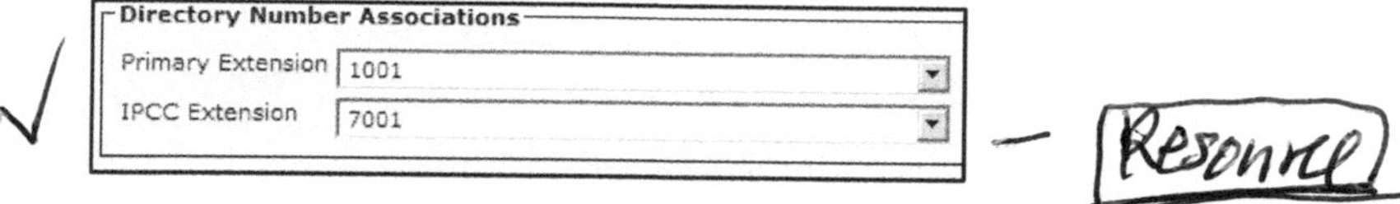

Figure 5-8 CUCM User Configuration

What matters here is the "IPCC Extension", which tells the system which line is the "ICD Line". If you don't have this set, the CUCM user will be disqualified to be a "Resource" on UCCX. For example, if you don't have the "IPCC Extension" set, you won't be able to find the corresponding user in the "Resource" list on UCCX. UCCX disqualifies the user as a resource (agent) because he/she doesn't have an IPCC extension.

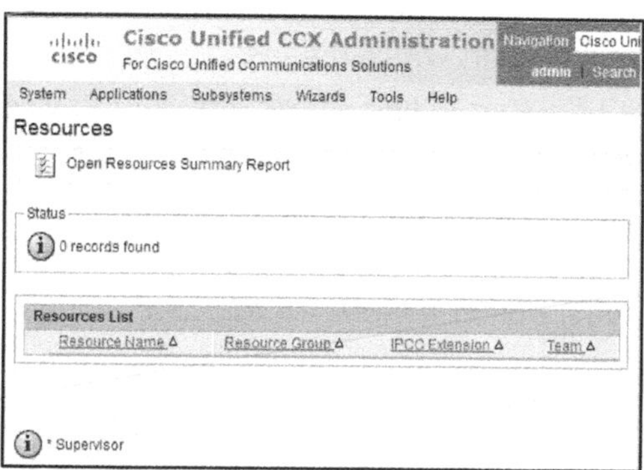

Figure 5-9 UCCX Resource List

CUCM: Provision Agent Phones

CUCM Tasks:

- **Provision phones (agent phones)**
- Provision end users (agents)

UCCX Tasks:

- Provision "Call Control Group" (CTI Ports)
- Provision "Resource" (agents)
- Provision "Contact Service Queue" (CSQ)
- Provision "Application"
- Provision "Triggers" (CTI Route Points)

What is special with a call center agent's phone? Nothing is special with the phone. But one of the lines requires special provisioning.

Phone status is one of the indicators of agent availability. UCCX monitors the phone status at line level. A single phone could have multiple lines. But only one of the lines will be monitored by UCCX. This line is referred as "ICD Line" by UCCX. This line is referred as "IPCC Extension" by CUCM.

CUCM Terminology	Corresponding **UCCX** Terminology
IPCC Extension	ICD Line

There is some special requirement for this line on CUCM:

1) This line has to be unique all over, which means:
   a. This line cannot be a shared line across different devices
   b. The directory number cannot be shared by multiple line appearance even if on the same device. (Some people use the same directory number in different partitions to create multiple line appearance. This is not supported by UCCX.)
2) The "Maximum Number of Calls" needs to be 2. The "Busy Trigger" needs to be 1. The "Max Number of Calls" controls total number of calls on the line (regardless incoming or outgoing). Incoming customer call will be counted as one. In case agent needs to transfer the call to a supervisor or another agent that will be another one. Thus the max number is set to 2. The "Busy Trigger" controls incoming calls. This is to make sure there can be only one incoming call on this line.

Multiple Call/Call Waiting Settings on Device SEP001EBE923926

Note:The range to select the Max Number of calls is: 1-200

Maximum Number of Calls* 2

Busy Trigger* 1 (Less than or equal to Max. Calls)

Figure 5-10 CUCM > Device > Phone > Line Configuration

Because of the above restrictions, it is a common practice to separate the ICD line from the primary (regular) line. For example, the regular line is with extension 1001. The ICD line is with extension 7001. Then apply the special settings to extension 7001.

Association

Modify Button Items

1 Line [1] - 1001 (no partition)

2 Line [2] - 7001 (no partition)

3 Add a new SD

4 Add a new SD

5 Add a new SD

Phone Type

Product Type: Cisco 7965

Device Protocol: SCCP

Real-time Device Status

Registration: Registered with Cisco U

IPv4 Address: 142.102.64.10

Active Load ID: SCCP45.9-3-1SR4-1S

Download Status: None

Figure 5-11 CUCM > Device > Phone Configuratoin

To provision agent phones, you may either pick from existing phone or create new phones. You may use the existing line appearance (extension) or add a new one as dedicated ICD line. Be sure to apply special settings to ICD lines:

- Uniqueness
- Max. Number of Calls = 2
- Busy Trigger = 1

After the phone was created/configured properly, we need to associate it to the "RmCm user" so UCCX and poll the status of the phone and control the phone. We go to **[CUCM > User Management > Application User > <*RmCm user*>]**. Select the agent phones from "Available Devices" list and move them into the "Controlled Devices" list. Then click the "Save" button to save changes.

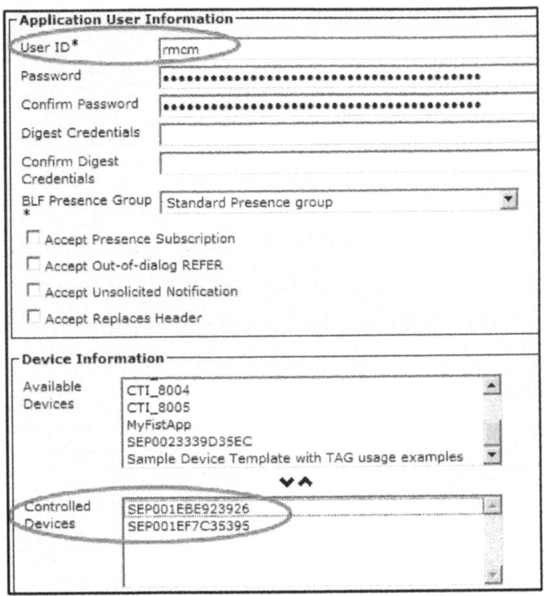

Figure 5-12 CUCM User Configuration

If you have many phones, and the phone you expect to see is not showing up on the "Available Devices" list, you'll have to use the "Find more Phones" button.

Associating agent phones to RmCm is very important. It is so important that UCCX won't allow an agent log into Agent Desktop if his/her phone is not associated with RmCm (usually referred as "RM JTAPI").

CUCM: Provision Agent User Accounts

CUCM Tasks:

- ✓ Provision phones (agent phones)
- ➢ **Provision end users (agents)**

UCCX Tasks:

- Provision "Call Control Group" (CTI Ports)
- Provision "Resource" (agents)
- Provision "Contact Service Queue" (CSQ)
- Provision "Application"
- Provision "Triggers" (CTI Route Points)

To provision agent user accounts, you may use existing end user accounts or create new ones. Apply the following settings to the user:

- Associate the phone to the user
- Specify the "Primary Extension" and "IPCC Extension"

Please note:

We associate the phone to an end user so that we can specify the end user's "Primary Extension" and "IPCC Extension". That is the purpose of the association. Don't confuse this association with the CTI device association, which is for the purpose of phone control.

UCCX: Provision Call Control Group

CUCM Tasks:

- ✓ Provision phones (agent phones)
- ✓ Provision end users (agents)

UCCX Tasks:

- ➢ **Provision "Call Control Group" (CTI Ports)**
- Provision "Resource" (agents)
- Provision "Contact Service Queue" (CSQ)
- Provision "Application"
- Provision "Triggers" (CTI Route Points)

As discussed before, UCCX "Call Control Group" is no more than a container for CTI ports. We associate a "Call Control Group" to an application or applications. Those applications will share the same pool of CTI ports. The number of CTI ports in that pool determines the number of concurrent calls the applications can handle.

However, the term "concurrent calls" is somehow misleading. UCCX only uses CTI ports before the call is handed off to an agent (when the caller is choosing menu options or waiting in the queue). Once the call is connected to an agent, the CTI port is released and put back into the pool.

The following two diagrams demonstrate the use of CTI ports.

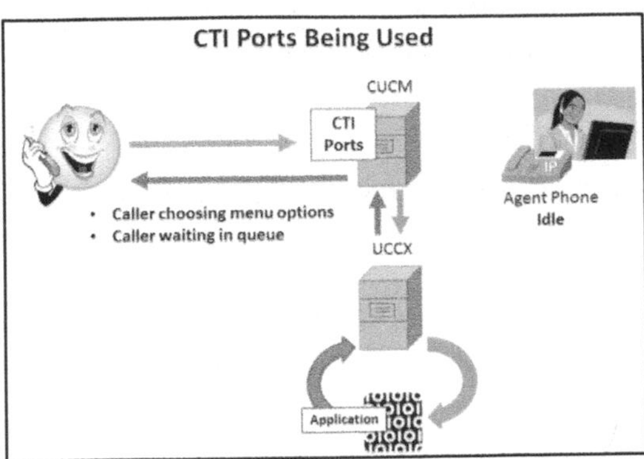

Figure 5-13 UCCX Handling the Call

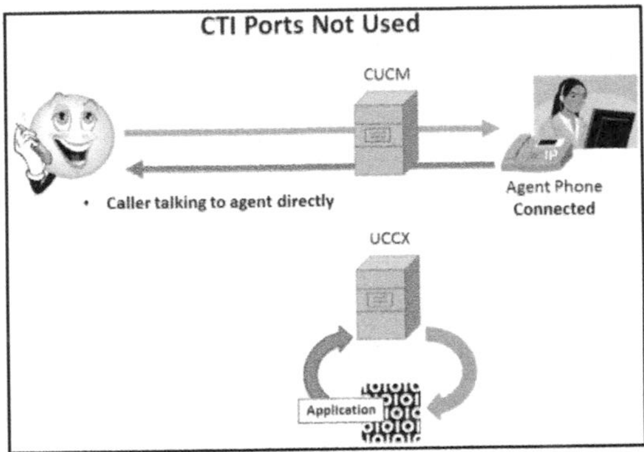

Figure 5-14 UCCX Handed Off the Call to Agent

Keeping these diagrams in mind will help you troubleshoot call issues as well. Say, the problem description was "when customer was talking to an agent, the call was dropped". If the description was accurate, the problem has nothing to do with UCCX. When the call was handed off to agent, UCCX is totally off the call flow (out of the picture).

When we create the "Call Control Group" from UCCX, it actually creates CTI ports on CUCM (via AXL integration).

To create "Call Control Group", we go to [**UCCX AppAdmin Portal > Subsystems > Cisco Unified CM Telephony > Call Control Group**].

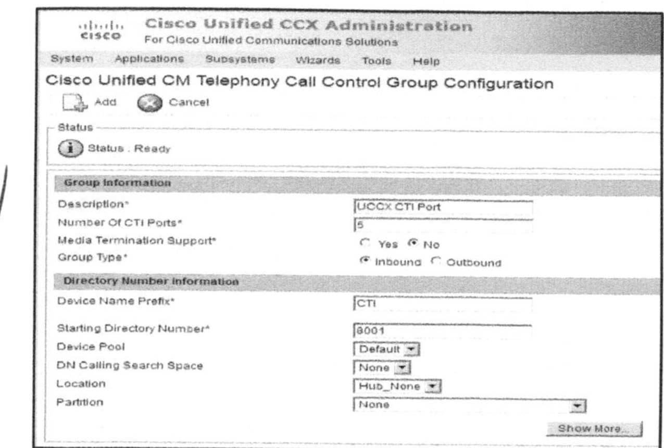

Figure 5-15 UCCX Call Control Group Configuration

Here are the parameter descriptions of a "Call Control Group".

Description	Self-explanatory. It will be used as CUCM device description.
Number of CTI Ports	The number of CTI ports you'd like to create for this group. It depends on how many "IVR port" the UCCX is licensed to use. And how many CTI ports have been created before.
Media Termination Support	This takes a little bit to explain. We will cover it later on. Use the default option of "No" is fine.
Group Type	Default is "inbound", means the CTI ports are used to receive customer calls. "Outbound" means call out to customer, which are normally used when "Call Me Back" option was chosen by customer.
Device Name Prefix	Name prefix being used to form the CTI port device names.
Starting Directory Number	Like phone device, each CTI port needs to have a directory number. Say, you specify the starting DN is 8001 and want to create 5 ports; their DNs will be from 8001 to 8005.
Device Pool, DN Calling Search Space, Location, Partition	These parameters are corresponding to the device settings on CUCM. A CTI port is just like an IP phone. These settings will impact the call behavior. For example, the CTI DN CSS (Calling Search Space) must be able to reach the agent phones DN partition. Otherwise, a call cannot be transferred from CTI port to agent.

Please note that even though we're creating the "Call Control Group" from UCCX, we are actually creating the CTI ports on CUCM. Think this part of UCCX as a "management front end" of CUCM.

When you hit the "Add" button, the following happens.

On UCCX:

- A Call Control Group is created with specific number of ports and parameters.

On CUCM:

- A number of CTI ports are created with specific parameters. You may find those CTI ports at [**CUCM > Device > Phone**] page.
- The newly created CTI ports are associated to the "Telephony User" (JTAPI user). You may see it at [**CUCM > User Management > Application User > *<JTAP user>***]

UCCX Call Control Group screen:

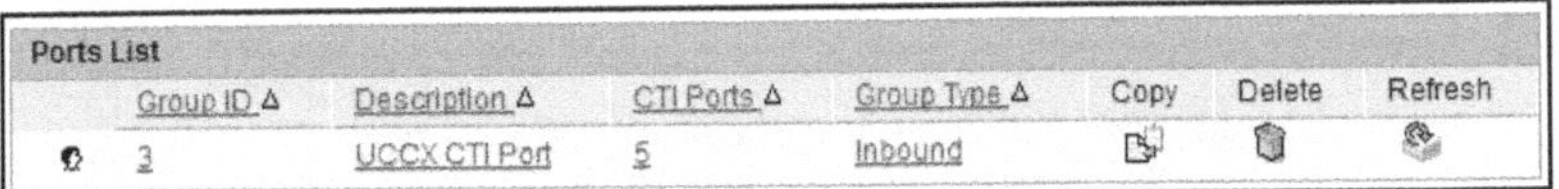

Ports List

	Group ID	Description	CTI Ports	Group Type	Copy	Delete	Refresh
	3	UCCX CTI Port	5	Inbound			

Figure 5-16 UCCX Call Control Group List

Don't worry about the "Group ID". It is just a system generated ID and doesn't have any significance in our configuration.

UCCX "Call Control Group" details (after creation):

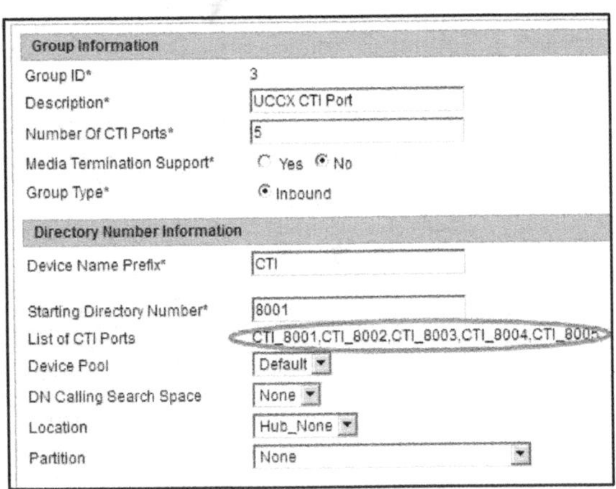

Group Information

Group ID*	3
Description*	UCCX CTI Port
Number Of CTI Ports*	5
Media Termination Support*	Yes / No (selected)
Group Type*	Inbound (selected)

Directory Number Information

Device Name Prefix*	CTI
Starting Directory Number*	8001
List of CTI Ports	CTI_8001,CTI_8002,CTI_8003,CTI_8004,CTI_8005
Device Pool	Default
DN Calling Search Space	None
Location	Hub_None
Partition	None

Figure 5-17 UCCX Call Control Group Created

Note the "List of CTI Ports" area has the CTI port device names listed.

CUCM Device List:

Device Name(Line)	Description	Device Pool	Device Protocol	Status	IPv4 Address
CTI_8001	UCCX CTI Port-1	Default	SCCP	Registered with 142.100.64.11	142.100.64.14
CTI_8002	UCCX CTI Port-1	Default	SCCP	Registered with 142.100.64.11	142.100.64.14
CTI_8003	UCCX CTI Port-1	Default	SCCP	Registered with 142.100.64.11	142.100.64.14
CTI_8004	UCCX CTI Port-1	Default	SCCP	Registered with 142.100.64.11	142.100.64.14
CTI_8005	UCCX CTI Port-1	Default	SCCP	Registered with 142.100.64.11	142.100.64.14
SEP001EBE923926	Agent1	Default	SCCP	Registered with 142.100.64.11	142.102.64.10
SEP001EF7C35395	Agent2	Default	SCCP	Registered with 142.100.64.11	142.102.64.12
SEP0023339D35EC	Customer	Default	SCCP	Registered with 142.100.64.11	142.102.64.11

Add New | Select All | Clear All | Delete Selected | Reset Selected | Apply Config to Selected

Figure 5-18 CUCM > Device > Phone List

Note the "Device Name" and "Description" are constructed with the parameters set on UCCX admin page.

CUCM Application User Details:

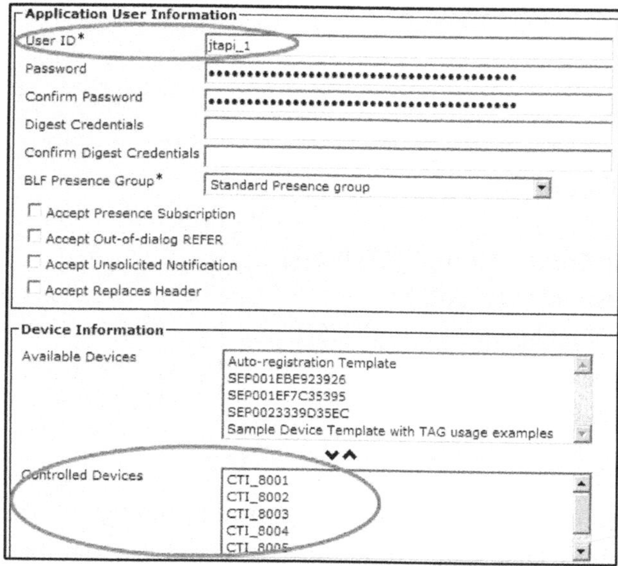
Application User Information
User ID* jtapi_1
Password
Confirm Password
Digest Credentials
Confirm Digest Credentials
BLF Presence Group* Standard Presence group
Accept Presence Subscription
Accept Out-of-dialog REFER
Accept Unsolicited Notification
Accept Replaces Header
Device Information
Available Devices
Auto-registration Template
SEP001EBE923926
SEP001EF7C35395
SEP0023339D35EC
Sample Device Template with TAG usage examples
Controlled Devices
CTI_8001
CTI_8002
CTI_8003
CTI_8004
CTI_8005

Figure 5-19 CUCM User Configuration

Note the newly created CTI ports in the "Controlled Devices" list.

At this point, we have successfully provision the UCCX "Call Control Group". Please note that you don't have to do this for each application. As a matter of fact, many UCCX deployments have only one "Call Control Group" for their whole life. You need more than one group only if you want to have different capacities for different applications.

Putting CTI ports into different groups give you more granular control. However, it might bring unbalanced utilization to the ports. For example, CTI ports in one of the groups are over utilized while the other group is underutilized.

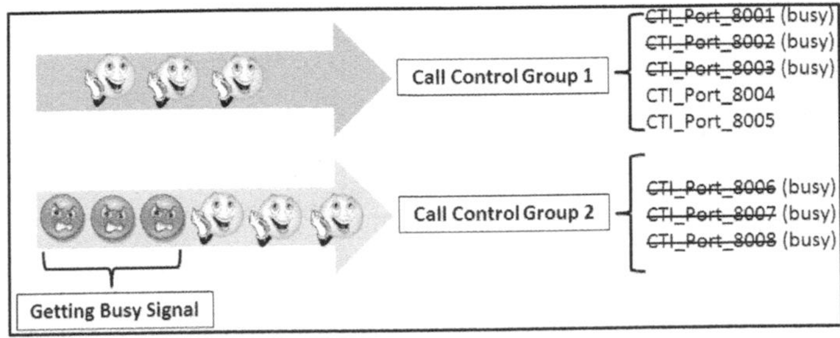

Figure 5-20 Two Call Control Groups

UCCX: Provision Resource (Agent)

CUCM Tasks:

- ✓ Provision phones (agent phones)
- ✓ Provision end users (agents)

UCCX Tasks:

- ✓ Provision "Call Control Group" (CTI Ports)
- ➢ **Provision "Resource" (agents)**
- Provision "Contact Service Queue" (CSQ)
- Provision "Application"
- Provision "Triggers" (CTI Route Points)

A "resource" means an agent in UCCX. UCCX synchronize the agent info (such as account name, first name, last name, etc.) from CUCM end user database. But not all CUCM end users are qualified as UCCX "resource". Only the users have "IPCC Extension" can become a "resource" (show up in the resource list). To see the resource list, you may go to [**UCCX AppAdmin Portal > Subsystems > RmCm > Resources**].

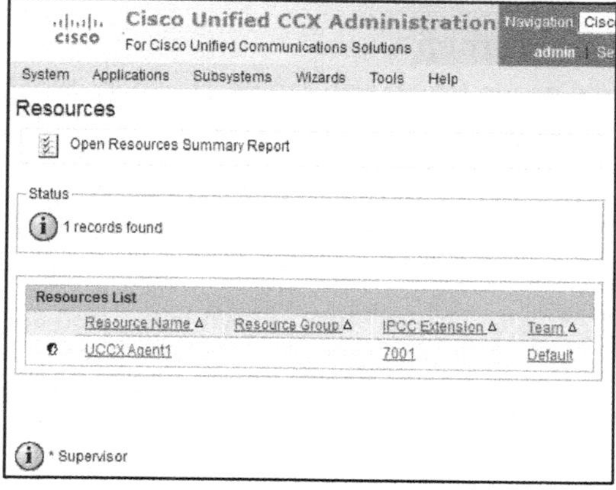

Figure 5-21 UCCX Resource List

Our ultimate goal is to associate resources to a CSQ (Contact Service Queue) so the agents and answer calls in a queue, which will be covered in next section.

Before we can associate the resource to a CSQ, the resource either has to be in a "Resource Group" or has to have some "Skills".

We will use "Resource Group" in this example because it is easier to set up. "Skill" gives us more flexibility to control resource but is also more complex. We will discuss "Skill" in later chapters.

Resource Group

Resource Group is a container for resources. There is no configurable parameter for resource group. All you need to do is to give it a name and save the configuration.

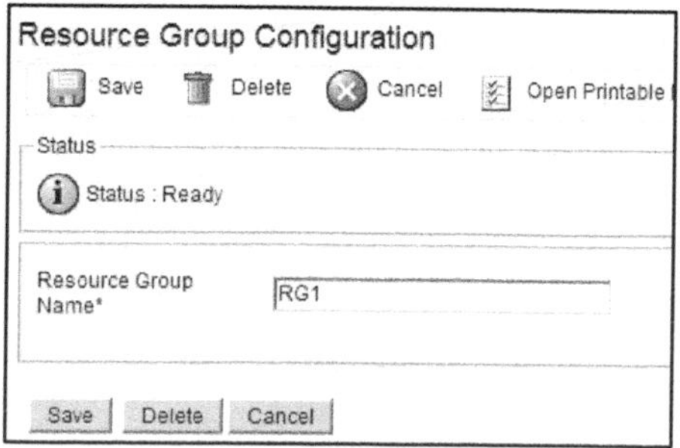

Figure 5-22 UCCX Creating Resource Group

Assign resource to a specific group

We can only assign resource group from resource perspective. Not from group perspective.

Go to [**UCCX AppAdmin Portal > Subsystems > RmCm > Resources**]. Then click on the resource you want to configure. On the "Resource Configuration" page, select desired appropriate group from "Resource Group" drop-down list. Then save the configuration.

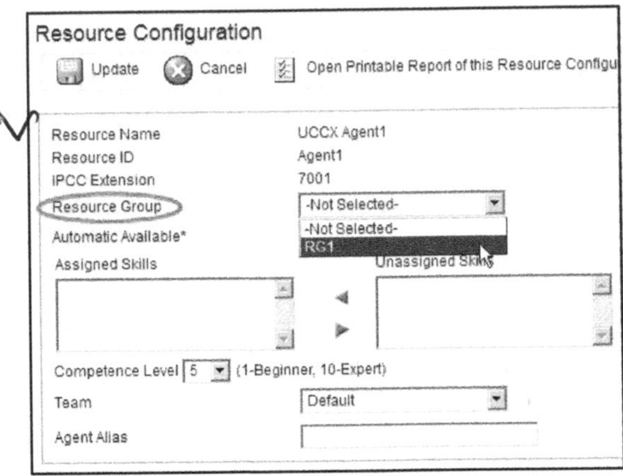

Figure 5-23 UCCX Resource Configuration

Don't worry about other parameters. We will discuss those later. Again, more groups/skills give you more granular control but make resource planning more complex. The best practice is to create groups/skills only when necessary.

UCCX: Provision "Contact Service Queue" (CSQ)

CUCM Tasks:

- ✓ Provision phones (agent phones)
- ✓ Provision end users (agents)

UCCX Tasks:

- ✓ Provision "Call Control Group" (CTI Ports)
- ✓ Provision "Resource" (agents)
- ➢ **Provision "Contact Service Queue" (CSQ)**
- • Provision "Application"
- • Provision "Triggers" (CTI Route Points)

When calls come into a call center, they are usually put into a queue. Callers wait in the queue until their calls get picked up by agents.

UCCX refers the queues as "Contact Service Queues" (CSQs). ICD application usually have at least one CSQ.

Parameters in CSQ determine which resources will serve the queue and how the calls will be distributed to resources.

To create a CSQ, we go to [**UCCX AppAdmin Portal > Subsystems > RmCm > Contact Service Queues**]. Click "Add New" button to add a new CSQ.

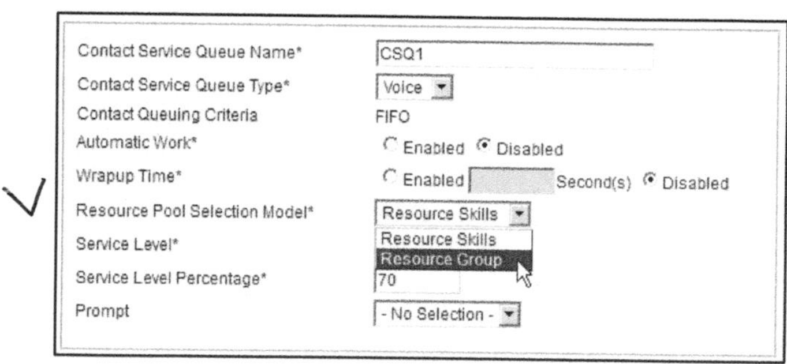

Figure 5-24 UCCX Creating CSQ

Enter a queue name in the "Contact Service Queue Name" field (for example "CSQ1"). Note the "Resource Pool Select Model" is "Resource Skills" be default. Since we are using "Resource Group" here in this example, let's choose "Resource Group" in the drop-down list. Leave other parameters as default. Then click "Next" button to go to the next screen.

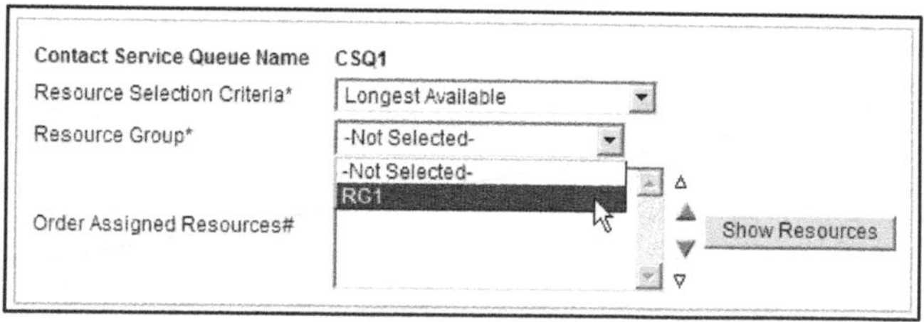

Figure 5-25 UCCX Creating CSQ (Continued)

Select the resource group we previously created (for example "RG1") from the drop-down list. Leave other parameters as default. Click "Add" button to create the CSQ. The finish screen would be like this:

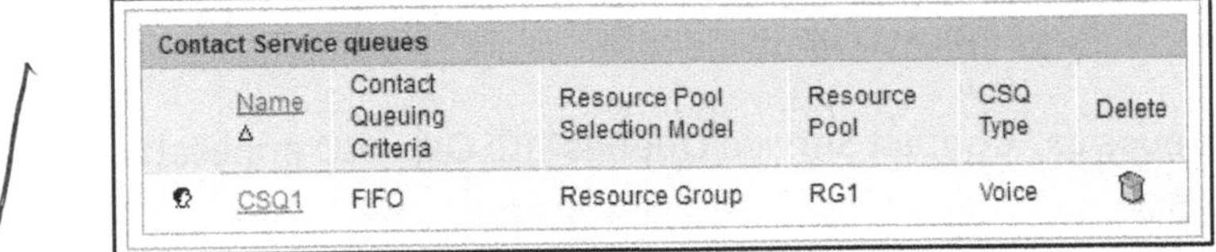

	Name △	Contact Queuing Criteria	Resource Pool Selection Model	Resource Pool	CSQ Type	Delete
	CSQ1	FIFO	Resource Group	RG1	Voice	

Figure 5-26 UCCX CSQ List

UCCX: Provision Application

CUCM Tasks:

- ✓ Provision phones (agent phones)
- ✓ Provision end users (agents)

UCCX Tasks:

- ✓ Provision "Call Control Group" (CTI Ports)
- ✓ Provision "Resource" (agents)
- ✓ Provision "Contact Service Queue" (CSQ)
- ➢ **Provision "Application"**
- Provision "Triggers" (CTI Route Points)

UCCX applications have intelligence to handle incoming calls. There are three different kind of applications:

- Cisco Script Application
- Busy
- Ring-No-Answer

In most (if not all) of the cases, you will be using "Cisco Script Application".

As the name indicates, a "Cisco Script Application" consists of a script (at least). Depending on the script, we might have to create prompts (audio files), documents, etc.

Fortunately, UCCX comes with some pre-built script. Thus we don't have to build a script from scratch for the purpose of this example. We are going to use a script called "ICD.aef".

Note: .aef stands for "Application Export File". It is the file format used by UCCX or Unity Express scripts.

To create an application, go to [**UCCX AppAdmin Portal > Application > Application Management**], then click "Add New" button.

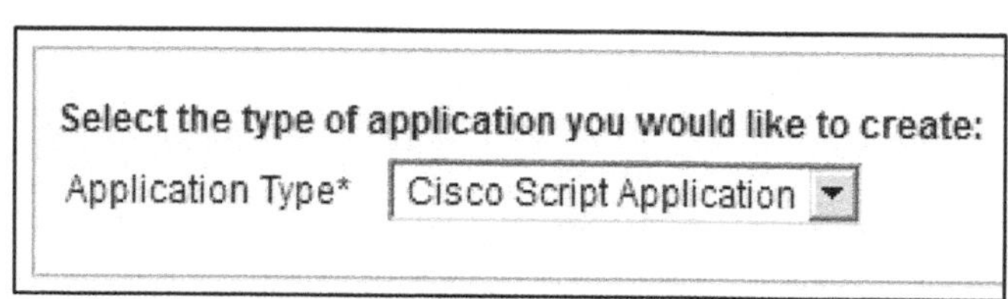

Figure 5-27 UCCX Creating Application

The first screen is to choose the Application Type. Note the default is "Cisco Script Application", which is exactly what we want. So just click the "Next" button to continue.

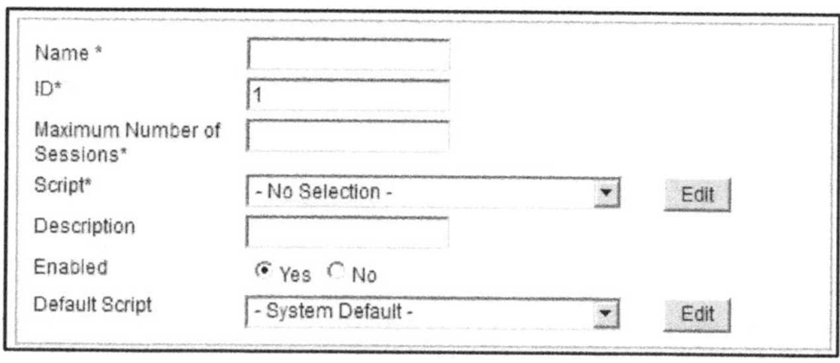

Figure 5-28 UCCX Creating Application (Continued)

On the next screen, you will enter a name for the application (for example "MyFirstApp").

You will also specify the Maximum Number of Sessions (for example "5"). There is no universal formula for this parameter. But if the application use at least one CTI port, this parameter should not be greater than the number of CTI ports assigned to this application.

You will choose "SSCRIPT[icd.aef]" from the Script drop-down list. Please note that once you select "SSCRIPT[icd.aef]", the page will automatically refresh and give you more script-specific parameters.

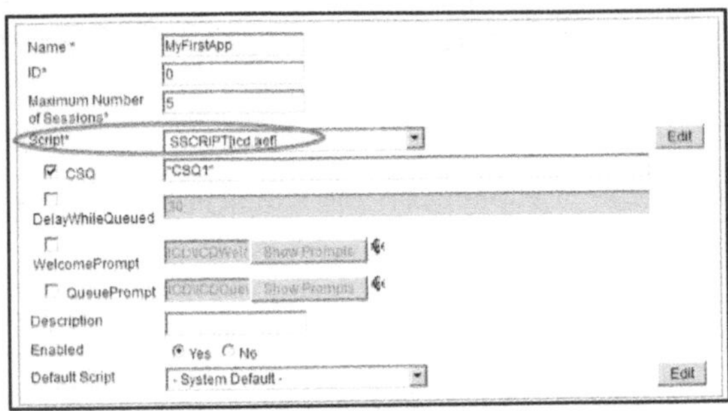

Figure 5-29 UCCX Creating Application - Script Selected

Each script-specific parameter has a checkbox. If the checkbox was checked, the script will use the parameter you entered here. If the checkbox was unchecked, the script will use default values (displayed in the grey-out area).

For icd.aef, we will have to modify at least one of the parameters – CSQ, because there is no default value for the CSQ parameter. We will check the checkbox next to CSQ and enter the CSQ we previously created (for example "CSQ1"). Please note the CSQ name has to be inside the quotation marks as shown on the example above.

Leave other parameters as default. Then click "Add" button. Now we have an application created on UCCX. But don't close the page yet. We will use the same page to continue the next task.

UCCX: Provision Triggers

CUCM Tasks:

- ✓ Provision phones (agent phones)
- ✓ Provision end users (agents)

UCCX Tasks:

- ✓ Provision "Call Control Group" (CTI Ports)
- ✓ Provision "Resource" (agents)
- ✓ Provision "Contact Service Queue" (CSQ)
- ✓ Provision "Application"
- ➢ **Provision "Triggers" (CTI Route Points)**

In previous steps, we created an UCCX application called "MyFirstApp". But how do we put this application in use? How do the customer calls hit this application?

For the customer calls to hit something, they need to have a destination number to call. This destination number is configured on Route Point device in CUCM. To link the calls hitting the route point to an application, we need a "trigger" configured on UCCX. To refresh our memory, here is the diagram again.

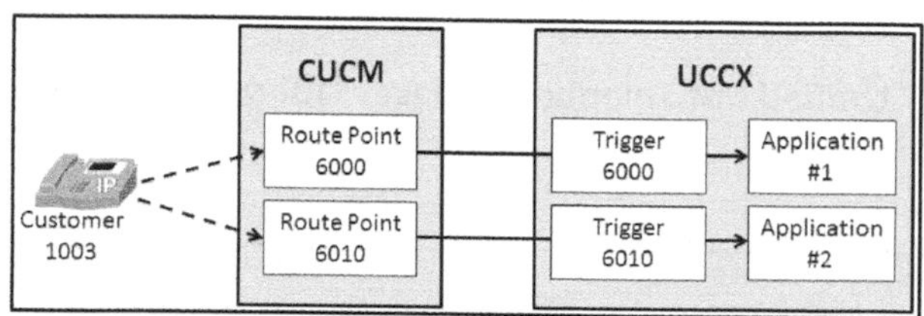

Figure 5-30 Route Point, Trigger and Application

Though route point is on CUCM while trigger is on UCCX, we can actually create them in one shot from UCCX. This makes our job easier and ensures configuration consistency.

There are two places on UCCX we can create a trigger:

- From [**UCCX AppAdmin Portal > Application > Application Management**]
- From [**UCCX AppAdmin Portal > Subsystems > Cisco Unified CM Telephony > Triggers**]

Since we just finish creating the application, let's create the trigger within the Application page.

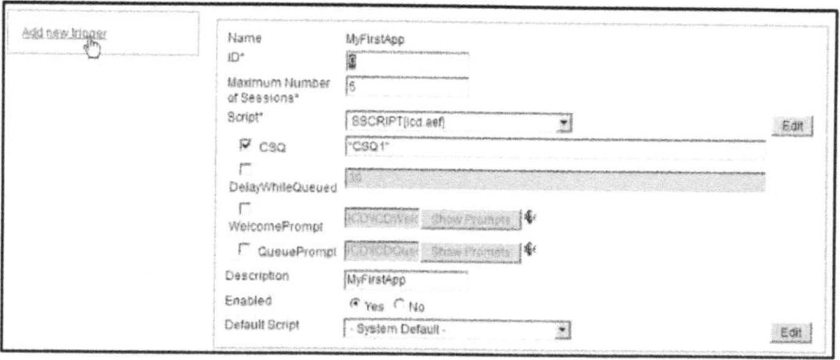

Figure 5-31 UCCX Creating Trigger within Application Page

Once an application is created, an "Add new trigger" link will appear on the left hand side within the page. Click on that link to create a trigger that associated with this application.

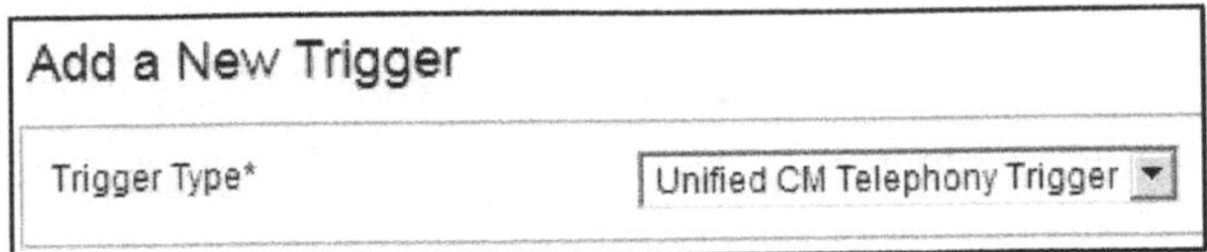

Figure 5-32 UCCX Creating Trigger

"Trigger Type" will be "Unified CM Telephony Trigger" for our application. Click "Next" to go to the next page.

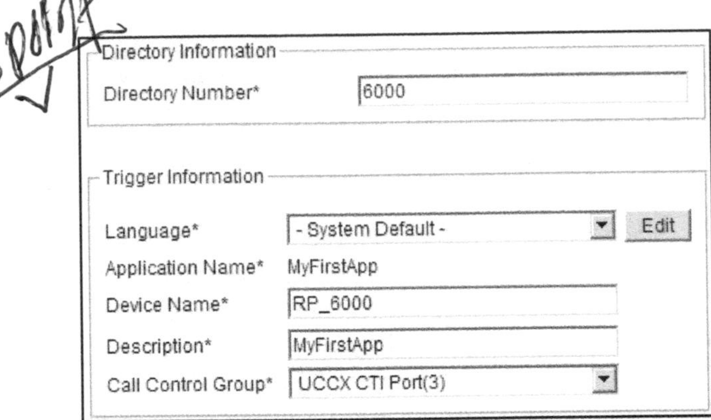

Figure 5-33 UCCX Creating Trigger (Continued)

Directory Number	Directory number of the route point. This is the destination number for the customer incoming calls.
Device Name	Device name for the route point on CUCM.
Description	Description of the route point on CUCM.
Call Control Group	The Call Control Group we previously created. The number 3 in the parentheses are the group ID, not the number of ports.

When we hit "Add" button on this page, the following happens:

On UCCX:

- A telephony trigger is created and associated with the application ("MyFirstApp" in our case)
- A call control group is associated to this trigger, which means the CTI ports in the group will be used to handle the calls hitting the trigger.

On CUCM:

- A CTI Route Point is created. You may find it at [CUCM > Device > CTI Route Points]

- The CTI Route Point is associated with the "Telephony User" (JTAPI user). You may find it at [**CUCM > User Management > Application User > *<JTAPI user>***].

UCCX Trigger details:

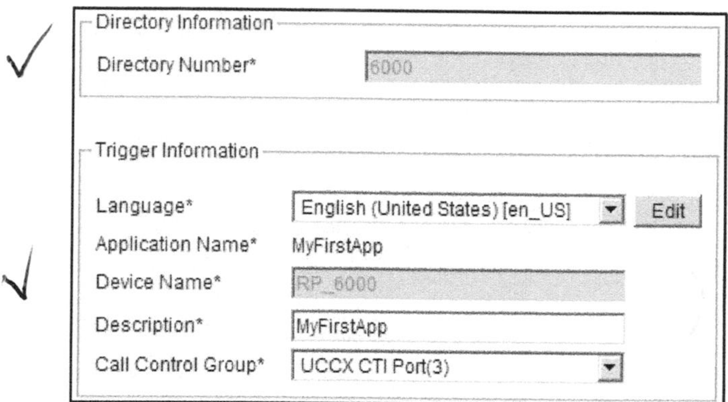

Figure 5-34 UCCX Trigger Created

Note the "Directory Number" and "Device Name" is grey-out once the trigger is created. To change those, you will have to delete the trigger and recreate.

[**CUCM > Device > CTI Route Points**] page:

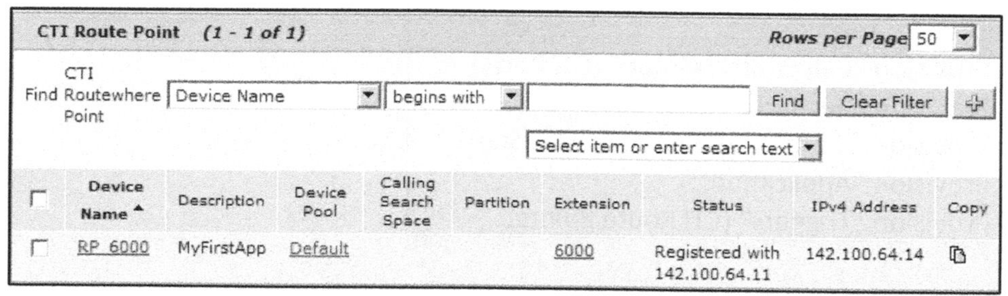

CTI Route Point (1 - 1 of 1) Rows per Page 50

Find CTI Routewhere Point [Device Name] [begins with] [ ] Find Clear Filter

Select item or enter search text

	Device Name ▲	Description	Device Pool	Calling Search Space	Partition	Extension	Status	IPv4 Address	Copy
	RP_6000	MyFirstApp	Default			6000	Registered with 142.100.64.11	142.100.64.14	

Figure 5-35 CUCM > Device > Route Point

[**CUCM > User Management > Application User > *<JTAPI User>***] page:

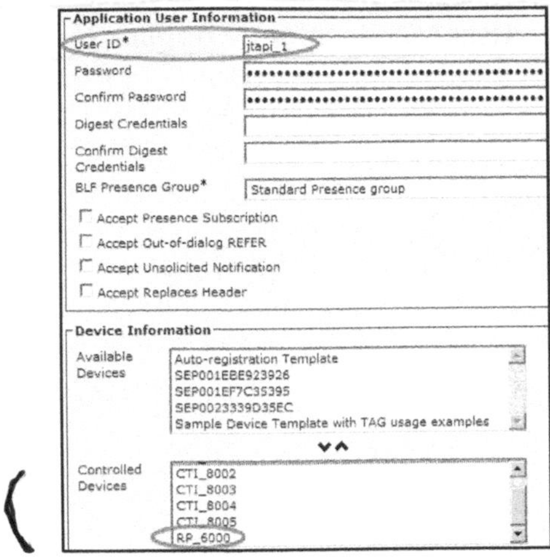

Figure 5-36 CUCM User Configuration

Note the newly created route point ("RP_6000") in the "Controlled Device" list.

CUCM Tasks:

- ✓ Provision phones (agent phones)
- ✓ Provision end users (agents)

UCCX Tasks:

- ✓ Provision "Call Control Group" (CTI Ports)
- ✓ Provision "Resource" (agents)
- ✓ Provision "Contact Service Queue" (CSQ)
- ✓ Provision "Application"
- ✓ Provision "Triggers" (CTI Route Points)

At this point, we have finish provisioning CUCM and UCCX servers. If you can't wait, you may pick up an IP phone and dial "6000".

You should hear a voice prompt *"Thank you for calling. All our representatives are assisting other callers at this time. Your call is very important to us. Please stay on the line and your call will be handled in the order it was received."*

If you look at the screen of the IP phone, you will notice the call is connected to one of the CTI ports (for example "8001", "8002", etc.) This is normal. Before the call is handed off to an agent, UCCX uses CTI ports to front end the call. Once the call is handed off to agent, you will see the screen display changes to the agent's extension.

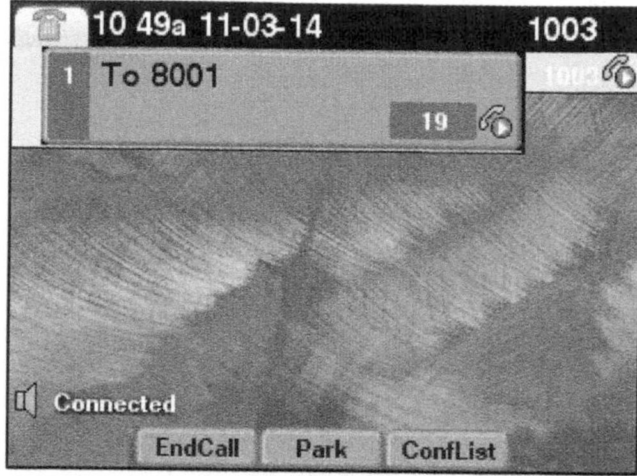

Figure 5-37 Customer Call Connected to CTI Port

Why the call was not delivered to the agent? The agents were not on the phone. Thus they should be available, shouldn't they?

Even though phone status is an important indicator of agent availability, it is not the sole indicator. There are some scenarios that the agent is not on the phone but not available to handle incoming call either. For example:

- Agent lunch time (or has to be away from the phone for whatever reason)
- Agent finished a customer call but needs time to enter information into the system (such as order info, etc.)
- Some other reasons that agent cannot take calls

UCCX gives agents the flexibility to indicate their availability. Agent can do it from Cisco Agent Desktop (CAD) or IP Phone Agent (IPPA). CAD and IPPA can also give agents useful information such as caller's account details, transaction history, etc.

If no agent has logged into CAD or IPPA, UCCX thinks no agent is available.

Provision Agent Desktop

You may download "CCX Desktop Suites" from UCCX server by going to [**UCCX AppAdmin Portal > Tools > Plug-ins**].

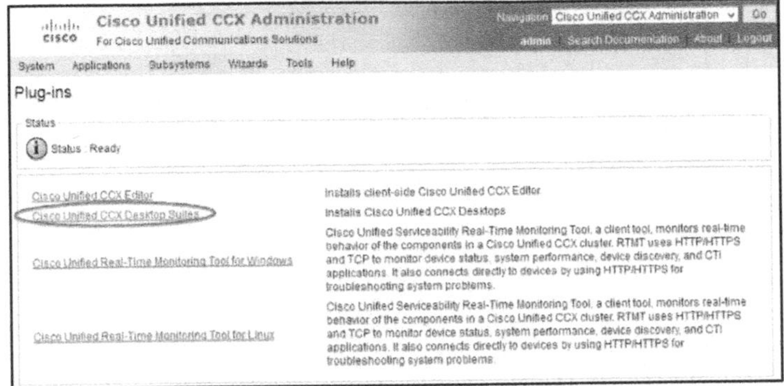

Figure 5-38 UCCX > Tools > Plug-ins

Client Configuration Tool

Before you install any "Desktop Suite" software for the first time, you should download and run the "CCX Client Configuration tool". This will set the site specific parameters in the installation files (such as server IP, etc.).

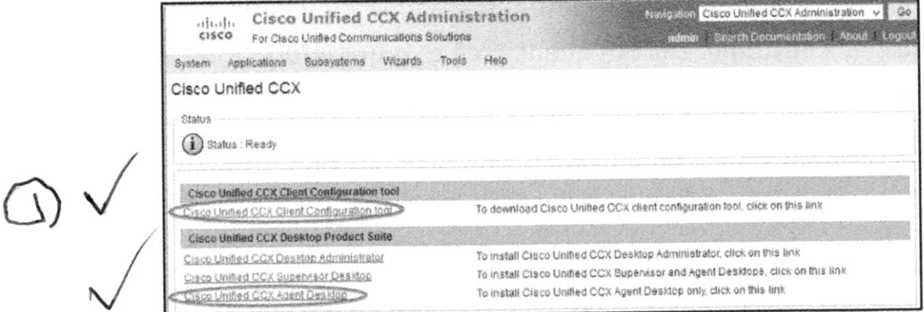

Figure 5-39 UCCX > Tools > Plug-ins > Desktop Suite

When you run the "Client Configuration tool", it'll ask you input the server IP:

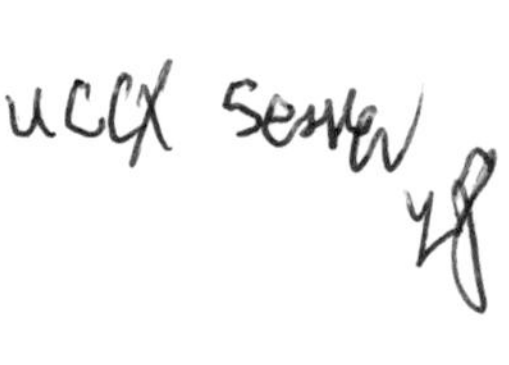

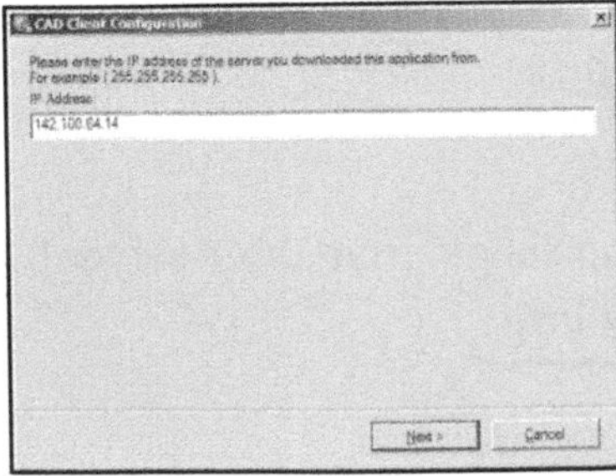

Figure 5-40 Client Configuration Tool - UCCX IP

Then it will download the client software (Agent Desktop, Supervisor Desktop and Administrator Desktop), set the parameters in the installation files, and upload them back to the server. When it is done, you will see a prompt like this:

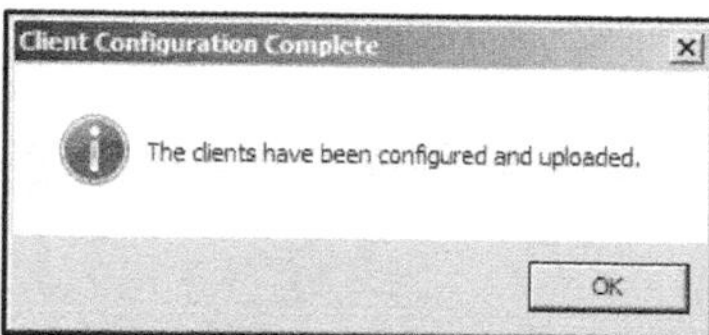

Figure 5-41 Client Configuration Tool - Confirmation

Install and Log Into Agent Desktop

Installation of Agent Desktop (CAD) is pretty straight forward. No parameter input is required other than clicking "Next" button.

When trying to log into agent desktop, you will be asked to enter user ID, password and extension.

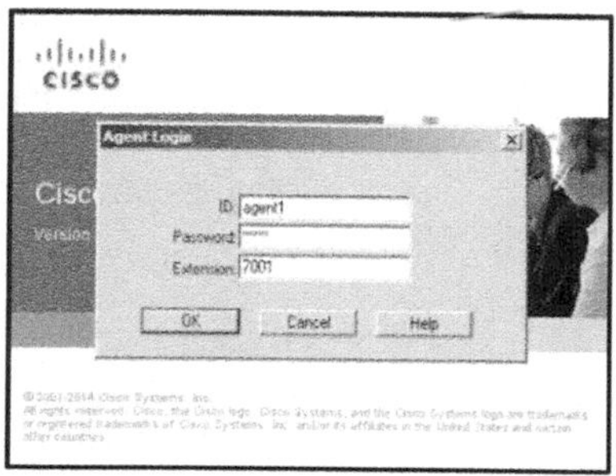

Figure 5-42 Agent Desktop - Login

User ID	Agent's CUCM user ID.
Password	Agent's CUCM user password.
Extension	Agent's IPCC Extension.

Above parameters are configured on [**CUCM > User Management > End User**] when creating/configuring the agent user. See "CUCM: Provision Agent User Account" section for details.

Here are some common seen errors during agent desktop logon.

"User ID, password, and extension is invalid"

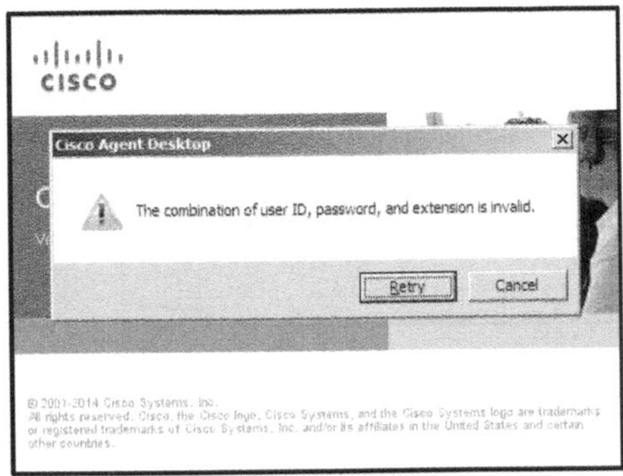

Figure 5-43 User ID/Password Invalid

Both user ID and password are case sensitive. For example, if the user ID on CUCM was "Agent1" but you entered "agent1", you won't be able to login. Also make sure you enter the "IPCC Extension", not the "Primary Extension" configured on CUCM.

"RM JTAPI" association error

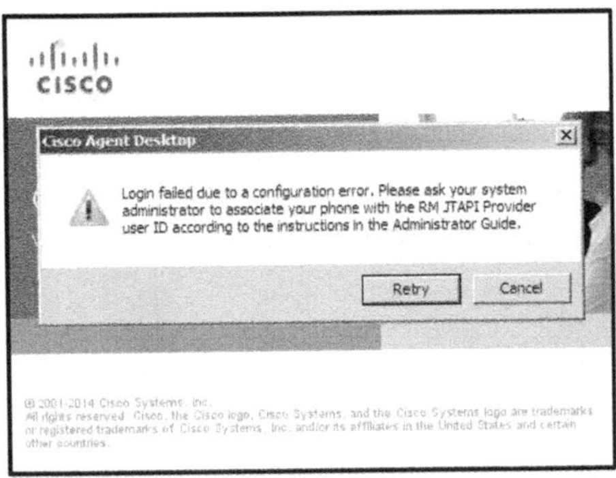

Figure 5-44 RMJTAPI Association Error

You will get this error if the agent's phone is not associated with the "RMCM" user. See "CUCM: Provision Agent Phone" for details.

If everything was configured properly, the agent desktop should log in in a few seconds. By default, the agent desktop starts as minimized. You may click the task bar icon to bring up the agent desktop.

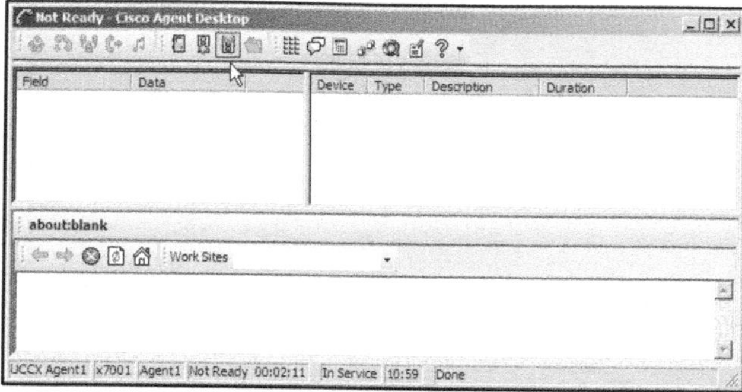

Figure 5-45 Agent Desktop

Agent Desktop State

There are different states for the agent desktop. Most frequently seen states are:

- Not Ready – Agent is not ready to handle calls
- Ready – Agent is ready to handle calls
- Working – Agent just finished a call and working on additional paperwork relevant to the call
- Reserved – UCCX has selected the agent and ringing his/her phone.
- Talking – Agent is talking on the phone.

"Working" state may or may not be present depending on business requirement and configuraiton.

By default, the agent desktop state is "Not Ready" after login. You may see this at the bottom of the window (status bar).

Agent may use the action buttons on the top to change his/her state. "Green traffic light" button stands for "ready". "Red traffic light" button stands for "not ready". UCCX will deliver the call to agent if his/her state is ready.

Let's click the "green traffic light" to make the agent desktop ready. Depending if there is any call waiting in the queue, agent desktop may behave differently.

If there is no call waiting in the queue, all you will notice is the agent state changed to "Ready" in the status bar.

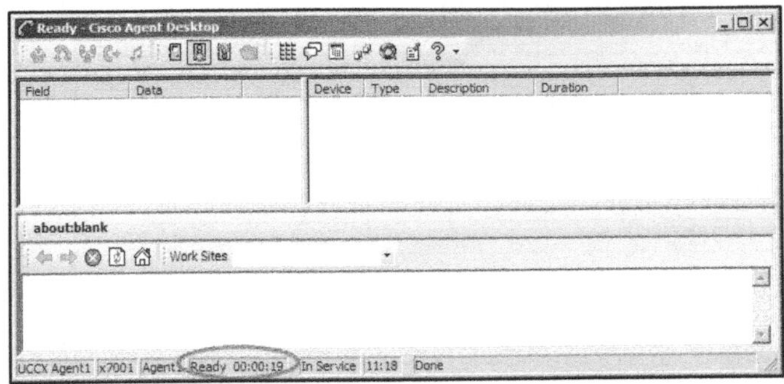

Figure 5-46 Agent Desktop in "Ready" State

If there are calls waiting in the queue and the agent change state from "not ready" to "ready", the call will be offered to the agent.

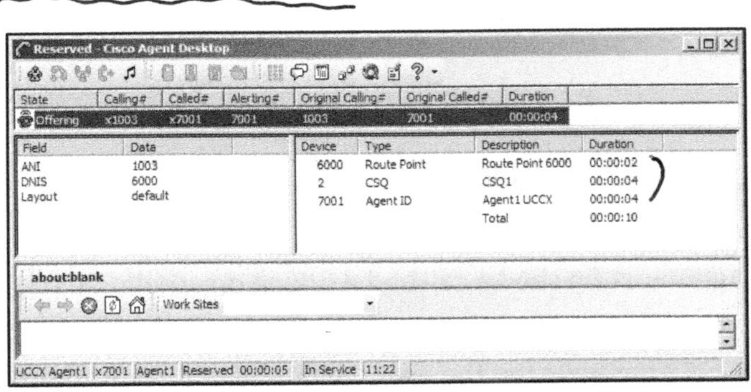

Figure 5-47 Agent Desktop in "Reserved" State

Agent desktop window is divided into multiple areas. The top area shows the call being offered (ringing).

The left area displays relevant info of the call. For example, ANI (Caller ID), DNIS (Dialed Number), etc. This area can be programmed to pull detailed information from database such as customer name, account number, street address, etc.

The right area displays the detailed call flow and the time spent on each step. In the example above, the call spent 2 seconds at route point, 4 seconds waiting in the queue, another 4 seconds ringing the agent's phone. Thus total wait time for the caller is 10 seconds.

The following chart may help you correlate the call state with caller's experience.

Call State	Caller Hears	Caller Sees
1. Call hits the Route Point	Usually nothing because it transits to next state very quickly	
2. Call hits CTI Port (in Queue)	UCCX Welcome Prompts or UCCX Music	CTI Port Directory Number
3. Call being offered to Agent	CUCM Music (Network MoH)	CTI Port Directory Number
4. Call is connected to Agent	Agent's voice	Agent's Directory Number

Here is what the agent desktop looks like when the call is connected to agent:

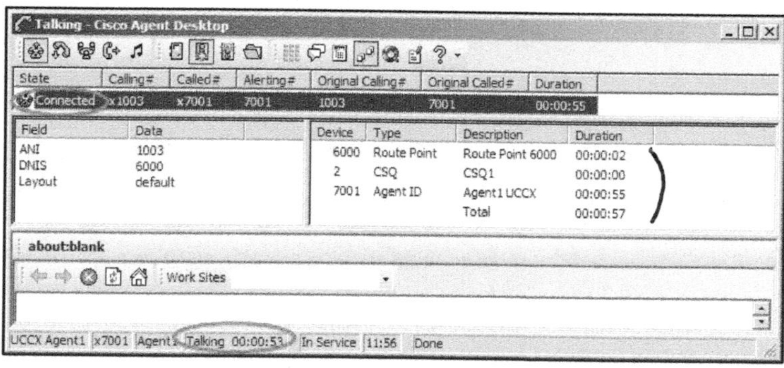

Figure 5-48 Agent Desktop in "Taling" State

At this point, you have successfully implemented your first UCCX application, which is an ICD (Intelligent Call Distribution) application. Though the application seems very simple and has limited features, it is actually the framework of any other real-life / complicated ICD applications.

Chapter 6 Script 101

Installing Script Editor

Most (if not all) UCCX intelligence is built on scripts. Though scripting is out of the scope of this book, it definitely helps us understand the system better by looking under the hood.

To open a script, you will need a CCX editor. You may download the editor from [**UCCX AppAdmin Portal > Plug-ins > Cisco Unified CCX Editor**].

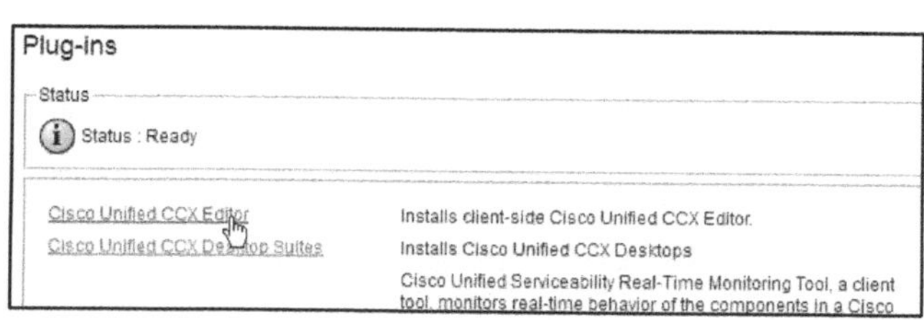

Figure 6-1 UCCX > Plug-ins

Launching Script Editor

When starting up the script editor, you will be asked to enter the UCCX address and admin credential.

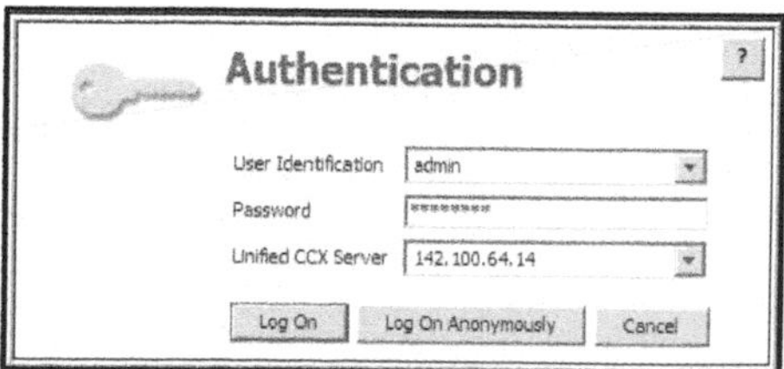

Figure 6-2 Script Editor Logon

You may have noticed that there is a "Log On" button and a "Log On Anonymously" button.

- **Log On** - If you have UCCX admin credential, the "Log On" button allows you to save scripts directly to UCCX repository.
- **Log On Anonymously** – If you don't have UCCX admin credential, the "Log on Anonymously" allows you use the script editor offline. You will have to manually upload the script from your local hard drive to UCCX server via UCCX admin web portal.

Note: To read/write scripts on UCCX server remotely, the script editor PC needs to be able to resolve UCCX by FQDN. For example, during UCCX installation, you entered hostname as "UCCX" and domain name as "example.local". The script editor PC needs to be able to resolve uccx.example.local to the IP address of the UCCX server. Otherwise, you won't be able to see the repository after log on. If you can't change the DNS server, the workaround is to change the local hosts file (on Windows, it is the C:\Windows\System32\Drivers\etc\hosts file).

After logon, you should have a screen like below:

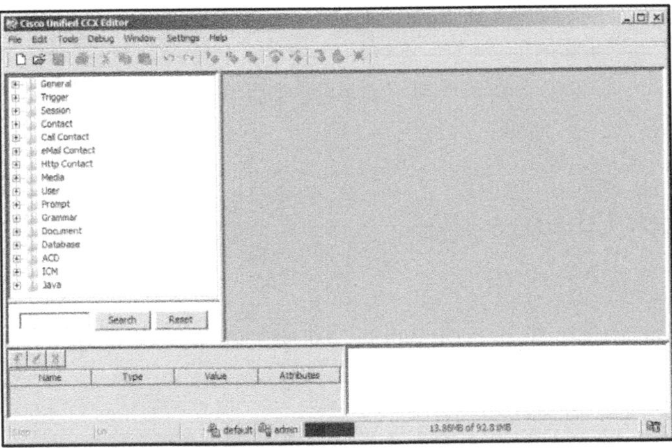

Figure 6-3 Script Editor After Logon

Opening a Script

Open the script "C:\Program Files (x86)\wfavvid_1051\Scripts\system\default\icd.aef". Please note the path will vary depending on your Operating System and UCCX version. For example, on 32-bit Windows you will have "Program Files" instead of "Program

Files (x86)". You will have "wfavvid_902" instead of "wfavvid_1051" if the UCCX version is 9.0.2 versus 10.5.1.

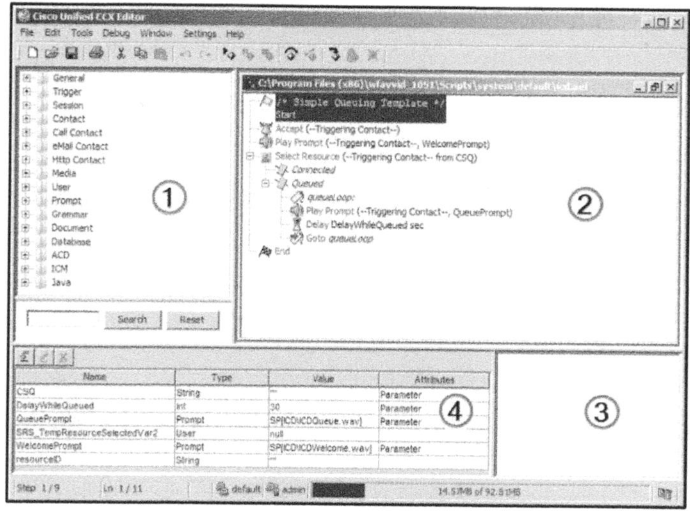

Figure 6-4 Script Editor Panes

The script editor window is divided into multiple areas (panes):

1. Palette Pane	Use the Palette pane to choose the steps you need to create your script.
2. Design Pane	Use the Design pane to create your script.
3. Message Pane	Use the Message pane to view messages when you are validating or debugging a script.
4. Variable Pane	Use the Variable pane to create, modify, and view variables for your script.

Palette Pane

Each command in the UCCX script is called a "step". Instead of typing the steps (as you would type the commands in other programming languages), you select a step from the Palette Pane, then drag-and-drop it into the Design Pane.

For detailed information regarding steps, please refer to UCCX documentations – "Editor Step Reference Guide".

Design Pane

Design pane is where you drop the steps and build your script. For some of the steps (like "Start" and "End" step) you may just drag-and-drop because there is not much you can configure (other than remarks and descriptions). For some other steps (like "Select

Resource" step) you will have to configure additional properties to make it work. To configure/change the properties of a step right-click on the step and choose "Properties" from context menu.

Message Pane

Script Editor will display messages in message pane when you validating or debugging a script.

Variable Pane

Variable pane is to create or modify the variables for the script. A variable can be defined as "Parameter".

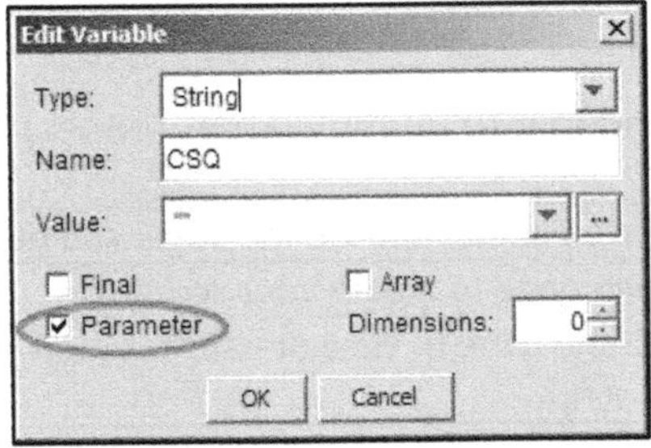

Figure 6-5 Variable

If a variable is defined as a "parameter", a UCCX administrator can define the initial value of the variable from UCCX Admin web portal. In the example of "icd.aef", we want to route the calls to a CSQ. Whenever we create a new CSQ or change the name of the CSQ, we need to reflect this change in the script. Instead of changing the script with script editor, we may pass the name of the CSQ to the script via UCCX Admin web portal as shown in the screen below.

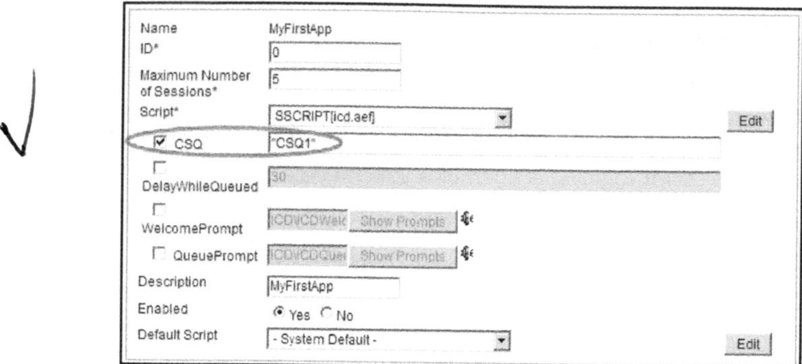

Figure 6-6 UCCX Application Configuration

ICD.aef

icd.aef is a system default script. It is a very good example for demonstrating UCCX functions and concepts. Many engineers use icd.aef as user acceptance test for UCCX installation.

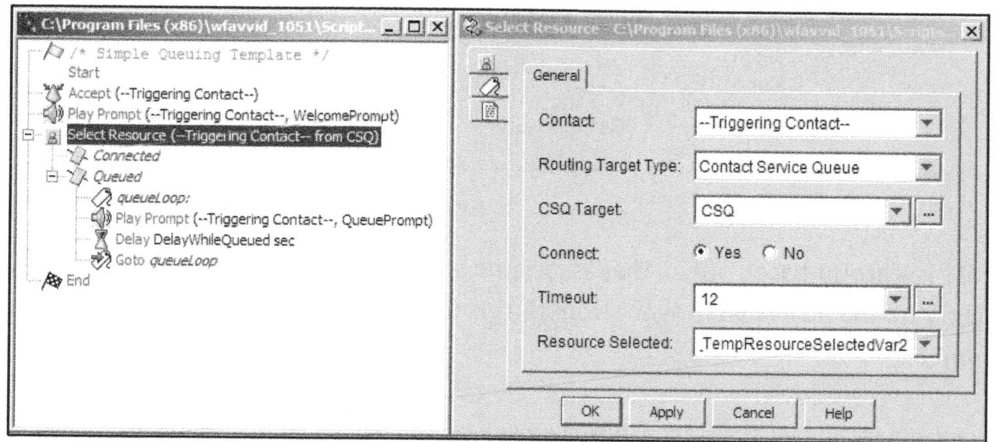

Figure 6-7 ICD.aef

Here is a brief explanation of each step in icd.aef.

Start	Every script should have "Start" as the first step.
Accept	After the Start step, the "Accept" step is normally the first step in a Cisco script, triggered by an incoming contact. A contact can be a telephone call, an e-mail message, or an HTTP request.

Play Prompt	Play back specific prompts (audio) to the caller.
Select Resource	Queues a call to a specific set of agents and optionally to connect the call to the agent the system chooses.
Delay	Pause the processing of a script for a specified number of seconds.
Goto	Cause the script logic to branch to a specified Label within the script.
End	Used at the end of a script to complete processing and free all allocated resources.

In English, the script logic is as below.

1. **Accept** - Accept incoming call.
2. **Play Prompt** - Play the prompt (audio) - "Thanks for calling".
3. **Select Resource** - Try to find an available resource from the contact service queue specified by variable "CSQ". The variable "CSQ" is a "parameter", which allows its value to be defined from UCCX Admin web portal. In our example, we define the value as "CSQ1". Thus the UCCX will try to find an available resource from "CSQ1". (Note the property "**CSQ Target**")

Contact Service queues

	Name △	Contact Queuing Criteria	Resource Pool Selection Model	Resource Pool	CSQ Type	Delete
	CSQ1	FIFO	Resource Group	RG1	Voice	

Figure 6-8 UCCX CSQ List

CSQ1 is a group-based queue that associated with the group RG1. Thus the UCCX will try to find an available agent from the group RG1, which has "Agent1" as its member.

If an agent is available, UCCX will try to connect the call to agent. (Note the "**Connect**" property). If the agent didn't answer the call in 12 seconds (note the "**Timeout**" property) UCCX will try to find another available agent.

There are two conditional branches in our "**Select Resource**" example above:

- **Connected** – If the call was connected to agent, UCCX has no control of the call anymore. But UCCX may perform other operations such as updating database, etc. Or does nothing, which ends the "**Select Resource**" step.

- **Queued** – If the call was not connected to agent (either no agent available or agent didn't answer the call) the step will be in "**Queued**" state. We usually play music and prompts in this branch to comfort the caller (note the "**Play Prompt**" step). As we don't know how soon agent will be available, we usually loop the prompt (note the "**Goto**" step).

Please note that we don't have to loop the "**Select Resource**" step itself. This is a little bit different from conventional programming language. Here is the internal logic of the "**Select Resource**" step:

1. If there is no available agent, the step will be in "**Queued**" state. It will perform whatever steps in the "**Queued**" branch. However, it will keep monitor the agents' status.
2. Once agent becomes available, the step will perform one of the following depending on the "**Connect**" property:
   a. If "**Connect = Yes**" it will have a "**Connected**" branch. UCCX will try to connect the call to agent. Once the call is connected to agent UCCX will perform the steps in "**Connected**" branch. If there is no step in "**Connected**" branch "**Select Resource**" will end.

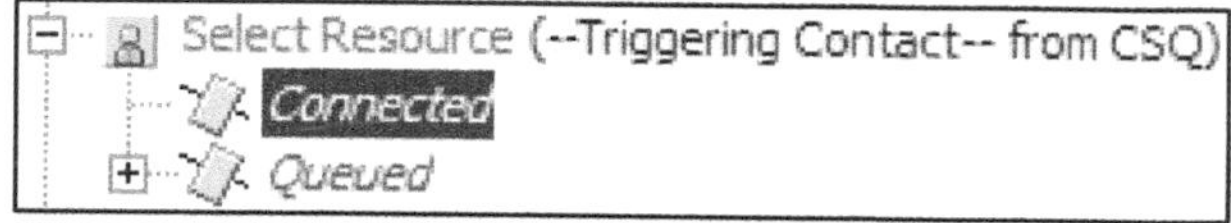

Figure 6-9 Select Resource - Connected

   b. If "**Connect = No**" it will have a "**Selected**" branch. UCCX will perform the steps in "**Selected**" branch. If there is no step in "**Selected**" branch "**Select Resource**" will end.

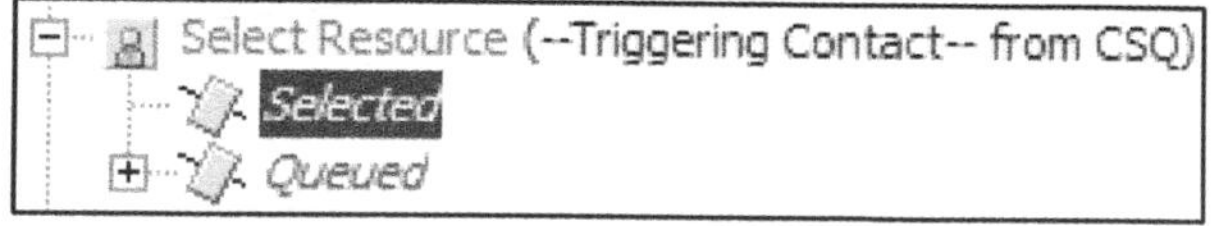

Figure 6-10 Select Resource - Selecte

Chapter 7 Resource Management

Resource management is very important in contact center. It determines how a call can be delivered to the best matched agent based on multiple factors such as language, specialties, skill level, etc.

Resource Group

Previously, we have discussed the concept of "Resource Group". We assign agents to resource groups. Then we associate CSQs to resource groups. Script routes calls to CSQs, in turn UCCX selects agents from resource groups as illustrated below.

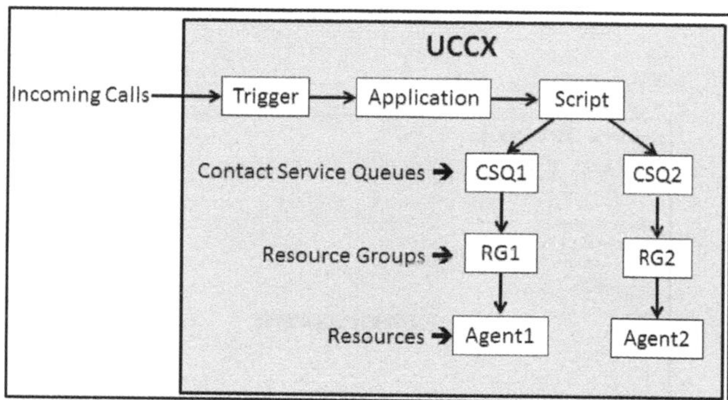

Figure 7-1 CSQ, Resource Groups and Resources

Create Resource Group

You create resource groups from [**UCCX AppAdmin Portal > Subsystem > RmCm > Resource Groups**]. All you need to enter is the group name.

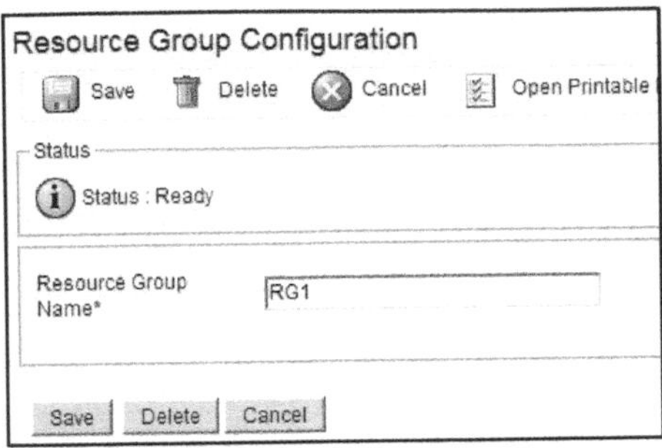

Figure 7-2 UCCX Creating Resource Group

Assign Agents to Resource Group

You assign agents to resource group from [**UCCX AppAdmin Portal > Subsystems > RmCm > Resources > <*Specific Resource*>**]. Each resource can be assigned to one resource group only.

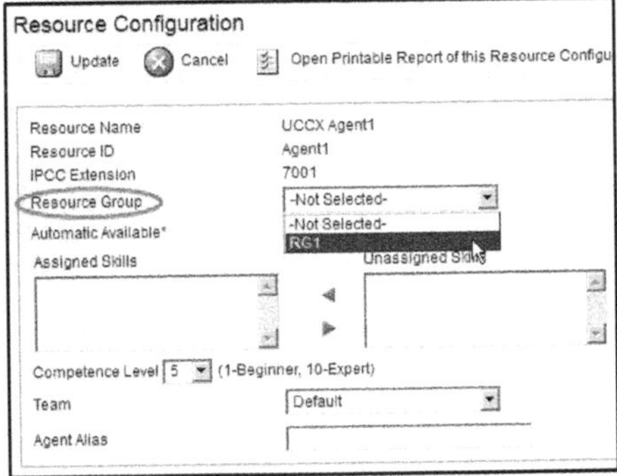

Figure 7-3 UCCX Assign Resource to Resource Group

Create Group-Based CSQ

You create CSQ from [**UCCX AppAdmin Portal > Subsystems > RmCm > Contact Service Queues**]. When creating CSQ, we have the option of choosing "Resource Pool Selection Model", either "Resource Skills" or "Resource Group". Choose "Resource Group" option to create a group-based CSQ.

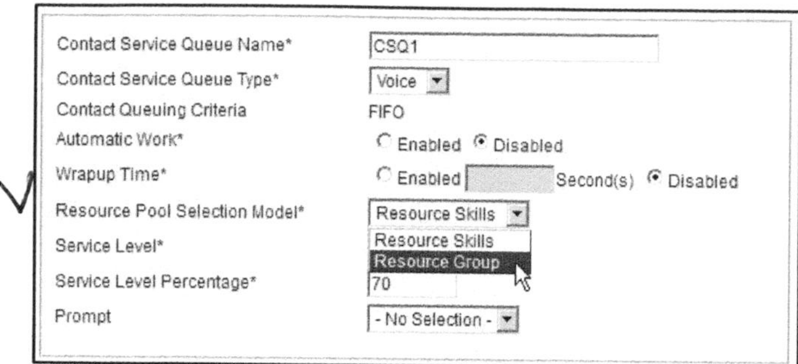

Figure 7-4 UCCX Creating Group Based CSQ

After choosing the "Resource Group" option, the next screen will give you a drop-down list of resource groups. Choose the resource group you want.

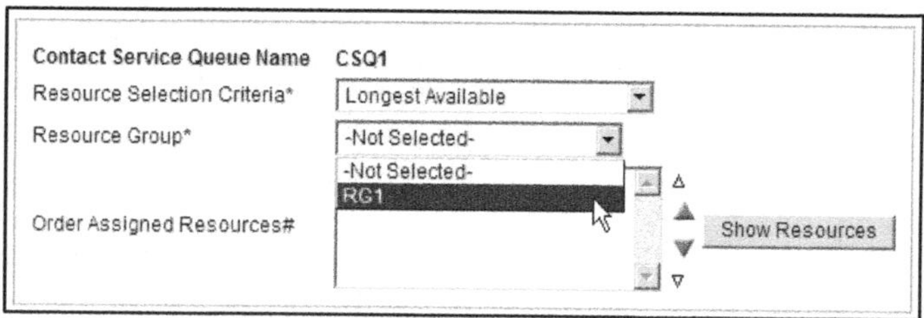

Figure 7-5 UCCX Creating Group Based CSQ (Continued)

Resource Group List:

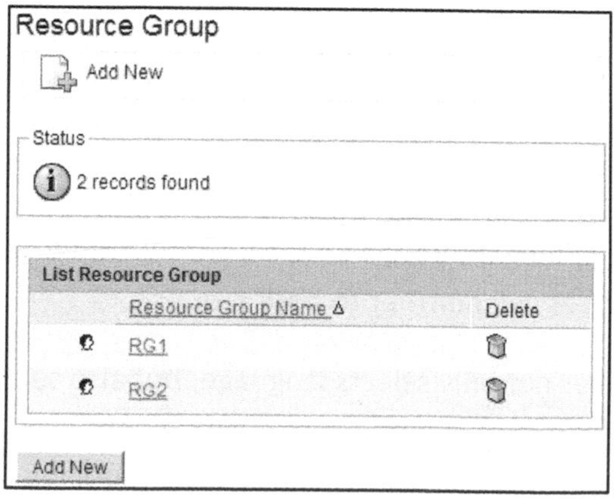

Resource Group

Add New

Status

2 records found

List Resource Group	
Resource Group Name ▵	Delete
RG1	
RG2	

Add New

Figure 7-6 UCCX Resource Group List

Resource List:

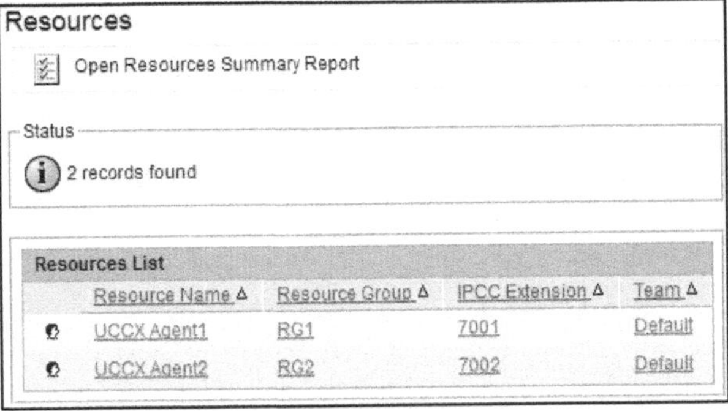

Figure 7-7 UCCX Resource List

CSQ List:

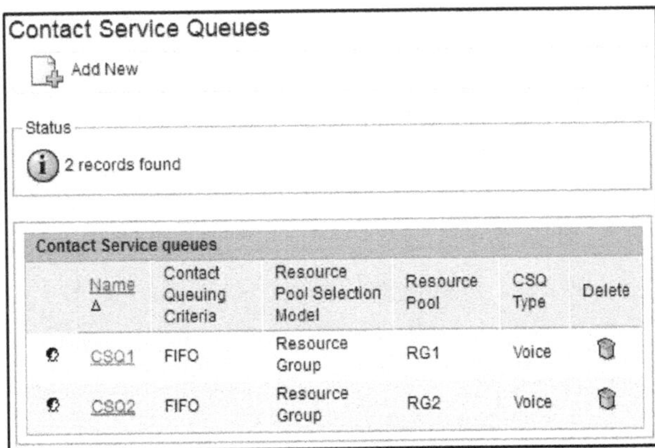

Figure 7-8 UCCX CSQ List

Resource group model is very simple. For example, we may assign some agents to "English Group" and some others to "Spanish Group". Then based on callers' language selection, we may route the calls to appropriate group.

However, each agent can belong to one group only. For example, if an agent can speak both languages, we cannot assign him/her to both groups.

In real-life scenarios, a caller not only selects language, but also selects the service he/she wants, such as "credit card application" versus "mortgage loan application". Different services require different skills. For the same reason, it is very difficult (if even possible) to manage resources with "resource group" only.

Skills

The concept of "skills" gives us more flexibility on resource management. Not only an agent can have multiple skills, but also we can assign different skill levels to the agent.

Below is an example of a "skill matrix", with 1 means least competent while 10 means most competent.

Skills / Agent	English	Spanish	Credit Card	Mortgage Loan
Agent1	10	8	10	6
Agent2	10	5	5	10
Agent3	6	10	10	7
Agent4	7	10	6	9

Once you have skills created and skill levels assigned to agents, you may create skill-based CSQs. For example:

CSQ Name	Required Skills
CSQ-English-CreditCard	English >= 8 and CreditCard >= 8
CSQ-Spanish-MortageLoan	Spanish >= 8 and MortgageLoan > = 8

With the above configuration, UCCX will try to locate an agent with required skills. If such an agent exists and is available, UCCX will try to deliver the call to the agent.

Create Skills

To create skills, you go to [**UCCX AppAdmin Portal > Subsystem > RmCm > Skills**].

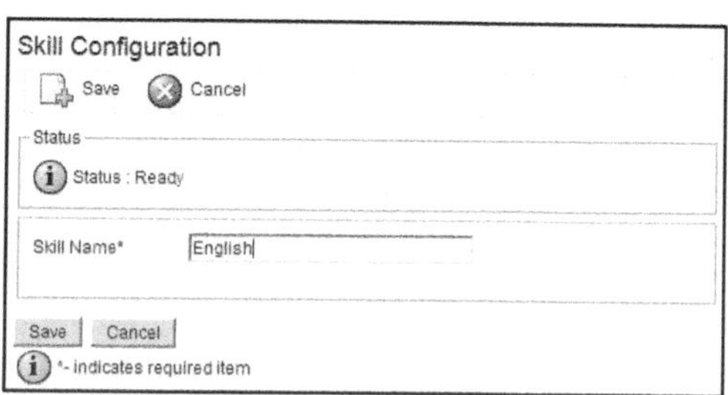

Figure 7-9 UCCX Creating Skill

All you need to do is to give a skill name (for example "English"). Repeat the same procedure for all the skills you want to create.

Skill List	
Skill Name∆	Delete
English	
Spanish	
CreditCard	
MortgageLoan	

Figure 7-10 UCCX Skill List

Assign Skill Level to Agents

After skills are created, you may assign skill levels to agents (resources). You do this from [**UCCX AppAdmin Portal > Subsystems > RmCm > Resources > <*Specific Resource*>**] page.

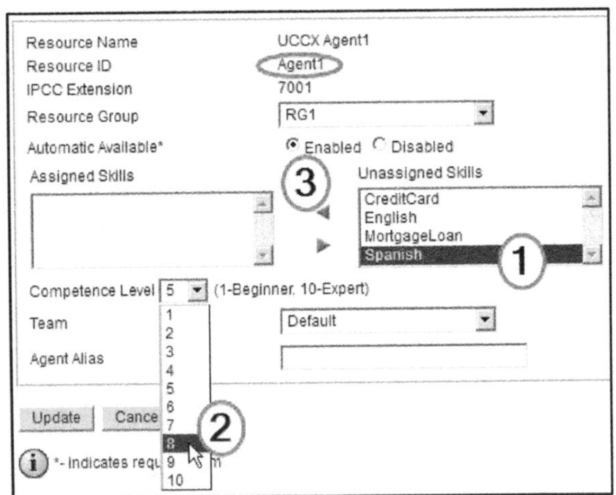

Figure 7-11 UCCX Resource Configuration

In the resource configuration page, perform the following steps to assign skill levels to resource:

1. Highlight the skill we want to assign.
2. Select the competence level from the drop-down list.
3. Click the triangle button to assign the skill level to "Assigned Skills" box.

For example, after adding "Spanish level 8" to resource "Agent1", you will have a screen like below:

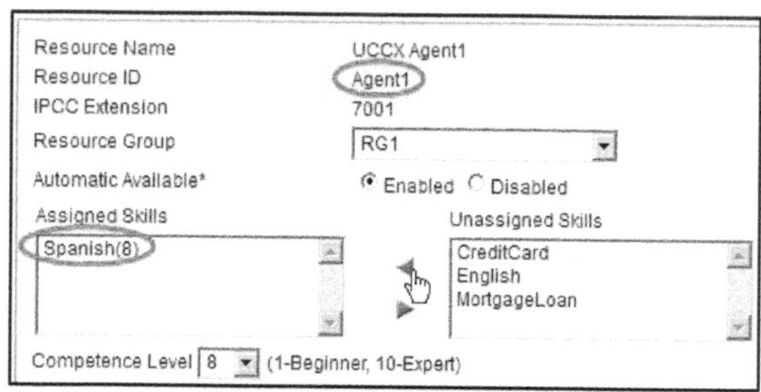

Figure 7-12 UCCX Resource Configuration (Skill Level Added)

Repeat the same procedure for each skill levels you want to assign. An agent can have multiple skills at the same time. The agent can also be part of a resource group while having multiple skills. However from a CSQ perspective, the CSQ can either be a group based queue or a skill based queue, but not both.

Create Skill Based CSQ

Just like group-based CSQ, you create the CSQ from [**UCCX AppAdmin Portal > Subsystems > RmCm > Contact Service Queues**]. To create skill-based CSQ, you choose "Resource Skills" from the "Resource Pool Selection Model" drop-down list.

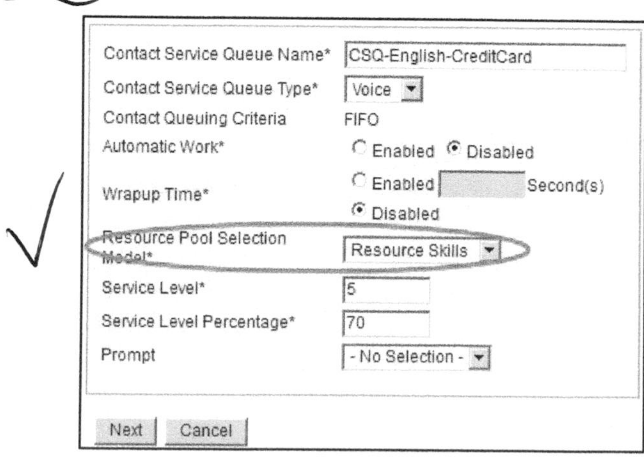

Figure 7-13 UCCX Creating Skill Based CSQ

On the next screen, you may highlight the skills needed for the queue then click "Add".

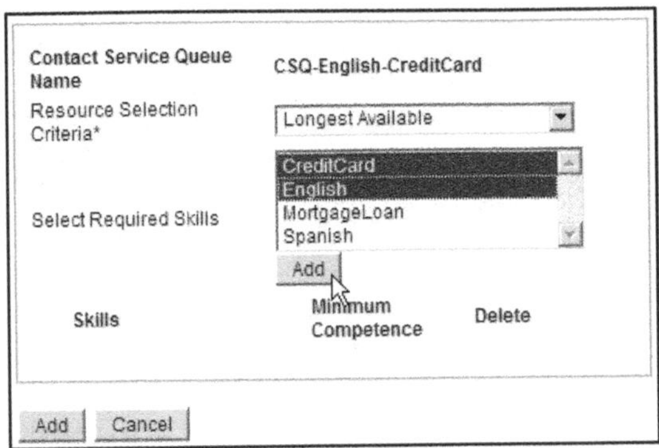

Figure 7-14 UCCX Creating Skill Based CSQ (Continued)

After needed skills are added, you may specify "Minimum Competence" for each skill. In the example below, we state that this CSQ requires an agent with English skill level 8 (or above) and CreditCard skill level 8 (or above). Agents are selected only if they meet both requirements.

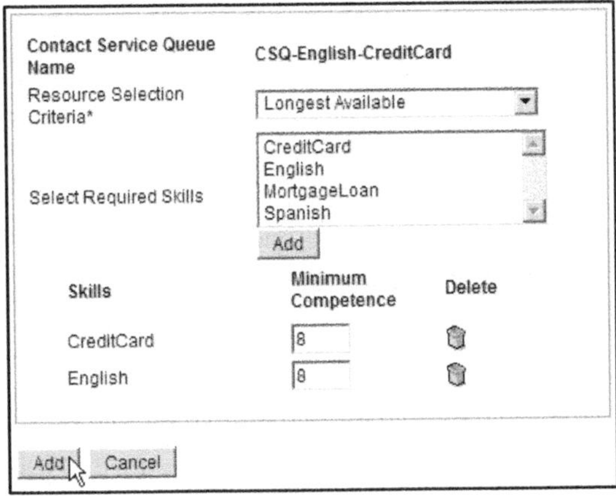

Figure 7-15 UCCX Creating Skill Based CSQ (Continued)

Below is the CSQ list after "CSQ-English-CreditCard" was created.

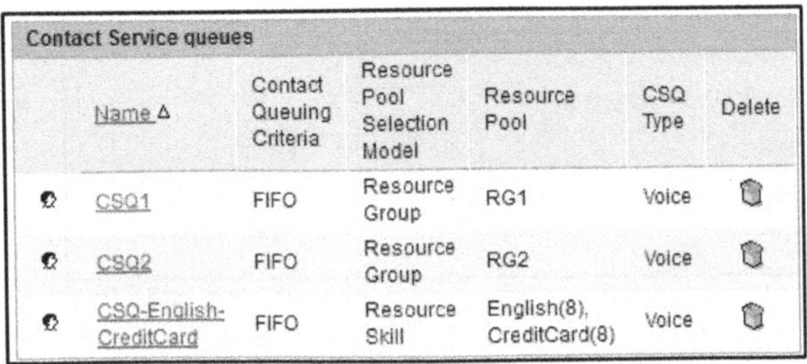

Contact Service queues

	Name Δ	Contact Queuing Criteria	Resource Pool Selection Model	Resource Pool	CSQ Type	Delete
	CSQ1	FIFO	Resource Group	RG1	Voice	
	CSQ2	FIFO	Resource Group	RG2	Voice	
	CSQ-English-CreditCard	FIFO	Resource Skill	English(8), CreditCard(8)	Voice	

Figure 7-16 UCCX CSQ List

The "Automatic" Options

There are a couple "automatic" parameters in resource and CSQ settings that will affect the behavior of agent state.

Automatic Available

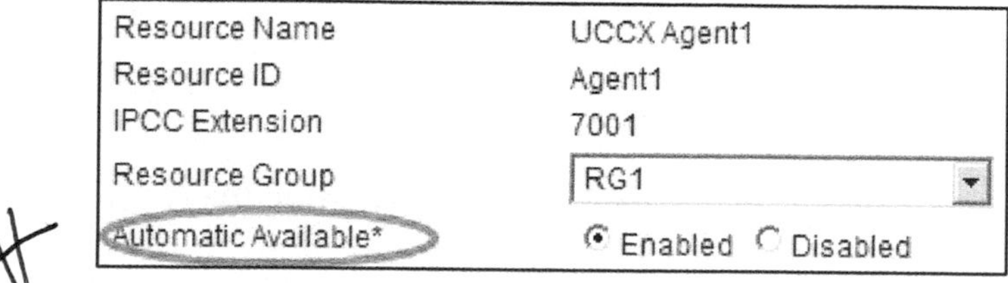

Figure 7-17 UCCX Resource Configuration

"Automatic Available" is a resource parameter. When enabled (which is default), it will put the agent into the Ready state after the agent finishes a call. When disabled, the agent will stays in "Not Ready" state after finishes a call. Agent will need to manually put himself/herself into Ready state with agent desktop.

Automatic Work

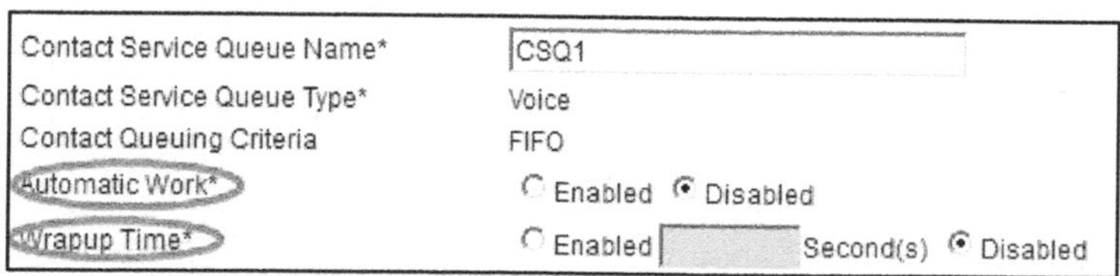

Figure 7-18 UCCX CSQ Configuration

"Automatic Work" is a CSQ parameter. It is usually used with the "Wrapup Time" parameter.

"Work" is another agent state besides "Ready" and "Not Ready". After finishing a call, the agent might need some time to update the customer record, finish the order, etc.

This is referred to as "Work" state. When agent is in "work" state, he/she won't be offered a new call.

- If "Automatic Work" is disabled (which is default), agent state will go into "Ready" or "Not Ready" after a call depending on "Automatic Available" parameter (see previous explanation).
- If "Automatic Work" is enabled, agent state will go into "Work" after a call. How long it will stay in "Work" depends on the "Wrapup Time" parameter.

Wrap-up Time

The activities of updating customer record or finishing the order after a call is usually referred as "wrap up".

- If "Wrapup Time" is disabled (which is default), agent may stay in "Work" stay as long as he/she wants.
- If "Wrapup Time" is enabled, 1 – 7200 seconds must be specified. After the "wrapup time", agent state will go into "Ready" or "Not Ready" after a call depending on "Automatic Available" parameter (see previous explanation).

From a call delivery perspective, "Work" state is pretty much the same as "Not Ready" state. Why bother introducing another state? This is more for billing and reporting purpose. As stated above, an agent might be wrapping up after a call. From a reporting perspective, it is "work" time and different with "not ready" (which is not considered as work time). If agents get paid or appraised by work time, this makes a big difference.

The decision chart is as below:

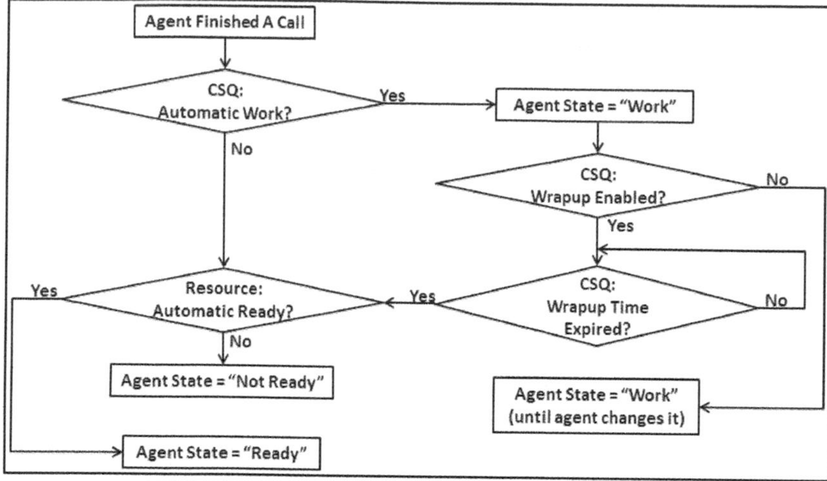

Figure 7-19 Agent State Decision Chart

Agent Based Routing Settings

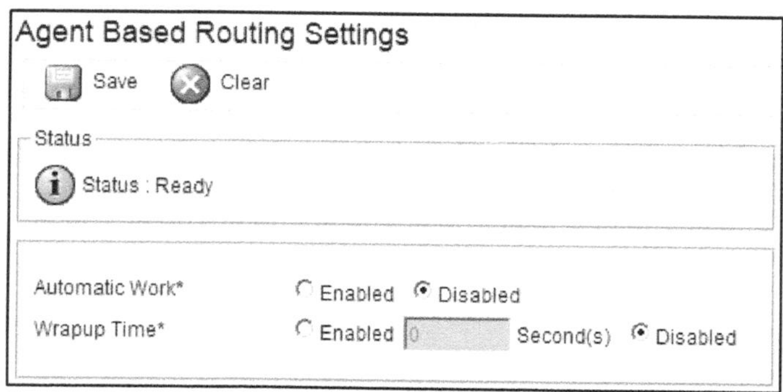

Figure 7-20 UCCX Agent Based Routing

What is "Agent Based Routing"? We normally route incoming calls to a CSQ so a group of agents can serve that queue. In some business cases, we might want to route incoming calls to a specific agent versus a queue. This is called "Agent Based Routing".

Since we route incoming calls to specific agent, CSQ is out of picture. Thus none of the CSQ parameters will apply, including the "Automatic Work" and "Wrapup Time" parameters. In that case, we set these parameters in [**UCCX AppAdmin Portal > Subsystems > RmCm > Agent Based Routing Settings**].

Chapter 8 Desktop Suite

UCCX won't be complete without "Desktop Suite". Desktop Suite is a set of applications that run on desktop computers to perform agent, supervisor, and administrator functions.

Until UCCX version 8.5, "Desktop Suite" is referred to the desktop applications developed by Spanlink, including:

- Cisco Agent Desktop (CAD)
- Cisco Supervisor Desktop (CSD)
- Cisco Desktop Administrator (CDA)

Call center agents use CAD to set their availability state, retrieve call related information, and collaborate with teammates and supervisors.

Call center supervisors use CSD to monitor the queues, listen/record agent/customer calls, create simple reports, etc.

Technical support personnel use CDA to configure desktop related functions and features.

Because "Cisco Agent Desktop" is the most commonly used application, we usually refer the classic desktop suite as CAD.

Cisco introduced a new desktop product called "Finesse" since UCCX version 8.5. Finesse is supposed to be the "next generation" desktop. UCCX allows you switch between CAD and Finesse. This has to be done from CLI (Command Line).

Due to the installation base of CAD and the feature gap between Finesse and CAD, many customers are still using CAD in the latest version of UCCX. This book will cover CAD mainly. Finesse will be covered in 2nd edition (or whenever Finesse totally takes over CAD).

To install the Desktop Suite go to [**UCCX AppAdmin Portal > Tools > Plug-ins > Cisco Unified CCX Desktop Suites**].

Note: You cannot install CSD if you already have CAD installed on the PC. However, if you uninstall CAD and install CSD, the installer will install CSD and CAD in one shot. This is because CAD is considered a component of CSD.

After installation, you will find the application shortcuts from [**Windows > Start > Programs > Cisco > Desktop**].

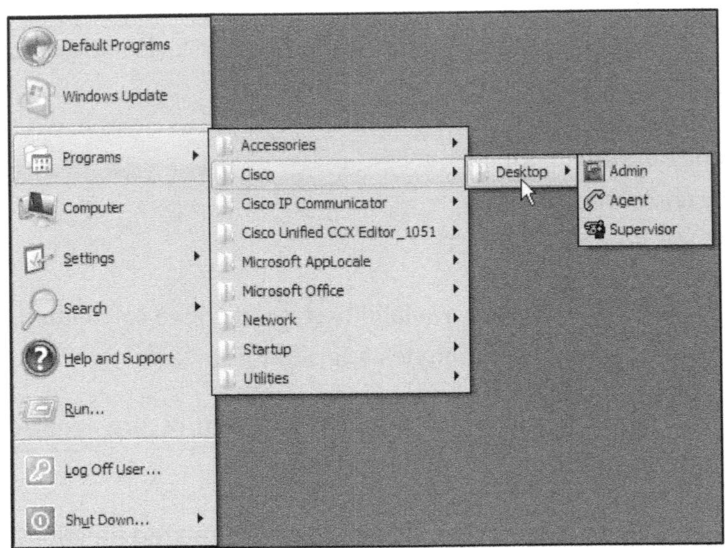

Figure 8-1 Windows Desktop Suite Shortcuts

Cisco Agent Desktop

Cisco Agent Desktop (CAD) is mainly used by call center agents to handles calls and set his/her availability state. However, CAD is more than that. It is highly customizable client software that can:

- Present incoming call related information (such as customer account information, home address, etc.) in "Enterprise Data" pane (text-based).
- Integrate with other applications/databases with a built-in web browser
- Receive team messages
- Call handling
    - Answer, Hold, Transfer, Conference
    - Make outbound calls
    - Alternating between calls

- Outbound Dialer (system initiated outbound calls)
- Chat (Instant Messaging)
- Email (Handle emails in queue)
- Record phone conversations
- Reason code (when transit to "Not Ready" state)

Please note that some of the function buttons will show up only after proper configuration. For example, the "Start Record"/"Stop Record" buttons won't show up until they are configured by administrator.

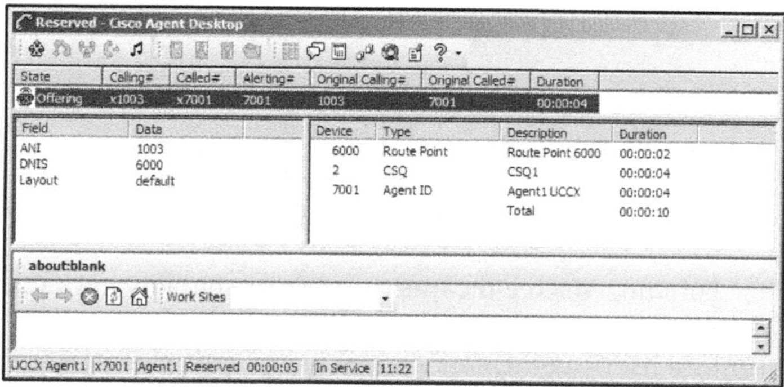

Figure 8-2 Agent Desktop

We are not going to go through each of the functions here because:

1) All configuration/customization is done from CDA (Cisco Desktop Administrator). There is not much we can configure from CAD (Cisco Agent Desktop).
2) This book is more focusing on configuring the application other than using the application.

Please refer to "Cisco Agent Desktop User Guide" for detailed explanation of all features and functions.

Cisco Supervisor Desktop

Before we can use CSD (Cisco Supervisor Desktop) we need to do some provisioning on UCCX server.

Give a user Supervisor permission

First of all, we need to designate some users as "supervisors". We do this from [**UCCX AppAdmin Portal > Tools > User Management > User View**].

Here is the current user list:

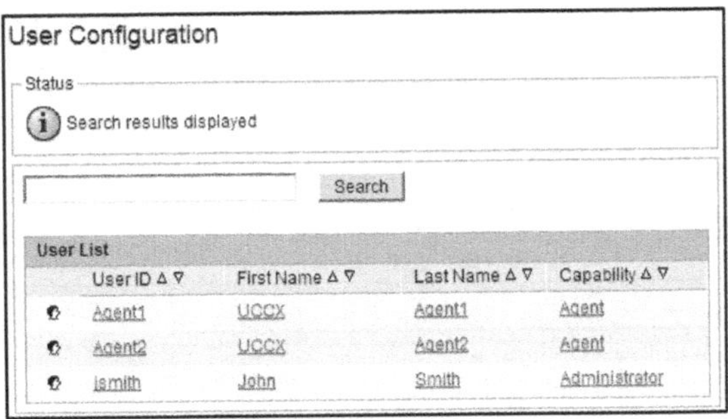
User Configuration

Status

Search results displayed

Search

User List

	User ID	First Name	Last Name	Capability
	Agent1	UCCX	Agent1	Agent
	Agent2	UCCX	Agent2	Agent
	jsmith	John	Smith	Administrator

Figure 8-3 UCCX User List

Note the "Capability" column, which indicates the user's capability in UCCX system.

Now we want to promote user "Agent2" as a supervisor. Let's click on the user ID "Agent2".

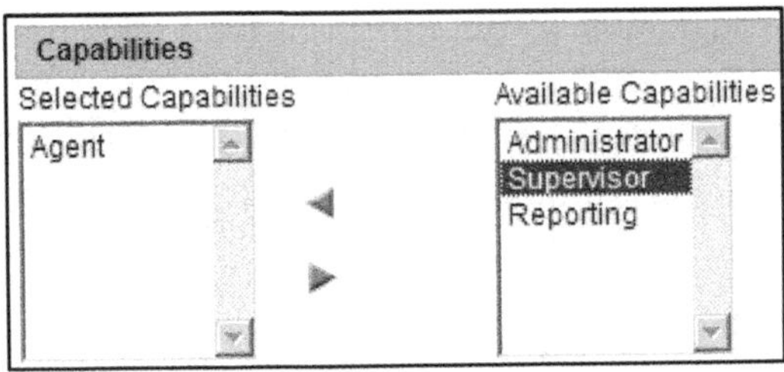

Figure 8-4 UCCX User Configuration

On the Agent2's user configuration page, we highlight "Supervisor" from "Available Capabilities" list and use the triangle button to move it to the "Selected Capabilities" list. Then click "Update". Now you see user Agent2 has both "Supervisor" and "Agent" capabilities.

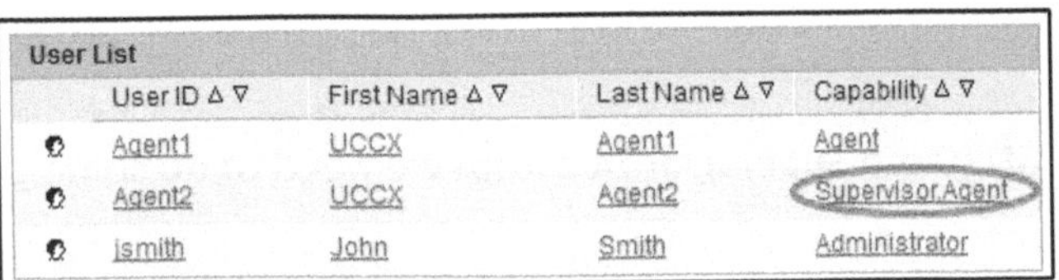
User List

	User ID	First Name	Last Name	Capability
	Agent1	UCCX	Agent1	Agent
	Agent2	UCCX	Agent2	Supervisor,Agent
	jsmith	John	Smith	Administrator

Figure 8-5 UCCX User List

A supervisor may or may not be taking customer calls. However, some of the supervisor features (such as "call intervention") requires agent desktop to work. Thus it is the best practice to have the supervisor log into CAD and CSD on the same computer. If you log into CSD without CAD login, you will get a warning like this:

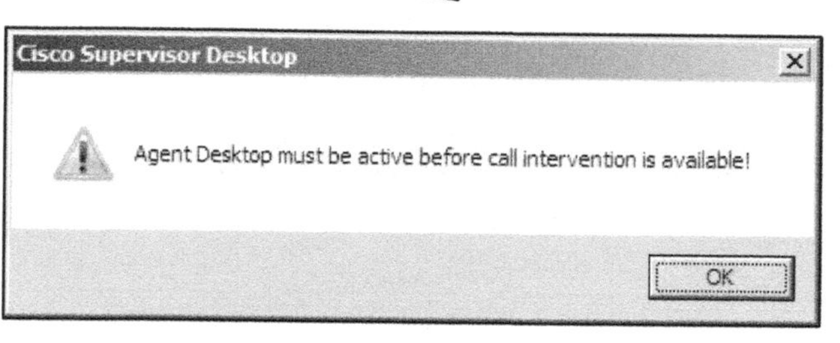

Figure 8-6 Running CSD without CAD

Assign supervisor to a team

Just like in real life, a supervisor may manage one or more teams. You may create teams in UCCX. Then assign agents and supervisors to one or more teams. By default, all agents are in a system generated team called "Default".

To see the team list you may go to [**UCCX AppAdmin Portal > Subsystem > RmCm > Teams**].

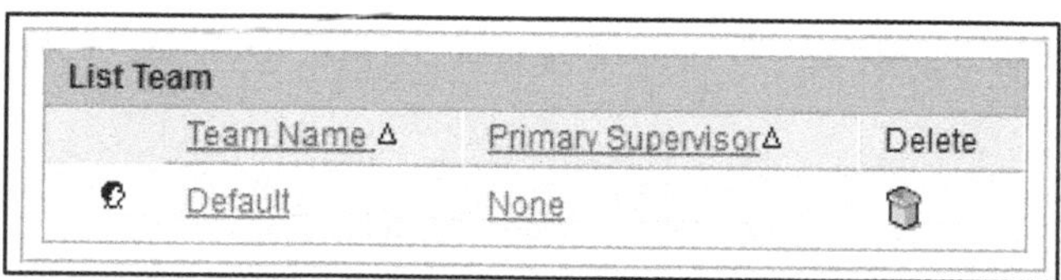

List Team

	Team Name ∆	Primary Supervisor∆	Delete
	Default	None	

Figure 8-7 UCCX Team List

By default, there is no supervisor assigned to the team. Thus you see the "Primary Supervisor" column shows "None". Let's click on the team "Default".

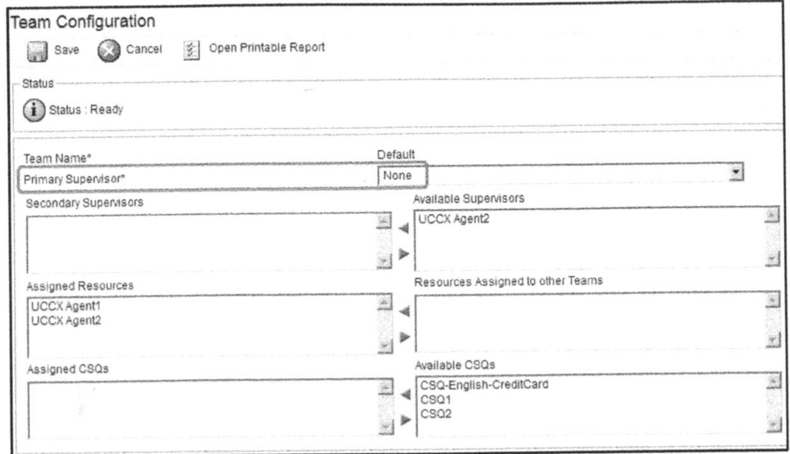

Figure 8-8 UCCX Team Configuration

Note the "Primary Supervisor" drop-down list is currently showing "None". Let's assign supervisor "Agent2" to this team. Let choose "UCCX Agent2" from the drop-down list and click "Save" button.

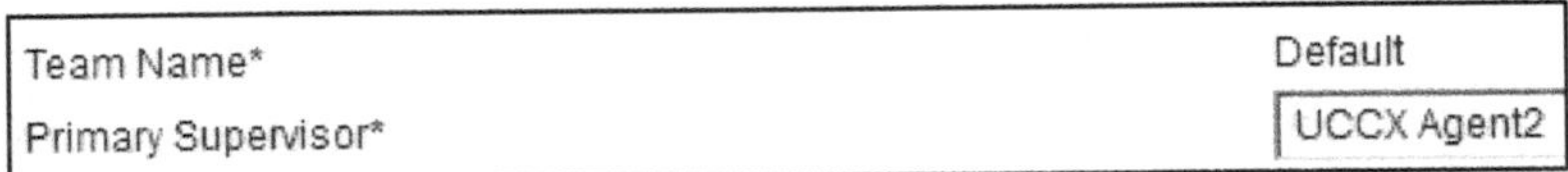

Figure 8-9 UCCX Assigning Supervisor to a Team

Back to the team list, you see the "Primary Supervisor" for "Default" team is "UCCX Agent2" now.

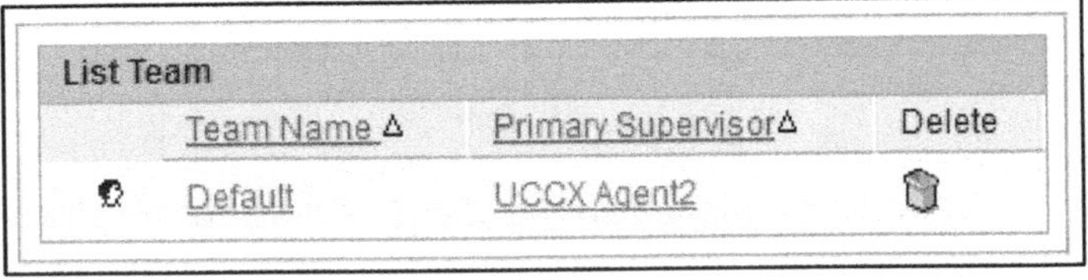

Figure 8-10 UCCX Team List (Supervisor Assigned)

If you don't assign supervisors to a team, the supervisor won't be able to do anything after logging into CSD (Cisco Supervisor Desktop).

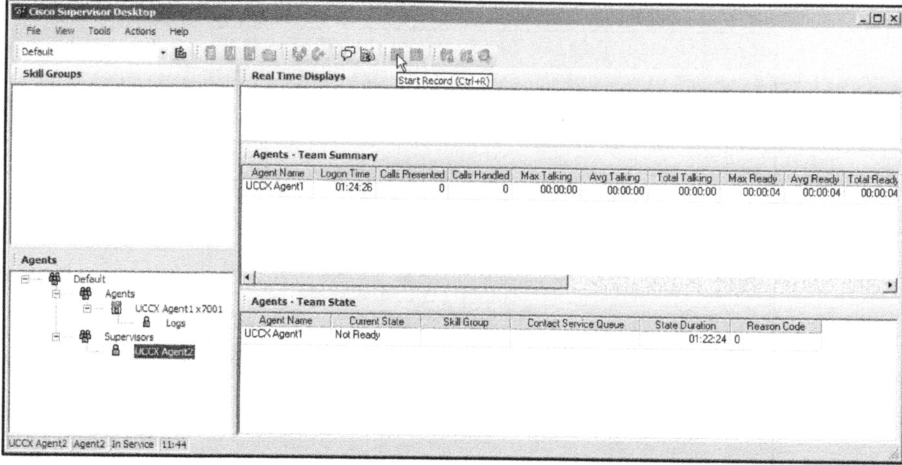

Figure 8-11 Supervisor Desktop

Note some of the buttons (such as recording and monitoring) are greyed out if have not been properly configured.

From CSD, the supervisor can:

- See agent status
- Change agent status
- Send messages to the team
- Barge in, intercept, and record calls
- Monitor/review agent e-mail
- Push a webpage to an agent
- Create supervisor workflow

Most of those features are self-explanatory. Using the Supervisor Work Flow Administrator feature, you can configure CSD to perform certain actions based on queue statistics.

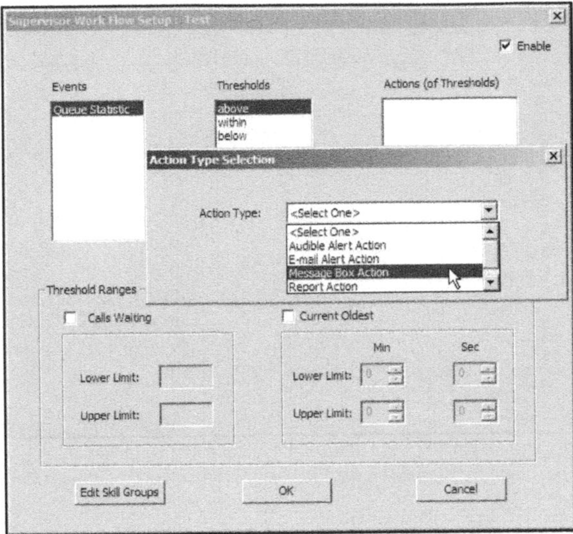

Figure 8-12 Supervisor Workflow

Cisco Desktop Administrator

CDA (Cisco Desktop Administrator) is used to configure or customize the functions and features of CAD and CSD. CDA used to be a single desktop application (just like CAD and CSD). In later version of UCCX, it was split into two parts:

- A web portal (referred to as "Cisco Desktop Administrator")
- A desktop application (referred to as "Cisco Desktop *Work Flow* Administrator")

Web Portal

To access the web portal, we choose "Cisco Desktop Administrator" from the upper right hand drop-down menu from the UCCX Admin web.

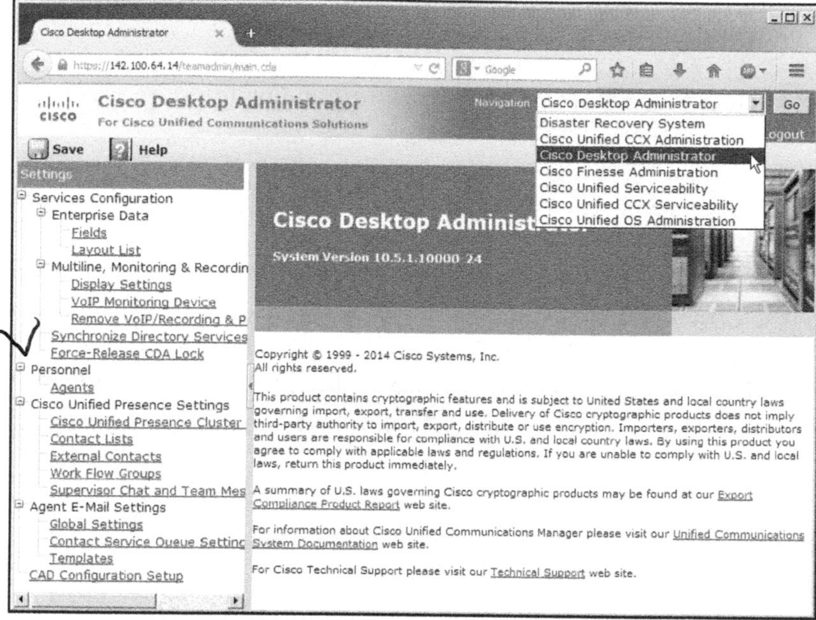

Figure 8-13 Desktop Administrator (CDA) Web Portal

CDA has navigation tree on the left just like its desktop siblings. CDA (both web portal and desktop application) is a single session application. If another CDA session is going on (or you didn't log off the previous session properly) you won't be able to make any changes. You will get a warning message as below:

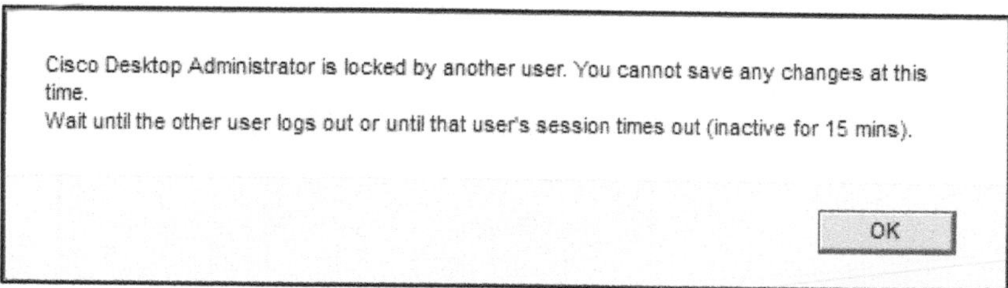

Figure 8-14 CDA Locked

You may force unlock from the navigation tree [**Service Configuration > Force-Release CDA Lock**].

There are five main branches in the navigation tree:

- Service Configuration
- Personnel
- Cisco Unified Presence Settings
- Agent E-Mail Settings

- CAD Configuration Setup

We will discuss each branch when we come to corresponding features.

Desktop Work Flow Administrator

Desktop Work Flow Administrator is an application running on desktop PC. It is a compliment of the CDA web portal.

"Work Flow" is a set of configuration that can be applied to agent desktops. You may create different Work Flow groups and apply to different agents. We will discuss Work Flow details in later chapters.

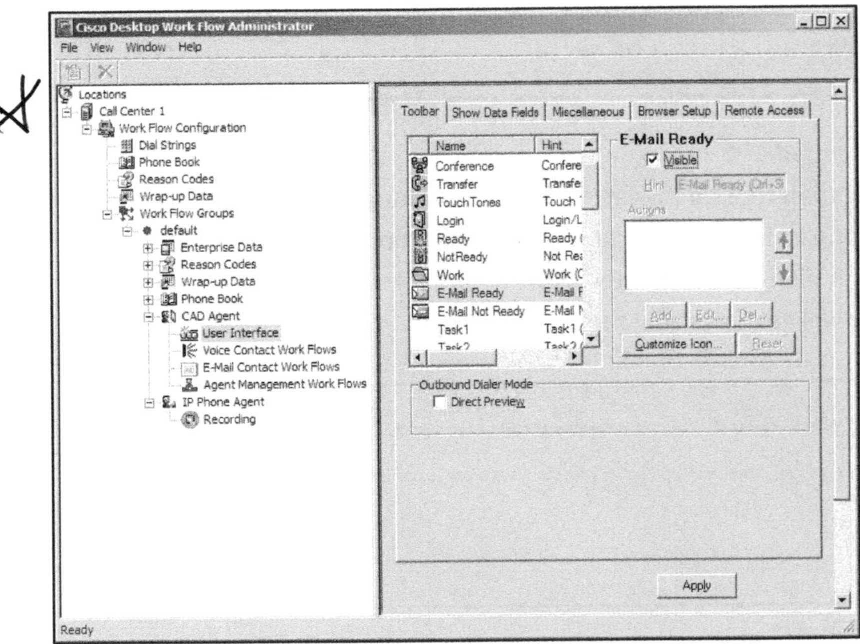

Figure 8-15 Desktop Work Flow Administrator

The Desktop Work Flow Administrator interface has two panes. The left pane is a navigation tree similar to that found in Windows Explorer. The right pane displays the settings for what you chose in the left pane (referred to as a "node").

When you select a "node" on the navigation tree, the Desktop Work Flow Administrator menu bar changes to reflect the available options of the node. For example, when you choose (highlight) the "Call Center 1" node, "setup" and "Desktop Administrator" menus are added to the menu bar:

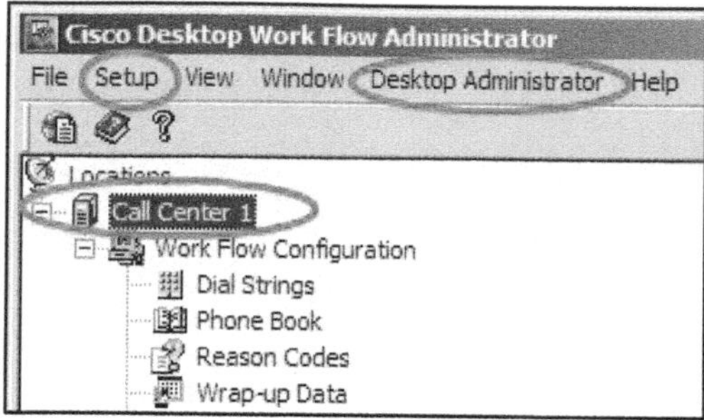

Figure 8-16 Desktop Work Flow Administrator - Node Based Menu Bar

By default, Desktop Work Flow Administrator is not protected by password. You may set a password by doing the following:

1. Highlight the "Call Center 1" node.
2. Click "Setup" menu, then click "Change Password".

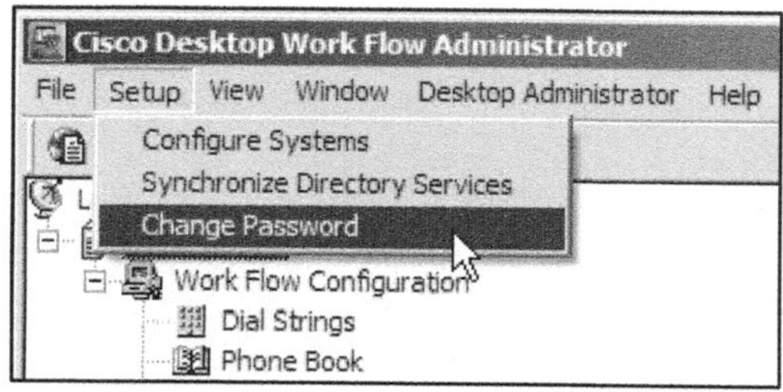

Figure 8-17 Desktop Work Flow Administrator - Change Password

If you set a password from Desktop Work Flow Administrator and forgot it, you may clear the password from CDA web portal [**"Cisco Desktop Administrator" web portal > CAD Configuration Setup > Reset Password**]

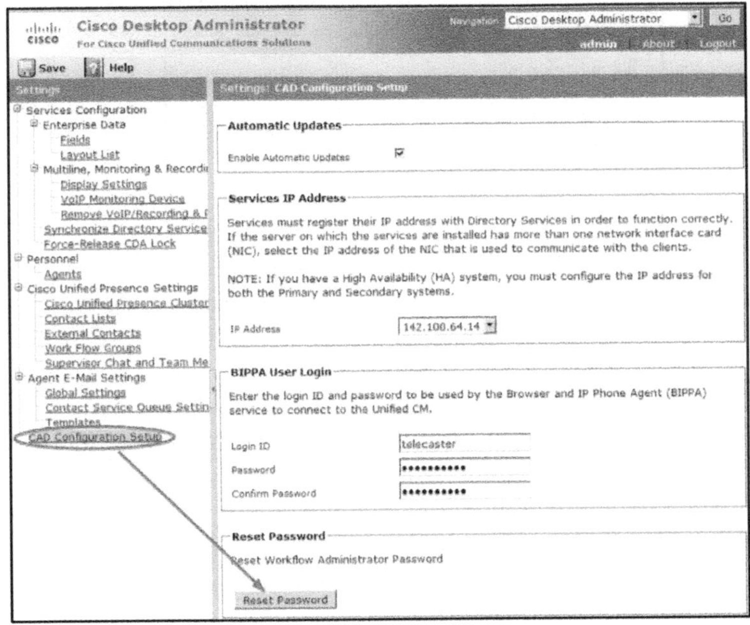

Figure 8-18 Reset Password for Work Flow Administrator

Chapter 9 IP Phone Agent

As you have already seen, agent desktop (CAD) is a powerful tool for agents to handle customer calls and collaborate with teammates and supervisors. But for budget limited call centers, we have the option of not using computers while still offering basic functions of the agent desktop. This is achieved by IPPA (IP Phone Agent).

Cisco IP phones are like mini computers. CUCM (CallManager) allows administrators to deploy IP phone services. End users can use the IP phone screen to access various functions such as check stock quotes, weather, etc. Those IP phone services are not limited to voice calls. Users can use the phone's LCD screen to view text or graphical information. Users can also interact with the service with phone's keypad or touch screen. Some of the popular IP phone services include IPMA (IP Manager Assistant), IPPA (IP Phone Agent), Corporate Directory, etc.

Call center agents may use IP phones as "mini desktops" to set their availability, view call related information, queue statistics, etc.

When combining Extension Mobility (EM) with IP Phone Agent (IPPA), call center agents may use any IP phone from any locations. This brings more flexibility to the call center.

Please note that IP phone agent is the alternative of agent desktop, which is the client side application. Whatever needed to provision the server side still apply, such as phone/user provisioning, resource/CSQ provisioning, etc.

IP Phone Agent provisioning can be summarized into the following steps:

1) Provision IPPA Phone Service (CUCM)
2) Subscribe IP phone to IPPA service (CUCM)
3) IP Phone Agent Logon (from IP Phone)

Provision Phone Service

To provision phone services, we go to [**CUCM > Device > Device Settings > Phone Services**].

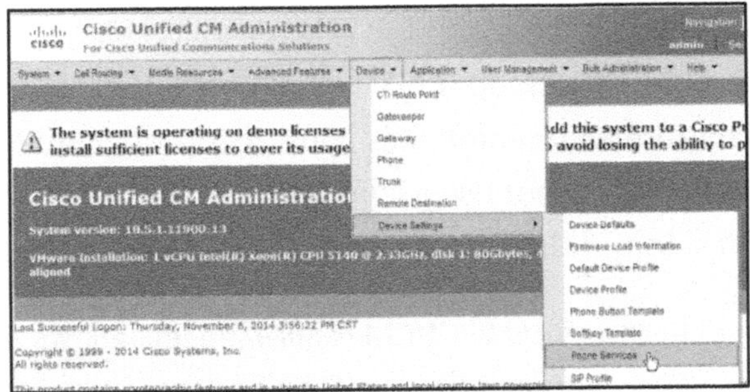

Figure 9-1 CUCM Phone Services

Click "Add New" button to add a new service.

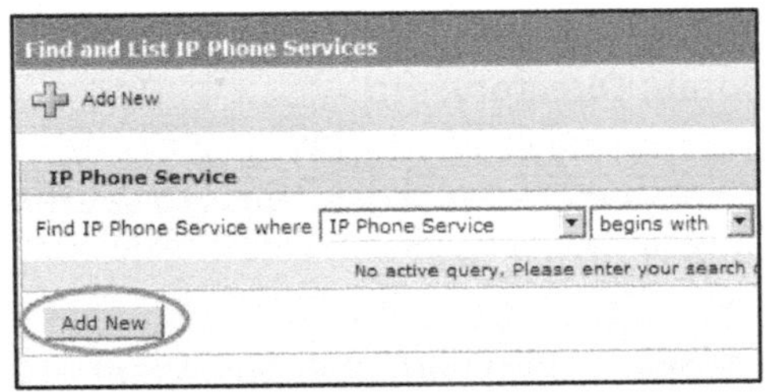

Figure 9-2 CUCM Add a New Phone Service

On the "IP Phone Services Configuration" screen, enter the following information then click "Save" button.

Service Name (Required)	Name of the service. Default is blank. Enter any name you like.
Service Description (Optional)	A description of the service. Default is blank.
Service URL (Required)	URL for the service. Default is blank. Enter the following URL between the quotation marks: "http://*ip-of-uccx*:6293/ipphone/jsp/sciphonexml/IPAgentLogin.jsp"
Service Category (Required)	XML Service (default)
Service Type (Required)	Standard IP Phone Service (default)
Enable	You need to check this box. (default is unchecked)

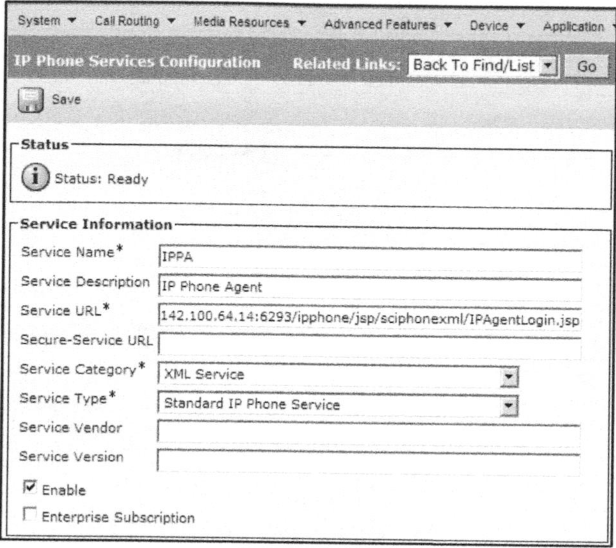

Figure 9-3 CUCM Creating Phone Services

After you click "Save" button, you will have the option to add parameters. We need to add three parameters for IP Phone Agent service:

Parameter Name	Display Name	Description
Ext	Extension	IPCC Extension
ID	User ID	Agent User ID
Pwd	Password	Agent Password

Please note that parameter names have to be entered exactly as shown above and also case sensitive because those are the exact parameters being used by the service. Display names can be anything you like.

Click the "New Parameter" button to create a new parameter. Enter appropriate information then click "Save" button to save the information.

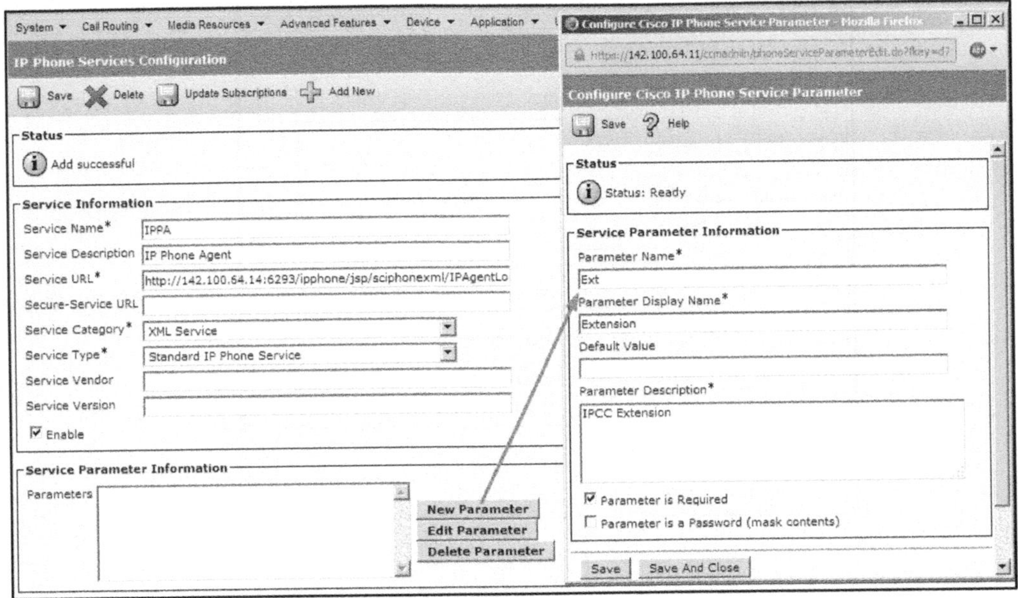

Figure 9-4 CUCM Adding Parameters to Phone Service

After saving the information, you will have the “Add New” button show up on the “Configure Cisco IP Phone Service Parameter” window. Use the “Add New” button to add additional parameters.

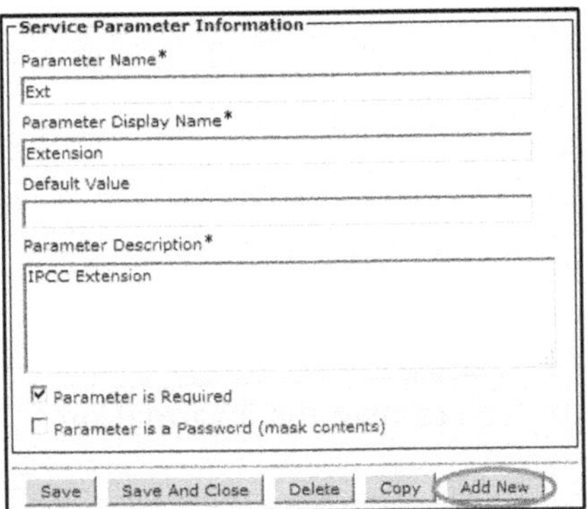

Figure 9-5 CUCM Add Additional Parameters

After finish adding all three parameters, you should have a screen like this:

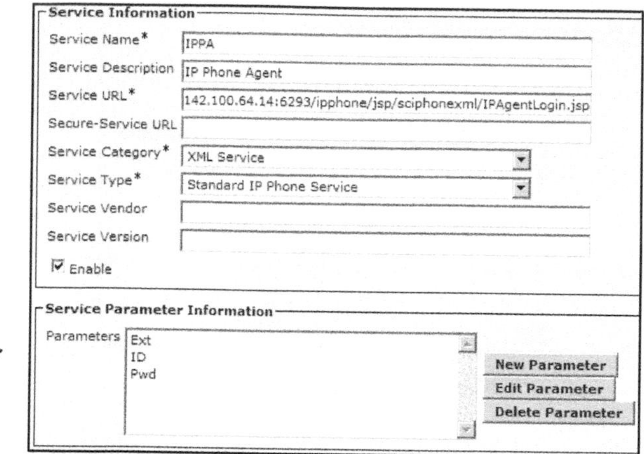

Figure 9-6 CUCM Finish Adding Parameters

Subscribe to IPPA service

For an IP phone to use the service, it has to subscribe to the service. We do this from phone configuration page [**CUCM > Device > Phone > *<Specific_ Phone>***]

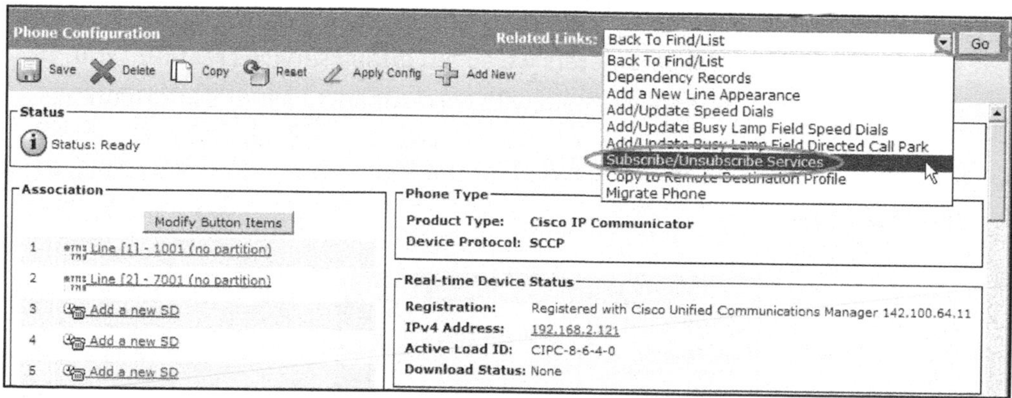

Figure 9-7 CUCM Phone Configuration Page

On the phone configuration page, choose "Subscribe/Unsubscribe Service" from the "Related Links" drop-down menu. Then click the "Go" button.

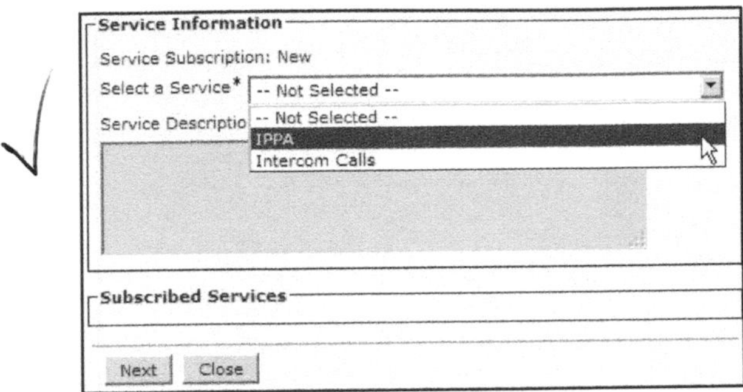

Figure 9-8 CUCM Phone Subscribing to Service

On next page you will choose "IPPA" from the drop-down list, which is the service we created previously. Then click "Next".

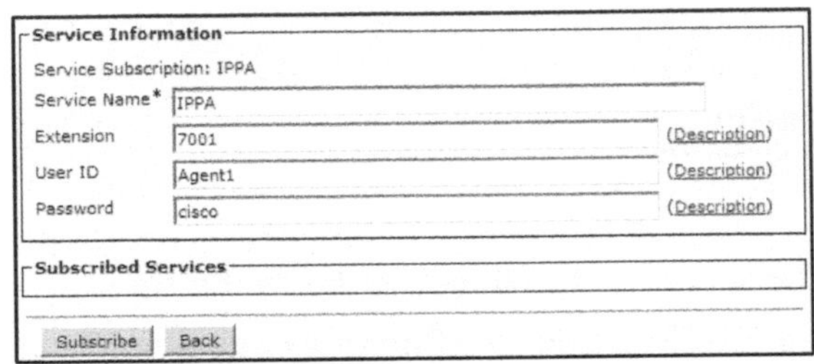

Figure 9-9 CUCM Phone Subscribing to Service (Continued)

On next screen, you will see the parameters we added during service creation. You may leave them blank or pre-populate them with corresponding agent's information.

- If you leave it blank, user will be asked for the login information every time, as illustrated below:

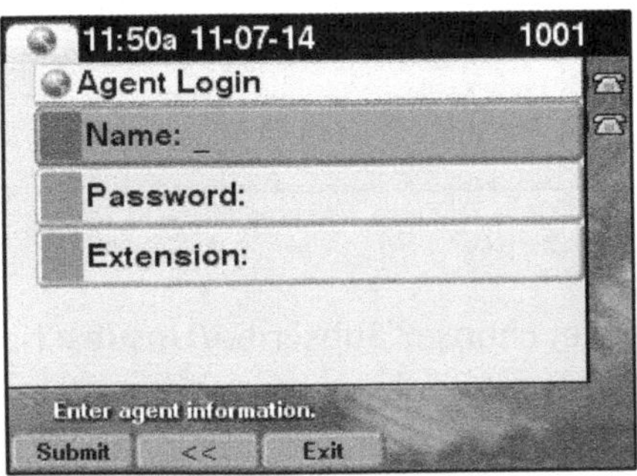

Figure 9-10 IPPA Agent Login

- If you pre-populate the login information, IPPA will go directly into the logged in state, as illustrated below:

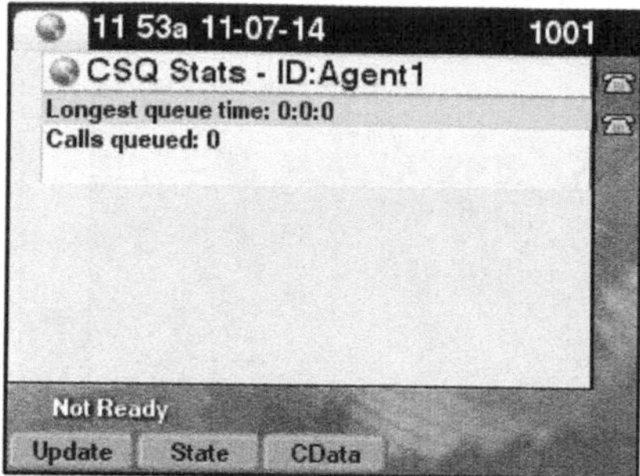

Figure 9-11 IPPA Logged In

In the case of IPPA (IP Phone Agent) service, we normally prepopulate the information during service subscription. So when agent hits the button on IP phone, it will automatically log into IPPA without asking for user ID and password. Because of this, IPPA is usually referred to as "One Button Login".

Please note that we are entering the parameter values during service subscription for a phone. The information is phone/agent specific. In another word, you will have to enter different information for different phones.

After entering the information, click "Subscribe" button to finish. You will notice "IPPA" shows up in the "Subscribed Services" box. That means we have successfully subscribed (associated) the IPPA service for this phone.

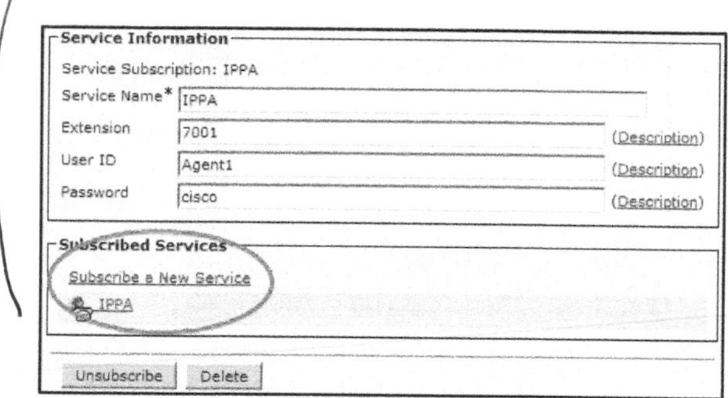

Figure 9-12 CUCM Phone - Subscribed Services

Agent Logon

To use the IPPA service, click the "Service" button on IP Phone.

Figure 9-13 IP Phone Service Button

If IPPA is the only service subscribed, the phone will automatically select that service and log in (with the information we pre-populated during subscription). You will see a screen like below:

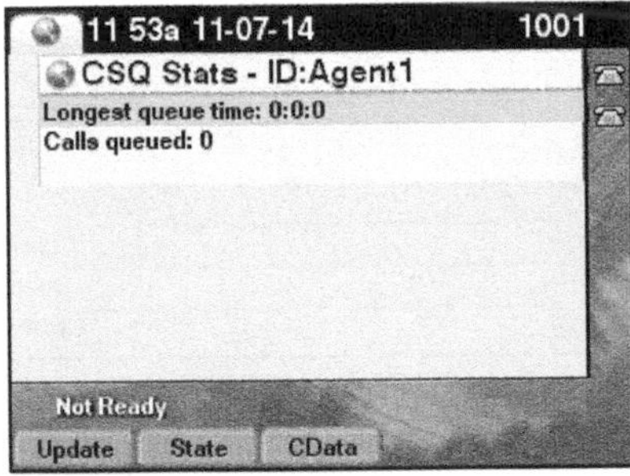

Figure 9-14 IPPA Logged In

You will see the agent state is "Not Ready". There are three soft keys:

- Update – Refresh the screen
- State – Change agent state (ready, not ready, logout, etc.)
- CData – Caller data (only available during an active call)

Agent may change his/her state with the "State" key.

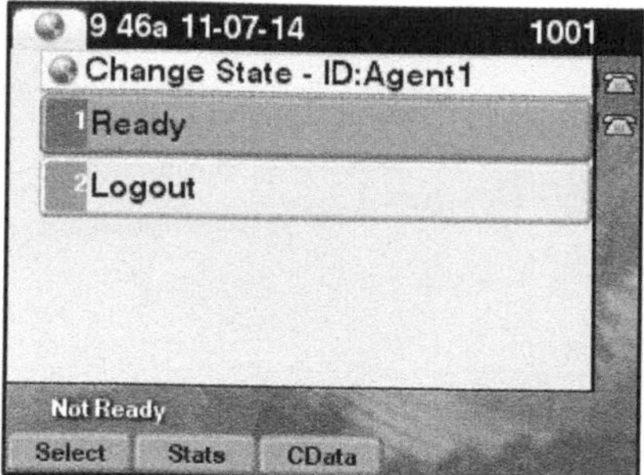

Figure 9-15 IPPA Changing State

Agent may monitor the queue statistics (number of calls waiting in queue, wait time, etc.)

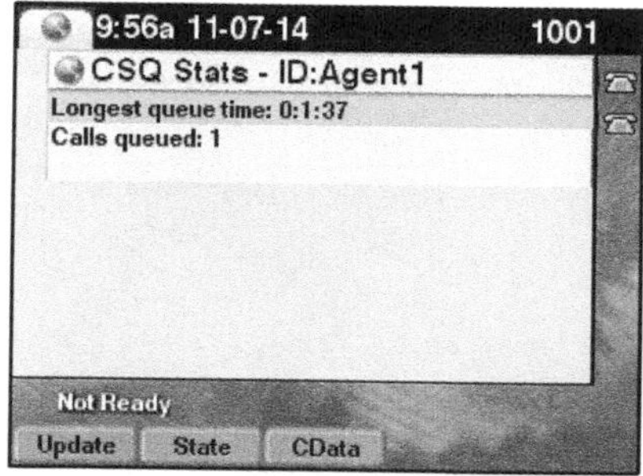

Figure 9-16 IPPA Queue Statistics

When there is an incoming call, agent may see the caller data with the "CData" key.

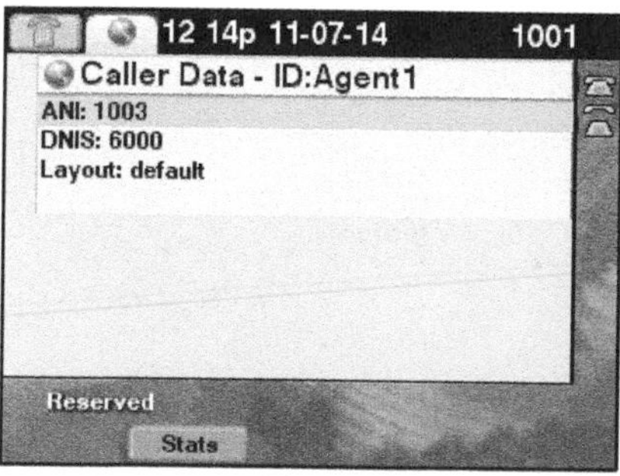

Figure 9-17 IPPA Caller Data

With proper scripting, we may display useful information in caller data such as account number, home address, etc. We will discuss the details in later chapters.

Chapter 10 Enterprise Data

In a call center environment, the more information agents have, the better they can serve the customer. Most of the call centers will use IVR (Interactive Voice Responder, also known as "automatic phone system") to collect some basic information before connecting customers to agents. For example, when you call a bank's service center, you will be asked to enter your account number, date of birth, etc. before you are connected to the agent.

When the call is being offered to agent, the information previously collected can be displayed on agent desktop (or IP phone). So the agent doesn't have to ask customer for the information again.

The information presented to agent is referred as "Enterprise Data" in UCCX (or "Caller Data" in IPPA).

To deliver Enterprise Data to agent, two parts of job need to be done:

1. Define the data format (fields and layouts) via CDA Web Portal
2. Populate the data via a script ("Set Enterprise Call Info" step)

Define Data Format

Fields

The term "field" is referring to a piece of information we want to deliver to agent desktop, for example, "Account_Number", "Home_Address", etc.

UCCX supports up to 256 fields. Each field has an "index number" ranging from 0 to 255. Index number 200 to 255 are reserved for system generated fields. Index number 0 to 199 can be used by administrator to define new fields.

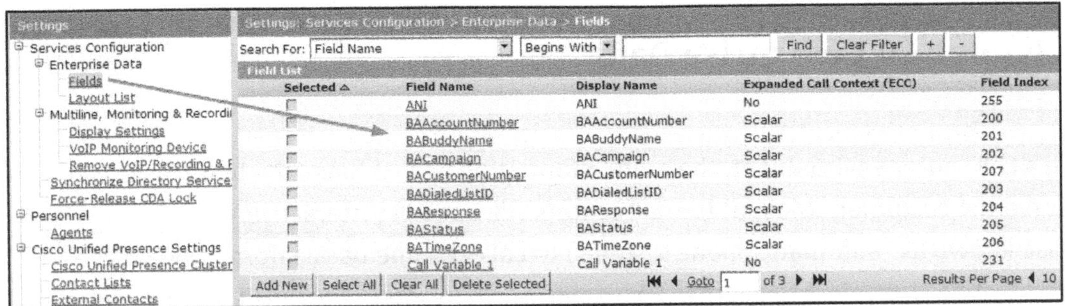

Selected	Field Name	Display Name	Expanded Call Context (ECC)	Field Index
	ANI	ANI	No	255
	BAAccountNumber	BAAccountNumber	Scalar	200
	BABuddyName	BABuddyName	Scalar	201
	BACampaign	BACampaign	Scalar	202
	BACustomerNumber	BACustomerNumber	Scalar	207
	BADialedListID	BADialedListID	Scalar	203
	BAResponse	BAResponse	Scalar	204
	BAStatus	BAStatus	Scalar	205
	BATimeZone	BATimeZone	Scalar	206
	Call Variable 1	Call Variable 1	No	231

Figure 10-1 CDA Web Portal > Service Configuration > Enterprise Data > Fields

Layouts

"Layout" is a container that contains multiple fields. When a script set the "layout" for a call, all the fields in the layout will be delivered to agent desktop.

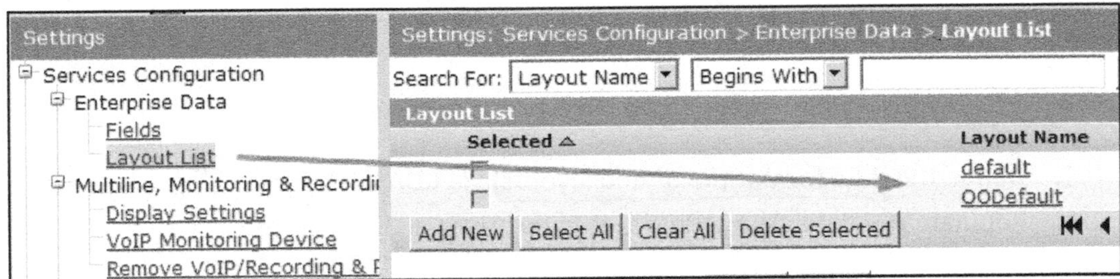

Figure 10-2 CDA Web Portal > Service Configuration > Enterprise Data > Layouts

UCCX has two system generated layouts – "default" and "OODefault". Content of the "default" and "OODefault" layouts are shown below.

Settings: Services Configuration > Enterprise Data > Layout List > default

General Information

Layout Name: default

Fields In Layout

Available:
200 BAAccountNumber
201 BABuddyName
202 BACampaign
203 BADialedListID
204 BAResponse
205 BAStatus
206 BATimeZone
207 BACustomerNumber
210 cisco.cem.Category
211 cisco.cem.MessageKey

Selected:
255 ANI
254 DNIS
252 Layout

Figure 10-3 "default" Layout

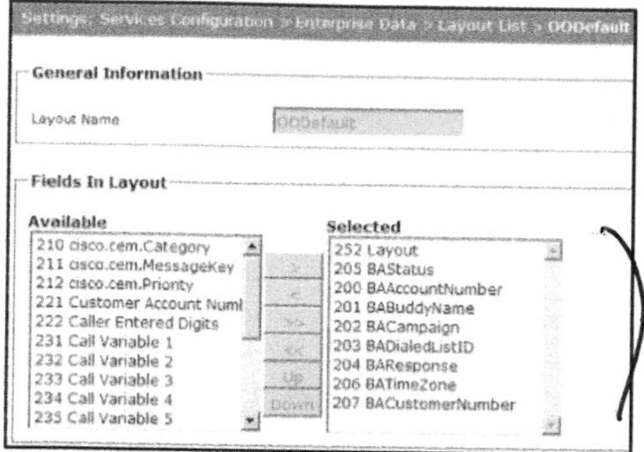

Figure 10-4 "OODefault" Layout

By default, "default" layout is used. That is why we are seeing "ANI", "DNIS" and "Layout" information on agent desktop whenever there's a calls being offered to the agent.

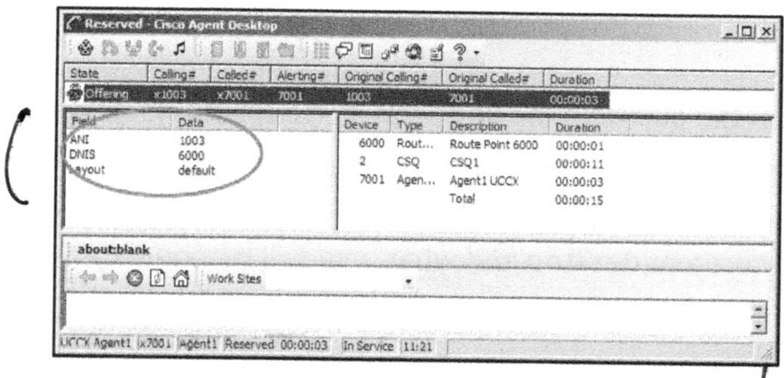

Figure 10-5 Agent Desktop - Enterprise Data

"Set Enterprise Call Info" Step

We define fields and layouts from CDA Web Portal. But to deliver the actual data to agent desktop, we need to do it from the script with "Set Enterprise Call Info" step.

"Set Enterprise Call Info" step is in the "Call Contact" category.

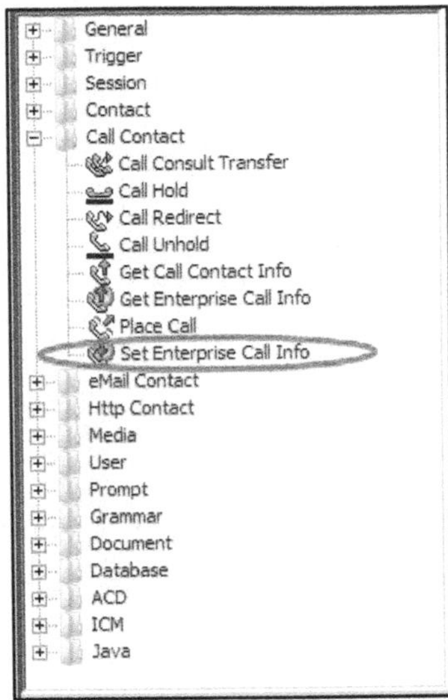

Figure 10-6 Script Editor - Set Enterprise Call Info

We drag this step from the palette pane and drop it into the design pane. Then we go to the properties of this step. In the properties, there is an "Expanded Call Variables" (ECC) tab that allows us add multiple ECC variables. Those variables determine which layout will be pushed to agent desktop and what data will be populated into which fields.

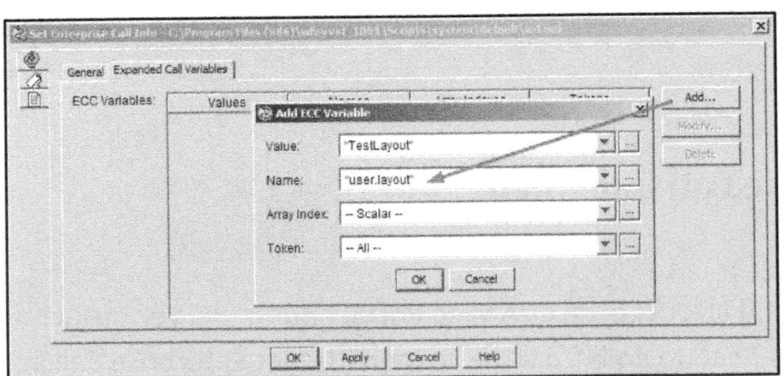

Figure 10-7 Set Enterprise Call Info - Variables

Example

Let say, we want to deliver the following information to agent desktop whenever the call is being offered to an agent:

Account Number	12345
Date of Birth	12/30/1987
Home Address	123 Main Street

In real life scenarios, the information will be dynamic and call specific (i.e. different caller will have different information). But for demonstration purpose, we will use static data in the example.

Define Fields

We will define three new fields – "AccNum", "DOB" and "HomeAddr" and give them index number 1 – 3 respectively.

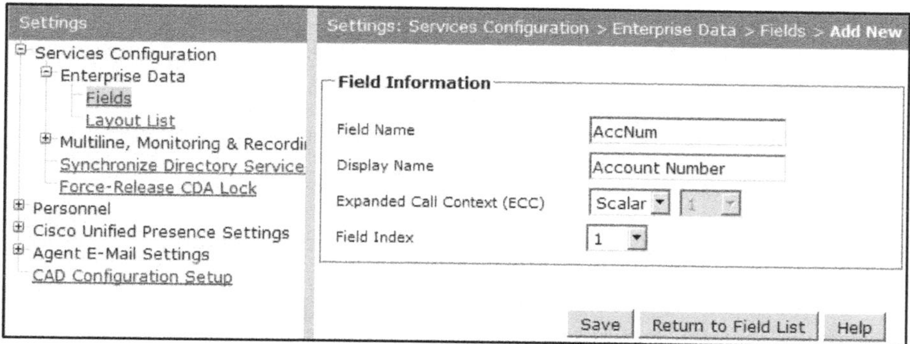

Figure 10-8 Adding New Fields

When finished, we should have three new fields like below:

Settings: Services Configuration > Enterprise Data > **Fields**

Search For: Field Index < 200 Find Clear Filter + -

Field List

Selected	**Field Name**	**Display Name**	**Expanded Call Context (ECC)**	**Field Index**
☐	AccNum	Account Number	Scalar	1
☐	DOB	Date of Birth	Scalar	2
☐	HomeAddr	Home Address	Scalar	3

Add New | Select All | Clear All | Delete Selected | Goto 1 of 1 | Results Per Pa

Figure 10-9 New Fields Created

Define Layout

Now we want to define a new layout called "TestLayout" which includes the three fields we just created.

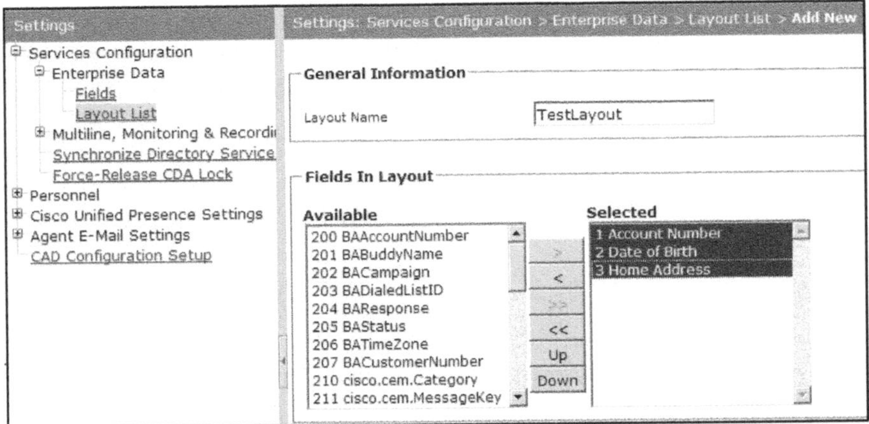

Figure 10-10 Creating a New Layout

Please note that not only we can choose what fields to be included in the layout but also we can arrange the fields in specific order. For example, if we want "Home Address" to be displayed on the top, we may highlight "Home Address" and use the "Up" button to move it up.

After the new layout is created, we should have a layout list like below:

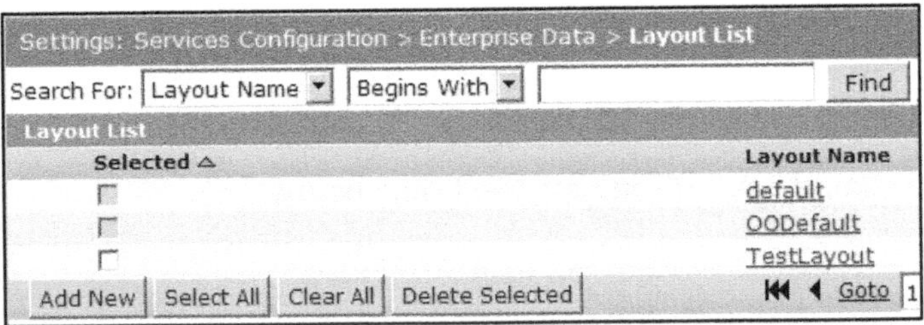

Figure 10-11 New Layout Created

Create a Test Script

Instead of creating a script from scratch, we may make a copy of the "icd.aef" script and add the "Set Enterprise Call Info" step to it.

1. We open the script "C:\Program Files (x86)\wfavvid_1051\Scripts\system\default\icd.aef" with script editor.

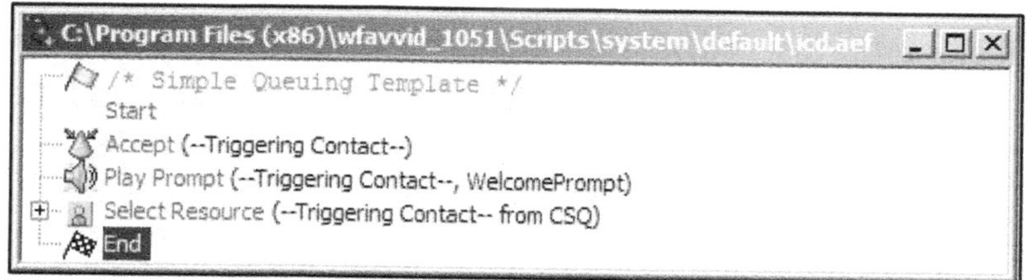

Figure 10-12 icd.aef Script

2. From palette pane, drag "Set Enterprise Call Info" step and drop it into the script right before "Select Resource" step.

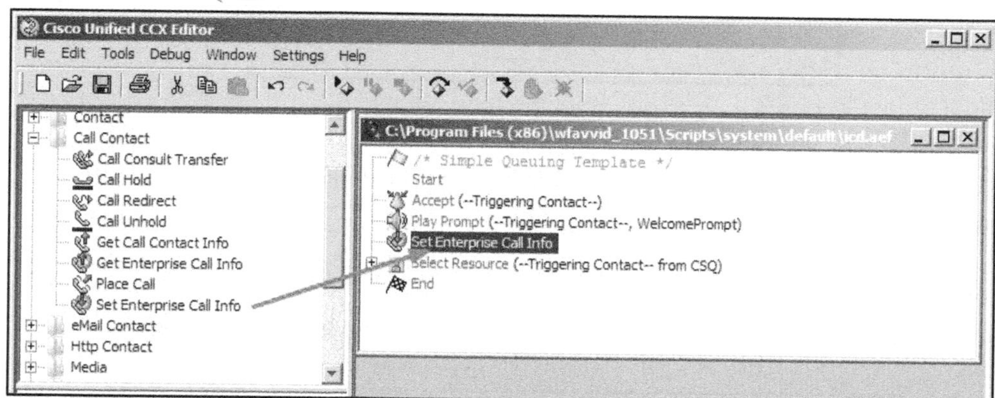

Figure 10-13 Set Enterprise Call Info

3. In design pane, right-click on the "Set Enterprise Call Info" step, choose "Properties" and go to "Expanded Call Variables" tab. Click "Add" button to add variables.

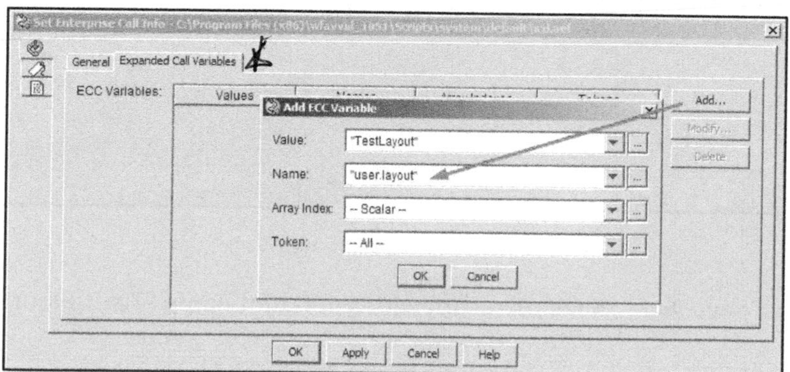

Figure 10-14 "user.layout" Variable

In the "Value" field, enter "TestLayout" (including the quotation marks). This is the layout we previously created.

In the "Name" field, enter "user.layout" (including the quotation marks). This is a special variable name that tells the system which layout we want to push to the agent desktop.

Leave others in default and click "OK" button. You will get a warning message like below:

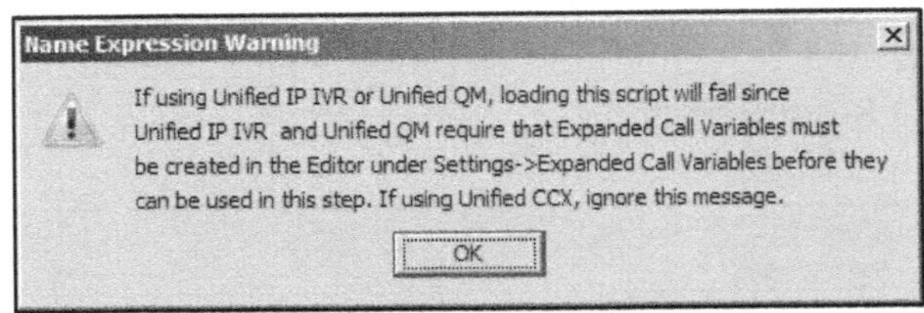

Figure 10-15 Warning that does not apply to UCCX

Since we are using UCCX, we may ignore this warning. Just click "OK" to dismiss the warning.

4. Repeat the same procedure to add "AccNum", "DOB" and "HomeAddr" variables and corresponding values. When finish, we should have a screen like below:

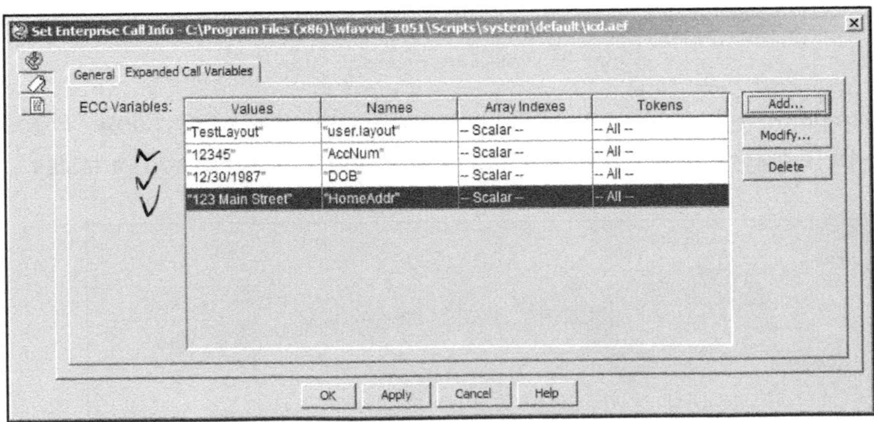

Figure 10-16 Expanded Call Variables

5. Go to [**File > Save As...**]. Save this script with a different name "TestLayout.aef".

Upload the Script

Go to [**UCCX AppAdmin Portal > Applications > Script Management**]. Click "Upload Scripts". Browse to the script we just created (TestLayout.aef). Click "Upload". Click "Return to Script Management". The page will refresh and you should see the new script showing up.

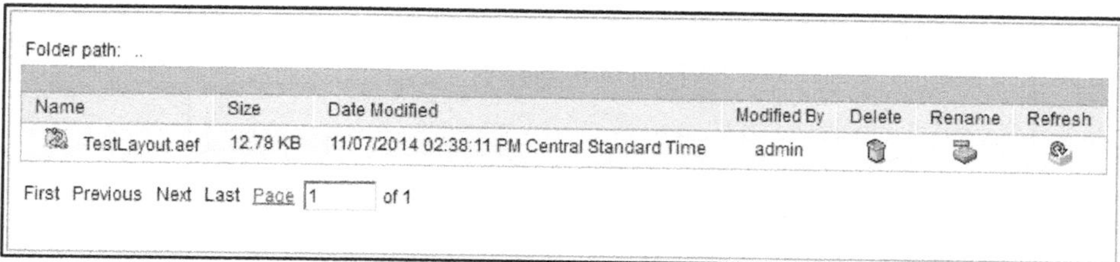
Folder path: ..

Name	Size	Date Modified	Modified By	Delete	Rename	Refresh
TestLayout.aef	12.78 KB	11/07/2014 02:38:11 PM Central Standard Time	admin			

First Previous Next Last Page 1 of 1

Figure 10-17 Script Uploaded

Modify the Application

To test the script, we will need an application. To save some time, we will modify the existing application instead of creating a new one.

We go to [**UCCX AppAdmin Portal > Applications > Application Management**]. Click the application we created before - "MyFirstApp". From the "Script" drop-down list, choose the script we just uploaded – "TestLayout.aef".

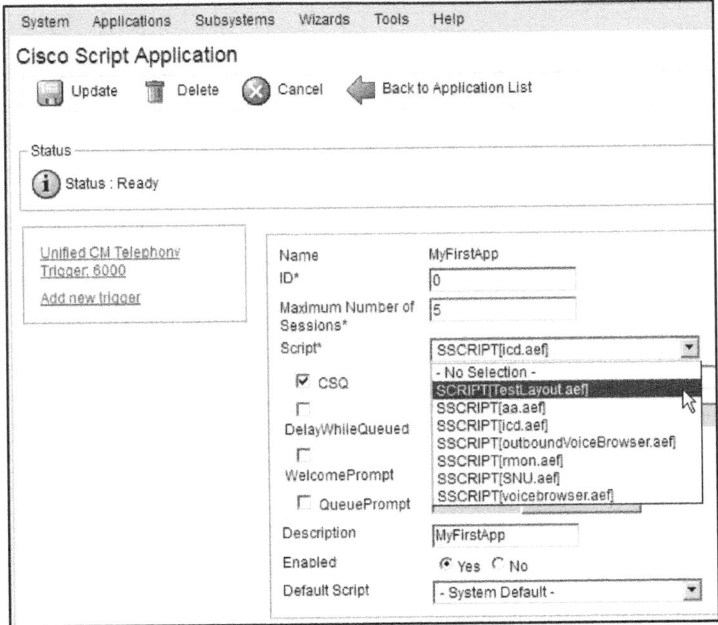

Figure 10-18 Modifying an Application

The page will refresh. You will have to check the checkbox next to CSQ and enter "CSQ1" (including quotation marks) into the field. Leave others in default and click "Update" button.

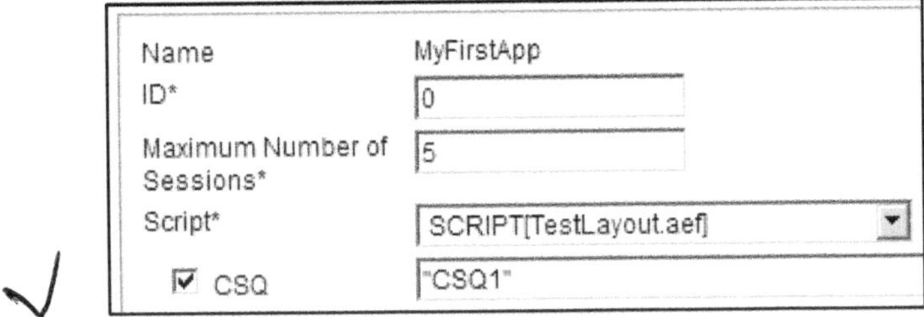

Figure 10-19 Set CSQ Value

Test the Application

Now let's log into agent desktop. Change the state to "Ready". From a non-agent phone, call the route point 6000. The call is offered to the agent. We see the following on agent desktop:

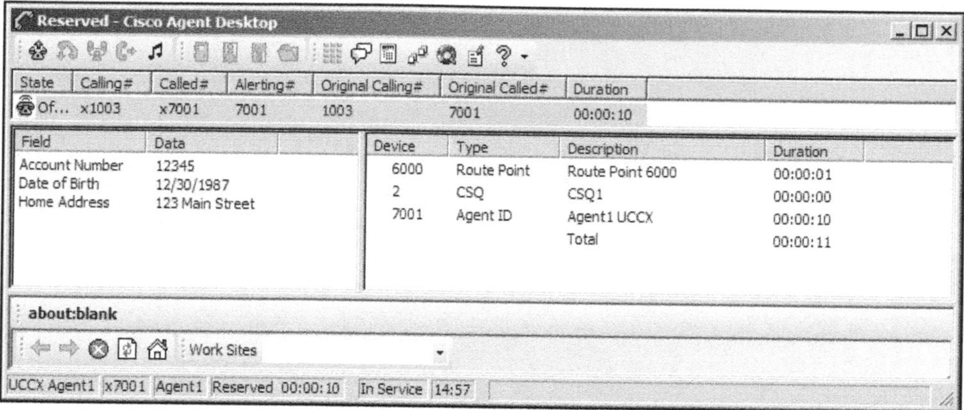

Figure 10-20 Enterprise Data on Agent Desktop

Note the Enterprise Data showing up on the left pane. It provides agent customer account number, date of birth and home address. If further integrated with database, the script could provide much more information regarding the customer. Agents will be able to better serve the customer with the information.

Same information is provided as "Caller Data" on IP Phone Agent (IPPA), as illustrated below:

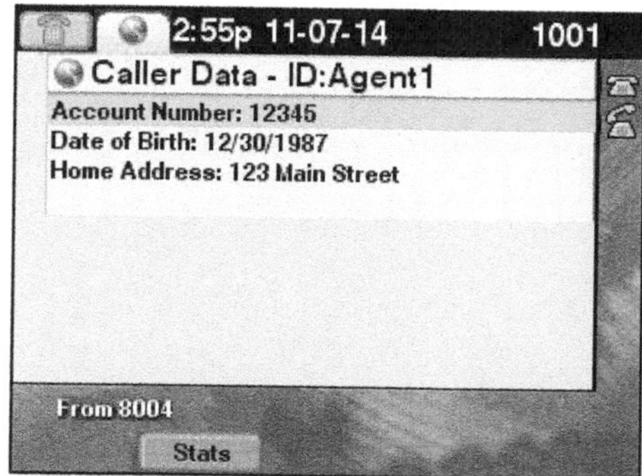

Figure 10-21 IP Phone Agent - Caller Data

Chapter 11 Customization and Automation

Call center agents use agent desktop (CAD) or IP phone agent (IPPA) to handle calls and perform other tasks such as update customer account information, place orders, etc. CAD or IPPA can be customized to meet business requirements. Routine tasks can also be automated with pre-defined rules (workflow). CAD can also be integrated with 3rd-party applications.

Most of the customization is done via CDA application. Some of the configuration such as "Phone Book", "Reason Codes" and "Wrap-up Data" has global configuration and group specific configuration. Different "Work Flow Groups" can be created to satisfy different business requirements. The "default" group was generated by system. All agents are in "default" group until they are re-assigned to a different group.

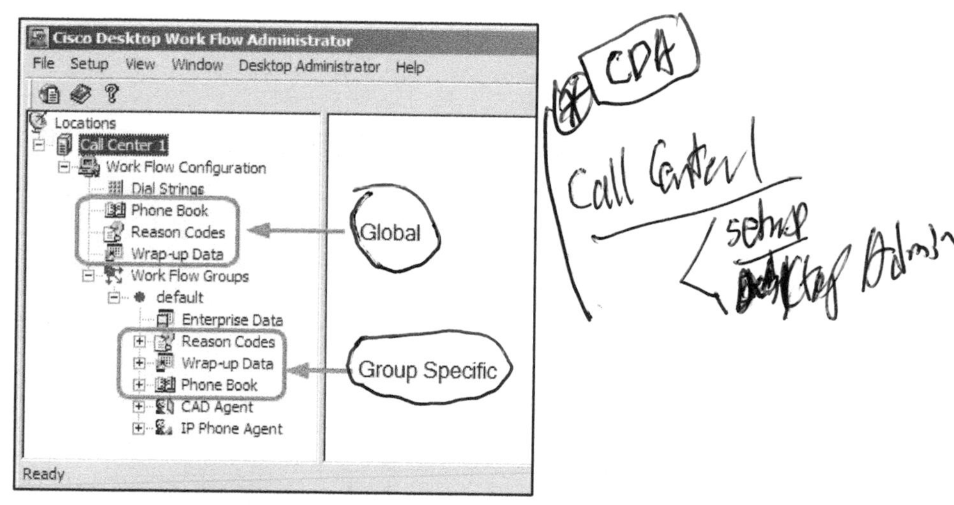

Figure 11-1 CDA App - Global vs. Group Specific Configuration

Dial String

"Dial Strings" option is used to configure the way desktop applications (mostly CAD) display and dial phone numbers. Though we may also do digit manipulation from CUCM or CME, "Dial Strings" settings give you another way to do it.

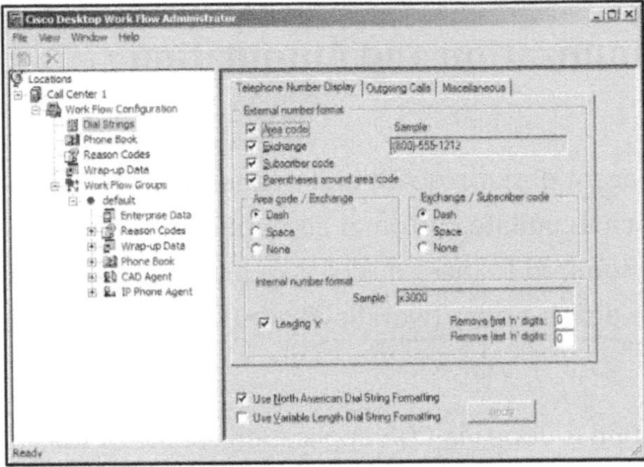

Figure 11-2 CDA - Dial Strings

Most of the settings in "Dial Strings" are self-explanatory. To avoid turning this book into a duplication of Cisco manual, we will skip the obvious.

Phone Book

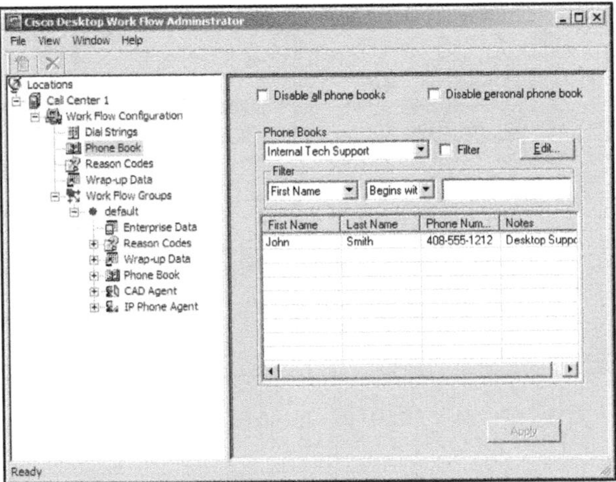

Figure 11-3 CDA - Phone Book

Agents have a number of phone number lists available to them:

- The Recent Call List, a dynamic list of up to 100 recently-called phone numbers kept by Agent Desktop
- A personal phone book, created and maintained by the agent (and enabled/disabled by the system administrator)

- Up to 256 phone books (includes **global phone books** and **work flow group phone books**). Each phone book supports a maximum of 3,000 directory entries.
- CAD supports in total up to 10,000 directory entries that includes global, work flow group, or personal phone book entries.
- Work flow group phone books, created by the system administrator with the work flow group Phone Book function

Global phone books, which are available to all agents, are created and maintained using the Phone Book node under the Work Flow Configuration node.

Work flow groups phone books, which are available to agents only in that specific work flow group, are created and maintained using the Phone Book node under the specific work flow group's node.

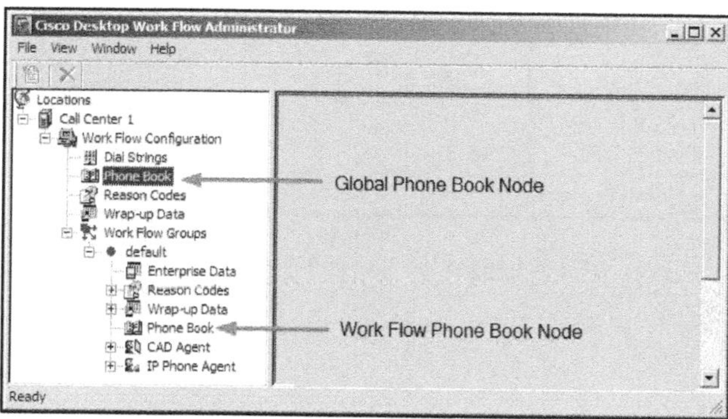

Figure 11-4 CDA - Phone Book Nodes

Reason Codes

Reason codes describe why an agent has changed to the Not Ready agent state or has logged out.

A maximum of 999 reason codes can be set up for CAD. IP Phone Agent has a limit of 100 reason codes.

Some reason codes are pre-defined (32, 33, 1000, 32749 – 23767). Addition reason codes can be created by administrator.

Global reason codes, which are available to all agents, are assigned using the Reason Codes node under the Work Flow Configuration node.

Work flow group reason codes, which are available only to agents in that specific work flow group, are assigned using the Reason Codes node under the specific work flow group's node.

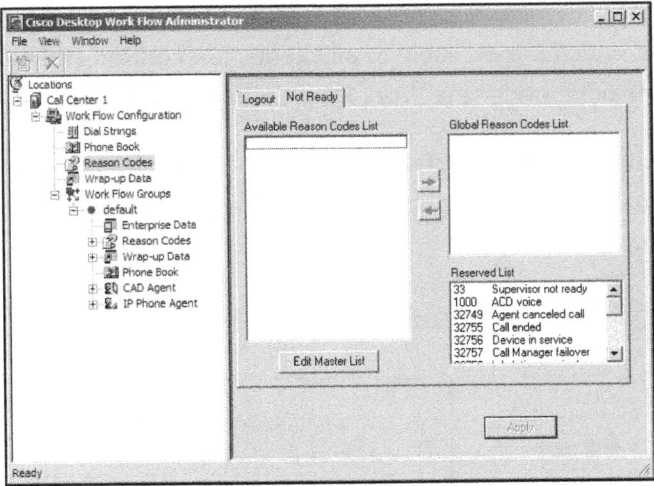

Figure 11-5 CDA - Reason Codes

Wrap-up Data

Wrap-up data descriptions are used by contact centers for purposes such as tracking the frequency of different activities and identifying the account to which to charge a call, among others. Wrap-up data is set up and maintained, and automated state changes are enabled, using the Wrap-up Data window. Wrap-up data descriptions are used for both calls and e-mails.

There is no limit on how many wrap-up data descriptions can be set up for CAD. IP Phone Agent has a limit of 100 wrap-up data descriptions.

Global wrap-up data descriptions, which are available to all agents, are created and assigned using the Wrap-up Data under the Work Flow Configuration node.

Work flow group wrap-up data descriptions, which are available to agents only in that specific work flow group, are created and assigned using the Wrap-up Data node under the specific work flow group's node.

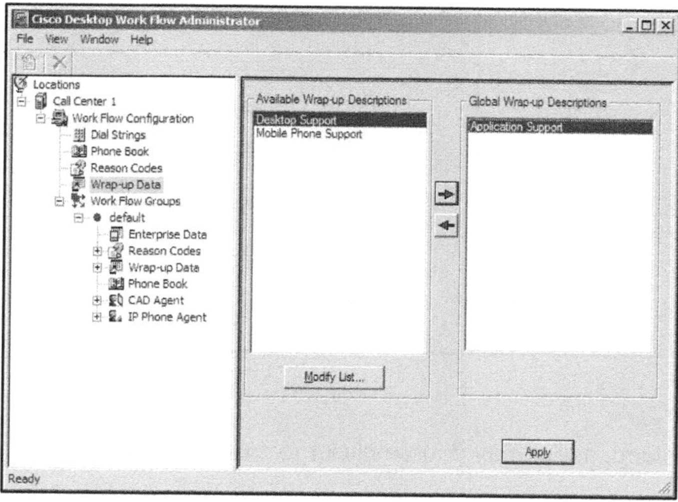

Figure 11-6 CDA - Wrap-up Data

Enterprise Data

We have discussed "Enterprise Data" in previous chapters. The "Enterprise Data" window in CDA enables you to:

- Configure Agent Desktop so that agents in the selected work flow group can edit enterprise data
- Set thresholds for call duration at a particular type of device while a call is in the contact center

Data

The Data tab controls whether or not an agent in the work flow group is allowed to edit the enterprise data displayed in Agent Desktop.

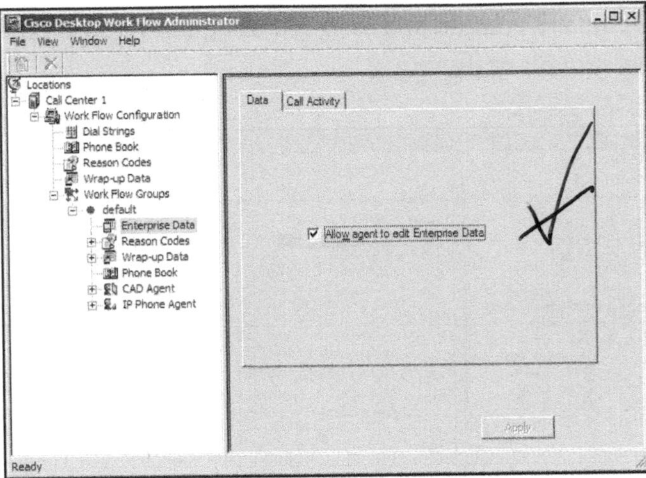

Figure 11-7 CDA - Enterprise Data > Data

If this option is enabled, agent may double-click the enterprise data fields in CAD to edit the data:

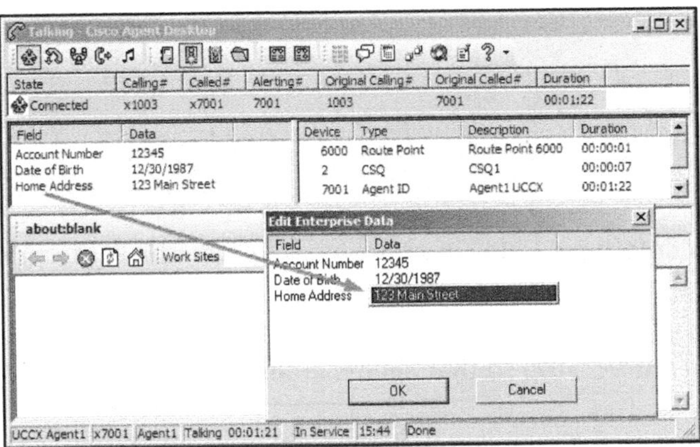

Figure 11-8 CAD - Edit Enterprise Data

Call Activity

The Call Activity tab enables you to set the thresholds for the selected work flow group for call duration at a particular type of device (CSQ and Agent) while a call is in the contact center.

If a call remains at a device longer than the defined Caution or Warning threshold, a Caution or Warning icon is displayed next to the device name in the Agent Desktop call activity pane.

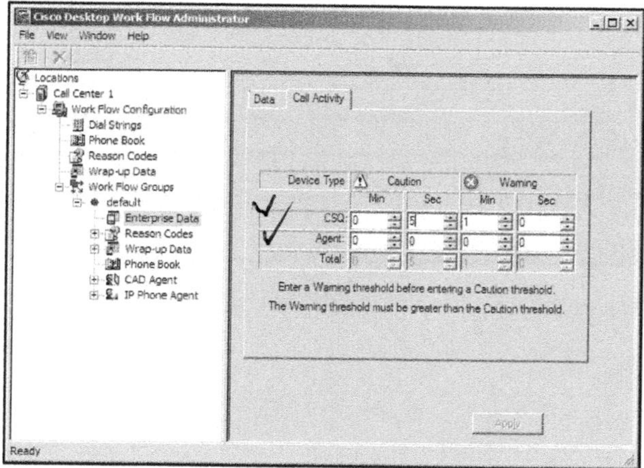

Figure 11-9 CDA - Enterprise Data > Call Activity

Here is the screen when the call exceeds the "caution" threshold.

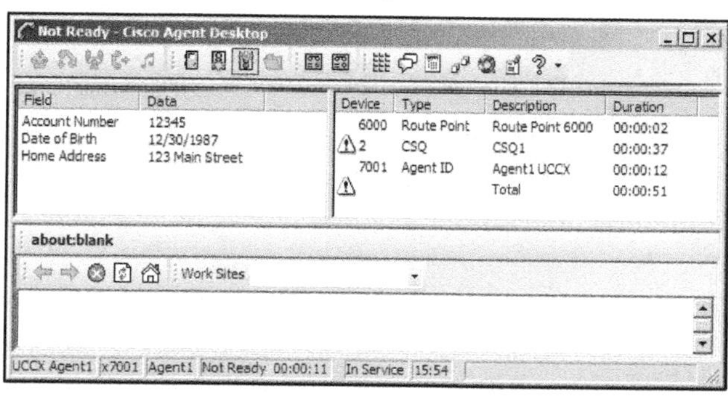

Figure 11-10 CAD - Call Exceeds "Caution" Threshold

Here is the screen when the call exceeds the "warning" threshold.

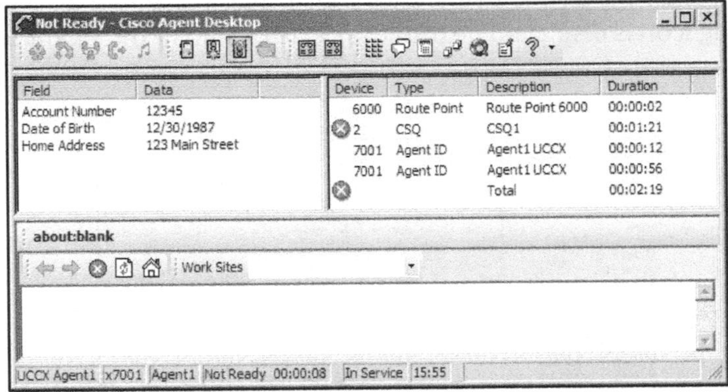

Figure 11-11 CAD - Call Exceeds "Warning" Threshold

CAD Agent

"CAD Agent" node enables you to configure various functions for each type of agent within the selected work flow group. "CAD Agent" node has four sub-nodes:

- User Interface
- Voice Contact Work Flows
- E-Mail Contact Work Flows
- Agent Management Work Flows

User Interface

The User Interface window enables you to configure the appearance and behavior of Agent Desktop.

Toolbar

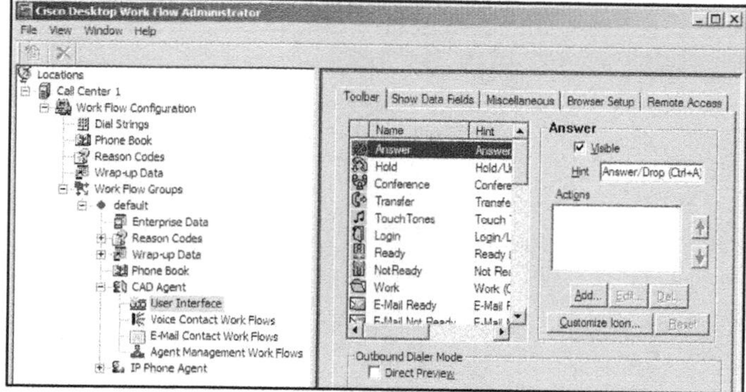

Figure 11-12 CDA > Work Flow Group > CAD Agent > User Interface > Toolbar

The Toolbar tab enables you to:

- Adding and Removing Toolbar Buttons
- Associating Actions with Task Buttons
- Changing a Task Button's Hint
- Customizing Button Icons
- Show Data Fields

Show Data Fields

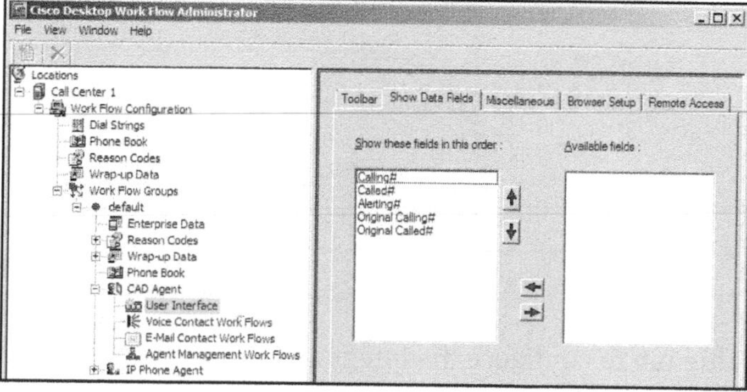

Figure 11-13 CDA > Work Flow Group > CAD Agent > User Interface > Show Data Fields

The Show Data Fields tab configures the data fields that appear in the contact appearance pane in Agent Desktop and enables you to rename data fields.

Miscellaneous

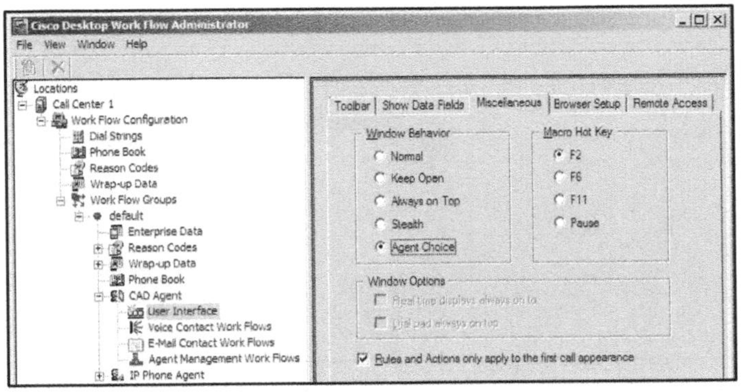

Figure 11-14 CDA > Work Flow Group > CAD Agent > User Interface > Miscellaneous

Use the Miscellaneous tab to configure other user interface options.

Browser Setup

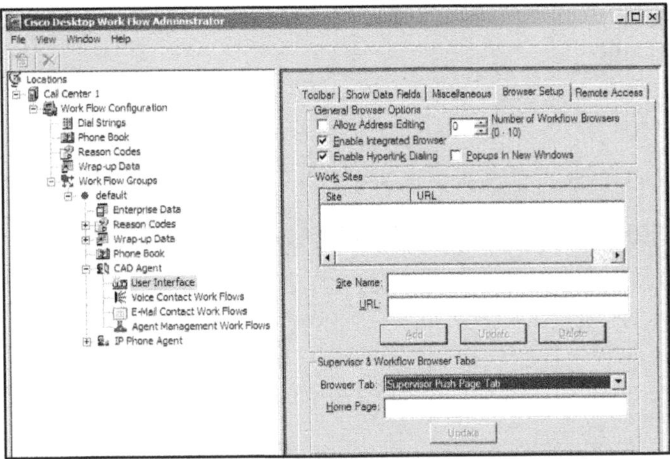

Figure 11-15 CDA > Work Flow Group > CAD Agent > User Interface > Browser Setup

Use the Browser Setup tab to configure the Integrated Browser portion of Agent Desktop. On this tab, you can do the following tasks:

- Enable/disable the integrated browser window
- Set the default web page displayed by the browser
- Enable up to 10 browser tabs
- Enable/disable popups to be displayed as a regular Internet Explorer popup window instead of a new tab in the integrated browser
- Enable/disable agents' access to other websites

- Add work sites (or "favorites") so agents can quickly access frequently-used websites
- Enable/disable hyperlink dialing

Remote Access

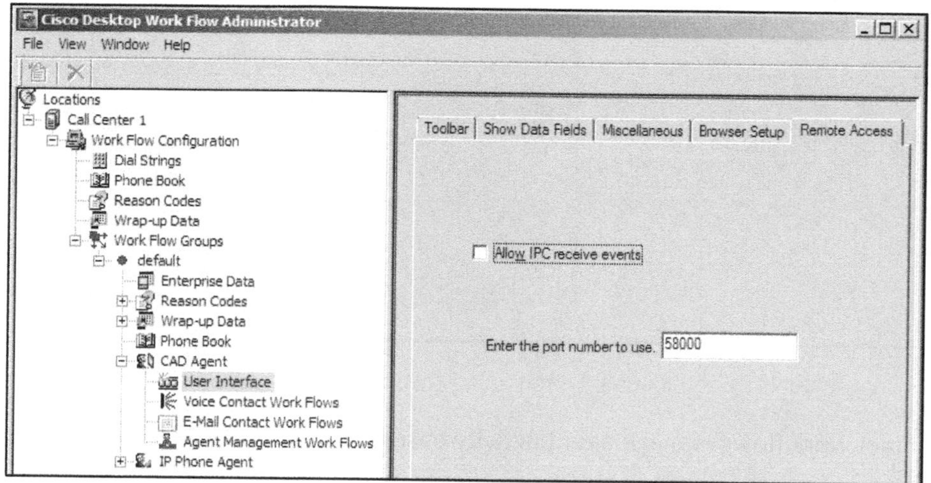

Figure 11-16 CDA > Work Flow Groups > CAD Agent > User Interface > Remote Access

The Remote Access tab is used to enable the IPC Receive Event feature and configure the port used by the feature. An IPC Receive Event occurs when a third-party application sends a message to Agent Desktop over a UDP socket. These messages must adhere to a predefined XML schema and cannot exceed 4000 bytes.

Voice Contact Work Flows

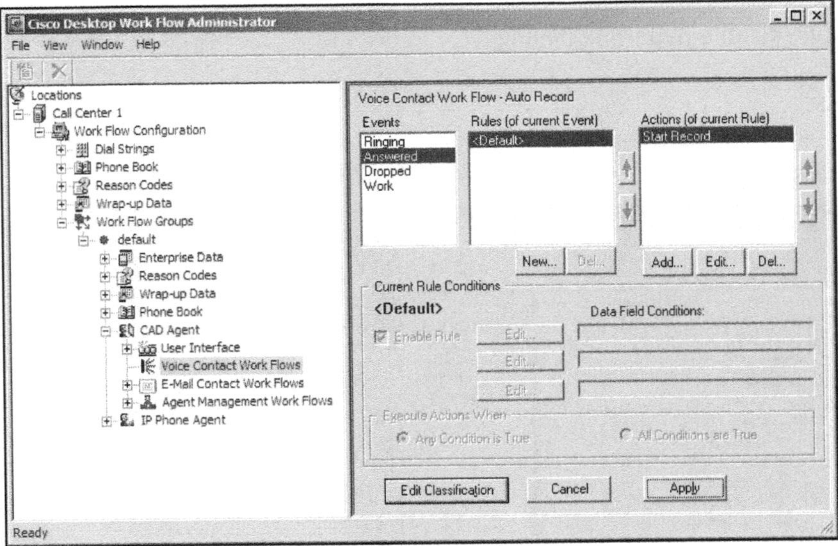

Figure 11-17 CDA > Work Flow Groups > CAD Agent > Voice Contact Work Flows

Voice contact work flows manage agent activity based on voice call events. Once a call is classified it is further filtered according to events, rules, and actions. Voice contact work flows are available to Agent Desktop agents.

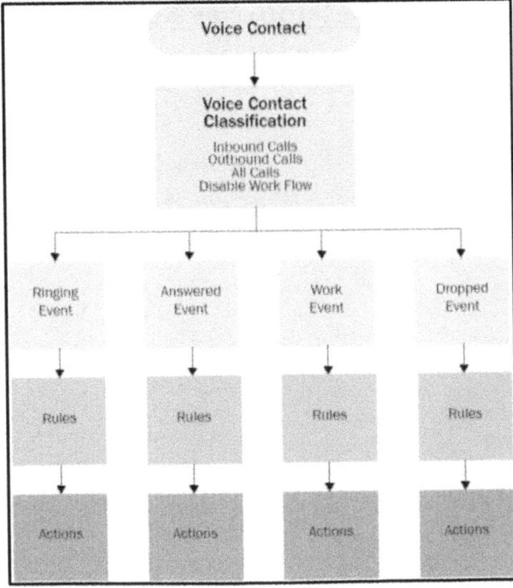

For example, a voice contact work flow could be set up as follows:

1. A call comes into the contact center and is routed to an agent in the Ready state.
2. The Voice Contact Classification filter determines which work flow to select. It examines the inbound call's enterprise data (original dialed number) and determines that it is a call for Product A technical support and thus meets the data conditions of Work Flow 1. The call is now subject to the second layer of filtering set up in Work Flow 1.
3. Work Flow 1 says that any ringing event on the Product A support line triggers an HTTP action. This action takes the customer-entered account information from the IVR (part of the call's enterprise data) and pops a web page in Agent Desktop's integrated browser that displays the customer's account information to the agent.
4. The agent answers the phone call and is ready to assist the customer.

E-Mail Contact Work Flows

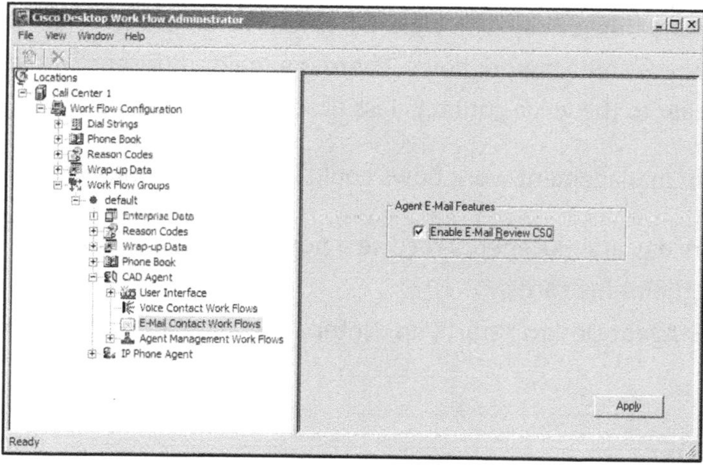

Figure 11-18 CDA > Work Flow Groups > CAD Agent > E-Mail Contact Work Flows

The E-Mail Contact Work Flows node is used to enable/disable the E-Mail Review CSQ for members of the work flow group. When this setting is enabled and the agent responds to an e-mail from a CSQ associated with Review CSQ, then all the agent replies to customer e-mails are automatically routed to Review CSQ, instead of sending them directly back to the customer. Agents with skill assignment for Review CSQ are responsible for reviewing and editing the content of the response before the e-mail reply is sent to the customer.

Agent Management Work Flows

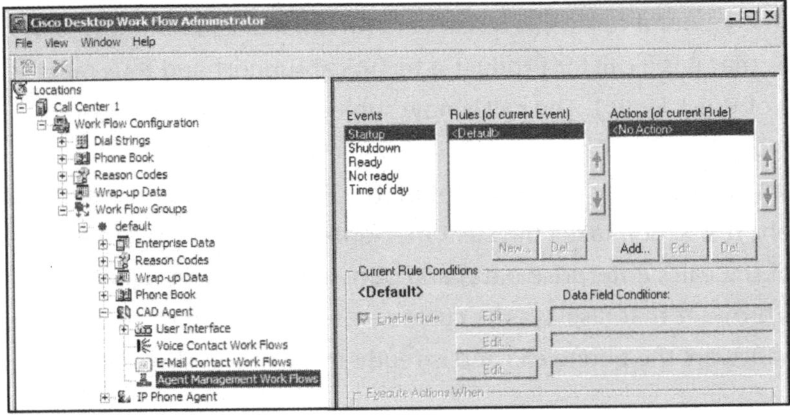

Figure 11-19 CDA > Work Flow Groups > CAD Agent > Agent Management Work Flows

Agent management work flows manage agent activity based on Agent Desktop activity, agent ACD states, and time of day. The work flows follow the event—rule—action behavior used by voice contact work flows. There is a major difference—there is no initial filtering similar to the voice contact classification applied to voice contacts.

For example, agent management work flows could be set up as follows:

- Every work day at 4:30, agents receive a popup message reminding them to complete their time cards.
- Whenever Agent Desktop starts up, Notepad is launched on the agent's desktop.

IP Phone Agent

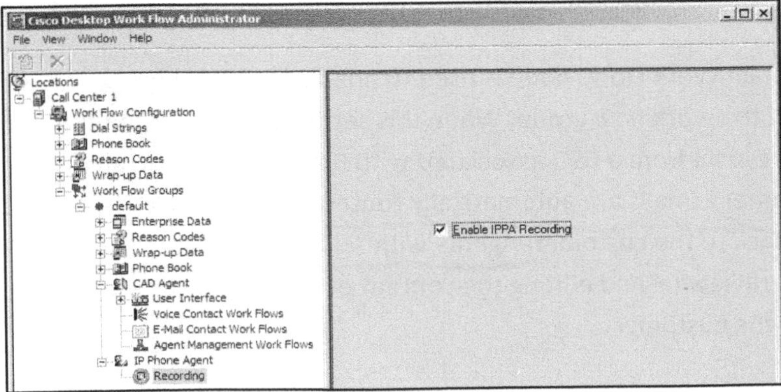

Figure 11-20 CDA > Work Flow Groups > IP Phone Agent > Recording

The Recording node under the IP Phone Agent node enables agent-initiated recording for agents who use the IP Phone Agent service.

When enabled, the IP Phone Agent service has soft key options for starting and stopping recording. The IPPA agent can then record his or her own phone conversations, and these recordings can be reviewed by the supervisor using Supervisor Record Viewer.

Example 1 – Enable Record Buttons for CAD

By default, agent desktop (CAD) does not have record button. Administrator may add the "Start Record" / "Stop Record" buttons to CAD so agents may record customer calls.

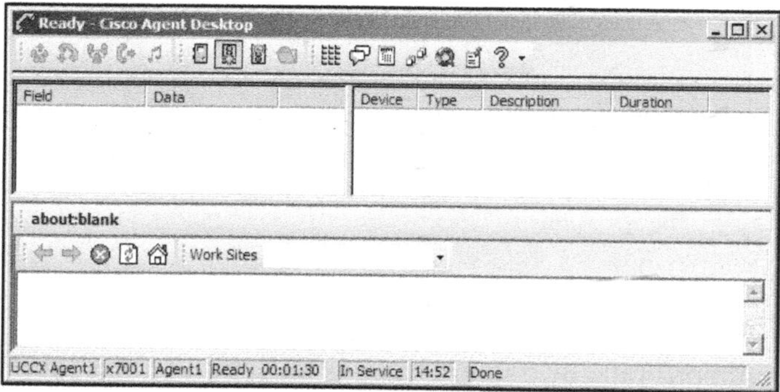

Figure 11-21 Default CAD Interface - No Record Button

1. Make a button visible on CAD

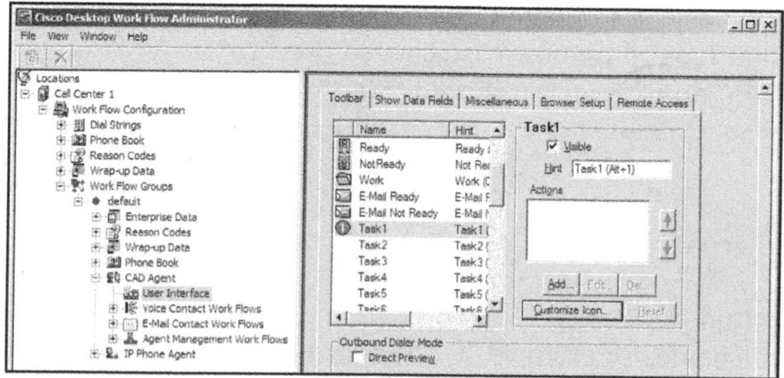

Figure 11-22 CDA > Work Flow Groups > CAD Agent > User Interface

Go to [**CDA > Work Flow Groups > *<specific group>* > CAD Agent > User Interface**]. Select the "Toolbar" tab. Highlight "Task1" then check the "Visible" checkbox. This makes the button visible on CAD interface. However, there is no action assigned to this button yet. Thus clicking the button does nothing.

2. Assign action to the button

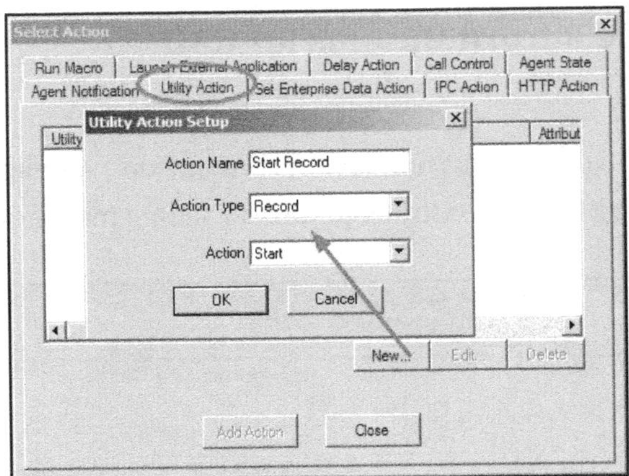

Figure 11-23 CDA > Work Flow Groups > CAD Agent > User Interface – Creating Actions

Click "Add" button below the "Actions" box. A "Select Action" window will pop up. Click on the "Utility Action" tab. By default, there is no action on this tab. We will create two actions – "Start Record" and "Stop Record". Then we will assign the actions to corresponding buttons.

To create a "Start Record" action, do the following:

2.1 Click "New" button.
2.2 Define an action name, for example "Start Record"
2.3 From the "Action Type" drop-down list, choose "Record"
2.4 From the "Action" drop-down list, choose "Start"
2.5 Click "OK" button

To create a "Stop Record" action, do the following:

2.1 Click "New" button.
2.2 Define an action name, for example "Stop Record"
2.3 From the "Action Type" drop-down list, choose "Record"

2.4 From the "Action" drop-down list, choose "Stop"
2.5 Click "OK" button

After the above steps, you should have "Start Record" and "Stop Record" actions on your "Utility Action" tab as below:

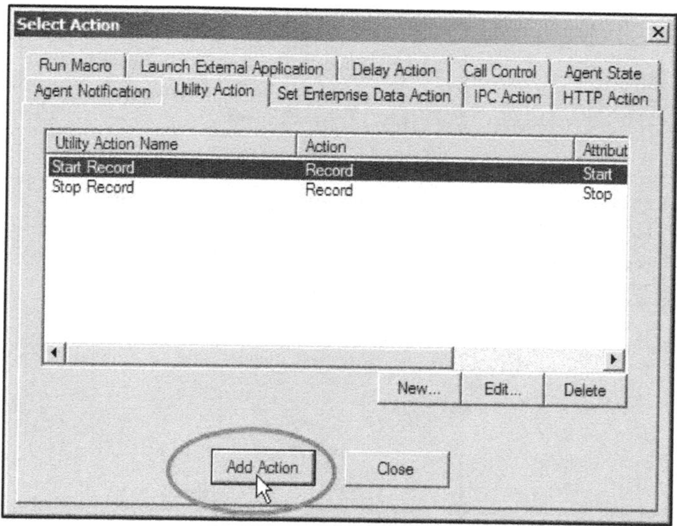

Figure 11-24 CDA > Work Flow Groups > CAD Agent > User Interface – Adding Action to Button

Highlight "Start Record" then click "Add Action" button. The "Select Action" window will disappear and you will return to the previous "Toolbar" tab. Shown as below:

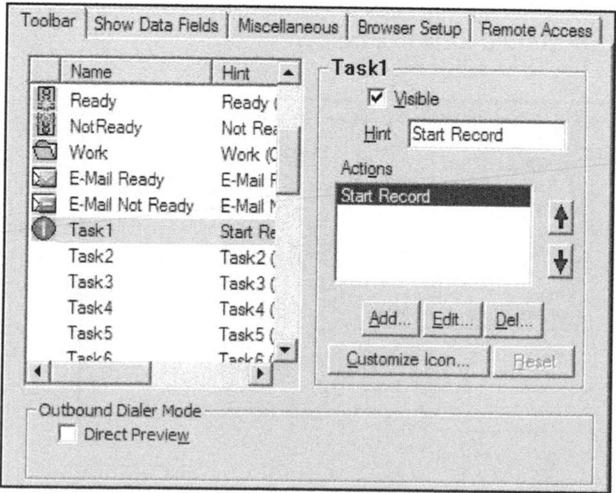

Figure 11-25 CDA > Work Flow Groups > CAD Agent > User Interface – Toolbar

You may follow similar procedures to assign "Stop Record" action to "Task2" button. Just make sure you choose "Stop Record" action from the "Utility Action" tab.

3. Customize the button icon

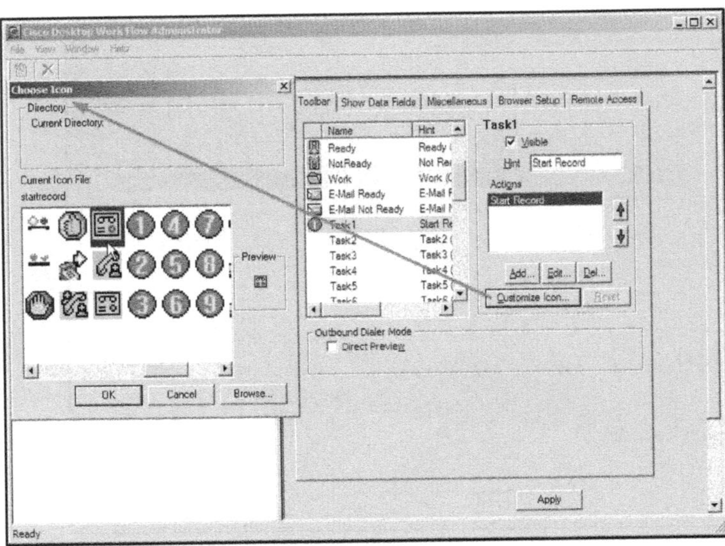

Figure 11-26 CDA > Work Flow Groups > CAD Agent > User Interface – Customizing Button Icon

Optionally, you may customize the button icon so it is more intuitive on the CAD user interface. For example, we may choose a recorder icon with a red dot to indicate "Start Record". Choose a recorder icon without the red dot to indicate "Stop Record". After customization, CDA should look like below:

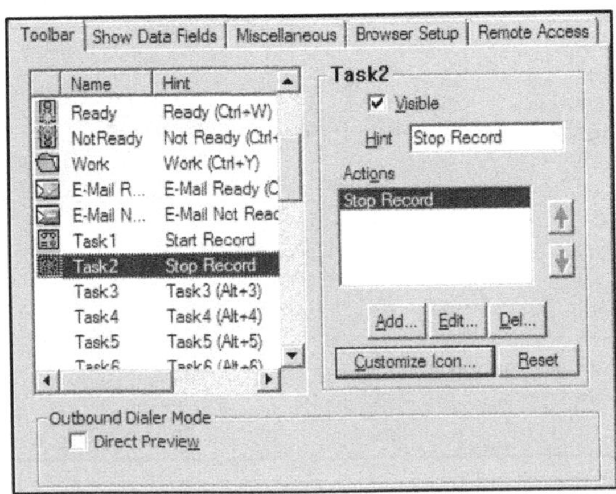

Figure 11-27 CDA > Work Flow Groups > CAD Agent > User Interface with Customized Icon

If everything was configured properly, agent desktop CAD will show the new button like below:

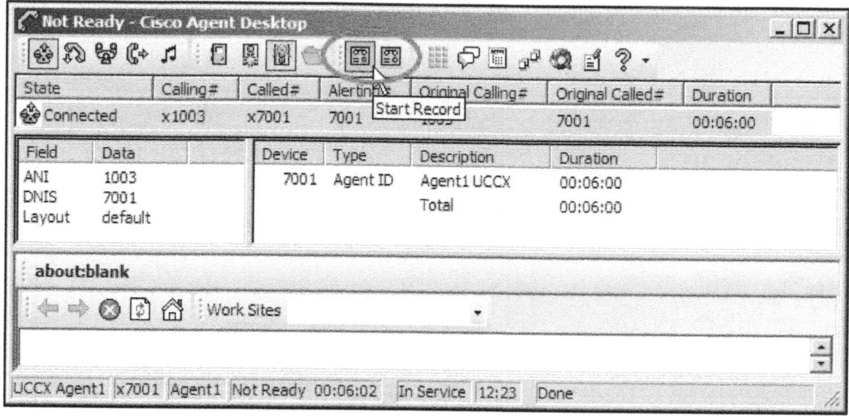

Figure 11-28 CAD with Record button

Example 2 – Configure Automatic Recording

UCCX/CAD does not have an "Automatic Record" function by default. But we can achieve that by using "Voice Contact Work Flows". This is a so-called "poor man solution" as it does not require additional investment on third-party recording solutions. However this method has its limitations. For example, it only works with CAD (Agent Desktop) but not IPPA (IP Phone Agent).

A "Voice Contact Work Flow" is a set of pre-programmed logics that is triggered by call events (such as call answered, call dropped). We may program the system so that when the call is answered, recording is automatically started. When call is dropped (disconnected), recording is automatically stopped.

Before configuring the "Voice Contact Work Flow", you'll have to define the "Start Record" and "Stop Record" action. See previous example for details.

Assuming "Start Record" and "Stop Record" actions have been defined, below are the procedures to configure "Voice Contact Work Flow".

Go to **Cisco Desktop Work Flow Administrator**, highlight "Voice Contact Work Flow" node under **[Call Center 1 > Work Flow Configuration > Work Flow Groups > default >**

CAD Agent] on the left pane. On the right pane, click "Add" button. In the popup window, enter a workflow name, for example "AutoRecord".

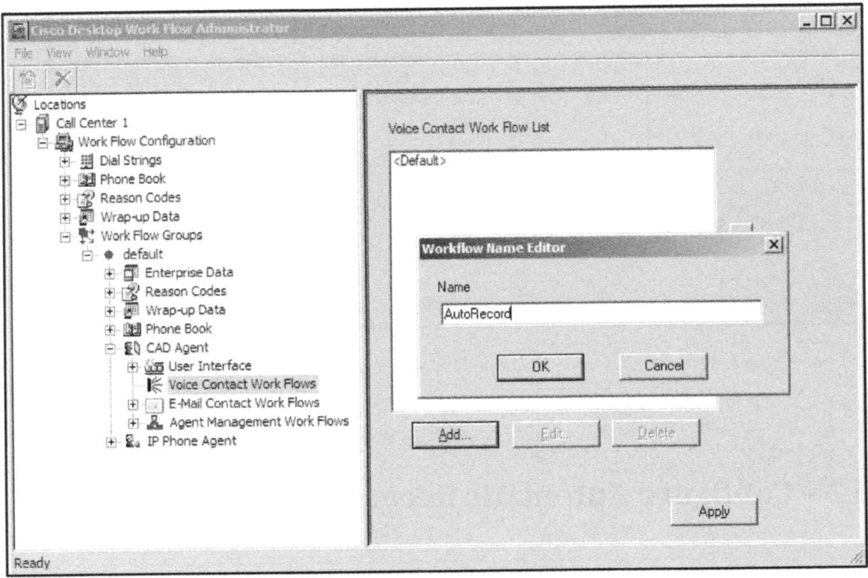

Figure 11-29 Adding a Work Flow

The next screen is to edit "Voice Contact Classification". You may just click "OK" to accept the default values. Default classification is for inbound calls only. You may click the drop-down menu to choose "outbound" or "all calls" (both inbound and outbound).

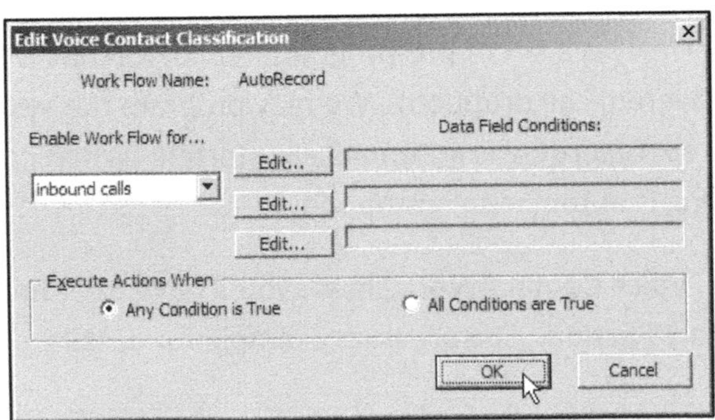

Figure 11-30 Voice Contact Classification

On the next screen, highlight "Answered" from "Events" list. Then click "Add" below the "Actions (of current Rule)" list. We are going to associate the "Start Record" action to the "Answered" event, which means when the call is answered by agent, system will start recording the call.

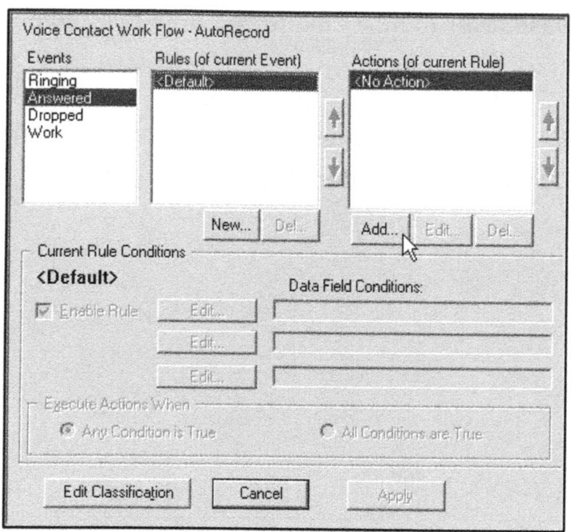

Figure 11-31 Configure Action for Event

On next screen, click the "Utility Action" tab, highlight "Start Record" action, click "Add Action". If you don't see any action listed, follow previous example to create them.

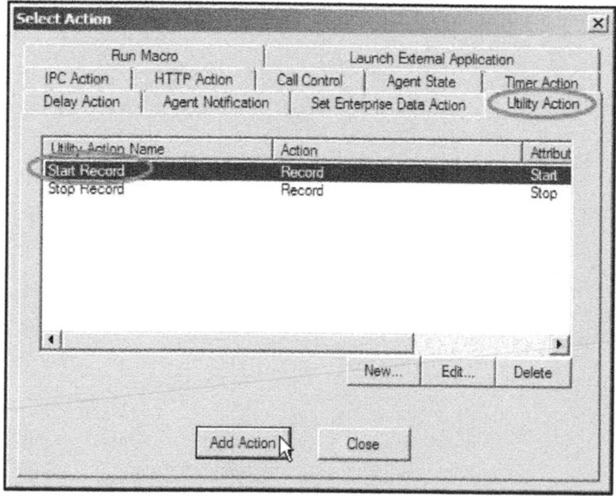

Figure 11-32 Select Action

Now we have associate the "Start Record" action with the "Answered" event. Follow the same procedure to associate "Stop Record" action to "Dropped" event. Highlight "Dropped" from "Events" list. Then click "Add" below the "Actions (of current Rule)" list. This time, select "Stop Record" action.

We have finished configuring “automatic record” work flow. However, the work flow is just to automate the recording process. The work flow itself does not have any recording capability. Please refer to next chapter for how to enable recording capability.

If recording capability was enabled, you may make some test calls and verify the recording files with **[CSD > Tools > Recorded Files]**.

Chapter 12 Silent Monitoring and Recording

Call monitoring and recording is an important function of call center for compliance or training purposes. There are many monitoring and recording solutions for UCCX. The two main categories are:

- UCCX Based
- CUCM Based

UCCX based solutions are usually used with CAD components. While CUCM based solutions are usually used with Finesse (next generation app). This book will cover UCCX based solution.

Monitoring

Monitoring is usually referred as "Silent Monitoring" because it allows supervisors to monitor agent calls without agent's awareness (agent notification is configurable though).

In call center environment, there are a couple of functions related to call monitoring or intervention:

- Monitor – Supervisor listens to agent/customer conversation silently.
- Remote Monitor - Supervisor listens to agent/customer conversation remotely (from any phone).
- Barge-In – Supervisor joins the call in the middle of agent/customer conversation (conference).
- Intercept – Supervisor takes over the call from agent.

Here is a comparison chart of these functions:

	Configuration Required?	**Audio Device**	**Agent Awareness?**	**Supervisor Action**
Monitor	Yes	Computer	No	Listen
Remote Monitor	Yes	Telephone (any kind)	No	Listen

Barge-In	No	IP Phone (in call center)	Yes	Conference
Intercept	No	IP Phone (in call center)	Yes	Takeover

How does monitoring work?

In a VoIP (Voice over IP) environment, voice conversations are encapsulated in IP packets. If we can make a copy of those packets and send to supervisor desktop, supervisor will be able to hear the voice conversation.

There are two options to do monitoring:

- Client-based Monitoring (default) – Agent desktop sends voice conversation to supervisor desktop.
- Server-based Monitoring – UCCX server relays voice conversation to supervisor desktop.

Each option has pros and cons based on different scenarios. Here is a comparison chart of these two options:

	Client-Based (default)	**Server-Based**
"Official" Name	**Desktop Monitor**	**VoIP Monitor**
LAN Switch Configuration	Not Required	Required
IPPA Support	No	Yes
Citrix Support	No	Yes
Multi-Network Segment Support	Yes	Additional servers might be needed in each segment
Configuration Steps	CUCM	LAN Switch, UCCX
Troubleshooting Areas	CUCM, Agent Computers	LAN Switch, UCCX
Who Mirrors Voice Traffic	Agent's IP Phone	LAN Switch
Who Sends Mirrored Traffic to Supervisor	Agent Desktop (CAD)	UCCX Server

Client-based Monitoring

Client-based (Desktop) monitoring requires minimal configuration (one parameter configuration on CUCM in best case scenario).

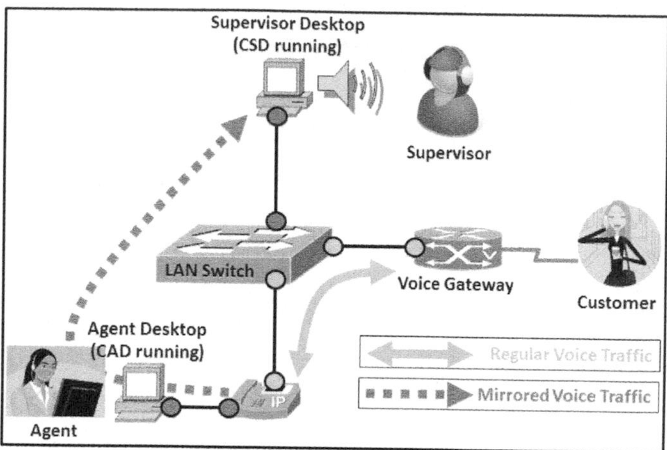

Figure 12-1 Desktop Monitoring

As the name indicates, "Desktop Monitoring" uses agent desktop software (CAD) to capture the voice conversation and send to supervisor desktop (CSD) upon request.

To achieve this, the following conditions need to be met:

1. Agent desktop PC connects to agent's IP phone.
2. Agent's IP phone was configured to clone voice traffic to PC port.
3. Agent desktop PC is able to handle packets not destined to it ("promiscuous mode" or "sniffing mode")

Cabling

When there is a PC and an IP phone, the common practice is to daisy-chain the PC to the phone, which means, connect the PC to the "PC port" of the phone, then connect the phone to the switch (as illustrated in "Figure 12-1 Desktop Monitoring" above).

By doing this, we save switch ports and infrastructure cabling. We also give the PC capability to "sniffer" the voice traffic.

CUCM Phone Configuration

By default, IP phone does not clone voice traffic to PC port. We will have to change it from [**CUCM > Device > Phone > *<Specific Phone>***].

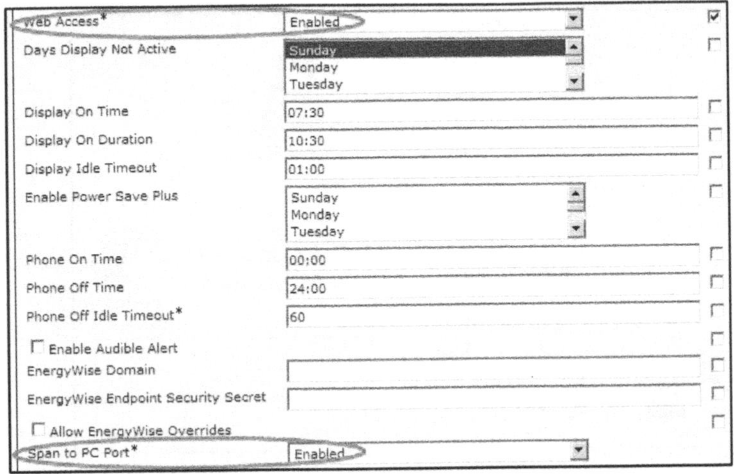

Figure 12-2 CUCM - Phone Configuration

Change the "Span to PC Port" parameter to "Enabled". Then click the "Apply Config" button. In some cases, IP phone is not getting the updated configuration from CUCM and won't do "Span to PC Port". The best way to verify is to look at the phone itself.

If you are local to the phone, press "Settings" button on the phone, go to [**Device Configuration > Ethernet Configuration**]. You should see a parameter called "Span to PC Port". Make sure it says "Yes".

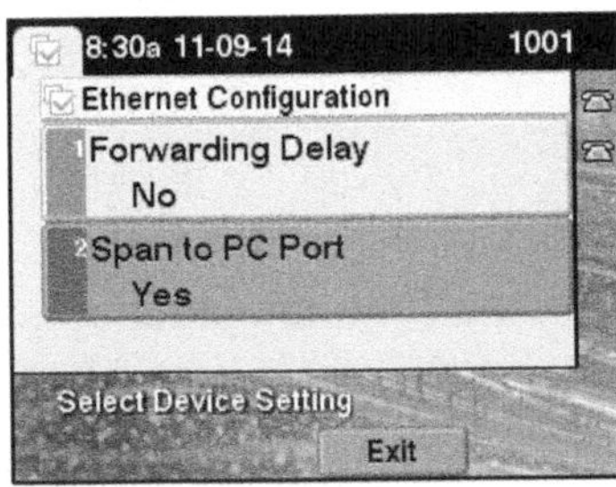

Figure 12-3 IP Phone Screen > Device Configuration > Ethernet Configuration

If you have "Web Access" enabled for the phone (see "Figure 12-2 CUCM - Phone Configuration") you may review this parameter remotely by going to **Error! Hyperlink reference not valid.**>. It is under "Network Configuration" on the IP phone web page. Search for "Span" and make sure it says "Yes".

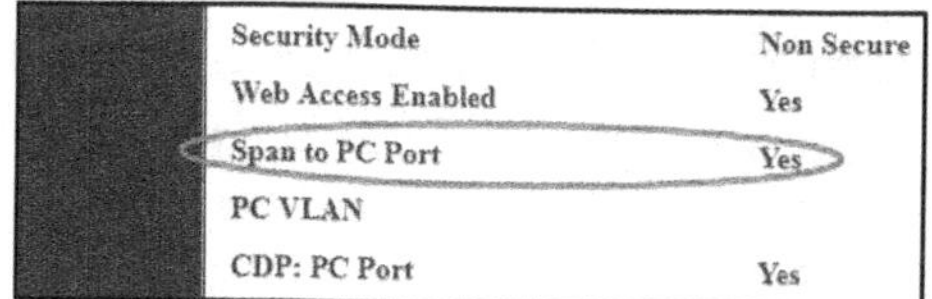

Figure 12-4 IP Phone Web Page > Network Configuration

Network Card Driver

When the "Span to PC Port" parameter is enabled, the phone will mirror the voice packets to the PC port. Those voice packets are with destination MAC address of the voice gateway instead of the PC. Some old network cards (or old driver) are not able to handle packets not destined to it. Those packets will be discarded at driver layer. In that case, agent desktop won't be able to capture voice packets and desktop monitoring won't work.

Sometimes, security/firewall software (such as McAfee Host Intrusion Prevention or Windows Firewall) will also filter out those packets.

Best way to verify is to run Wireshark on the PC and see if it can capture any voice packets.

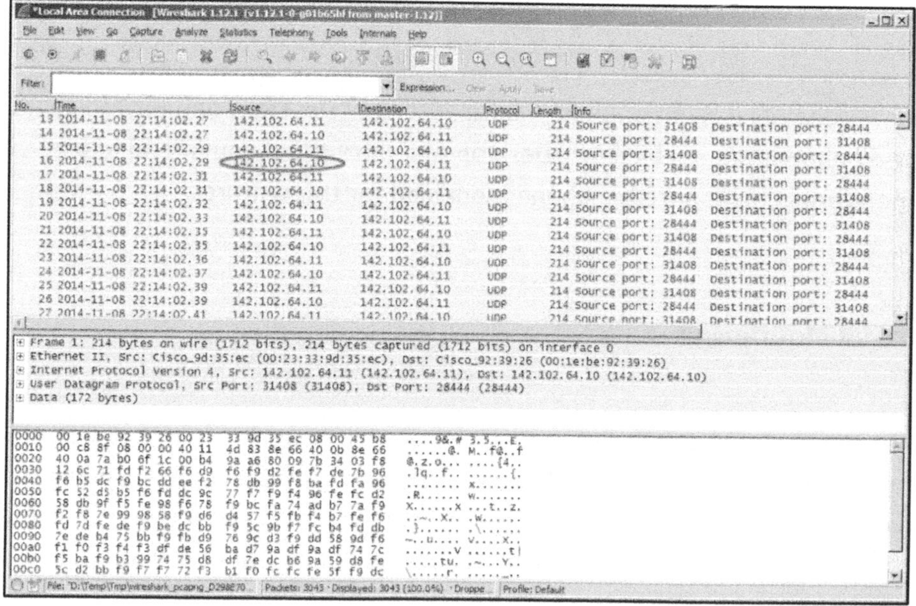

Figure 12-5 Wireshark - Voice Packets

Voice packets are usually UDP or RTP packets with source or destination IP address of the phone. In above example, phone's IP address is 142.102.64.10.

UCCX Settings

By default, UCCX enables "Desktop Monitoring". We don't have to do anything on UCCX server. However, it is one of the places you want to check during troubleshooting.

Go to [**CDA Web Portal > Service Configuration > Enterprise Data > Multiline, Monitoring & Recording > VoIP Monitoring Device**].

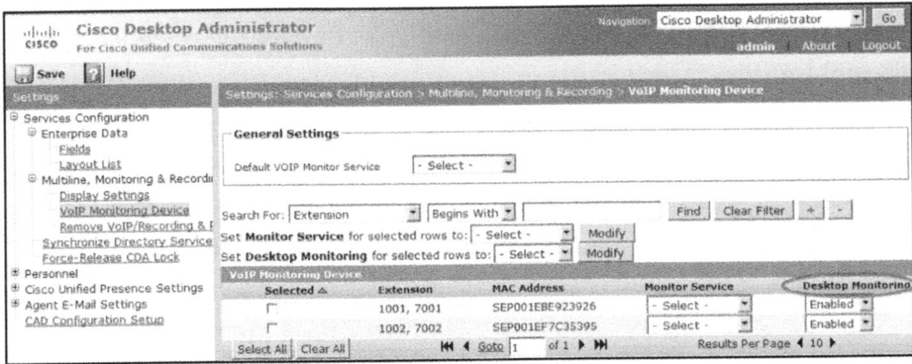

Figure 12-6 VoIP Monitoring Device List

This page has a list of all agent phones. Please note the "Desktop Monitoring" column. By default, all phones are enabled for "Desktop Monitoring". If you intend to use desktop monitoring, make sure the phone is enabled for this feature.

Server-based Monitoring

Server-based (VoIP) monitoring relies on switch port mirroring, in Cisco terms, SPAN (Switch Port Analyzer). We configure the switch to mirror all voice conversations to UCCX server. UCCX server, upon request, relays appropriate conversation to supervisor desktop. Supervisor desktop software plays the conversation out to the computer's sound card.

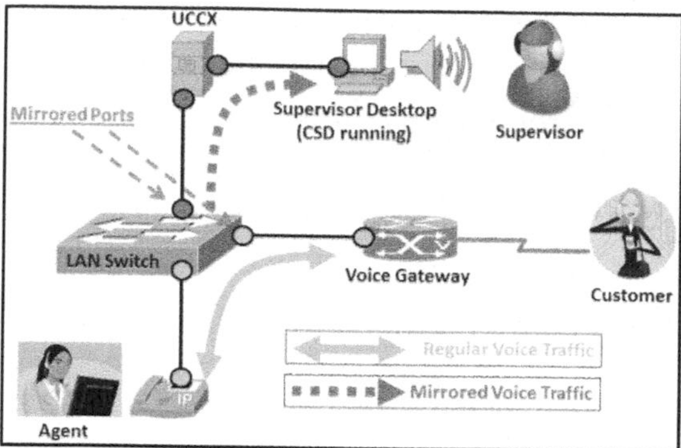

Figure 12-7 Server Based Monitoring

Switch Port Mirroring

The common practice is to mirror the voice gateway port (source) to the UCCX port (destination). This is because:

1. Switch allows limited number of mirror sessions. If we were to mirror every phone ports we would run out of mirror sessions very quickly.
2. All agent-customer conversations go through voice gateway. Thus the gateway port is the best place to mirror.

Different switches may have different command syntax for port mirroring. In the example of Cisco IOS, the commands would be similar to below:

```
monitor session 1 source interface g1/0/1 both
monitor session 1 destination interface g1/0/24 ingress vlan 10
```

The first command is to specify the source port (the switch port connecting to voice gateway). The "both" keyword means we are mirroring inbound and outbound traffic.

The second command is to specify the destination port (the switch port connecting to UCCX server). The "ingress" keyword allows the port receive data from UCCX server. Without "ingress" keyword, the "monitor destination" port does not allow data traffic from UCCX to switch. The "vlan" keyword specifies the VLAN UCCX server should be in.

When UCCX server is in virtualization environment, configuration would be a little bit tricky, especially when trunk port was involved. Cisco recommends the following:

- Dedicated physical NIC, vSwitch and port group for the UCCX server
- "Promiscuous Mode" on vSwitch or port group level
- Physical port should be configured as access port versus trunk port

For more details, please see "UCCX SPAN-Based Silent Monitoring Configuration Example" on http://www.cisco.com/c/en/us/support/docs/customer-collaboration/unified-contact-center-express/118160-configure-uccx-00.html

UCCX Server Configuration

To configure server-based monitoring, we go to [**CDA Web Portal > Service Configuration > Multiline, Monitoring and & Recording > VoIP Monitoring Device**].

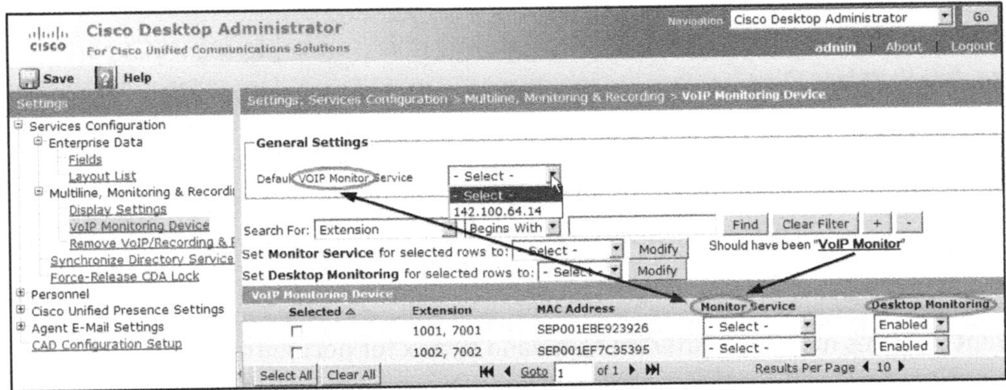

Figure 12-8 CDA Web Portal - VoIP Monitor

Note the "Monitor Service" column. It should have been "VoIP Monitor Service" to distinguish itself from "Desktop Monitoring" and be consistent across the web page.

In the scenario of server-based monitoring, there could be more than one "VoIP Monitor" server. Each agent phone can be monitor by one server only. You may use the "Monitor Service" column to specify which phone is monitored by which server.

There are three ways to associate a phone to a monitor server:

- Option 1: Use the drop-down menus in the "Monitor Services" in the "Monitor Service" column to dedicate a monitor server for each phone. You have to do this on each phone one-by-one.

- Option 2: Select the phones you want to modify. Then use the "Set Monitor Service for selected rows" on the top of the screen. This can make changes to multiple phones in one shot.
- Option 3: Set the "Default VoIP Monitor Service" in "General Settings" box on the top. Then leave the drop-down menus blank. Phones with blank drop-down menus will default to the "Default VoIP Monitor Service". Please refer to "Figure 12-13 Combination of Desktop and Server Monitoring" to see when the "Default" will take effect.

In our example below, we have only one monitor server (142.100.64.14). We want to use server-based VoIP Monitor only for all phones. Here is the configuration screen.

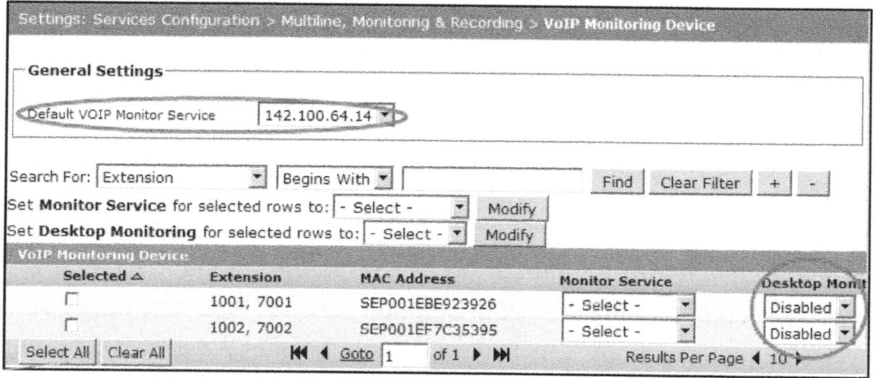

Figure 12-9 Server-based VoIP Monitor

Client-based vs. Server-based

Generally speaking, client-based monitoring is recommended because:

- It requires minimal configuration (only the "Span to PC Port" parameter on CUCM).
- It puts fewer loads on the UCCX server as the mirrored voice session bypass UCCX server.

Whenever possible, we should use client-based (desktop) monitoring. However, there are some scenarios that server-based (VoIP) monitoring is the only option.

IP Phone Agent (IPPA)

As discussed before, IP Phone Agent (IPPA) does not use computer. Without a computer, there will be no agent desktop (CAD) to capture the voice packets. In this case, server-based monitoring is the only choice.

Citrix

In a Citrix environment, the agent desktop (CAD) is actually running from the Citrix server versus the local computer. Since the CAD is not directly connected to the phone, it cannot capture the voice packets. In this case, server-based monitoring is the only option.

Remember that you may have some phones doing client-based (desktop) monitoring while others doing server-based (VoIP).

Additional Monitor Servers

Server-based (VoIP) monitoring requires SPAN session to the "monitor server". A monitor server is a server running the "VoIP Monitor" service. You may have "VoIP Monitor Service" running without "CRS Engine". That becomes a dedicated "monitor server". There could be more than one monitor server in a UCCX cluster.

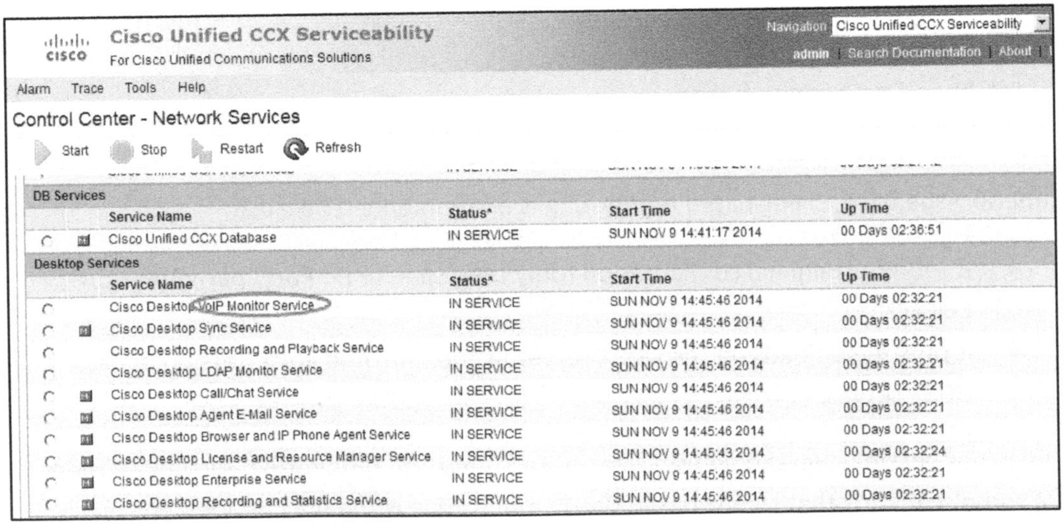

Cisco Unified CCX Serviceability
For Cisco Unified Communications Solutions
Navigation Cisco Unified CCX Serviceability
admin | Search Documentation | About

Alarm Trace Tools Help

Control Center - Network Services

Start Stop Restart Refresh

DB Services

Service Name	Status*	Start Time	Up Time
Cisco Unified CCX Database	IN SERVICE	SUN NOV 9 14:41:17 2014	00 Days 02:36:51

Desktop Services

Service Name	Status*	Start Time	Up Time
Cisco Desktop VoIP Monitor Service	IN SERVICE	SUN NOV 9 14:45:46 2014	00 Days 02:32:21
Cisco Desktop Sync Service	IN SERVICE	SUN NOV 9 14:45:46 2014	00 Days 02:32:21
Cisco Desktop Recording and Playback Service	IN SERVICE	SUN NOV 9 14:45:46 2014	00 Days 02:32:21
Cisco Desktop LDAP Monitor Service	IN SERVICE	SUN NOV 9 14:45:46 2014	00 Days 02:32:21
Cisco Desktop Call/Chat Service	IN SERVICE	SUN NOV 9 14:45:46 2014	00 Days 02:32:21
Cisco Desktop Agent E-Mail Service	IN SERVICE	SUN NOV 9 14:45:46 2014	00 Days 02:32:21
Cisco Desktop Browser and IP Phone Agent Service	IN SERVICE	SUN NOV 9 14:45:46 2014	00 Days 02:32:21
Cisco Desktop License and Resource Manager Service	IN SERVICE	SUN NOV 9 14:45:43 2014	00 Days 02:32:24
Cisco Desktop Enterprise Service	IN SERVICE	SUN NOV 9 14:45:46 2014	00 Days 02:32:21
Cisco Desktop Recording and Statistics Service	IN SERVICE	SUN NOV 9 14:45:46 2014	00 Days 02:32:21

Figure 12-10 VoIP Monitor Service

In some cases, we might not be able to create a SPAN session between the source port (voice VLAN) and the destination port (monitor server) because RSPAN is not available (or not allowed). In that case, we will have to put an additional monitor server local to the source port.

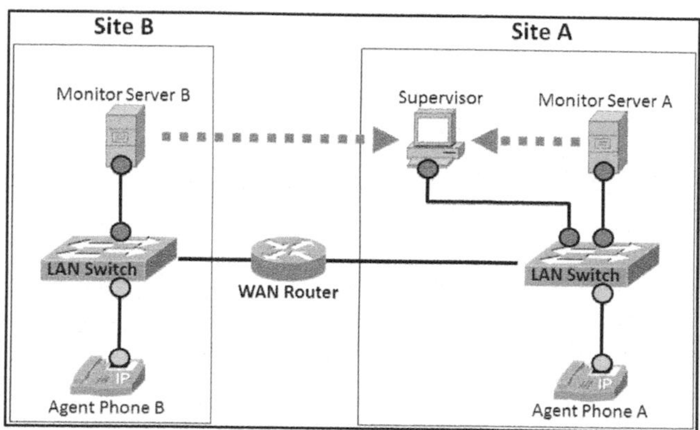

Figure 12-11 Multiple Monitor Servers

Additional servers add CAPEX (capital expense) and OPEX (operational expense) to the picture.

Supportability

Though server-based (VoIP) monitoring requires more configurations, the scope is relatively static (and small). The scope is limited to the LAN switch and monitor server. In most cases, we will have only one switch and one server to support. If server-based monitoring works for one agent, it will work for all agents.

On the other hand, though client-based (desktop) monitoring requires minimal configuration, the scope is relatively dynamic (and large). Depending on the business, the scope could be hundreds of computers with various brands, operating systems, drivers and 3rd-party security software. Desktop monitoring could work for some agents but not the others. In that case, you will have to troubleshoot hundreds of desktop computers versus one server.

Mix and Match

If client-based (desktop) monitoring is recommended, we only use server-based (VoIP) monitoring when we have to. Would there be any scenario that we want to enable both?

Yes, we may enable both for redundancy. If both are enabled, client-based monitoring takes precedence. Server-based monitoring will be used only if desktop monitoring fails.

Remember the "VoIP Monitor" configuration page on CDA Web Portal?

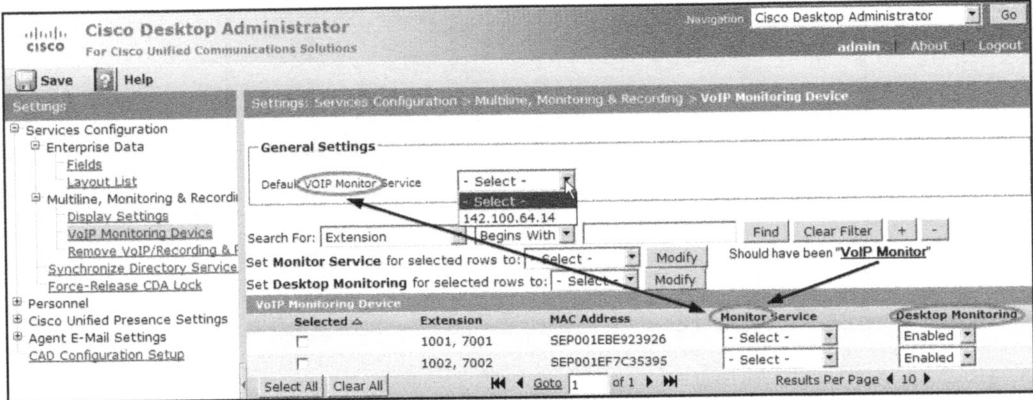

Figure 12-12 CDA Web Portal - VoIP Monitoring Device

There are three important parameters on this page:

- Monitor Service (should have been "VoIP Monitor) – we refer this as "**Specific VoIP**" in the table below.
- Desktop Monitoring – we refer this as "**Desktop Monitor**" in the table below.
- Default VoIP Monitor Service – we refer this as "**Default VoIP**" in the table below.

Specific VoIP	Desktop Monitor	Default VoIP	Effect on Devices
No	No	No	Monitoring fails if there are multiple VoIP monitor services; monitored by default VoIP Monitor service if there is one VoIP Monitor service in the system.
Yes	No	No	Monitored by specific VoIP Monitor service; no backup in case of failure.
Yes	Yes	No	Monitored by Desktop Monitor; backed up by specific VoIP Monitor service.

Yes	No	Yes	Monitored by specific VoIP Monitor service; no backup in case of failure.
No	Yes	No	Monitored by Desktop Monitor; no backup in case of failure. If there is only one VoIP Monitor service in the system, it serves as backup.
No	Yes	Yes	Monitored by Desktop Monitor; backed up by default VoIP Monitor service.
No	No	Yes	Monitored by default VoIP Monitor service; no backup in case of failure.
Yes	Yes	Yes	Monitored by Desktop Monitor; backed up by the specific VoIP Monitor service. If the selected VoIP Monitor service fails, there is no backup.

Figure 12-13 Combination of Desktop and Server Monitoring

For each device, look up the three parameters combination in the table above. Then you may determine the expected effect.

Recording

Recording is another feature of UCCX. It records agent-customer conversations (either manually or automatically). Supervisor may load the recordings from server and listen to the conversation in a later time.

Recording function is provided by "Recording Sever". A recording server is a server with "Recording and Playback" service running. If the "Recording and Playback" service is running on a server without CRS engine, it is a dedicated recording server.

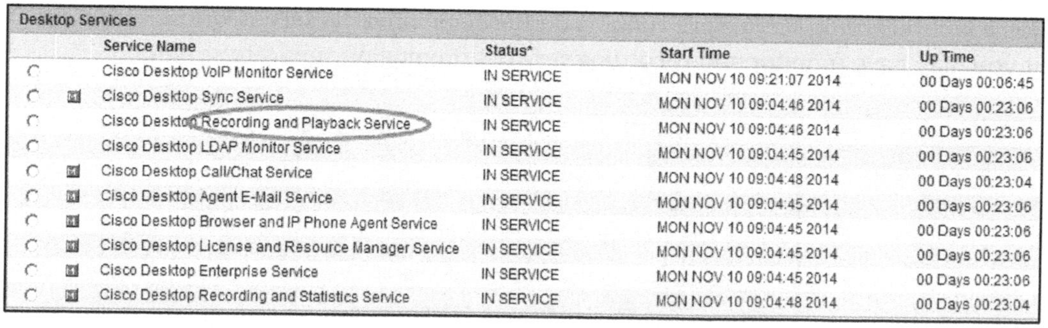

Desktop Services

Service Name	Status*	Start Time	Up Time
Cisco Desktop VoIP Monitor Service	IN SERVICE	MON NOV 10 09:21:07 2014	00 Days 00:06:45
Cisco Desktop Sync Service	IN SERVICE	MON NOV 10 09:04:46 2014	00 Days 00:23:06
Cisco Desktop Recording and Playback Service	IN SERVICE	MON NOV 10 09:04:46 2014	00 Days 00:23:06
Cisco Desktop LDAP Monitor Service	IN SERVICE	MON NOV 10 09:04:45 2014	00 Days 00:23:06
Cisco Desktop Call/Chat Service	IN SERVICE	MON NOV 10 09:04:48 2014	00 Days 00:23:04
Cisco Desktop Agent E-Mail Service	IN SERVICE	MON NOV 10 09:04:45 2014	00 Days 00:23:06
Cisco Desktop Browser and IP Phone Agent Service	IN SERVICE	MON NOV 10 09:04:45 2014	00 Days 00:23:06
Cisco Desktop License and Resource Manager Service	IN SERVICE	MON NOV 10 09:04:45 2014	00 Days 00:23:06
Cisco Desktop Enterprise Service	IN SERVICE	MON NOV 10 09:04:45 2014	00 Days 00:23:06
Cisco Desktop Recording and Statistics Service	IN SERVICE	MON NOV 10 09:04:48 2014	00 Days 00:23:04

Figure 12-14 Recording and Playback Service

Unlike "Monitor Server", there can be only one "Recording Server" in a UCCX cluster. However, the UCCX post-install initialization process always activates monitoring and recording service by default. You may use the "CDA Web Portal" to remove those services from specific servers.

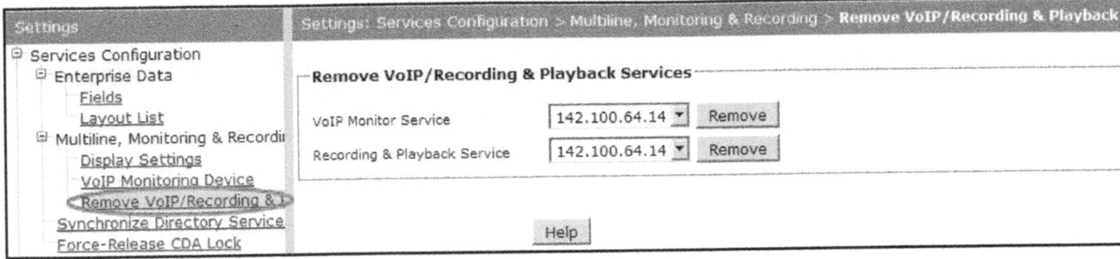

How does recording work

"Recording" does not have any configurable parameters. "Recording" relies on "Monitoring" to work, which means you should configure and test monitoring before using recording.

The "monitoring entity" (either a monitor server or an agent desktop) sends the audio stream to recording server. Recording server saves the audio as files in hard drive for later playback.

Recording Server in Server-Based Environment

In a server-based (VoIP Monitor) environment, audio streams are captured by the monitor server(s) and forwarded to recording server. In our reference lab, the monitor service and recording service are running on the same physical server with CRS engine. But you may have monitor and recording services running on separate servers.

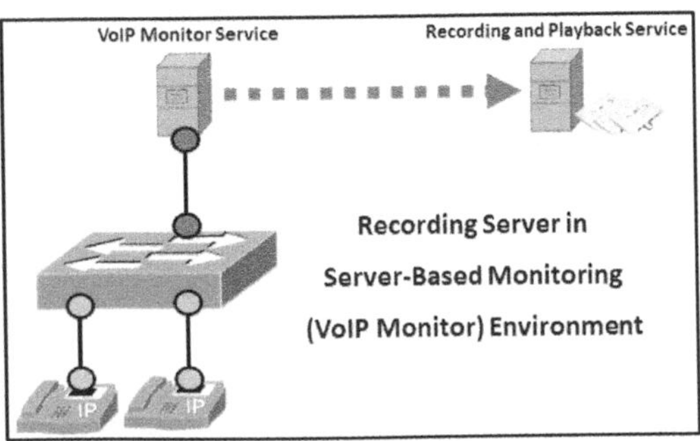

Figure 12-15 Recording Server with Server-based Monitoring

Recording Server in Client-Based Environment

In a client-based (Desktop Monitoring) environment, audio streams are captured by the agent desktop computers and forwarded to recording server.

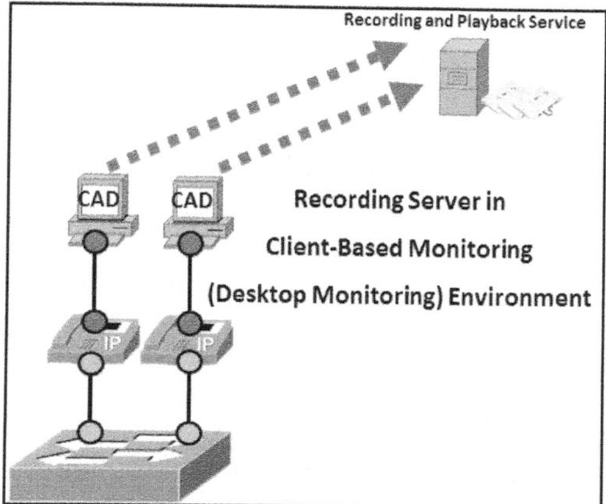

Figure 12-16 Recording Server in Client-based Environment

Manual Monitoring or Recording

Monitoring

Monitoring is done from Supervisor Desktop (CSD). Highlight the agent you want to monitor in supervisor desktop. Then click "Start Voice Monitor" button from the action bar. Audio will come out of supervisor desktop speaker. Click the "Stop Voice Monitor" button to stop.

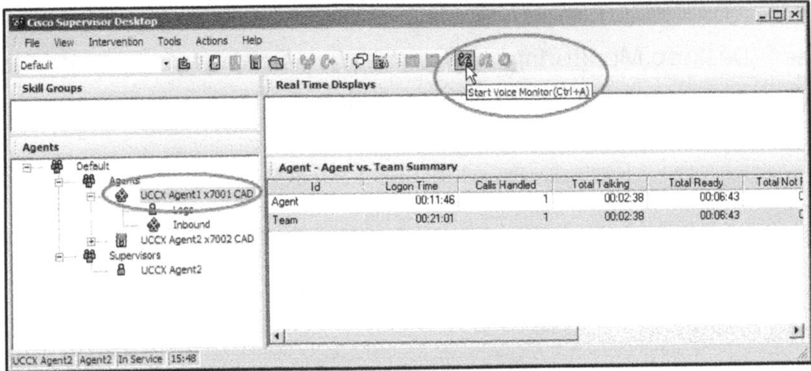

Figure 12-17 Voice Monitor

Manual Recording - Supervisor

Recording can be done from either supervisor desktop (CSD) or agent desktop (CAD). Different from monitoring, we highlight <u>specific call</u> versus agent in supervisor desktop. Then click "Start Record" button. To stop record, click "Stop Record" button.

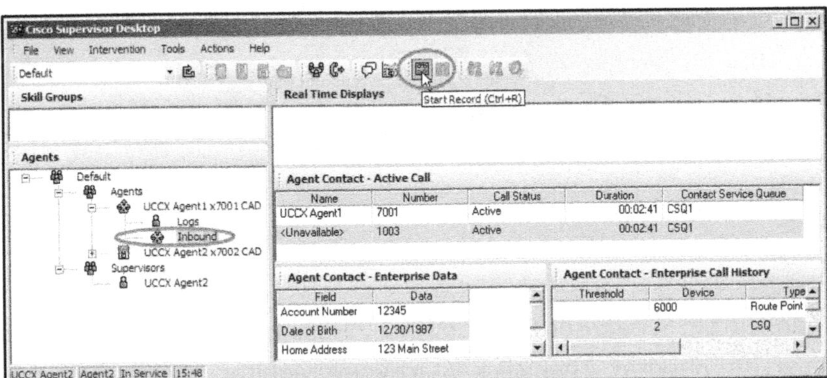

Figure 12-18 Voice Recording

Playback – Supervisor

To play back recordings go to [**Supervisor Desktop > Tools > Recorded Files**].

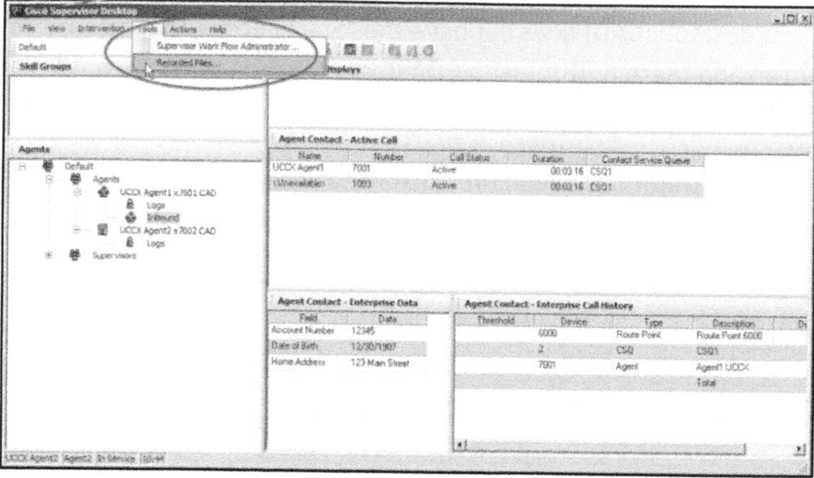

Figure 12-19 CSD > Tools > Recorded Files

You will see the "Supervisor Record Viewer". Each file is labeled with agent ID, team, time, duration. Choose the file you want to play then click the "Play" button. You may also save the files to the local hard drive by clicking on the "Play and Save" button. The length of time the recording is archived: Normal is 7 days, Extended is 30 days.

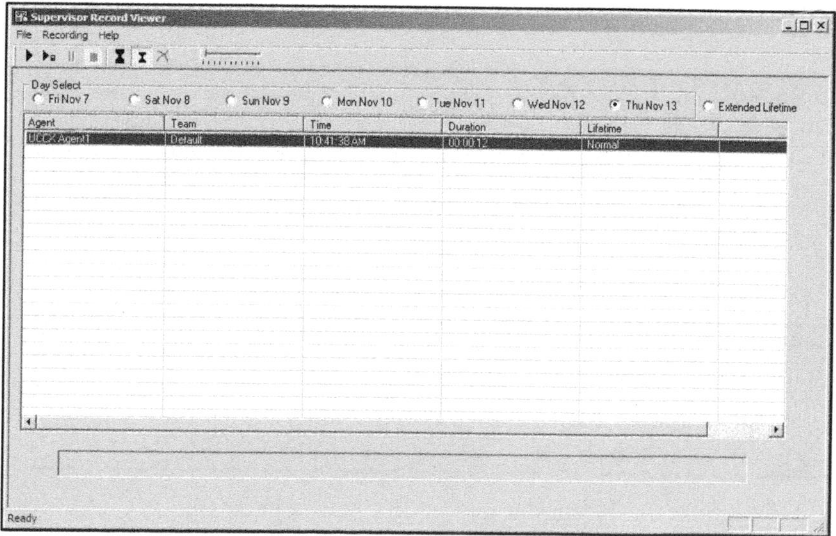

Figure 12-20 Supervisor Record Viewer

Manual Recording – Agent

By default, agent desktop (CAD) does not have the "Start Record/Stop Record" buttons. Administrator can add these buttons with CDA (Cisco Desktop Work Flow Administrator) application.

Assuming the administrator has added the buttons to agent desktop, agents may use the "Start Record" and "Stop Record" button in a call conversation.

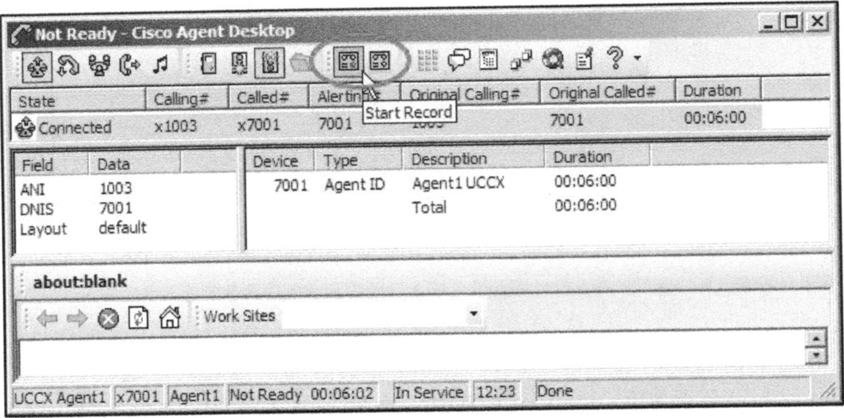

Figure 12-21 Agent Desktop with Start/Stop Record Buttons

Once agent hits the "Start Record" button, the icon will be changed to indicate the call is being recorded.

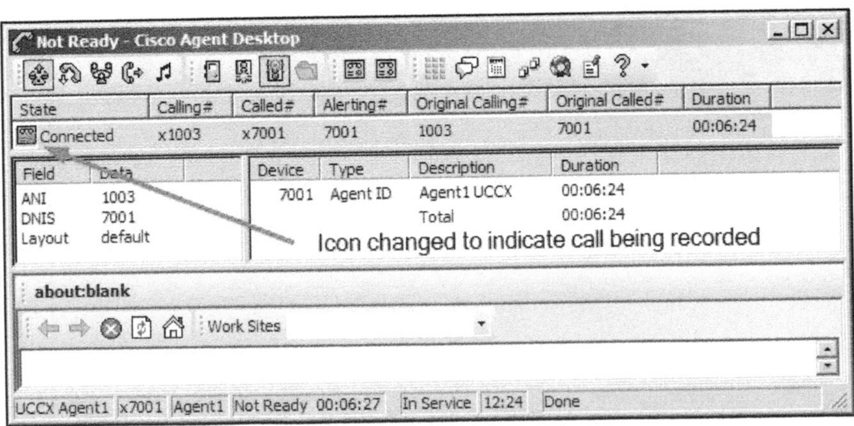

Figure 12-22 Icon Changed When Call Being Recorded

Unfortunately, agent desktop does not have the capability to playback recorded files. Only supervisors can play recorded files with supervisor desktop. Agent initiated recordings are not different from supervisor initiated recordings. "Supervisor Record Viewer" cannot tell which recording was initiated by whom.

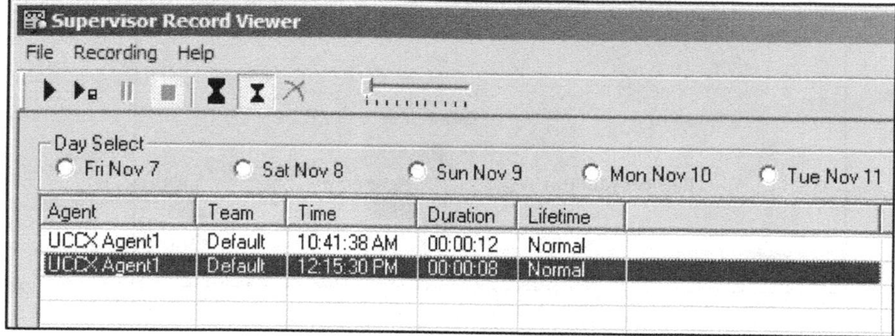

Figure 12-23 Supervisor Viewing Agent Initiated Recordings

Automatic Recording

Some of the call centers require all customer calls to be recorded. The easiest way to do this is to create an automatic workflow for agent desktop. Then the call is connected, agent desktop starts recording. When the call is disconnected, agent desktop stops recording. Please refer to previous chapter for details.

Remote Monitor

As previously discussed, both server-based and client-based monitoring are based on packet capture. They require supervisor desktop (CSD) and a computer to be functioning. There are some cases that CSD or computer is not available. In those cases, "Remote Monitor" allows supervisor use just a phone to monitor agent-customer conversation. It doesn't have to an IP phone. It could be a cell phone, a legacy home phone, etc.

Figure 12-24 Remote Monitor

Remote Monitor is nothing more than "conferencing". The differences between Remote Monitor and traditional call conferencing are:

- Remote Monitor is initiated by a supervisor who is outside of the current agent-customer conversation.
- Remote Monitor is established by a UCCX script. Thus UCCX application, trigger, etc. have to be provisioned.
- Remote monitor can be conducted without agent's awareness (silent monitoring)

Summary of steps are:

1. Create Remote Monitor application
2. Create Trigger
3. Provision Supervisor
4. Assign Resources and CSQs to Remote Supervisor

Create Remote Monitor Application

- ➢ **Create Remote Monitor application**
- Create Trigger
- Provision Supervisor
- Assign Resources and CSQs to Remote Supervisor

Follow normal procedures to create an UCCX application. For detailed steps please refer to "UCCX: Provision Application" on page 62.

Make sure to choose the system script "rmon.aef". This script handles incoming calls from supervisors and "bridge" the supervisor's call with agent/customer calls so that the supervisor can hear the agent/customer conversation.

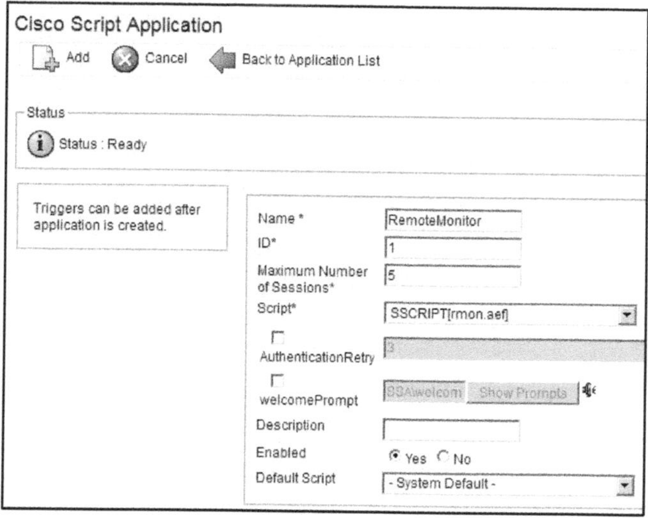

Figure 12-25 Creating "Remote Monitor" Application

Create Trigger

- ✓ Create Remote Monitor application
- ➢ **Create Trigger**
- Provision Supervisor
- Assign Resources and CSQs to Remote Supervisor

Follow normal procedures to create a Telephony Trigger for the "Remote Monitor" application. For detailed steps please refer to "UCCX: Provision Triggers" on page 64.

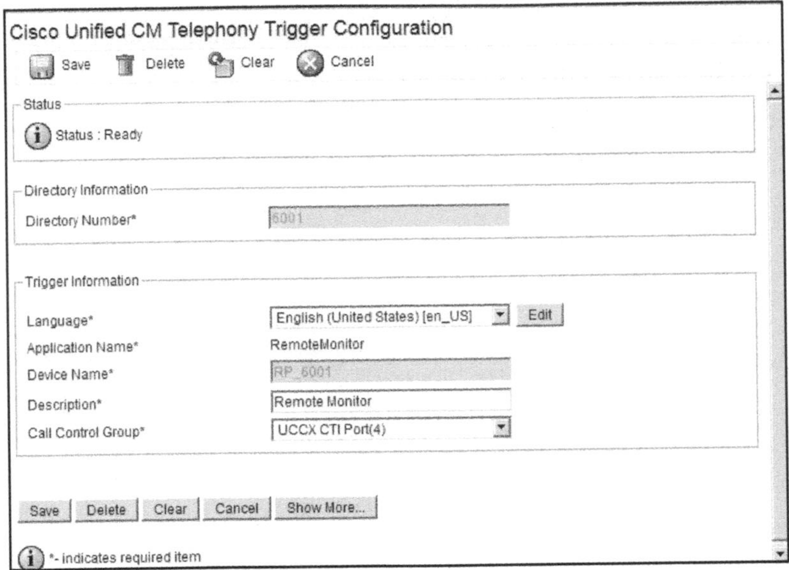

Figure 12-26 Trigger for "Remote Monitor"

Provision Supervisor

- ✓ Create Remote Monitor application
- ✓ Create Trigger
- ➢ **Provision Supervisor**
- • Assign Resources and CSQs to Remote Supervisor

Follow normal procedures to provision supervisors. For detailed steps please refer to "Give a user Supervisor permission" on page 100. When provisioning supervisors for "Remote Monitor" purpose, the user ID needs to be all digits. This is because the remote supervisor will need to key in his/her user ID on the phone. UCCX mandates digit user IDs so they can be entered easily.

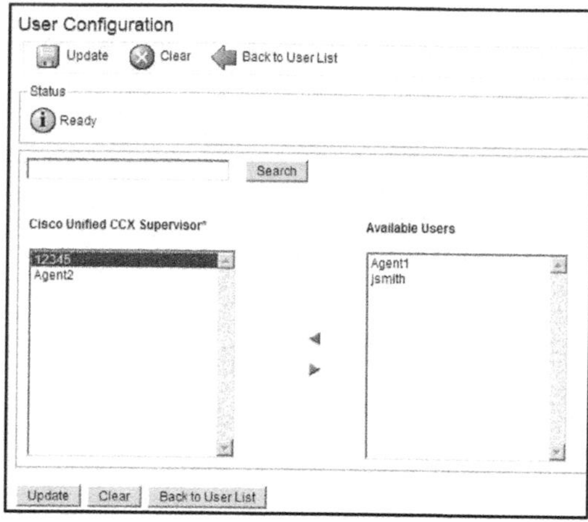

Figure 12-27 Supervisor with digit ID

Assign Resources and CSQs to Remote Supervisor

- ✓ Create Remote Monitor application
- ✓ Create Trigger
- ✓ Provision Supervisor
- ➢ **Assign Resources and CSQs to Remote Supervisor**

This step is unique to Remote Supervisor. We have to tell the system which agents or CSQs are allowed to be monitored by remote supervisor. To do this, we go to "Subsystem > RmCm > Remote Monitor". Please note that even though we have more than one supervisors in the system, this page will only display the supervisors who have all-digit user IDs.

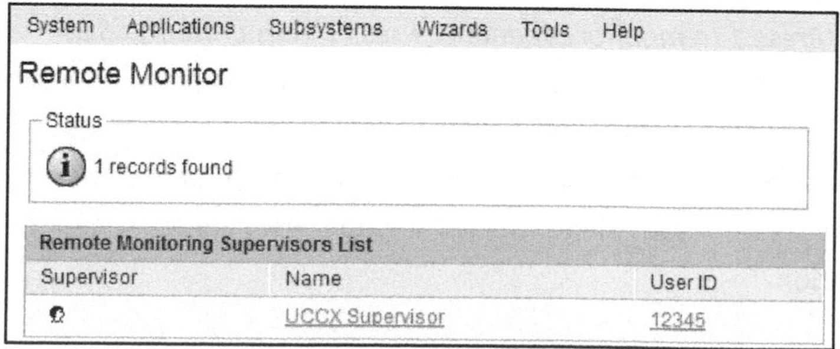

Figure 12-28 Supervisor with all-digit User IDs

Click on the supervisor you want to configure, then choose the agents and/or CSQs you want to assign to this supervisor.

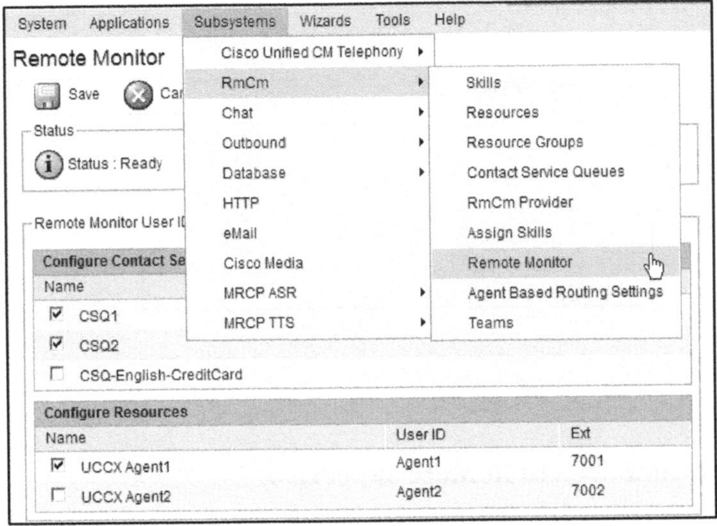

Figure 12-29 Assign Agents and/or CSQs to Supervisor

Use Remote Monitor

1) Supervisor calls into the Route Point (trigger).
2) System: *"Welcome to remote monitoring. Please enter your user ID followed by the # key."*
3) Supervisor enters his/her user ID and # key.
4) System: *"Please enter your PIN followed by the # key."*
5) Supervisor enters his/her PIN and # key.
6) System: *"Press 1 to monitor an agent. Press 2 to monitor a CSQ."*
7) If supervisor chose 1, system will ask for agent extension. If supervisor chose 2, system will ask for CSQ ID.
8) If the entered agent extension or CSQ was allowed to be monitored by the supervisor, system will bridge the call so supervisor can hear agent/customer conversation.

CSQ ID

You might wonder how to find out the "CSQ ID" for a specific CSQ. To do that, we log into the "**https://<ip_of_UCCX_server>/appadmin**" web page with the remote supervisor's credential. After login, you'll see a web page with limited menus like below.

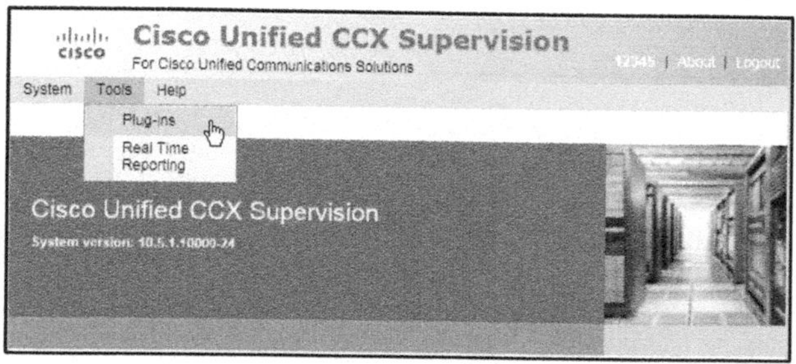

Figure 12-30 "AppAdmin" page with Supervisor Credential

Go to "Tools > Plug-ins". Then click on "Cisco Unified CCX Desktop Suites".

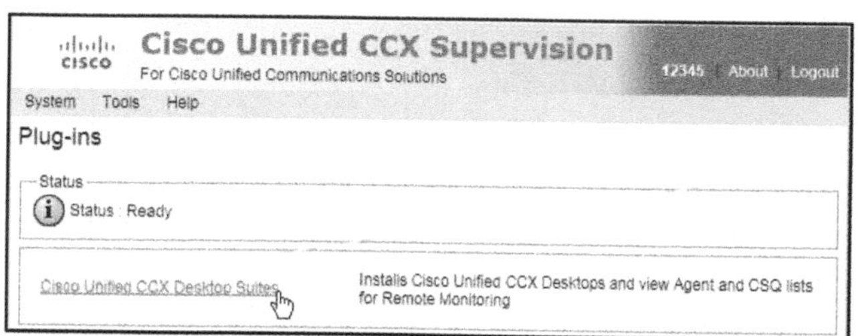

Figure 12-31 Tools > Plug-ins

Click on "View CSQ".

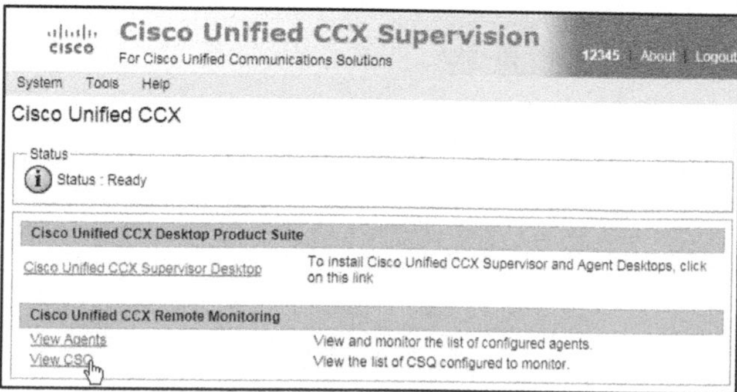

Figure 12-32 Cisco Unified CCX Desktop Suites

You will find the CSQ ID in the "id" column.

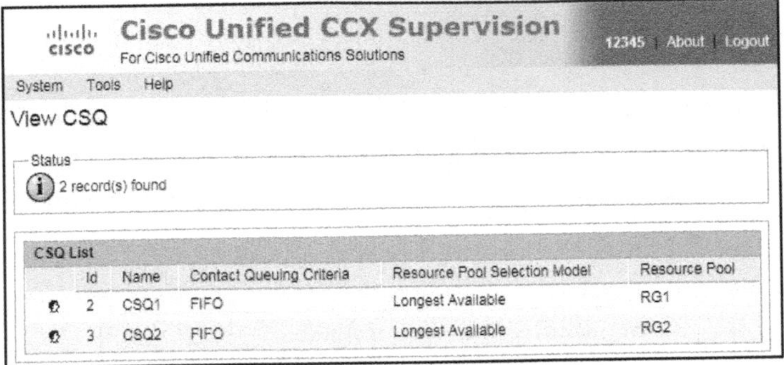

Figure 12-33 View CSQ

Chapter 13 E-Mail

There are two different "E-Mail" features in UCCX. They are independent to each other.

- **Server E-Mail a.k.a. "eMail Subsystem"**
  Allows the UCCX applications (scripts) create and send emails.
- **Agent E-Mail**
  Allows agents handle customer emails in a CSQ (Customer Service Queue) style, just like customer cals.

Server E-Mail

Server E-Mail configuration is relatively simple – just specify email server and email address.

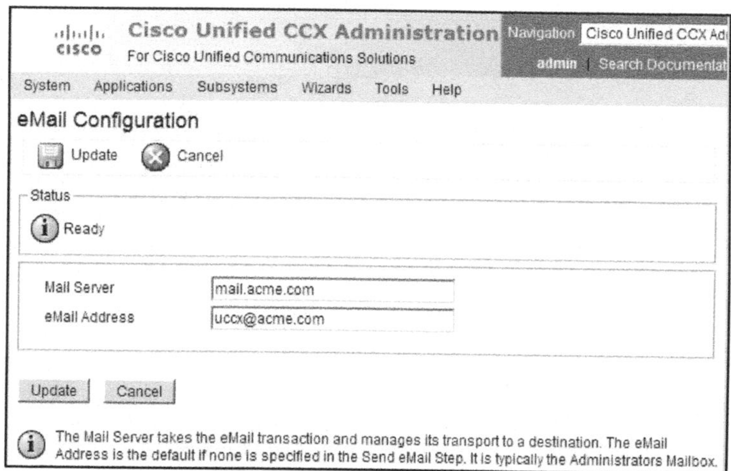

Figure 13-1 Server E-Mail Configuration

"Send eMail" step in UCCX script will use the above information to send email.

UCCX server uses SMTP protocol to communicate with the mail server. Most of the mail servers nowadays require some kind of authentication from the SMTP client to prevent SPAM. As you can see from the UCCX Admin portal, there's nowhere to configure username/password. Thus the authentication can only be done by adding the UCCX server's IP to the mail server's trust list. The procedure is mail server specific. Please refer to the mail server documentation for detail instructions.

Agent E-Mail Overview

Call Centers have evolved from voice-only to multi-media such as email, web-chat, etc. That's why we use the term "Contact Center" versus "Call Center" because the word "call" usually indicates "voice".

Customers may contact the company by email. Emails will go into a queue just like phone calls. Contact center agents serve the email queues just like they serve the phone call queues.

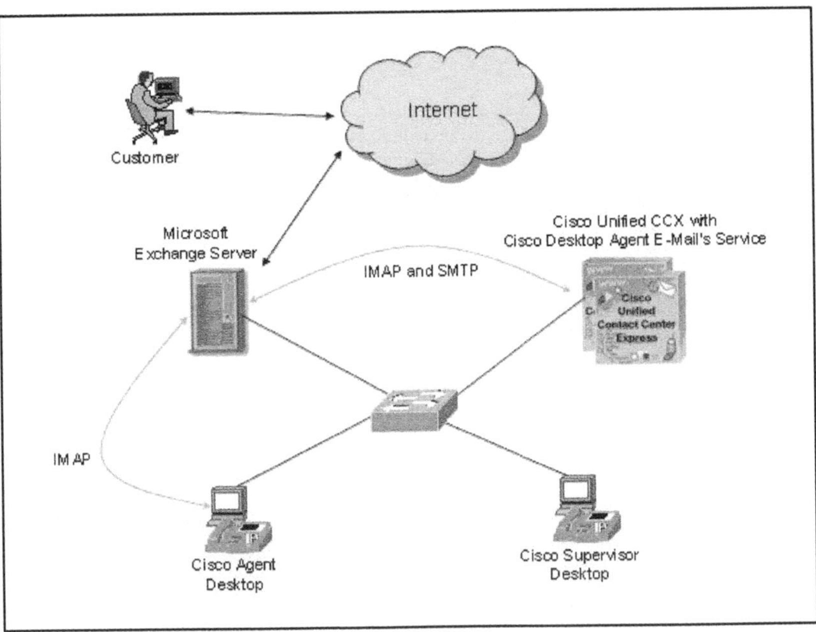

Figure 13-2 Email Queue

CSD includes real-time displays and information that enable supervisors to manage email CSQs and their email capable agents. When creating a CSQ in Unified CCX Administration, you designate the CSQ as either email or voice. A single CSQ cannot be both an email CSQ and a voice CSQ. Agent association with email CSQs is done in the same manner as voice CSQs.

The agent states READY and NOT READY for email and voice are independent of each other. An agent can handle both emails and voice calls simultaneously. An agent can receive emails only if he manually moves himself to email READY state. Only agents that have been assigned to at least one email CSQ will see the email functionality in CAD. Only supervisors that service at least one email capable team or at least one email capable agent will see email functionality in CSD.

The Agent email feature requires the use of an external mail store (Microsoft Exchange is supported). This mail store is not provided, installed, or configured as part of the CAD installation.

Agent email uses the IMAPv4 (for message retrieval) and SMTP protocols (for message sending). These protocol types must be enabled in the mail server and host/IP information must be specified using Cisco Desktop Administrator. These protocol types are not typically enabled by default. CAD and the Cisco Desktop Agent email Service make IMAP connections to the mail store. Cisco Desktop Agent E-mail Service also makes an SMTP connection to the mail store. Agent E-mail supports both secure and plain text connections to the mail store.

CAD components (Cisco Agent Desktop and Cisco Desktop Agent E-mail Service) will connect to the mail store using a single dedicated mail store account. This account must be created by the mail store administrator.

CAD must be configured to use this account through Cisco Desktop Administrator. This account should be a dedicated account, and not used for purposes other than the Agent E-mail feature.

While CAD uses a single email account, it can, and typically will, have multiple distribution list addresses associated with that user. This email account and corresponding distribution lists must be configured manually by the mail store administrator. Routing information for the distribution list addresses can then be specified using Cisco Desktop Administrator.

Review CSQs can be associated with normal email contact CSQs. Emails sent from a Contact CSQ associated with a Review CSQ will be transferred to the Review CSQ. Members of a Review CSQ who receive emails transferred in this manner will be able to perform all of the normal email operations on the message, including editing the draft, and transferring, requeuing, and sending the message.

Messages sent from a review CSQ will be sent using the configured email address of the original CSQ, which the message was sent from.

The following steps describe how an email is routed using the Agent E-mail feature:

1) The Cisco Desktop Agent E-mail Service on the Unified CCX server connects to the mail store (IMAP and SMTP) on startup.
2) An email-capable agent in the email CSQ logs in using CAD. CAD connects to the Cisco Desktop Agent E-mail Service and to the mail store (IMAP).
3) The agent goes to an email ready state. CAD requests an email from the Cisco Desktop Agent E-mail Service.
4) A customer sends an email to, for example, sales@companyname.com.
5) The website sales@companyname.com is a distribution list with the Agent E-mail account as the only member. Microsoft Exchange presents the email to that account's inbox.
6) The Cisco Desktop Agent E-mail Service has been monitoring the Agent E-mail account inbox, and sees the new email. Based on the routing rules specified in Cisco Desktop Administrator, it sees that emails to sales@companyname.com are associated with the email CSQ and that an agent in the email CSQ is in the Ready state. The service then assigns the email to the agent and notifies the agent.
7) CAD receives notification of the assignment and retrieves the email from the mail store directly.
8) The agent is presented with the e-mail from the customer.
9) The agent authors a response and presses the Send button.
10) If review CSQs are enabled, the message is routed to the review CSQ before final approval is sent out.
11) The agent's response is saved to the outbox folder on the mail store using IMAP commands.
12) The Cisco Desktop Agent E-mail Service periodically checks the outbox folder and sends all messages in it.

Agent E-Mail Configuration

Agent E-Mail configuration consists of the following steps:

1. Mail store configuration (Microsoft Exchange)
2. Global Settings (CDA Web Portal)
3. Create Contact Service Queue (UCCX Admin Web Portal)
4. Contact Service Queue Settings (CDA Web Portal)

Why E-Mail Contact Service Queue (CSQ) has to be created and configured in two different places? Remember the UCCX engine (routing) portion was written by Cisco and the Agent portion was written by Spanlink/Calabrio? The integration on admin interface is not there yet.

Mail store configuration (Microsoft Exchange)

- ➢ **Mail store configuration (Microsoft Exchange)**
- Global Settings (CDA Web Portal)
- Create Contact Service Queue (UCCX AppAdmin Portal)
- Contact Service Queue Settings (CDA Web Portal)

The most detailed configuration guide for Microsoft Exchange is in the "Cisco CAD Installation Guide". There is a dedicated chapter named "Configuring Agent E-Mail". It covers in-depth details on Microsoft Exchange, certificates, Java, etc. Please refer to the CAD installation guide for details.

Global Settings (CDA Web Portal)

- ✓ Mail store configuration (Microsoft Exchange)
- ➢ **Global Settings (CDA Web Portal)**
- Create Contact Service Queue (UCCX AppAdmin Portal)
- Contact Service Queue Settings (CDA Web Portal)

After configuration Microsoft Exchange server, we'll have to tell UCCX server about the mail server such as IP/DNS name of the mail server, credentials to authenticate with the mail server etc. This is done via the [**CDA Web Portal > Agent E-Mail Settings > Global Settings**].

Please note that if you want to use IMAP over SSL (port 993), you'll have to import the MS Exchange certificate into UCCX so UCCX server trust the Exchange server. Certificate import is out of the scope of this book. Please refer to Cisco documentations.

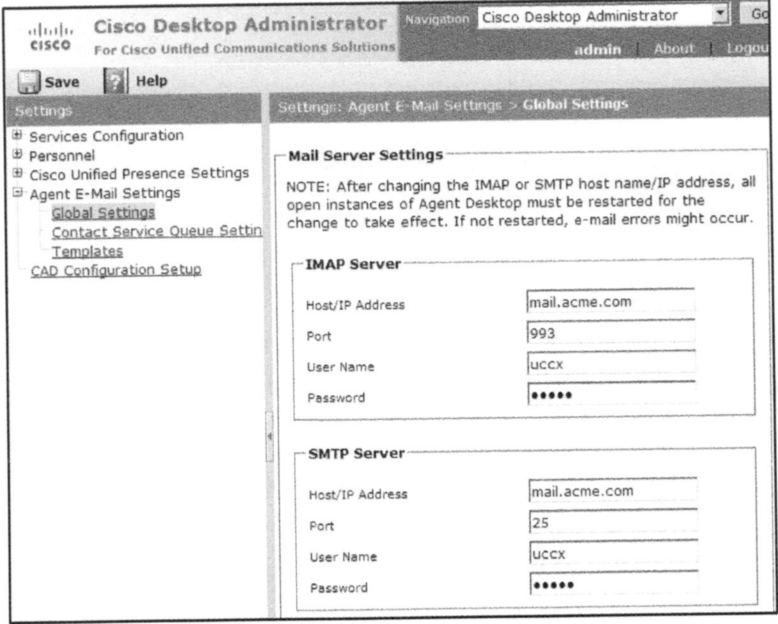

Figure 13-3 Agent E-Mail Global Settings

Create Contact Service Queue (UCCX AppAdmin Portal)

- ✓ Mail store configuration (Microsoft Exchange)
- ✓ Global Settings (CDA Web Portal)
- ➢ **Create Contact Service Queue (UCCX AppAdmin Portal)**
- • Contact Service Queue Settings (CDA Web Portal)

The procedure to create an E-Mail CSQ is the same as creating a voice CSQ except that we choose "Email" versus "Voice" from the drop-down menu. Please refer to [UCCX: Provision "Contact Service Queue" (CSQ)] on page 60 for details.

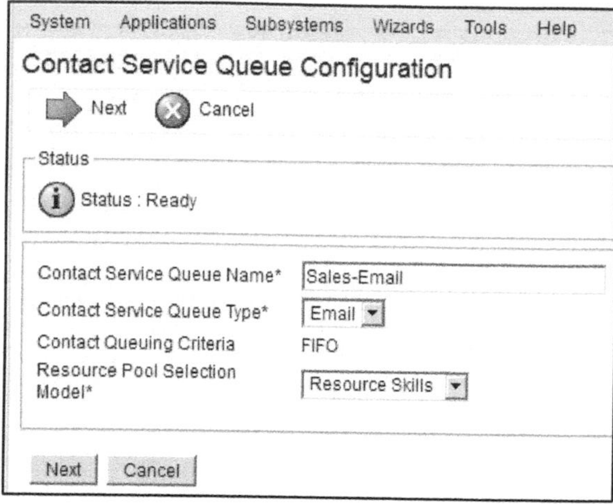

Figure 13-4 Creating Email CSQ

Contact Service Queue Settings (CDA Web Portal)

- ✓ Mail store configuration (Microsoft Exchange)
- ✓ Global Settings (CDA Web Portal)
- ✓ Create Contact Service Queue (UCCX AppAdmin Portal)
- ➢ **Contact Service Queue Settings (CDA Web Portal)**

After CSQ is created, we need to map a specific email address (e.g. sales@acme.com) to a specific CSQ (e.g. "Sales-Email" CSQ). This is done on the [**CDA Web Portal > Agent Email Settings > Contact Service Queue Settings**]. Please note that only the email CSQs will show up here.

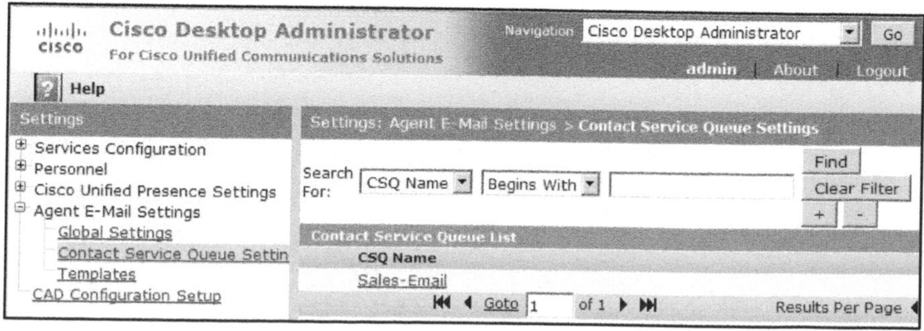

Figure 13-5 CDA > Email CSQs

Click on the CSQ you want to configure. You'll get to the CSQ settings page.

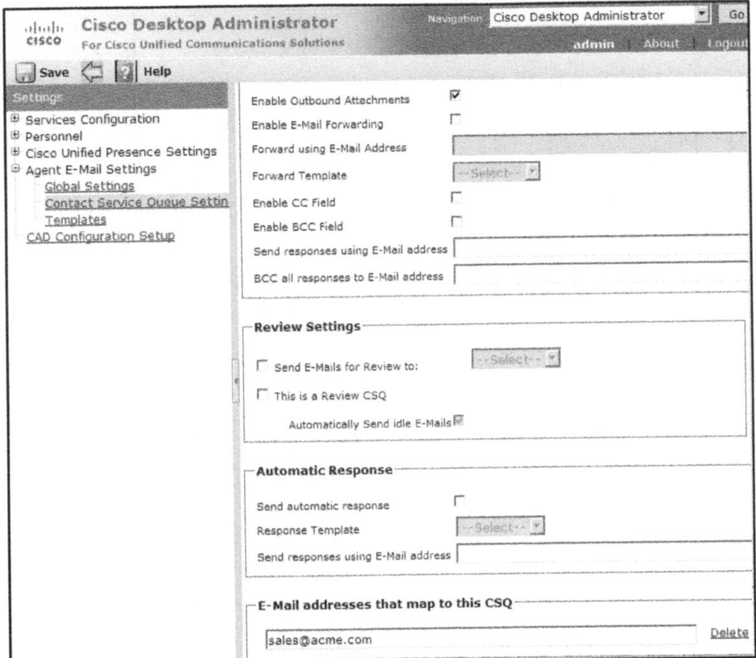

Figure 13-6 Email CSQ Settings

The most important setting is at the bottom, which maps an email address to the CSQ. In the example above, all customer emails sent to sales@acme.com will be put in the "Sales-Email" CSQ". Optionally, you may configure "Review CSQ" so that response emails can be reviewed by supervisors before being sent to customers.

Chapter 14 Web Chat

Web Chat Overview

More and more companies are providing web chat features on their support websites. Web chat is a good supplement to voice and email. When customer initiates a web chat request, the request can be put into a contact service queue (CSQ). Agents serve the web chat CSQ just like the way they serve the voice CSQ.

Please note:

1. Web chat requires an additional server called "Cisco SocialMiner".
2. On UCCX AppAdmin portal, there's a separate menu to create web chat CSQs (and all web chat related configurations).

General steps of deploying web chat are as below:

1. Install Cisco SocialMiner Server
2. Integrate UCCX with SocialMiner
3. Create Chat CSQ
4. Create Chat Widget

Install Cisco SocialMiner Server

- ➢ **Install Cisco SocialMiner Server**
- Integrate UCCX with SocialMiner
- Create Chat CSQ
- Create Chat Widget

SocialMiner server installation is pretty straight forward. The installation process is very similar to CUCM or UCCX.

If you install SocialMiner server on VMware ESXi, you will have to disable LRO (Large Received Offload) on the ESXi host. Otherwise, you may experience intermittent network issues. Potential error messages that may be seen with this issue include:

- A timeout occurred loading the application. Refresh the browser or try again later. If problem persists, you may need to check your network connectivity.
- Your browser is currently not receiving real-time updates. Please try to refresh or contact your system administrator.

To disable LRO, follow procedures below:

1. Log in to the ESXi host or vCenter Server by using the vSphere Client.
2. Navigate to the host in the inventory tree, and on the Configuration tab click Advanced Settings under Software.
3. Select Net and scroll down until you reach parameters starting with Vmxnet.
4. Set the following LRO parameters from 1 to 0:
   - Net.VmxnetSwLROSL
   - Net.Vmxnet3SwLRO
   - Net.Vmxnet3HwLRO
   - Net.Vmxnet2SwLRO
   - Net.Vmxnet2HwLRO
5. Reboot the ESXi host to apply the changes.

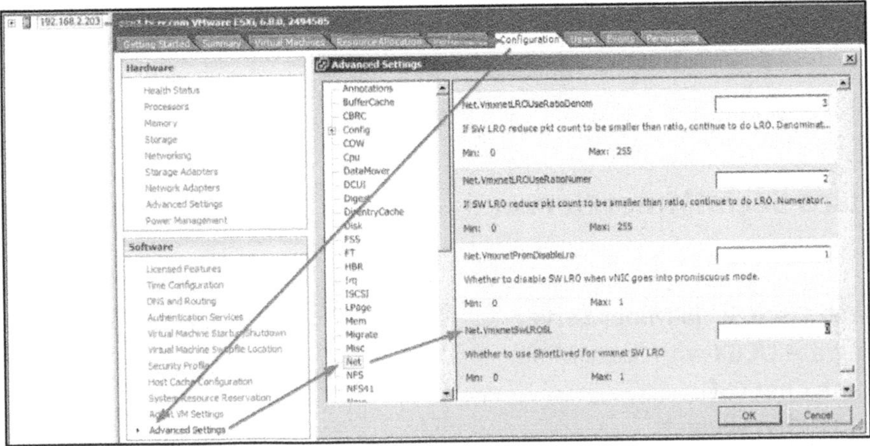

Figure 14-1 Turn off LRO in ESXi Host

Integrate UCCX with SocialMiner

- ✓ Install Cisco SocialMiner Server
- ➢ **Integrate UCCX with SocialMiner**
- Create Chat CSQ
- Create Chat Widget

Once SocialMiner server is installed, we need to integrate UCCX with SocialMiner. All integration tasks can be done from UCCX. You don't have to log onto SocialMiner server at all.

Go to [**UCCX AppAdmin portal > Subsystems > Chat > SocialMiner Configuration**]. Enter the hostname of the SocialMiner server and username/password of SocialMiner administrator.

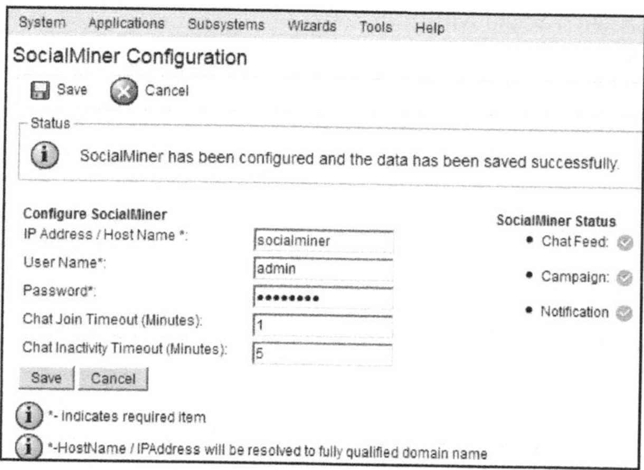

Figure 14-2 Integrate UCCX with SocialMiner

Please note that DNS plays an important role here. Make sure the hostname entered here can be resolved by DNS. Otherwise, the integration will fail.

Once you hit the "Save" button, the system will tell you if it succeeds or not. If it succeeds, UCCX will create a "Chat Feed" and a "Campaign" on SocialMiner server. Don't worry if you're not familiar with those terminologies as they are not relevant in this chapter.

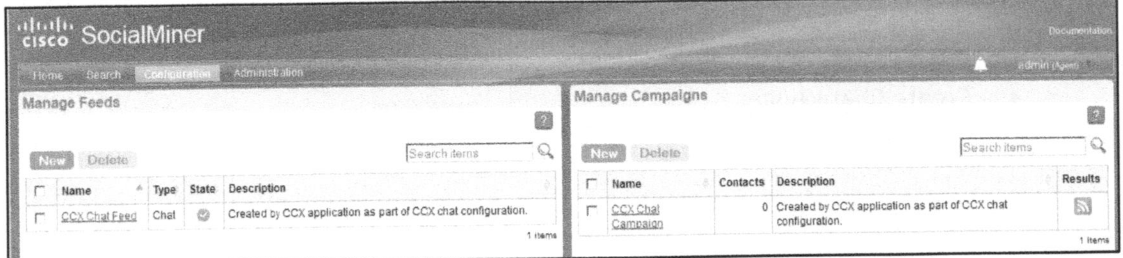

Figure 14-3 "Chat Feed" and "Campaign" Created on SocialMiner Server

Create Web Chat CSQ

- ✓ Install Cisco SocialMiner Server
- ✓ Integrate UCCX with SocialMiner
- ➢ **Create Chat CSQ**
- • Create Chat Widget

In a perfect world, all CSQs (voice, email and chat) should be created from the same menu. Unfortunately, we are not in a perfect world. Web chat was added to UCCX as a very different component. Thus it has its menus in a different place. To create a chat CSQ, go to [**UCCX AppAdmin portal > Subsystems > Chat > Chat Contact Service Queues**].

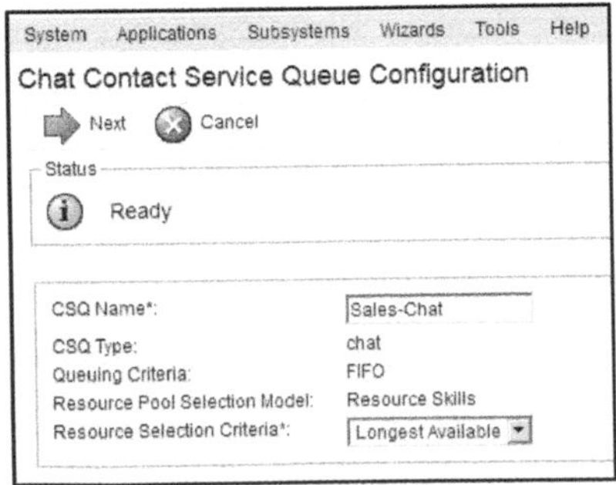

Figure 14-4 Creating Chat CSQ

Chat CSQ is skill-based. We specify the minimal skill required to serve the CSQ.

Create Chat Widget

- ✓ Install Cisco SocialMiner Server
- ✓ Integrate UCCX with SocialMiner
- ✓ Create Chat CSQ
- ➢ **Create Chat Widget**

A "Chat Widget" is actually a HTML form that collects user information and associates the chat request to a CSQ.

Just like voice queues, the more information collected, the better the system can route the customer to the right agent. For example, in the form below, system asks for customer's name and the reason/problem he/she requesting a chat.

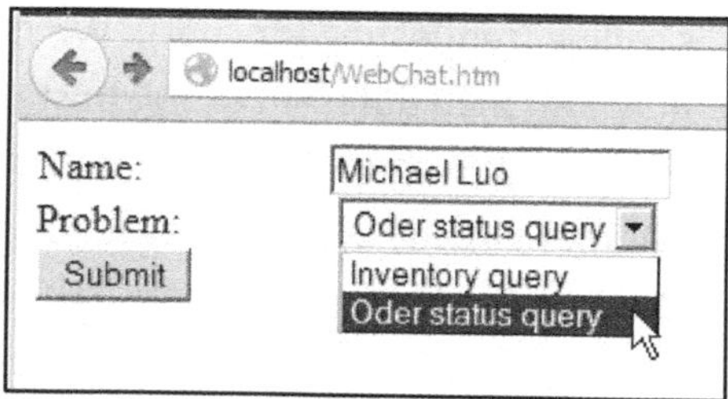

Figure 14-5 Example of a Chat Request Form

Based on the reason/problem, system can route the customer to different CSQs that better serves the customer.

UCCX has a "Chat Widget List" menu that can help us build HTML forms with some pre-defined fields (such as Name, Phone, Address, etc.). Once the form is built, we may copy the HTML code to the corporate web server as the chat request form.

To create a "Chat Widget", go to UCCX AppAdmin > Subsystems > Chat > Chat Widget List. Click "Add New" button to create a new widget (web form).

In the example below, we just select "Name" as the user form field.

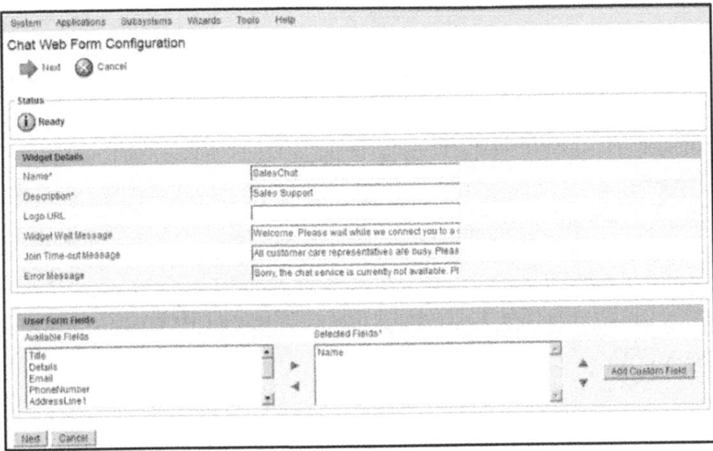

Figure 14-6 Creating a New Widget (Web Form)

On next screen, we may create some "Problem Statements". "Problem Statements" specify the reason customer is calling (requesting for chat). We may have more than one problem statement. We may also map different problem statements to different CSQs. For example, if customer wanted to check if an item is in stock, it can be handled by the general sales CSQ. If customer already placed an order and would like to check the order status, it can be handled by a "ordering" CSQ, etc. This is where a web form actually ties to a CSQ.

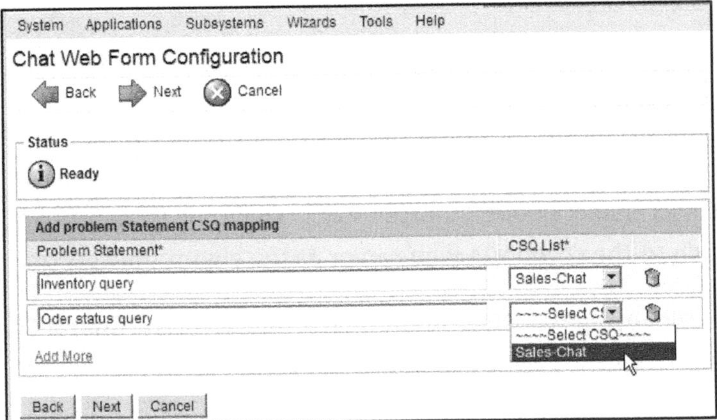

Figure 14-7 Problem Statements

The next screen is a preview of the web form. If it looks good, you may click the "Finish" button.

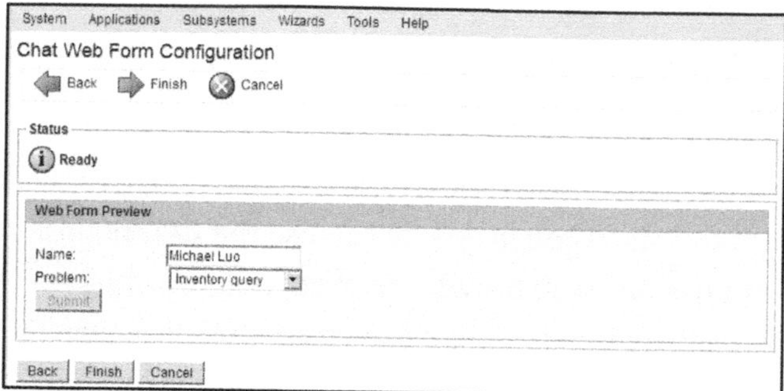

Figure 14-8 Web Form Preview

Next screen is the generated HTML code that you can copy to the corporate web server.

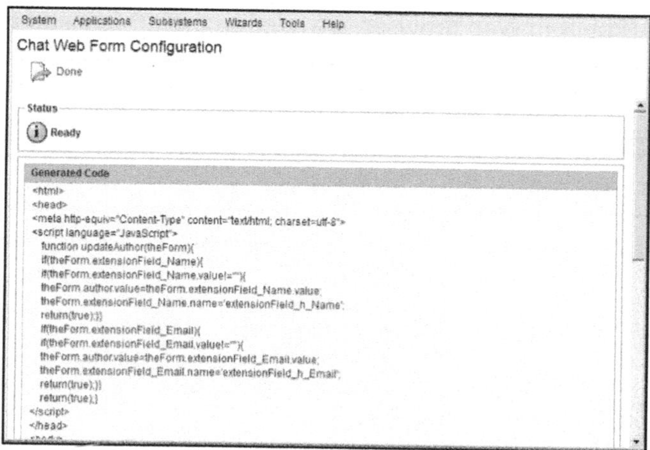

Figure 14-9 Generated HTML Code

Click "Done" button to close the "Generated Code" screen. You will be brought back to the "List Chat Web Forms" screen, where you can see the newly created web form. You may always come to this screen to retrieve the HTML code.

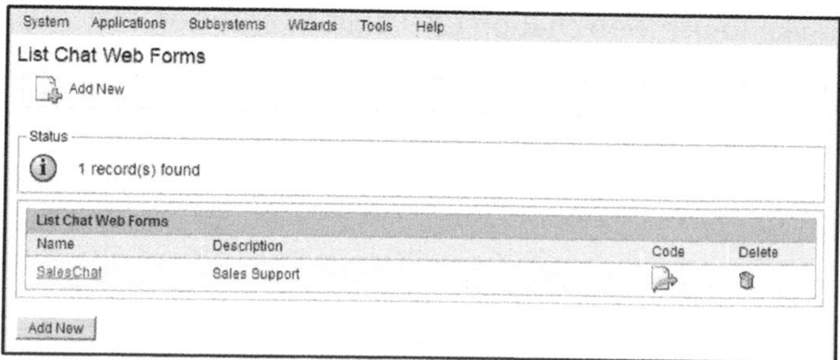

Figure 14-10 List Chat Web Forms

Agent Web Chat Interface

Agents use web chat interface (**https://*address-of-uccx-server*/agentdesktop**) to handle incoming chat requests. Though agents can use the CAD built-in browser, they don't have to. They can use any web browser to access the URL above. Please note the agent web chat availability is independent to voice / email availability. So far, there is no way to synchronize one type of availability to another.

CAD Built-In Web Browser

If we want to use CAD built-In Web Browser, we need to use CDA to add the web chat URL to the CAD Interface.

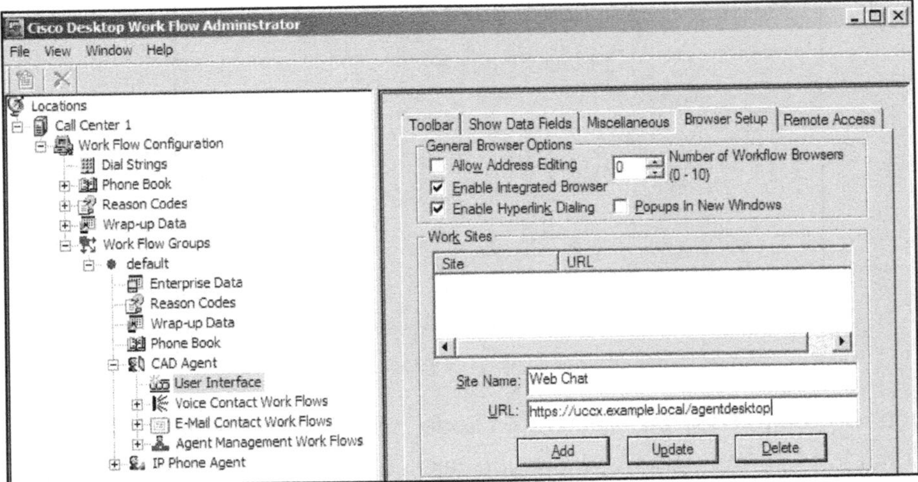

Figure 14-11 Add Web Chat URL to CAD Interface

Here's what it looks like to use web chat on CAD built-in browser.

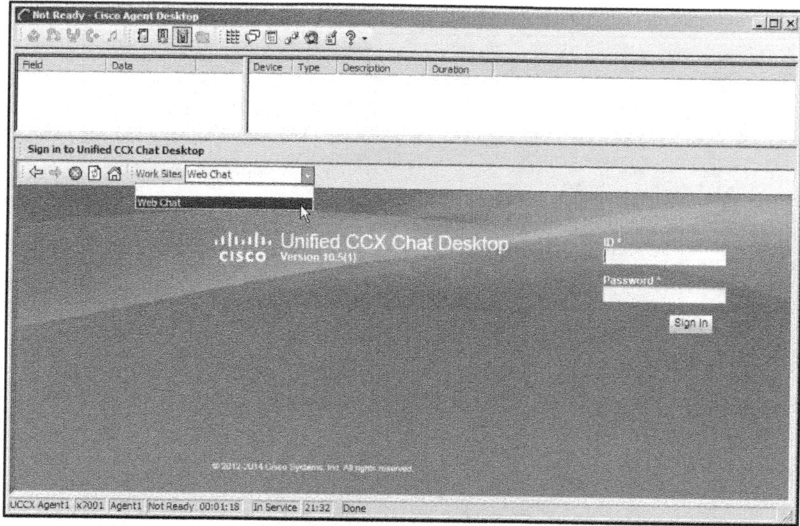

Figure 14-12 Web Chat on CAD Built-In Browser

Standalone Browser

Agents may also use standalone web browsers (such as Internet Explorer, Firefox, etc.) to log into web chat interface.

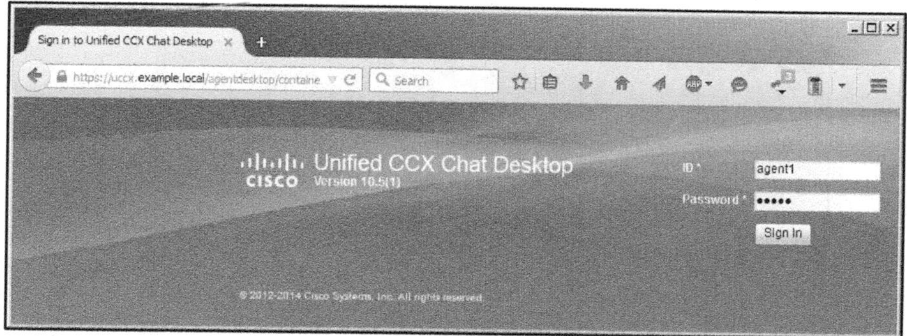

Figure 14-13 Web Chat on Standalone Browser

Agents may toggle the state between "Ready" and "Not Ready".

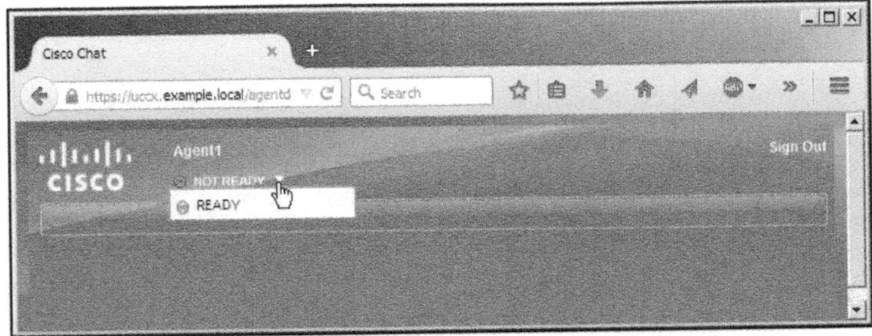

Figure 14-14 Web Chat Agent State

When there is an incoming chat request, agent state will change to "Busy".

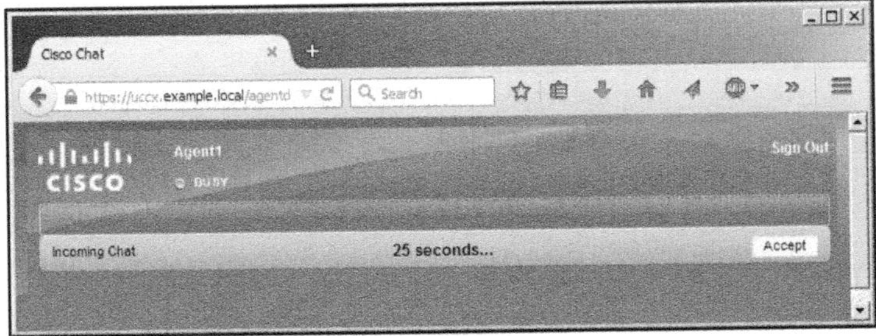

Figure 14-15 Incoming Chat Request

When agent accepts the chat request, he/she can see the information submitted via the web form ("customer name" in this example).

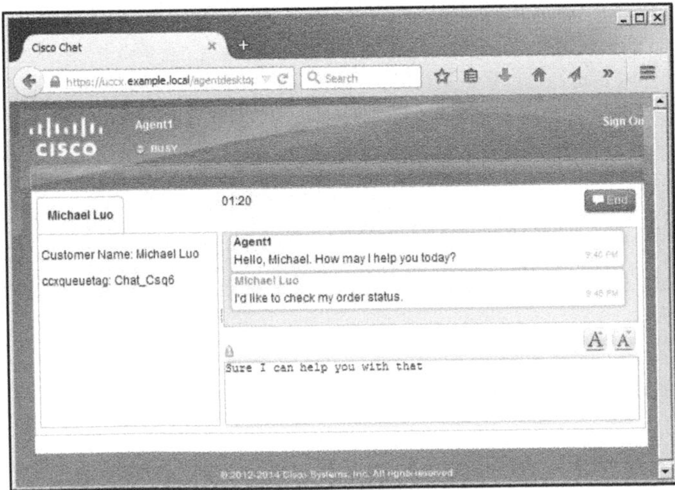

Figure 14-16 Agent/Customer Chat

Chapter 15 Outbound Dialer

Overview

Have you ever received a telemarketing call? Originally, those telemarketing calls were initiated by human beings (agents). Now with contact center technologies, calls can be initiated by computer systems. The benefits are:

1. The calls can target specific customers (or potential customers) based on the information in database such as gender, age, income, occupation, etc.
2. The system can filter out fax machine or answer machines so only the calls answered by live person are presented to live agents. This saves a lot on human resource.

UCCX refers this feature as "Outbound Dialing".

Basic Concepts

Campaign

Campaign is the base unit of outbound dialing. Each campaign serves a specific purpose. For example, we may have a "survey" campaign that calling customers to do marketing survey. We may have a "direct sale" campaign that calling customer to sell products/services. Different campaigns have different targeted customers. Thus each campaign may have different contact list and/or different CSQs.

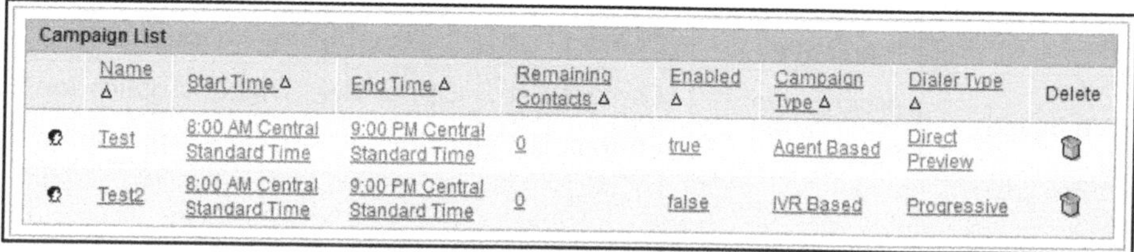

Campaign List

	Name Δ	Start Time Δ	End Time Δ	Remaining Contacts Δ	Enabled Δ	Campaign Type Δ	Dialer Type Δ	Delete
	Test	8:00 AM Central Standard Time	9:00 PM Central Standard Time	0	true	Agent Based	Direct Preview	
	Test2	8:00 AM Central Standard Time	9:00 PM Central Standard Time	0	false	IVR Based	Progressive	

Figure 15-1 Campaign List

Campaign can be configured from [**UCCX AppAdmin Portal > Subsystem > Outbound > Campaigns**]

Campaign Types

When creating a campaign in UCCX, you may choose from two campaign types: "Agent Based" or "IVR Based".

Please don't be misled by the words "agent based" and "IVR based". They only indicate the type of resource that will ***first*** handle the calls.

An "IVR based" campaign may need agent resource depending on the user input. Here is an example of IVR based campaign:

1) A gentleman received a call on his home phone
2) He answered the call
3) He heard a recording "*We are with ABC bank and would like to get your feedback on our service. Please press 1 to talk to a customer representative or press 2 to decline.*" Up to this point, the call was handled by IVR, which is why this campaign is classified as "IVR based".
4) If the gentleman pressed 1, an agent is needed to handle the call. That is controlled by the script. A CSQ is needed at this point.

On the other hand, an "Agent Based" campaign may need IVR/scripts if we want to use scripts to handle abandoned calls or answering machines.

The table below lists the mandatory and optional components needed for each type of campaigns.

Campaign Type	Dialer Type	Contact List?	CSQ?	Trigger/Application?
Agent Based	Direct Preview	Contact List	CSQ	n/a
	Progressive	Contact List	CSQ	Optional
	Predictive	Contact List	CSQ	Optional
IVR Based	Progressive	Contact List	Optional	Trigger/Application
	Predictive	Contact List	Optional	Trigger/Application

Contact List

A contact list is an internal database associated with a specific campaign. We build the contact list by importing CSV (Comma Separated Values) file into the campaign. Please make contact is not on the "National Do Not Call List". In United States, there is a "National Do Not Call List". People who do not want to be called by telemarketing may register their names and phone numbers to the list. Telemarketing companies are not allowed to call those numbers by law.

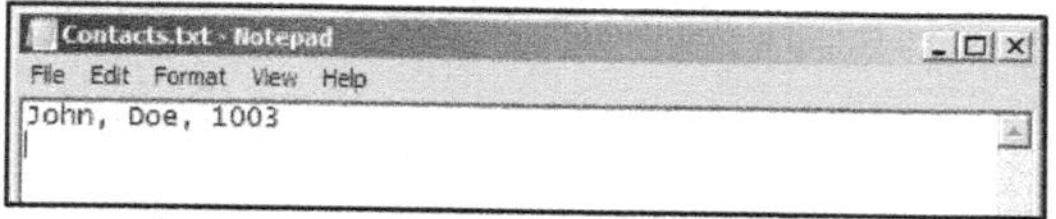

Figure 15-2 Contact List CSV Example

Contact list can be imported from campaign configuration page.

Area Codes

Government regulation also dictates what time companies can conduct telemarketing calls (usually 8AM to 9PM local time). UCCX uses area code to determine time zone of the called party.

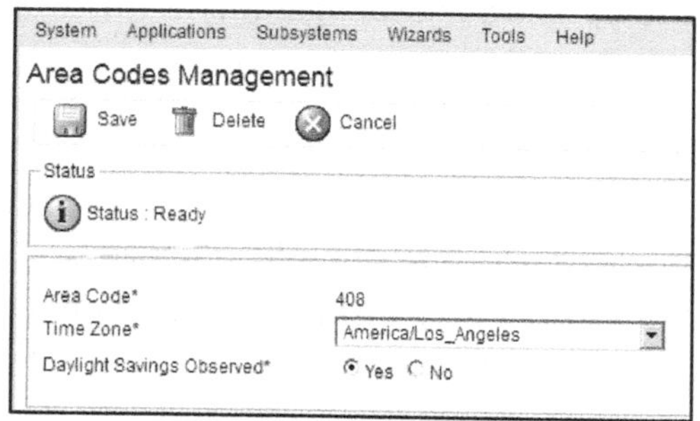

Figure 15-3 Area Code to Time Zone Mapping

Area codes can be configured from [**UCCX AppAdmin Portal > Subsystem > Outbound > Area Codes**]

CPA (Call Progress Analysis)

Contact Center resources (agents and IVR ports) are valuable resources. If we "pre-screen" the outbound calls before presenting them to resources we could save a lot of money. For example, we want agents talk to live persons but not answering machines. CPA (Call Progress Analysis) can help us distinguish live persons from answering machines. CPA is a feature of SIP Gateways.

There are three primary functions in CPA:

- Answering machine detection (AMD)
- Fax/modem detection
- Answering machine terminating tone detection

There are complex algorithms implemented to make these distinctions, but, from a functional stand point:

- A live party answer is expected to be a short salutation, then a period of silence.
  Example: "Hello" + silence
  Example: "Hello, Johnson residence" + silence
- An answering machine is expected to be a longer salutation, then no silence.
  Example: "You've reached the Miller's residence, please leave a message after the beep"
- An answering machine terminating tone detect is expected to be detection of the answering machine, then silence, then a terminating tone.
- A fax detect is recognition of the fax tone.

The ability to make these distinctions might be difficult, so you might need to adjust timing parameters in order to optimize the configuration.

SIP Gateway

SIP gateway is the voice gateway in the case of outbound dialing. UCCX use the CPA (Call Progress Analysis) feature on the SIP gateway to determine if the answering party is a live person or a fax / answering machine.

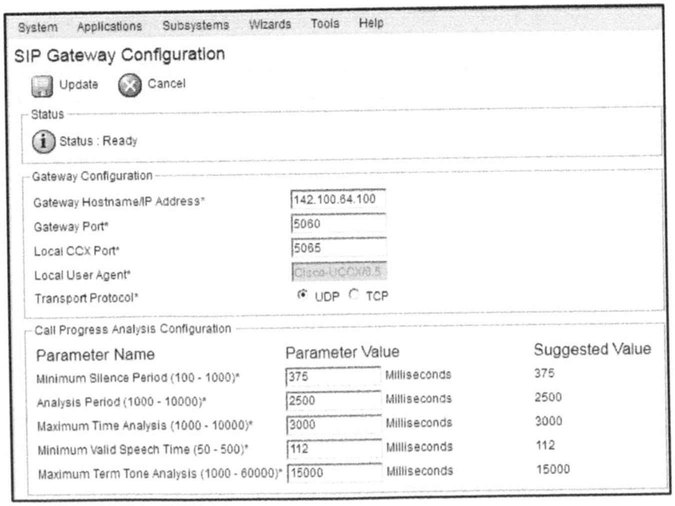

Figure 15-4 SIP Gateway Configuration

SIP Gateway can be configured from [**UCCX AppAdmin Portal > Subsystem > Outbound > SIP Gateway**]

Please understand that UCCX use SIP gateway mainly for "call screening" purpose (CPA). Once the answering party type is determined, the call will be transferred to CUCM for further processing. Here is the work flow:

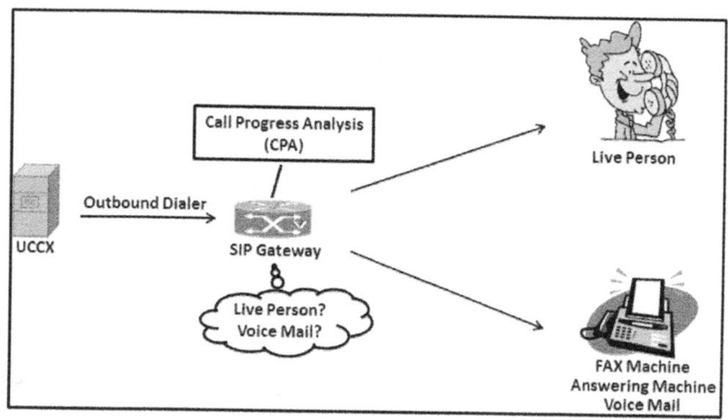

Figure 15-5 UCCX calls contacts via SIP gateway

Step 1: UCCX outbound dialer calls contacts via SIP gateway. No CUCM is involved at this point. Call is answered by the contact. With the parameters configured on UCCX and the CPA (Call Progress Analysis) feature on SIP gateway, UCCX determines if the contact is a live person, a fax or voicemail / answering machine.

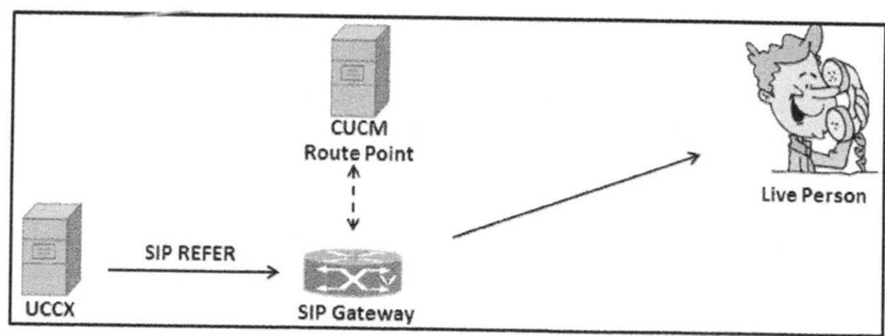

Figure 15-6 Transfer the call to CUCM Route Point

Step 2: Based on the contact type, UCCX may decide to use contact center resource (agents or IVR ports) to handle the call. If so, UCCX will send a SIP REFER message to SIP gateway, requests the call to be transferred to CUCM Route Point.

Why transfer the call to CUCM while UCCX already "has" the call? Because UCCX was not designed to have full set of call control features and has limited control on phones and media resources. Also UCCX applications/scripts are usually associated with CUCM route points. Transfer the call to CUCM route point is the easiest way to trigger UCCX applications/scripts.

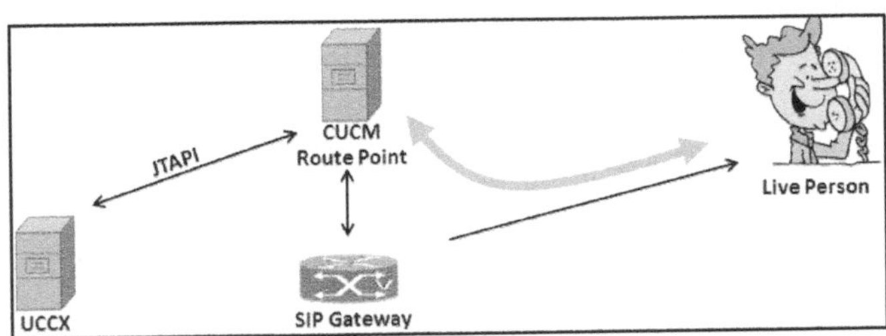

Figure 15-7 Route Point triggers UCCX scripts via JTAPI

Step 3: When the call is transferred to CUCM Route Point, it is just like any regular incoming call hits the Route Point. Route Point triggers UCCX scripts via JATPI protocol.

Abandoned Calls

With CPA, contact center may use its resource more efficiently. Instead of reserving resource before making the call, contact center may reserve resource after identifying a valid call. However, there is a side effect to that. What if no resource was available after identifying a valid call? Contact center would have to drop the call. This is defined as "abandoned call".

The ratio of abandoned calls over all outbound calls is defined as "abandon rate". Government regulation on abandon rate is usually less than 3%.

We cannot predict the "successful rate" of outbound calls. The only way to guarantee a zero percent abandon rate is to reserve resource before making the call (we call it "Direct Preview" in UCCX). Yet this defeats the purpose of CPA and makes contact center very inefficient (we have to over-provision resources).

LPA (Line Per Agent) and LPP (Line Per Port)

Since the successful rate of outbound calls is always less than 100%, contact center usually "over-subscribes" resources. For example, when contact center has 10 agents or IVR ports available it will make 12 outbound calls. If 10 of the 12 calls are valid calls, the resource utilization rate will be 100% (ideal situation). If less than 10 calls are valid, the resource will be underutilized. If more than 10 calls are valid, there will be abandoned calls.

The oversubscription rate is referred to as LPA (Line Per Agent) in Agent Based campaigns and LPP (Line Per Port) in IVR Based campaigns. In our example above, the LPA or LPP is 1.2. Please note the LPA/LPP is based on ***available*** resource, not the total number of resource. For example, a contact center has 100 agents. 50 of them are available. If LPA was set to 1.2 contact center system will try to dial 50 x 1.2 = 60 outbound calls at that moment. Contact center system monitors available resource real time to determine number of calls to make.

The higher the LPA/LPP is, the higher the abandon rate will be. The lower the LPA/LPP is, the lower the abandon rate will be. The lowest LPA/LPP is 1, whereas abandon rate will be 0.

Progressive and Predictive

As discussed above, LPA/LPP will impact abandon rate. However there is no formula for LPA/LPP and abandon rate. i.e. we cannot predict abandon rate based on the value of LPA/LPP because the "successful rate" on call screening is unpredictable. Then how do we set the appropriate value for LPA/LPP to achieve a desired abandon rate?

In UCCX, there are two options (dialer types) that use LPA/LPP to control outbound call behavior.

Progressive

If we chose the "progressive" dialer, we will set the LPA/LPP value manually. Whenever we want to change the value, we will have to change it manually. Consider it as a static oversubscription ratio.

Predictive

If we chose the "predictive" dialer, we will set the initial value of LPA/LPP. UCCX then automatically adjust the LPA/LPP value based on the abandon rate. Predictive dialer is self-adaptive.

For detailed explanation of the progressive and predictive algorithm please refer to "Cisco Unified Contact Center Express Design Guide > Features > Unified CCX Outbound Dialer".

Dialer Types

Different types of outbound dialers have different call behaviors. UCCX supports three dialer types:

- Progressive
- Predictive
- Direct Preview

We have discussed "progressive" and "predictive". What is "Direct Preview"?

"Direct Preview" is a dialer with LPA value hardcoded to 1, which means no oversubscription on resource. Also, "Direct Preview" does not use any CPA feature, which means agents might be connected to answering machines or fax machines. "Direct Preview" is only used with Agent Based campaigns. It cannot be used with IVR based campaigns.

Finesse vs. CAD

As discussed in previous chapters, Finesse is the next generation desktop application for UCCX while CAD is the traditional client. Some of the outbound features (Agent Based Progressive or Predictive Dialing) are only available with Finesse. If Finesse was not activated, you won't be able to see the corresponding feature options.

The screen below shows the "Dialer Type" options for agent based campaign. When Finesses is deactivated (which is the default), only "Direct Preview" option is visible. "Progressive" or "Predictive" option is hidden from the drop-down list.

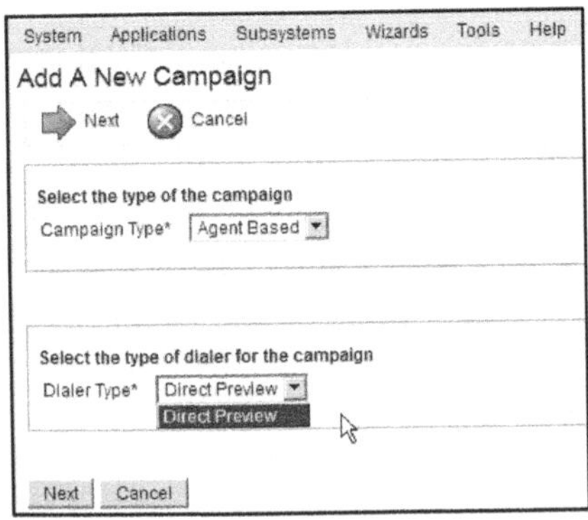

Figure 15-8 Finesse Deactivated (Default)

You may use "`utils uccx finesse activate`" command on the CLI to activate Finesse. Reboot is required to take effect.

```
admin:utils uccx finesse activate
Unified CCX currently does not support concurrent use of Cisco Agent/Supervisor
Desktop and Cisco Finesse.
If you are using Cisco Agent/Supervisor Desktop, deactivate Cisco Finesse servic
e.

Do you want to proceed? (yes/no) yes

Cisco Finesse activation in progress...
Cisco Finesse activated successfully.

If this is a HA deployment, run this command on both Unified CCX nodes.

Please reboot the system for the changes to take effect

admin:_
```

Figure 15-9 Activating Finesse from CLI

When Finesse is activated, you will see the "Progressive" and "Predictive" options for "Agent Based" campaigns.

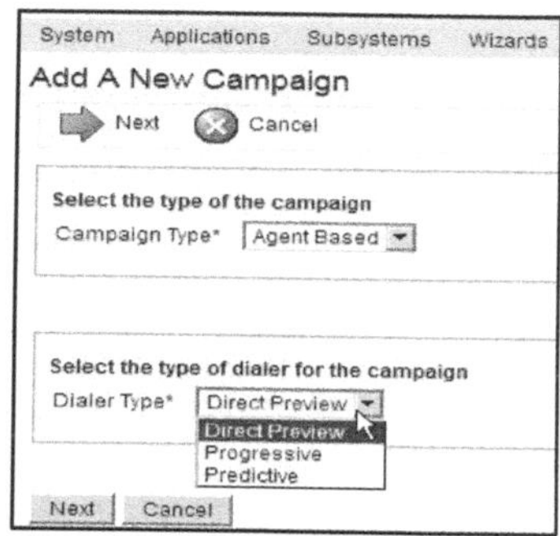

Figure 15-10 with Finesse Activated

Preparation

Before we actually create and configure campaigns we have to do preparation work.

Licensing

Go to [**UCCX AppAdmin Portal > System > License Information > Display License(s)**] to review outbound license. If you plan to use IVR based outbound dialer, make sure you have outbound IVR ports. If you plan to use agent based outbound dialer, make sure you have outbound agent seats.

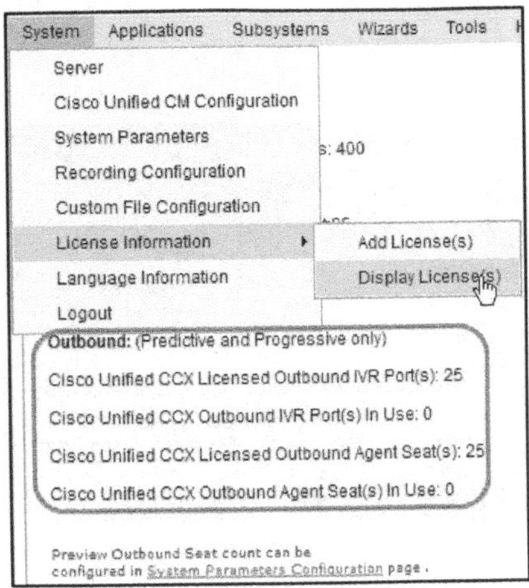

Figure 15-11 License Information

Outbound IVR Ports

Outbound IVR ports are created through [**UCCX AppAdmin Portal > Subsystems > Cisco Unified CM Telephony > Call Control Group**]. Please refer to [**UCCX: Provision Call Control Group**] on page 53 for details.

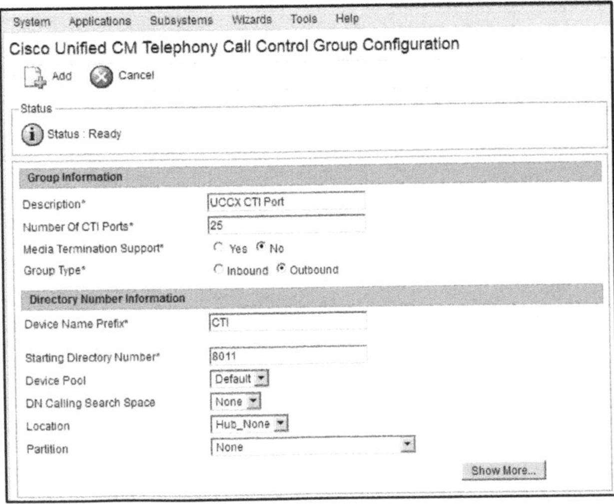

Figure 15-12 Creating Outbound Call Control Group

The only difference here is to choose "outbound" as Group Type.

CSQs

You may use inbound CSQs previously created. Or you may create dedicated CSQs for outbound calls. Please refer to [**UCCX: Provision "Contact Service Queue" (CSQ)**] on page 60 for details.

Scripts, Applications and Triggers

If you plan to use progressive or predictive dialing (IVR based or agent based), you would normally use scripts, application and triggers. Please refer to previous chapters for details.

If you plan to use Preview Dialer, you don't need any script, application or trigger.

Global Configuration

There are four menu items under [**UCCX AppAdmin Portal > Subsystems > Outbound**]:

- General
- Campaigns
- Area Codes
- SIP Gateway Configuration

"General", "Area Codes" and "SIP Gateway Configuration" are global configuration, which means they apply to any campaigns

We may create campaigns under the "Campaigns" menu. There are five different types of campaigns based on "Campaign Type" and "Dialer Type".

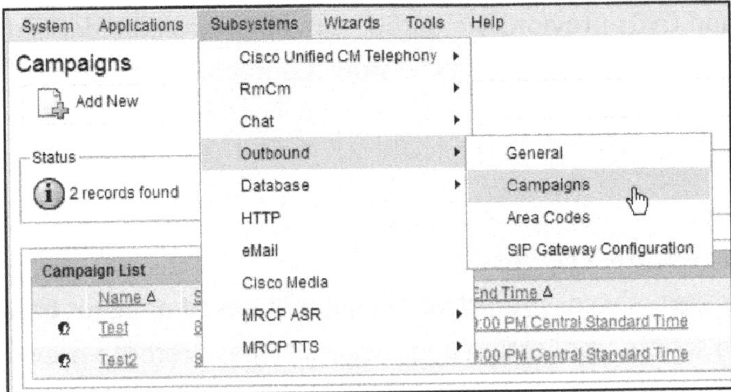

Figure 15-13 Outbound Subsystem

General Configuration

The most important item on "General" menu is "Assigned CSQs". Only the CSQs listed under "Assigned CSQs" will be available in campaigns. If you leave it as default (empty "Assigned CSQs") you won't be able to configure any campaign.

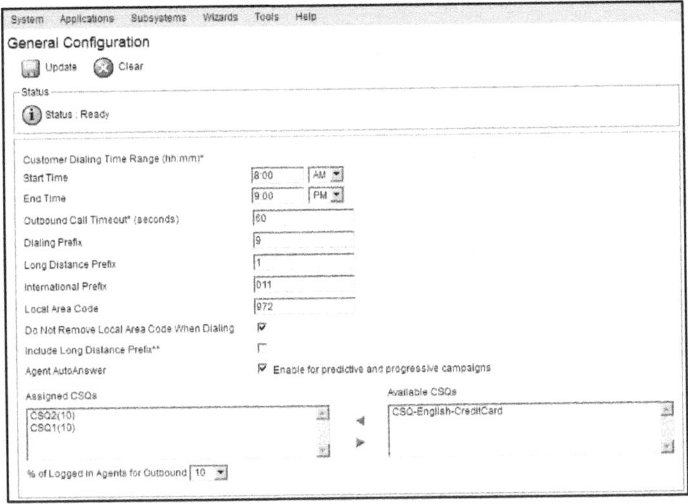

Figure 15-14 Outbound > General

Area Codes

As mentioned before, area codes are used to map phone numbers to time zones. UCCX comes with United States area codes pre-installed. You may add or change area code to time zone mapings.

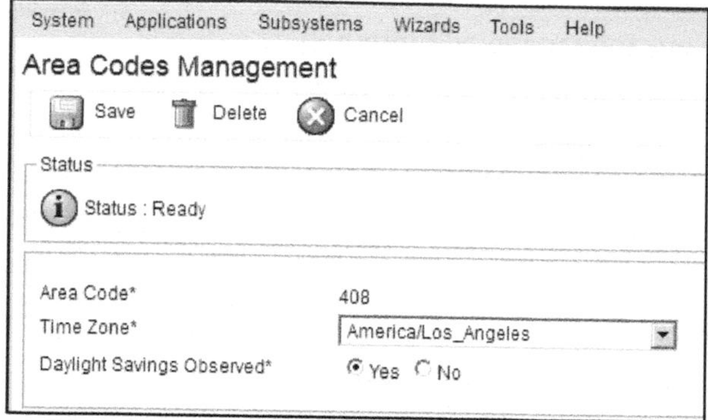

Figure 15-15 Area Codes Management

SIP Gateway Configuration

SIP Gateway Configuration is used for CPA (Call Progress Analysis). Please refer to product documentation for parameter explanations.

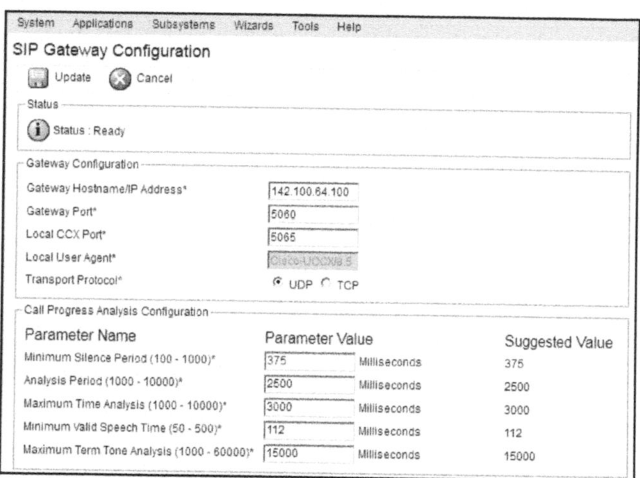

Figure 15-16 SIP Gateway Configuration

General Workflow

One-time global configuration

1. Make sure licensing is ready
2. Create outbound Call Control Group (usually one-time)
3. General outbound parameters

4. Area code to time zone mapping (optional)
5. SIP Gateway parameters

Per campaign configuration

1. Determine campaign type and dialer type (choose one out of five)
2. Create CSQ (unless you want to use inbound CSQ for outbound dialing).
3. If new CSQs were created, add them to outbound general configuration [**UCCX AppAdmin Portal > Subsystems > Outbound > General**]
4. Create new applications and triggers (except for Preview Dialer).
5. Create new campaign and configure campaign-specific parameters

We have discussed "one-time global configuration" in this chapter.

For "per campaign configuration", we have covered item 1 in this chapter and items 2-4 in "Intelligent Call Distribution" chapter.

In following sections, we will focus on item 5 (campaign-specific configuration). Since "Direct Preview" is the simplest dialer type, we will discuss it first. Remember "Direct Preview" dialer can be used with Agent Based campaign only.

(Agent Based) Direct Preview Dialer

Direct Preview Dialer is the simplest outbound dialer. It does not use any IVR, trigger, script or SIP gateway. When agent is available, Direct Preview Dialer will present a contact's information to agent desktop for preview. If agent clicks "Accept", call will be dialed out to contact and agent phone will ring. Agent picks up the phone to connect to the contact.

Preparation

Enable "Direct Preview" for CAD

If you are using CAD you need to enable "Direct Preview" on CAD. Go to [**Cisco Desktop Work Flow Administrator > Call Center 1 > Work Flow Configuration > Work**

Flow Groups > Default > CAD Agent > User Interface]. Enable "Direct Preview" on the right panel.

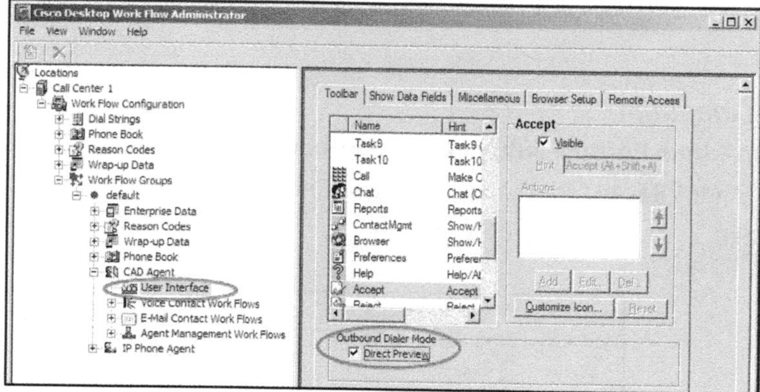

Figure 15-17 Enable "Direct Preview" on CAD

Please note:

Among three agent-based dialers (Direct Preview, Progressive, and Predictive), CAD only supports "Direct Preview", while Finesse supports all three.

Prepare CSQ

As discussed before, you need to have CSQs in the Outbound General Configuration. Make sure the CSQ you want to use is on the "Assigned CSQs" list. You may create new/dedicated CSQs or use existing CSQs.

System Applications Subsystems Wizards Tools Help

General Configuration

Update Clear

Status

Status : Ready

Customer Dialing Time Range (hh:mm)*

Start Time	8:00 AM
End Time	9:00 PM
Outbound Call Timeout* (seconds)	60
Dialing Prefix	9
Long Distance Prefix	1
International Prefix	011
Local Area Code	972
Do Not Remove Local Area Code When Dialing	☑
Include Long Distance Prefix**	☐
Agent AutoAnswer	☑ Enable for predictive and progressive campaigns

Assigned CSQs	Available CSQs
CSQ2(10) CSQ1(10)	CSQ-English-CreditCard

% of Logged in Agents for Outbound 10

Figure 15-18 Outbound > General

Campaign-Specific Configuration

Step 1: Create Campaign

Go to [**UCCX AppAdmin Portal > Subsystems > Outbound > Campaigns**]. Click "Add New". Choose "Agent Based" for Campaign Type. Choose "Direct Preview" for "Dialer Type". Click "Next".

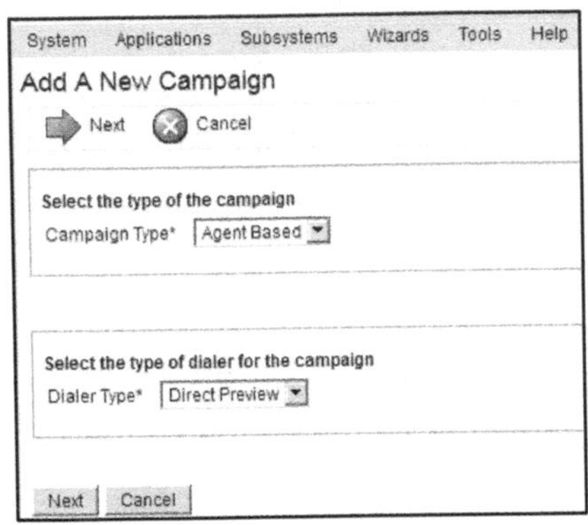

Figure 15-19 Add A New Campaign

On the next screen, enter the Campaign Name and move the CSQ you want to the "Assigned CSQs" list. Then click "Add".

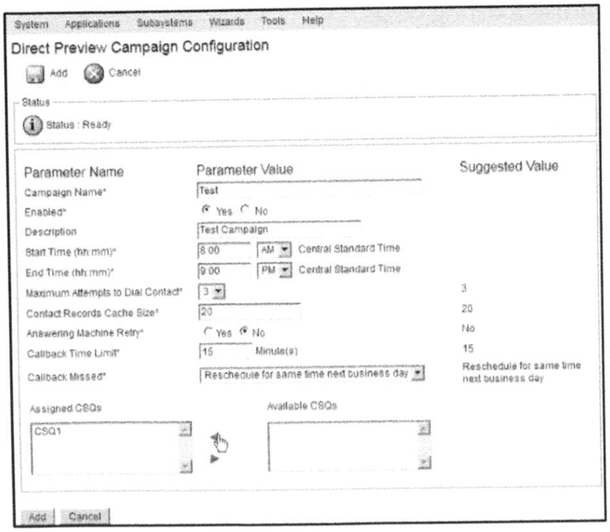

Figure 15-20 Direct Preview Campaign Configuration

Step 2: Import Contacts

We need to tell UCCX what numbers to dial for this campaign. For testing purpose, we create a contacts.txt file with only one line in it "John, Doe, 1003" (without the quotation marks). John is the first name. Doe is the last name. 1003 is the phone number.

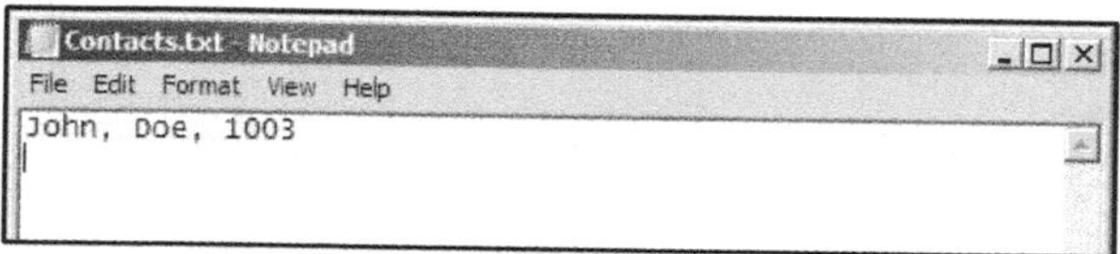

Figure 15-21 Contacts.txt

Save the contacts.txt file to your computer's hard drive. Go to [**UCCX AppAdmin Portal > Subsystems > Outbound > Campaigns**]. Click on the campaign we just created. Click "Import Contacts". Choose "First Name" from 1st drop-down menu from the top. Choose "Last Name" from 2nd drop-down. Choose "Phone1" from 3rd drop-down. Click "Browse" to choose contacts.txt file we created. The screen will lok like below:

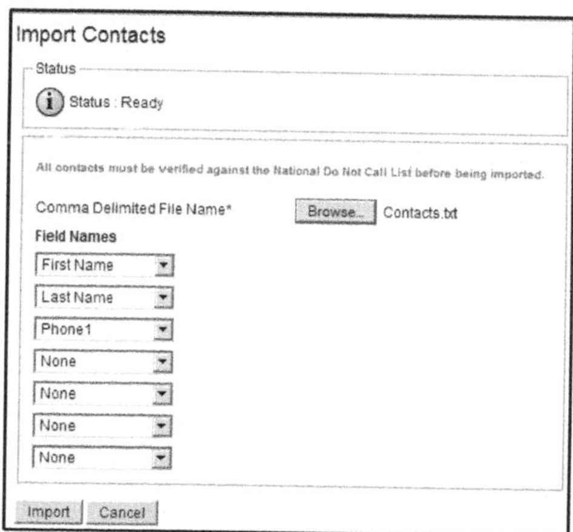

Figure 15-22 Import Contacts

If everything looks good click "Import" button. Go back to the "Campaign Configuration" page and set the "Enabled" to "Yes". A campaign cannot be enabled without contact list.

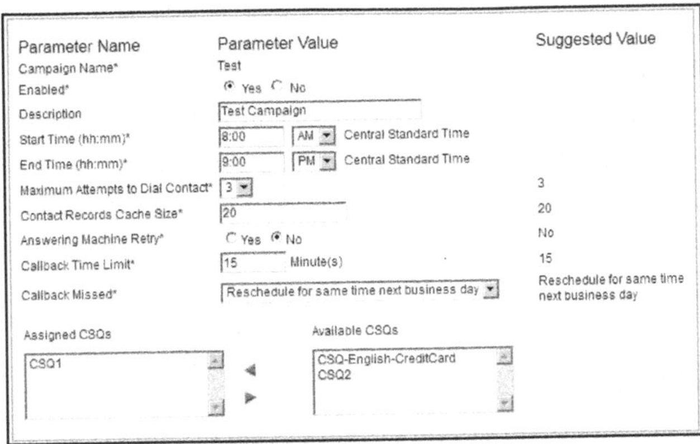

Figure 15-23 Enable Campaign

That is it! You have finished creating a campaign to use outbound dialer!

Test the campaign

Choose an agent that is capable of serving the outbound CSQ. Please refer to previous chapters on how to assign agents to CSQ and how to see which agents are capable of serving which CSQ.

Log into CAD with the agent credential and go to "Ready" state. Once the agent goes to "Ready" state the CAD will receive an "offer" with contact's information (first name, last name, and phone number) like the screen below. Agent state is "Reserved". Call state is "Offering".

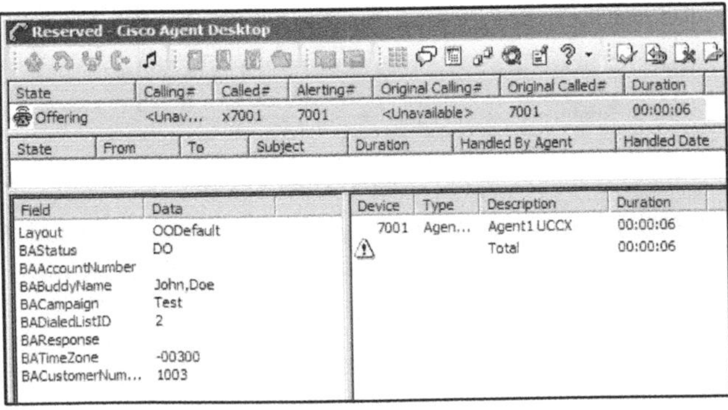

Figure 15-24 Contact being offered to agent

Agent clicks "Accept" button from the tools bar on the top (a piece of paper with green checkmark).

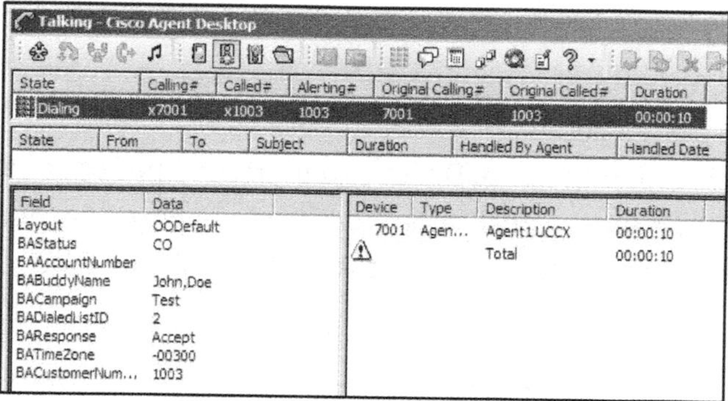

Figure 15-25 Dialing contact

Agent state changes from "Reserved" to "Talking". Call state changes from "Offering" to "Dialing". At this moment, the contact's phone will ring. The agent's phone will play ring-back tone.

If the contact answers the call, call state will change to "Connected".

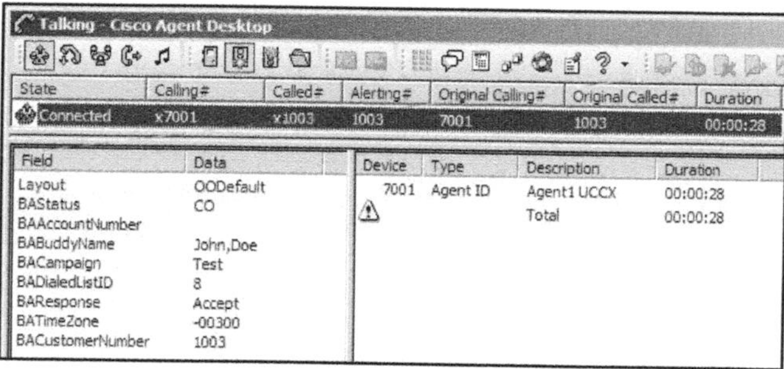

Figure 15-26 Call Connected

Agent Based Campaign

Agent Based Campaigns require agents to handle calls. Agent selection is based on CSQs. Thus you need to prepare CSQs before creating campaigns.

If you plan to use scripts to handle answering machine or abandoned calls, you also want to prepare the scripts, applications and triggers. For example, if an answering machine answered the call, the script may leave a message to let the contact know what the call was about. If a live person answered the call but no agent is available, the script may play an apology and give the person options for call back, etc.

Agent Based Progressive Dialer

To create an "Agent Based Progressive Dialer", go to [**UCCX AppAdmin Portal > Subsystem > Outbound > Campaigns**], click "Add New". Choose "Agent Based" from "Campaign Type" drop-down. Choose "Progressive" from "Dialer Type" drop-down. Then click "Next".

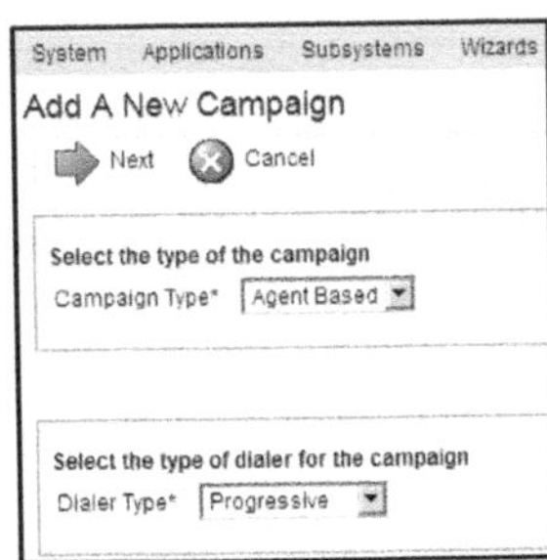

Figure 15-27 Agent Based Progressive

Next page is campaign specific parameters. Since this is a very long page we will divide it into multiple sections.

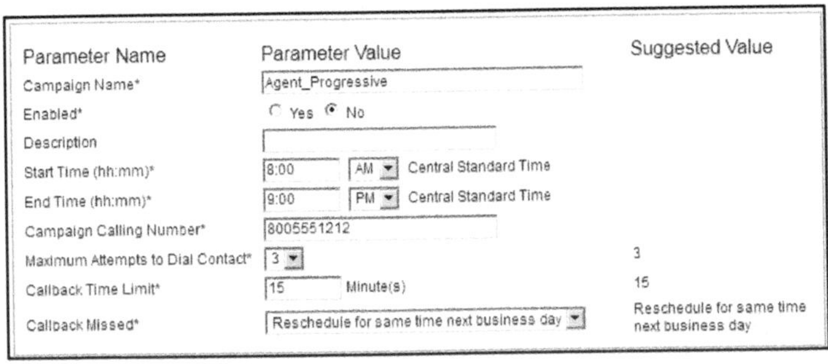

Figure 15-28 Section 1: General Parameters

The first section is general parameters. Most parameters are self-explanatory. Note the "Campaign Calling Number" is the caller ID, not the destination number to dial.

Dialing Options

Lines Per Agent(1-3)*	1.0	
Handle Low Volume as Voice	Yes / No	
Answering Machine Treatment	Transfer To IVR / End Call Trigger* : 6002 AppName : OB_IVR_Progressive	Transfer To IVR
Abandoned Call Treatment	Transfer To IVR / Abandon Call Trigger* : 6002 AppName : OB_IVR_Progressive	Transfer To IVR

Figure 15-29 Progressive Dialing Options

The second section is dialing options.

The default LPA (Lines Per Agent) value is set to 1. You may change it to any value between 1 and 3.

Optionally, you may use UCCX applications to handle answering machines or abandoned calls. For example, when CPA detects an answering machine, instead of dropping the call, an UCCX application may leave a message. If there is no agent available when a live person answers the call, an UCCX application may play apologizing message and give the person some self-service options, etc. If you plan to use these options, scripts, applications and triggers should be created in the "preparation" before configuring the campaign.

Dial Settings

No Answer Ring Limit*	15	Second(s)	15
Abandoned Call Wait Time*	2	Second(s)	2

Retries

No Answer Delay*	60	Minute(s)	60
Busy Signal Delay*	60	Minute(s)	60
Customer Abandoned Delay*	0	Minute(s)	0
Dialer Abandoned Delay*	0	Minute(s)	0

Figure 15-30 Dial and Retry Settings

The third section is dial and retries settings which controls the dial and retry timers. You may leave them as default.

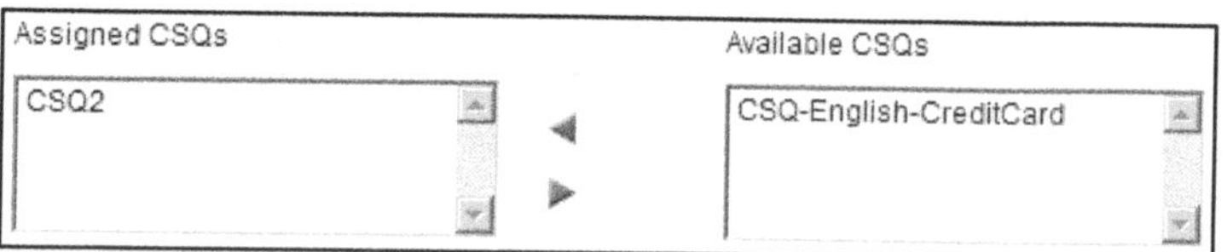

Figure 15-31 Assigned CSQs

The fourth section is assigned CSQs. Keep in mind that CSQs have to be added to the "Outbound > General" settings before you can see them here.

Agent Based Predictive Dialer

To create an "Agent Based Predictive Dialer", go to [**UCCX AppAdmin Portal > Subsystem > Outbound > Campaigns**], click "Add New". Choose "Agent Based" from "Campaign Type" drop-down. Choose "Predictive" from "Dialer Type" drop-down. Then click "Next".

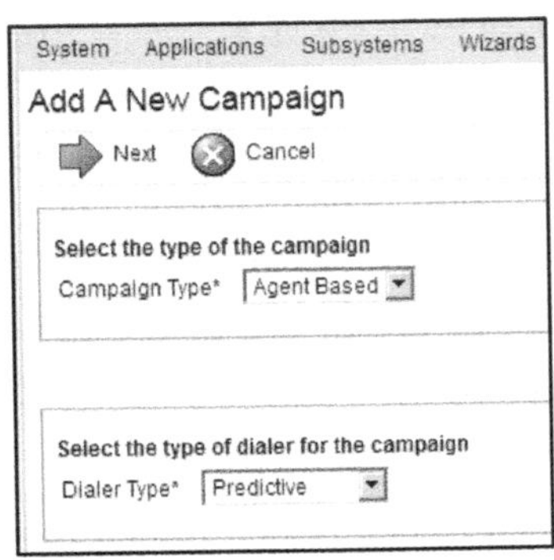

Figure 15-32 Agent Based Predictive

Next page is campaign specific parameters. Most of the parameters are identical to "progressive" dialer. Thus we will only discuss the ones that are different.

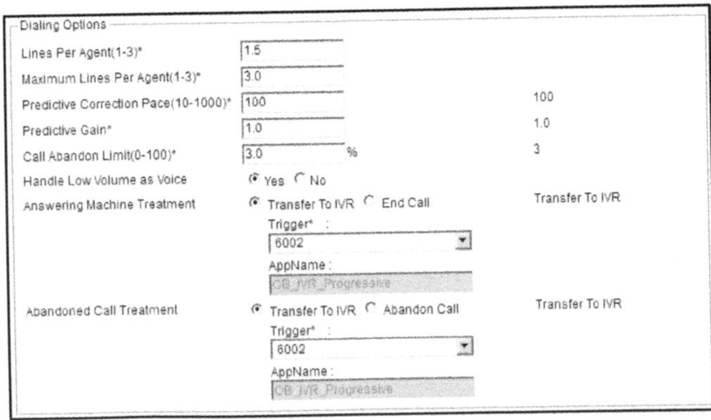

Figure 15-33 Predictive Dialing Options

The only different section in predictive dialer is the "Dialing Options".

Lines Per Agent

For predictive dialer, default value of "Lines Per Agent" is set to 1.5 while progressive dialer has default LPA value of 1.

Maximum Lines Per Agent

Remember predictive dialer will adjust the LPA automatically. "Maximum Lines Per Agent" parameter defines the upper limit of the LPA value.

Predictive Correction Pace

Remember predictive dialer will adjust the LPA automatically based on abandon rate. The dialer has to make enough calls so the abandon rate reflects the actual situation. For example, if the dialer only made two calls and both of them were abandoned, we cannot say the abandon rate was 100%, because two calls are not a big enough sample.

"Predictive Correction Pace" defines how big of a sample is big enough. i.e. The predictive algorithm starts correcting the LPA value only when the number of calls answered by live voice reaches the value defined by the "Predictive Correction Pace". Default value is 100, meaning the predictive dialer starts correcting the LPA value when the number of call answered by live person reaches 100.

Consecutive corrections happen after the Predictive Correction Pace is divided by 4, the number of live voice calls.

Predictive Gain

The amount of correction given by the predictive algorithm is controlled by the Predictive Gain as well. The correction factor is multiplied by the Predictive Gain and then it is added to the Lines Per Port of the previous iteration.

It is advisable not to change the Correction Pace and Predictive Gain values unless there is an urgent need to control the output of the predictive algorithm

Call Abandon Limit

The maximum abandon rate allowed. This has to be compliant with government regulations.

IVR Based Campaign

IVR based campaign is very similar with agent based campaign except that it uses IVR (Interactive Voice Responder) to handle calls. This is usually used for customer surveys where customers can use the keypad on the phone to rate their satisfaction score.

IVR Based Progressive Dialer

To create an "IVR Based Progressive Dialer", go to [**UCCX AppAdmin Portal > Subsystem > Outbound > Campaigns**], click "Add New". Choose "IVR Based" from "Campaign Type" drop-down. Choose "Progressive" from "Dialer Type" drop-down. Then click "Next".

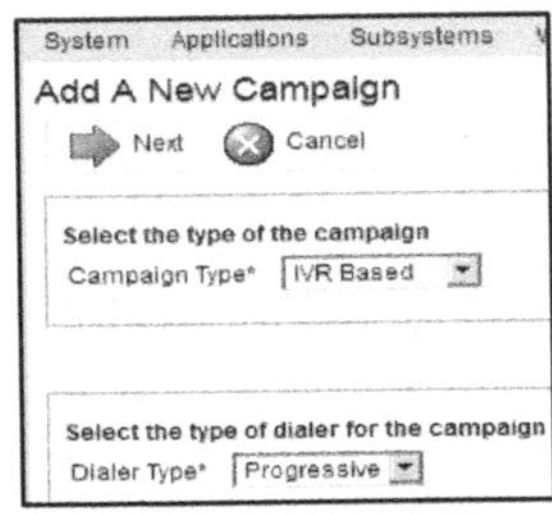

Figure 15-34 IVR Based Progressive

Next page is campaign specific parameters. Most of the parameters are identical to "Agent Based Progressive" dialer. Thus we will only discuss the ones that are different.

The first different section is the general parameters.

Parameter Name	Parameter Value	Suggested Value
Campaign Name*	OB_IVR	
Enabled*	○ Yes ◉ No	
Description		
Start Time (hh:mm)*	8:00 AM Central Standard Time	
End Time (hh:mm)*	9:00 PM Central Standard Time	
Campaign Calling Number*	8005551212	
Application Trigger*	6002	
Application Name	OB_IVR_Progressive	
Maximum Attempts to Dial Contact*	3	3
Callback Time Limit*	15 Minute(s)	15

Figure 15-35 IVR Based Progressive - General Parameters

Note that there is an "Application Trigger" in general parameters. This parameter is mandatory versus optional in "Agent Based Progressive Dialers". This is because to have IVR handle the calls, you need to have an application.

The second different section is dialing options.

Dialing Options

Number Of Dedicated Ports*	0	
Lines Per Port(1-3)*	1.0	
Handle Low Volume as Voice	Yes / No	
Answering Machine Treatment	Transfer To IVR / End Call	Transfer To IVR

Figure 15-36 IVR Based Progressive - Dialing Options

Number of Dedicated Ports

Number of dedicated IVR ports that you want to reserve for this campaign based on the number of CTI ports available in the outbound call control group for the campaign duration. That is, the total number of dedicated IVR ports for the selected campaign cannot exceed the maximum licensed ports for Outbound IVR minus the sum total of IVR ports dedicated to other campaigns running at the same time.

Lines Per Port

"Line Per Port" is the "oversubscription" ratio for IVR ports. i.e. number of outbound calls to dial per each available IVR port. See LPA/LPP explanation in "Basic Concepts" section.

Answering Machine Treatment

Note that there is no application triggers for answering machines or abandoned calls.

For "Answering Machine", you have two options – either transfer to IVR or end the call. If you chose "Transfer to IVR", it will be transferred to the application trigger that was configured in general parameters section (see above).

For "Abandoned Calls" (caused by no IVR ports), the only option is to end the call. Thus no configurable parameter is available.

IVR Based Predictive Dialer

To create an "IVR Based Predictive Dialer", go to [**UCCX AppAdmin Portal > Subsystem > Outbound > Campaigns**], click "Add New". Choose "IVR Based" from "Campaign Type" drop-down. Choose "Predictive" from "Dialer Type" drop-down. Then click "Next".

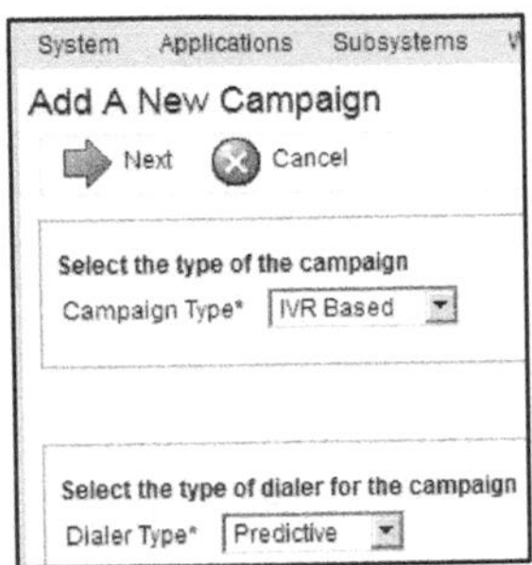

Figure 15-37 IVR Based Predictive

Next page is campaign specific parameters. Similar to "IVR Based Progressive Dialer", you have to configure application trigger in the general parameter section.

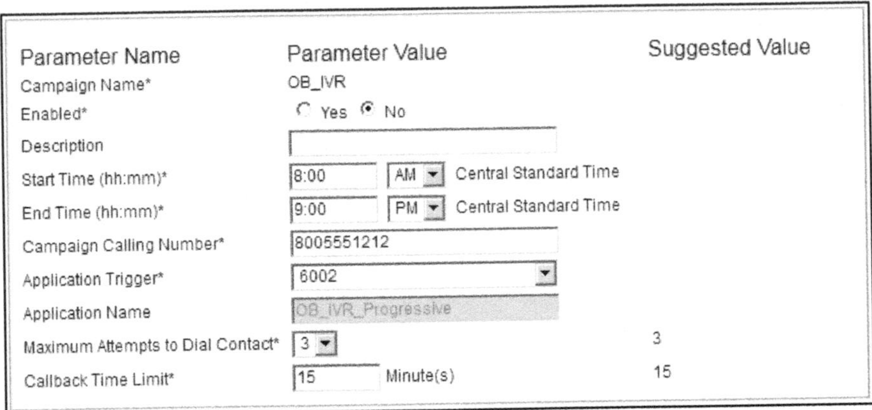

Figure 15-38 IVR Based Predictive - General Parameters

IVR Based Predictive Dialing options are very similar to Agent Based Predictive. Please refer to previous sections for explanation of each parameter.

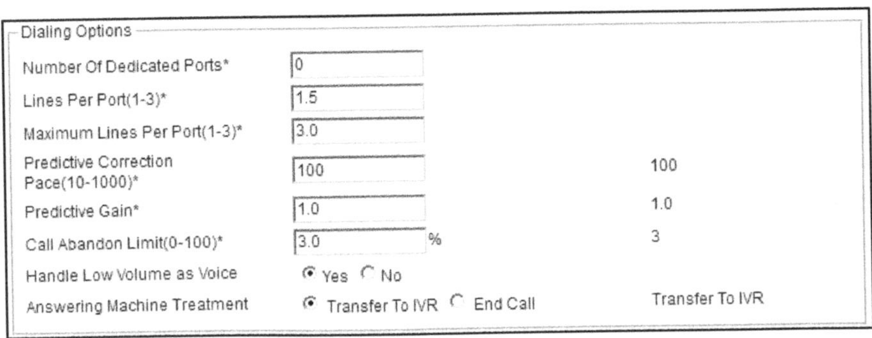

Figure 15-39 IVR Based Predictive - Dialing Options

Chapter 16 HTTP Trigger

HTTP Trigger Overview

HTTP trigger allows you to better integrate contact center functions with your web sites. For example:

1. Customer logs into online banking to review account activities.
2. Customer has question regarding one of the transactions.
3. Customer clicks on the "Call Me Now" button on the web page.
4. The backend system tries to find the best agent based on customer information, such as:
    a. Customer's preferred language
    b. The account (checking, saving, credit card) customer was reviewing when requesting the call
    c. Other information.
5. So that when customer receives the call, the agent already knows which account customer was having questions with.

UCCX intelligence was built on scripts. A script can be triggered by phone calls or online activities. That's why UCCX supports two kinds of triggers:

- Telephony Trigger
- HTTP Trigger

To understand how HTTP triggers work, you need to have some basic knowledge about HTTP, for example

- Hyperlinks or web buttons
- "HTTP GET" and "HTTP POST"
- Web Forms

General steps of deploying HTTP triggers are:

1. Create a script
2. Create an application to use the script
3. Create a HTTP trigger for the application

4. Build a web page to "call" the HTTP trigger

Create a script

- ➢ **Create a script**
- Create an application to use the script
- Create a HTTP trigger for the application
- Build a web page to "call" the HTTP trigger

We have discussed how to use script editor to create scripts. Please refer to [Script 101] on page 77 for details.

For demonstration purpose, we create a very simple script here called "WebCall.aef". This script does nothing but to return a file called "Test.html" to the requester via HTTP protocol.

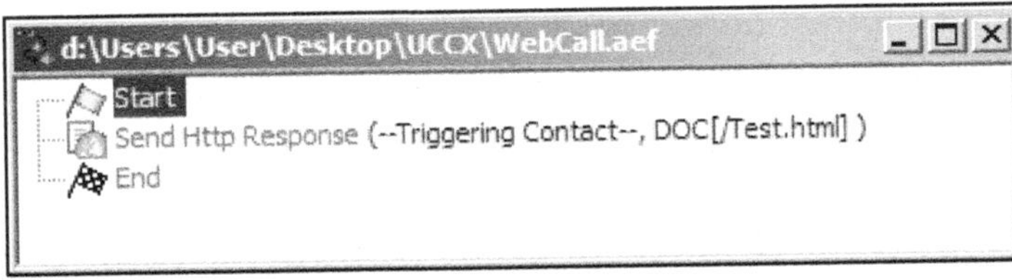

Figure 16-1 Sample Script

Content of the "Test.html" file is as below:

```
<html>

<center><font size="6">This is a test <u>HTML</u> document.</font></center>

</html>
```

Figure 16-2 Sample HTML File

We upload the "WebCall.aef" to UCCX via [**UCCX AppAdmin Portal > Applications > Script Management**].

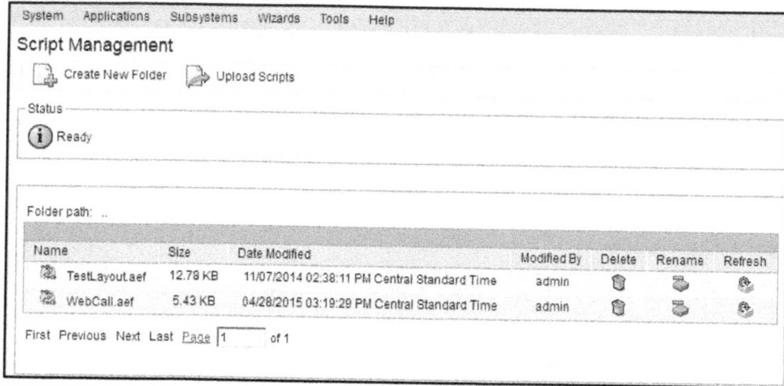

Figure 16-3 Script Management

We upload the "Test.html" to UCCX via [**UCCX AppAdmin Portal > Applications > Document Management**]. We may put the document into "default" folder.

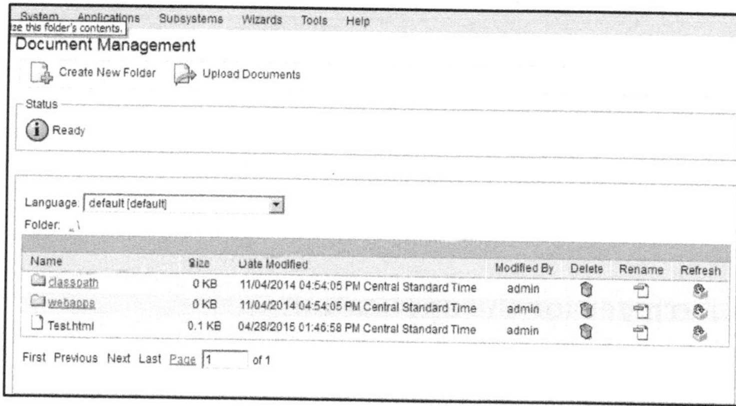

Figure 16-4 Document Management

Create an application to use the script

- ✓ Create a script
- ➢ **Create an application to use the script**
- Create a HTTP trigger for the application
- Build a web page to "call" the HTTP trigger

We have discussed how to create an application. Please refer to [UCCX: Provision Application] on page 62 for details. We are going to name our application "WebCall" and choose the "SCRIPT[WebCall.aef]" from drop-down menu.

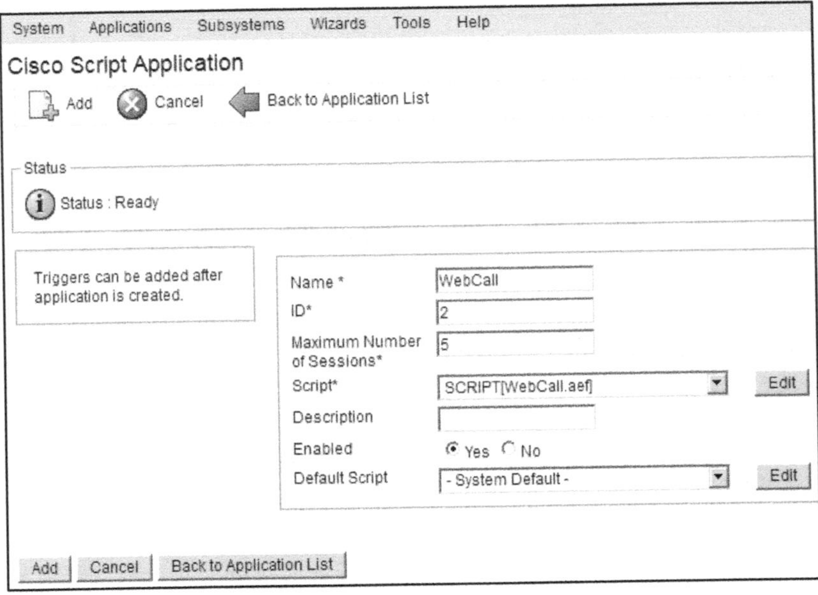

Figure 16-5 Creating Application

Create a HTTP trigger for the application

- ✓ Create a script
- ✓ Create an application to use the script
- ➢ **Create a HTTP trigger for the application**
- • Build a web page to "call" the HTTP trigger

After creating the application, we may click the "Add new trigger" link on the page.

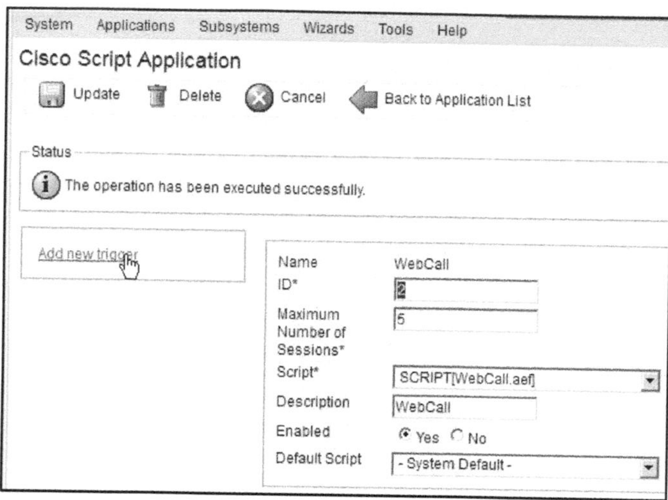

Figure 16-6 Add New Trigger

We will choose "Cisco HTTP Trigger" as the trigger type.

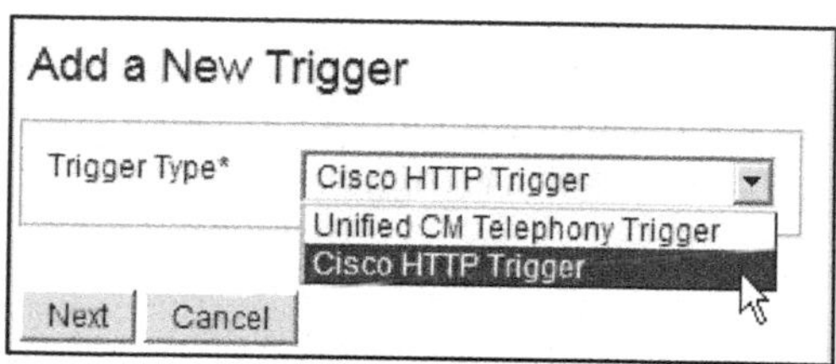

Figure 16-7 Trigger Type

On the next page, we enter an arbitary URL (Uniform Resource Locator) in the URL field. Please note:

1. You are creating a new URL. This URL could be anything. It does not have to match any pre-existing files or configuration.
2. Most special characters are not allowed in URL. To keep it simple, use only alphanumerical characters.

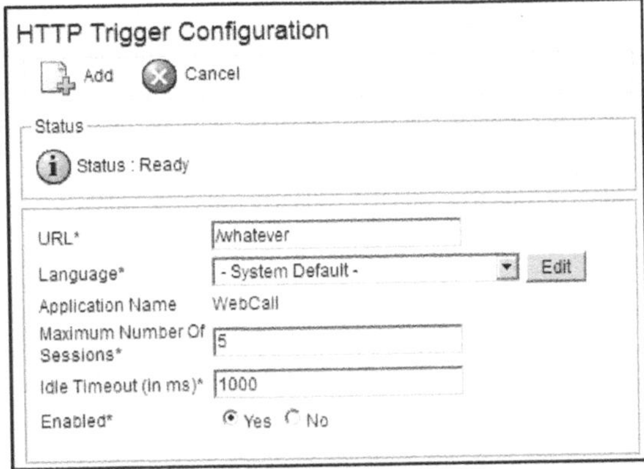

Figure 16-8 Creating HTTP Trigger

Build a web page to "call" the HTTP trigger

- ✓ Create a script
- ✓ Create an application to use the script
- ✓ Create a HTTP trigger for the application
- ➢ **Build a web page to "call" the HTTP trigger**

Now we have the application and HTTP trigger created. How do we use it? To use a HTTP trigger, a HTTP GET or HTTP POST has to hit the UCCX server on port 9080. This is how we "call" the HTTP trigger.

For example, on your company website, you may build create a button and associate it with a hyperlink like <a href="http://name-of-uccx-server:9080/whatever">. Please note we are referencing the HTTP trigger we created in previous step. We are not referencing any UCCX application, script or document.

When a customer clicks on the button on your website, the web browser will initiate a HTTP GET to the HTTP server on port 9080 with URL "/WebCall". This will trigger the UCCX run the script "WebCall.aef". The script will return a HTTP response to the customer's web browser. Result is as below.

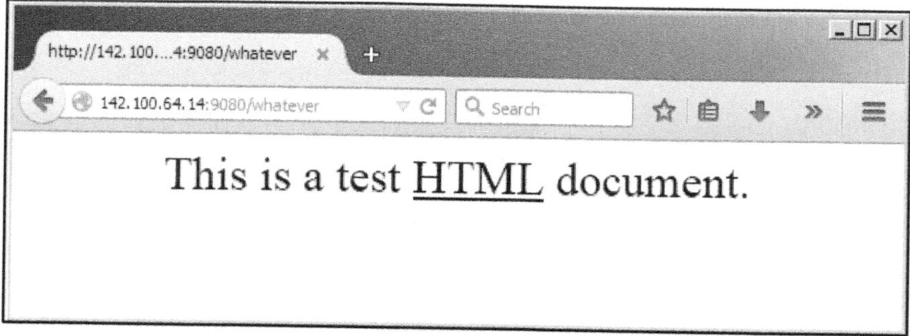

Figure 16-9 HTTP Trigger Result

You might wonder why take the trouble to create scripts, documents and applications. We may achieve the same result with simple, static HTML coding.

A UCCX script can provide dynamic results based on customer input. And the result is not limited to a web page. It can be a phone call to customer. Or anything you can do with the UCCX script language.

For a better, take a look at the "Script Repository" on Cisco.com. There are two scripts in the "release1" folder:

- webcallback.aef
- webcallbackQueueing.aef

The above scripts allow customer enter a callback number on the web page. Then initiate a call from within UCCX. Below is a screenshot of the webcallbackQueueing.aef script.

```
/* Accept the incoming call because it is the "phantom call" representing the web callback request */
Accept (--Triggering Contact--)
Delay 4 sec
Get Call Contact Info
/* Use Get Contact Info to retrieve the "Implementation ID" that will be used to retrieve the web callback session */
Get Contact Info (--Triggering Contact--)
/* Use the "Implementation ID" to retrieve the session, but not create a new session */
session = Get Session (media_id)
/* Use Get Session Info to retrieve the values initially passed in from the HTML form requesting a callback */
Get Session Info (session)
/* Map the values from the HTML form to variables that will be shown on the agent's desktop
    You will also need to create an ECC variable for the custom layout to be shown on the agent's desktop
    but the custom layout must be created in the Cisco Desktop Administrator */
Set Enterprise Call Info (--Triggering Contact--) Variables Used:name,numberToCall,description,"webcallback"
Queue:
Select Resource (--Triggering Contact-- from csq)
End
```

Figure 16-10 WebCallBack Example

Chapter 17 Database Subsystem

Overview of Database Subsystem

Most companies store customer information on database servers such as Oracle Database, Microsoft SQL, etc. UCCX scripts can query external databases to make use of the customer information.

In order for scripts to use external database, "Database" subsystem has to be configured on UCCX server first.

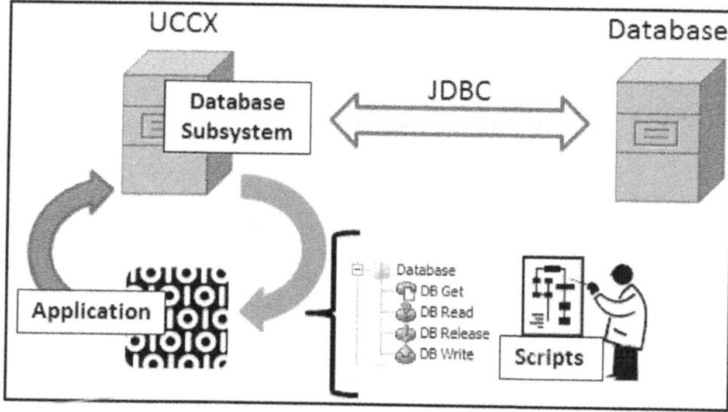

Figure 17-1 Database Subsystem

General steps of configuring database subsystem are as below:

1. Prepare Database Server
2. Upload JDBC Driver to UCCX Server
3. Configure Data Source
4. Test Data Source

Prepare Database Server

- ➢ **Prepare Database Server**
- Upload JDBC Driver to UCCX Server
- Configure Data Source
- Test Data Source

Preparing database server is out of the scope of this book as they are vendor/product specific. Generally speaking, we need to take care of the following:

1. Network communication between UCCX server and database server.

   Make sure they can reach each other and the database access ports are not blocked by firewall.

2. Authentication and authorization.

   Make sure database server support the authentication method UCCX is going to use. Make sure appropriate database access permission is granted. For example, Microsoft SQL server needs to enable "mixed mode" in authentication as UCCX cannot use "Windows authentication".

Upload JDBC Driver to UCCX Server

- ✓ Prepare Database Server
- ➢ **Upload JDBC Driver to UCCX Server**
- Configure Data Source
- Test Data Source

UCCX use JDBC (Java Database Connectivity) to talk to database server. Different database server (e.g. Oracle, DB2, Sybase, MS SQL) requires different JDBC driver on UCCX. Interestingly, UCCX server does not have any driver preloaded. We will have to find the driver ourselves and upload it to UCCX server. We will use MS SQL as an example.

We go to [**UCCX AppAdmin Portal > Subsystems > Database > Drivers**]. There is a drop-down menu called "Driver class name" that has the following selections:

- com.ibm.db2.jcc.DB2Driver – for IBM DB2
- oracle.jdbc.driver.OracleDriver – for Oracle
- net.sourceforge.jtds.jdbc.Driver – for Microsoft SQL
- com.sybase.jdbc2.jdbc.SybDriver – for Sybase

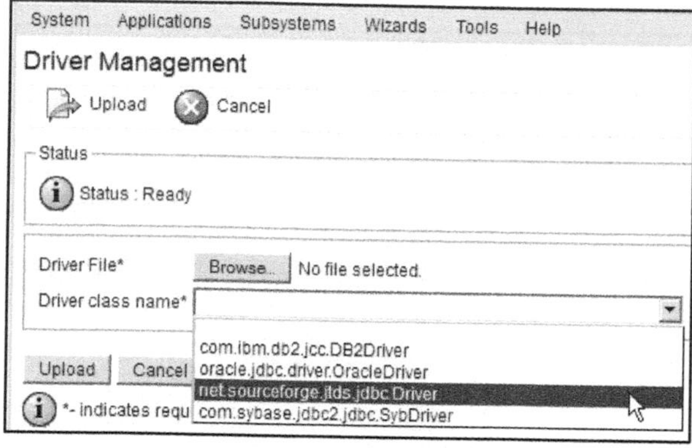

Figure 17-2 JDBC Drivers

We have to find the corresponding driver that matches the database server. Then upload it to UCCX server via this web page. When doing the upload, we need to tell UCCX which type it is.

We search Internet for "jdts" and "SQL". Found the driver on sourceforge.

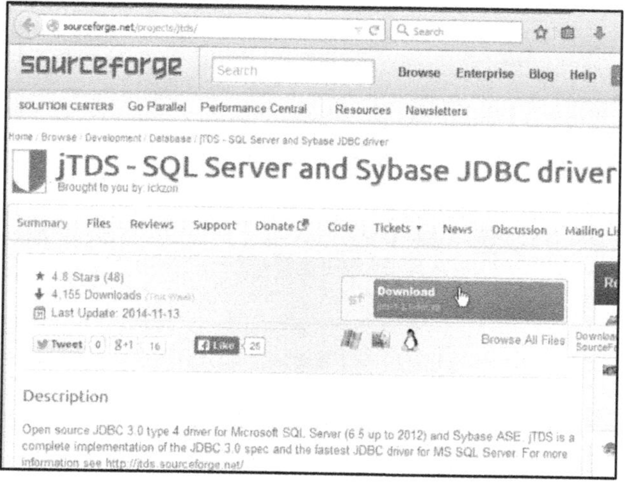

Figure 17-3 JDBC Driver for MS SQL

We download the driver (archive) and extract jtds-1.3.1.jar file from the archive, save it to our desktop. That is the only driver we need.

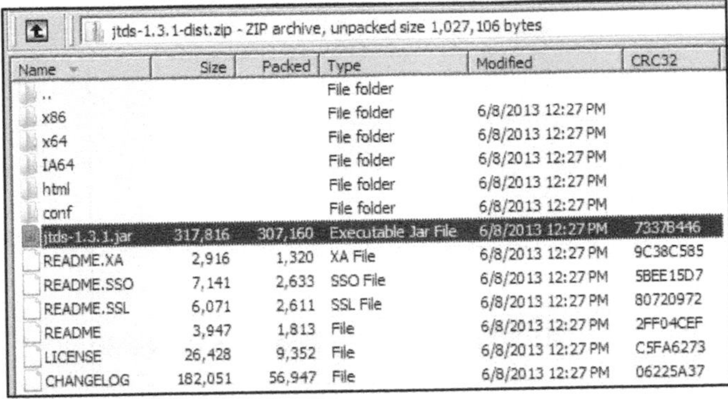

Figure 17-4 jar File in Archive

On UCCX web page, click "Browse" button > browse to the location where we save the jar file then choose it. From the drop-down menu, choose "net.sourceforge.jtds.jdbc.Driver" then click "Upload" button.

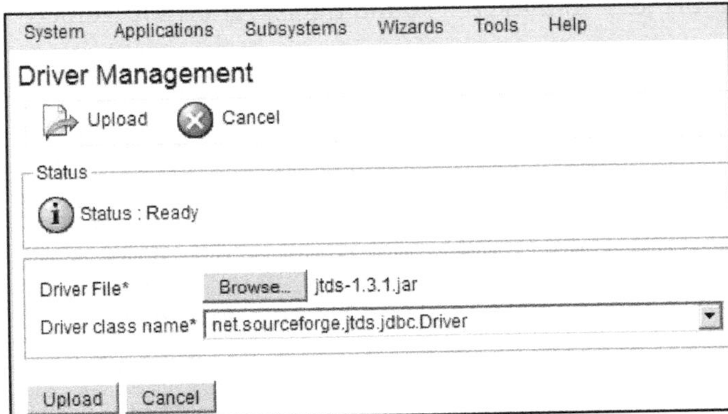

Figure 17-5 Driver Upload

You should see a screen like below after uploading the driver.

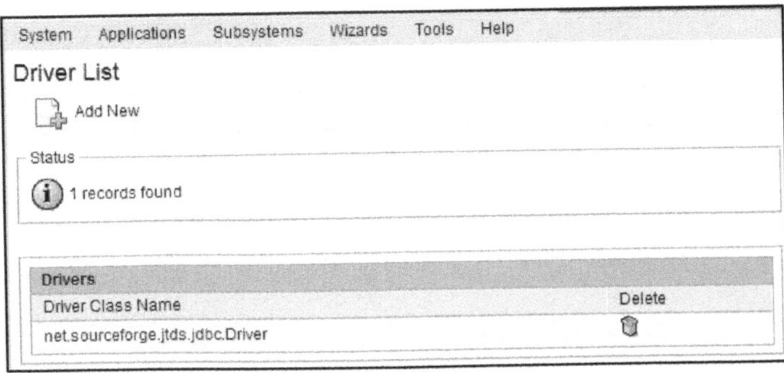

Figure 17-6 Driver Uploaded

Configure Data Source

- ✓ Prepare Database Server
- ✓ Upload JDBC Driver to UCCX Server
- ➢ **Configure Data Source**
- • Test Data Source

After uploading the JDBC driver, we will configure data source in the database subsystem so UCCX knows where to reach out for the database server. We may configure multiple data sources on UCCX server if needed.

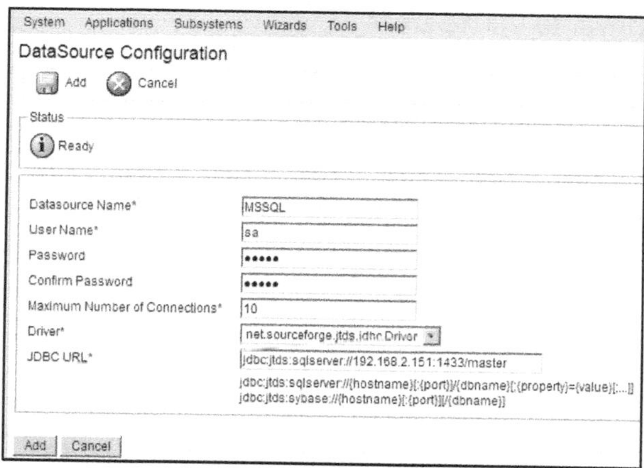

Figure 17-7 Configuring Data Source

"Datasource Name" could be any name you like. It does not have to match with server name. We use "MSSQL" here as an example.

"User Name" and "Password" is the credential to access database server. You should have pre-configured this on the database server and give it appropriate permissions.

"Maximum Number of Connections" depends on the application requirement. For testing purpose, we set it to 10 here.

Choose "net.sourceforge.jtds.jdbc.Driver" from the "Driver" drop-down list. If you haven't uploaded any driver yet, you won't see any selectable options in this drop-down.

Enter the JDBC URL following the onscreen syntax. In our example, it is "jdbc:jtds:sqlserver://192.168.2.151:1433/master". "192.168.2.151" is the IP of the database server. "1433" is the TCP port that the database server is listening on. "master" is the database name.

Click "Add" button. UCCX server will test the connection and let you know if it failed or succeeded.

Test Data Source

- ✓ Prepare Database Server
- ✓ Upload JDBC Driver to UCCX Server
- ✓ Configure Data Source
- ➢ **Test Data Source**

After configuring the data souce, we may test it from UCCX AppAdmin portal or Script Editor.

Test from UCCX AppAdmin Portal

From AppAdmin portal, we may click the "Test Connection" button on the DataSource Configuration page, like the screen below.

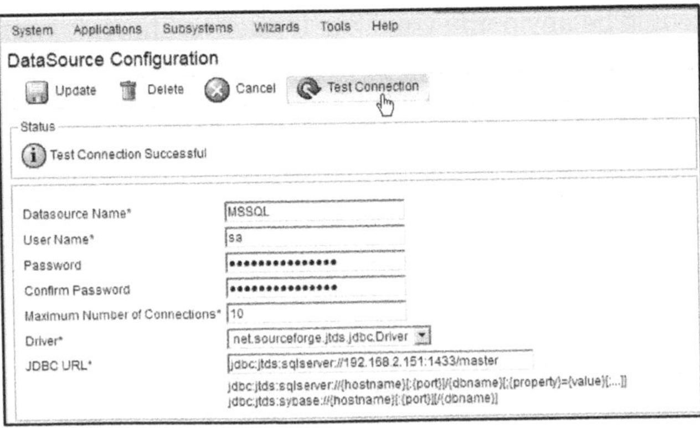

Figure 17-8 Test Data Source from AppAdmin Portal

Test from UCCX Script Editor

If you want to test from UCCX script editor, make sure the editor has network connectivity to UCCX and database server.

Create a new script with "DB Read" step in it. Right-click the "DB Read" step and choose "Properties". On "General" tab, click the "Refresh Database Schema" button. Editor will take a while to pull the information from servers.

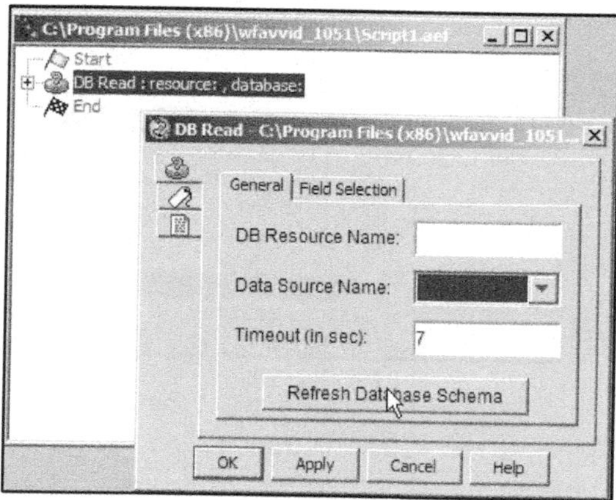

Figure 17-9 DB Read Step

Now if we click the "Data Source Name" drop-down menu, we will see the DSN (Data Source Name) we just created on UCCX server, which is "MSSQL".

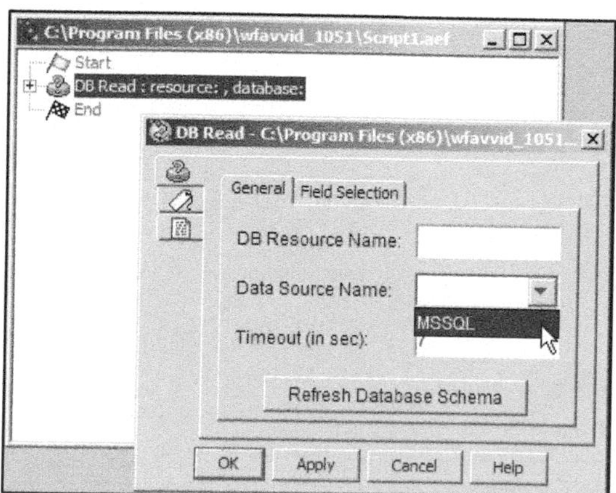

Figure 17-10 Data Source Name Pulled from UCCX Server

If we want to futher test it we may go to "Field Selection" tab. We may either browse the tables from the "Show all fields (select table/view)" drop-down menu. Or we can actually run some SQL query to see if database access permission was set up properly. "Number of rows returned" is the result of the SQL query.

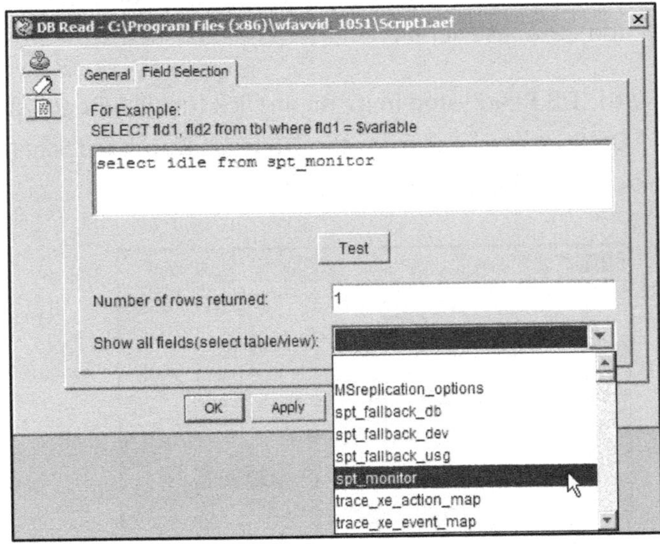

Figure 17-11 Field Selection Tab

Chapter 18 Reporting

Overview

Reporting is very important to contact center operations. Many business decisions are based on metrics reported such as wait time in queue, rate of abandoned calls, etc.

UCCX separates reporting functions into three categories:

- Realtime Report – Realtime statistics, such as number of calls in queue, number of agents logged in, etc.
- Realtime Snapshot – Used by 3rd-party wallboard systems.
- Historical Report – Detailed report for a specific period of time

Realtime Report

Realtime report can be accessed from [**UCCX AppAdmin Portal > Tools > Realtime Reporting**].

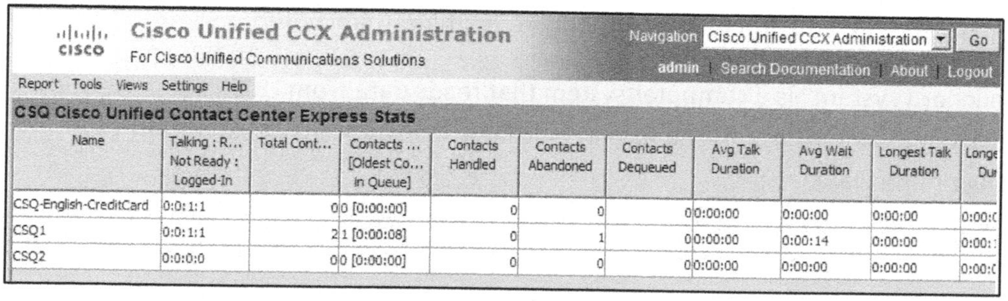

cisco **Cisco Unified CCX Administration**
For Cisco Unified Communications Solutions
Navigation Cisco Unified CCX Administration Go
admin | Search Documentation | About | Logout
Report Tools Views Settings Help

CSQ Cisco Unified Contact Center Express Stats

Name	Talking : R... Not Ready : Logged-In	Total Cont...	Contacts ... [Oldest Co... in Queue]	Contacts Handled	Contacts Abandoned	Contacts Dequeued	Avg Talk Duration	Avg Wait Duration	Longest Talk Duration	Longe Dur
CSQ-English-CreditCard	0:0:1:1	0	0 [0:00:00]	0	0	0	0:00:00	0:00:00	0:00:00	0:00:
CSQ1	0:0:1:1	2	1 [0:00:08]	0	1	0	0:00:00	0:00:14	0:00:00	0:00:
CSQ2	0:0:0:0	0	0 [0:00:00]	0	0	0	0:00:00	0:00:00	0:00:00	0:00:

Figure 18-1 Built-in Realtime Report Example

To access the built-in realtime report, we use web browsers with Java plug-in. UCCX use self-signed certificates. Java plug-in by default won't trust self-signed certificates. You will have to adjust the Java security settings on the client computer. You might want to lower the Java security and add UCCX server to the Java "Exception Site List".

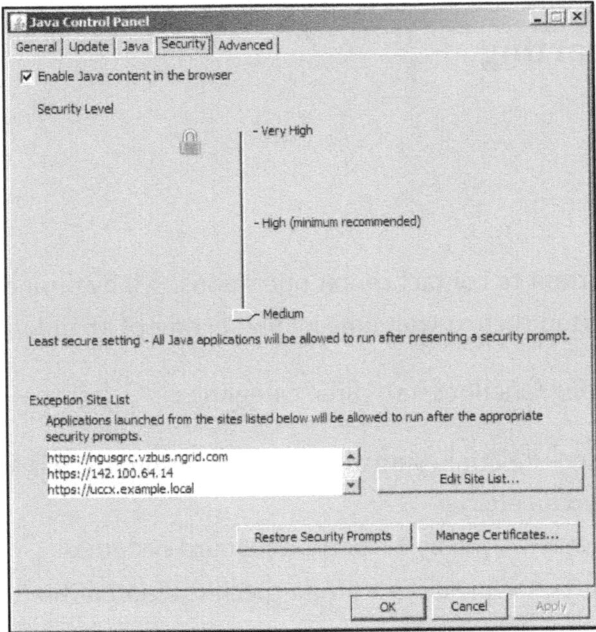

Figure 18-2 Java Settings in Windows Control Panel

Realtime Snapshot

Realtime snapshot is used by 3rd-party wallboard systems. If you don't plan to use wallboard system, you don't have to configure realtime snapshot.

A "wallboard system" is a computer system that reads data from UCCX database and displays the data in a customized format on a large display (usually flat screen TVs hanging on the wall).

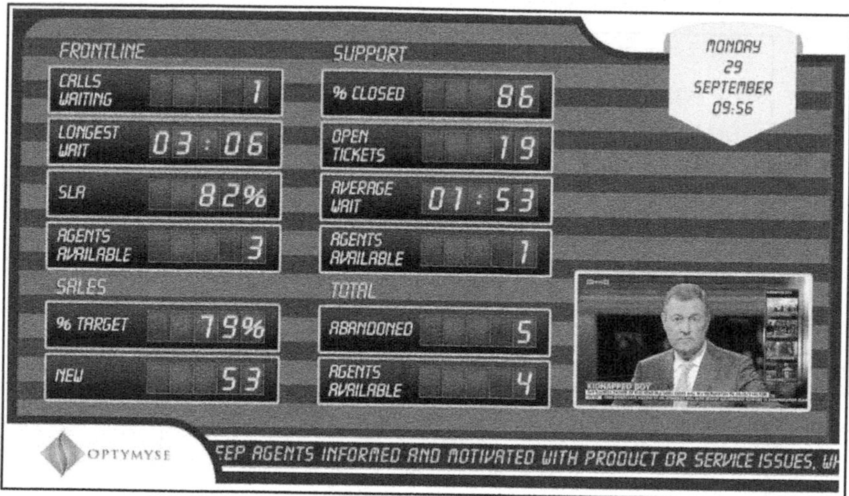

Figure 18-3 Wallboard System Example

Realtime Snapshot consists of two UCCX database tables – "RtCSQsSummary" and "RtICDStatistics". If configured, UCCX will write realtime statistics into these two tables in specific interval (5, 10, 15, 20 or 25 seconds). That is why it is called "snapshot".

For security reason, 3rd-party wallboard systems are only allowed to read the two snapshot tables and nothing else.

General steps of configuring realtime snapshot are as below:

1. Configure Real Time Snapshot (UCCX side)
2. Configure wallboard password (UCCX side)
3. Configure DSN (wallboard side)

Configure Real Time Snapshot (UCCX side)

- ➢ **Configure Real Time Snapshot (UCCX side)**
- Configure wallboard password (UCCX side)
- Configure DSN (wallboard side)

To configure the real time snapshot, go to [**UCCX AppAdmin Portal > Tools > Real Time Snapshot Config**]

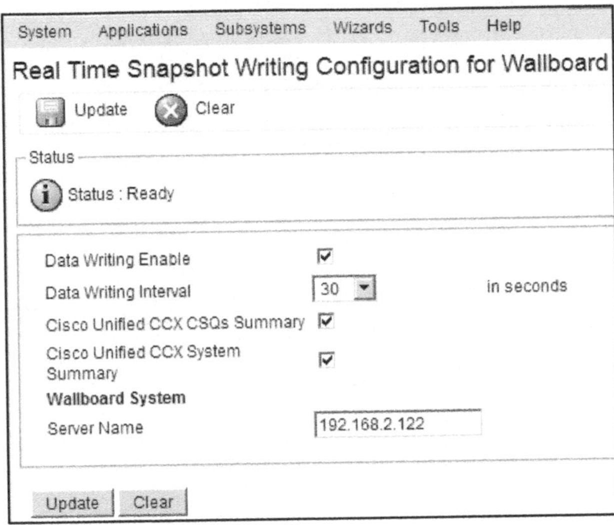

Figure 18-4 Real Time Snapshot Configuration

Enable all checkboxes. For your reference, the relationship between menu items and databases tables is as below:

Menu Items	Database Tables
UCCX CSQs Summary	RtCSQsSummary
UCCX System Summary	RtICDStatistics

The "Server Name" here is actually a white list (allow list) of wallboard systems. Only the IP addresses on the list can access the snapshot database table above. This is for security reason. You may separate multiple IP addresses with comma.

To verify the white list, you may try to access an UCCX URL from the wallboard system. The URL is "http://address-of-uccx-server/uccx/isDBMaster". For example:

- We configured 192.168.2.122 on the white list ("wallboard system server name").
- Our UCCX server IP address is 142.100.64.14

If we access URL "http://142.100.64.14/uccx/isDBMaster" from 192.168.2.122, we'll see a page with XML file like below:

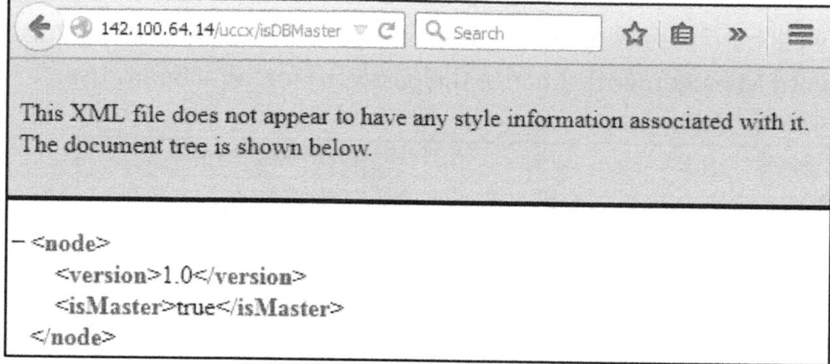
This XML file does not appear to have any style information associated with it. The document tree is shown below.

```
- <node>
    <version>1.0</version>
    <isMaster>true</isMaster>
  </node>
```

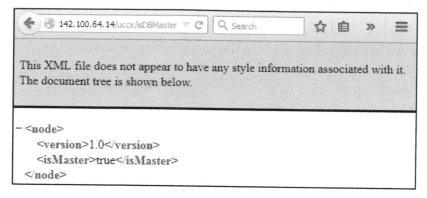

Figure 18-5 IP on White List

If we access URL "http://142.100.64.14/uccx/isDBMaster" from another IP address, we'll see a page with 404 (Request cannot be completed) message like below:

Figure 18-6 IP not on White List

Configure Real Time Snapshot (UCCX side)

- ✓ Configure Real Time Snapshot (UCCX side)
- ➢ **Configure wallboard password (UCCX side)**
- Configure DSN (wallboard side)

To configure wallboard password on UCCX side we go to [**UCCX AppAdmin Portal > Tools > Password Management**]. Change the password for "WallBoard User".

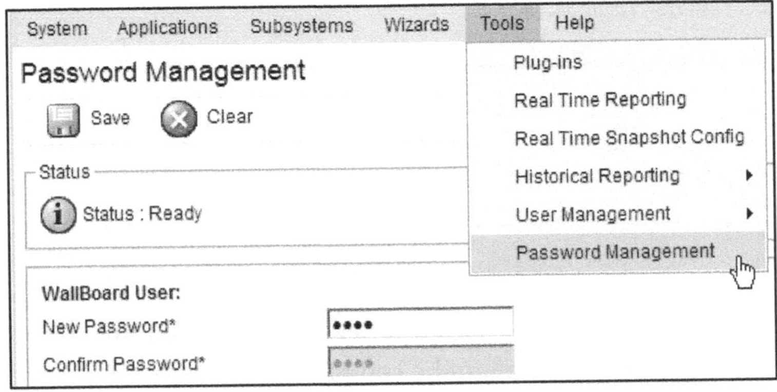

Figure 18-7 Wallboard Password

Please note that you can only change the password. You cannot change the username. The username is hardcoded to "uccxwallboard".

Configure DSN (wallboard side)

- ✓ Configure Real Time Snapshot (UCCX side)
- ✓ Configure wallboard password (UCCX side)
- ➢ **Configure DSN (wallboard side)**

Wallboard system uses ODBC client to access UCCX database. As UCCX uses Informix database system, Informix ODBC driver needs to be installed on wallboard side. General procedures as below:

Step 1 Install the wallboard software and IBM Informix ODBC Driver (IDS Version 3.0.0.13219 and above) on the wallboard client desktop.

Note You can download the Informix ODBC driver from the following URL: http://www14.software.ibm.com/webapp/download/search.jsp?rs=ifxdl. Download the IBM Informix Client Software Development Kit (CSDK) Version 3.00 or higher for the operating system you are installing with the wallboard client. More information about the CSDK can be found at the following URL:http://www.ibm.com/software/data/informix/tools/csdk/.

Step 2 Select Start > Settings > Control Panel.

Step 3 From the Control Panel menu, select Administrative Tools > Data Sources ODBC to launch the OBDC Data Source Administrator.

Step 4 Click the System DSN tab. Then click Add to open the Create New Data Source dialog box.

Step 5 Scroll down to locate and select the IBM INFORMIX ODBC DRIVER.

Step 6 Click Finish to open the IBM Informix Setup dialog box.

Step 7 On the General tab, enter and apply a Data Source Name and Description.

Step 8 On the Connection tab, enter the values for the fields as shown in the table below:

Field	Description
Server Name	This is the instance name of the Informix database. Informix database instance name can be formed using Host Name of the Unified CCX server by following these conventions: • Convert all upper case letters to lower case. • Replace hyphens with underscore. • Add the letter "i" as a prefix to the instance name, if the hostname starts with a number. • Append the letters "_uccx" to the instance name. For example, if the hostname is "802UCCX-Ha-Node1", enter "i802uccx_ha_node1_uccx" in the Server Name field.
Host Name	Enter the hostname of the primary Unified CCX server.
Service	Enter *1504*.
Protocol	Enter *onsoctcp*.
Options	Leave blank.
Database Name	Enter *db_cra*.
User ID	Enter *uccxwallboard*. This is the user id of the Unified CCX database created for wallboard.
Password	The password for the wallboard user that has been configured. You can change the password by going to Tools > Password

	Management submenu option from the Unified CCX Administration menu bar.

Step 9 Click Apply.

Step 10 Click the Environment tab and enter the values for the following fields:

Field	Description
Client Locale	Enter *en_US.UTF8.*
Database Locale	Enter *en_US.UTF8.*

Step 11 Click OK.

Step 12 Return to the Connection tab and click Apply and Test Connection.

If the phrase "Test completed successfully" is returned, click OK.

If the test is unsuccessful, return to the configuration sequence and fix any errors.

Historical Report

CUIC (Cisco Unified Intelligence Center)

Historical report can be accessed through CUIC (Cisco Unified Intelligence Center). CUIC is a powerful reporting tool that can be co-locating with UCCX server or acting as a standalone server. By default, CUIC collocates with UCCX and can be access through the URL https://*<address-of-uccx>*:8444/cuic.

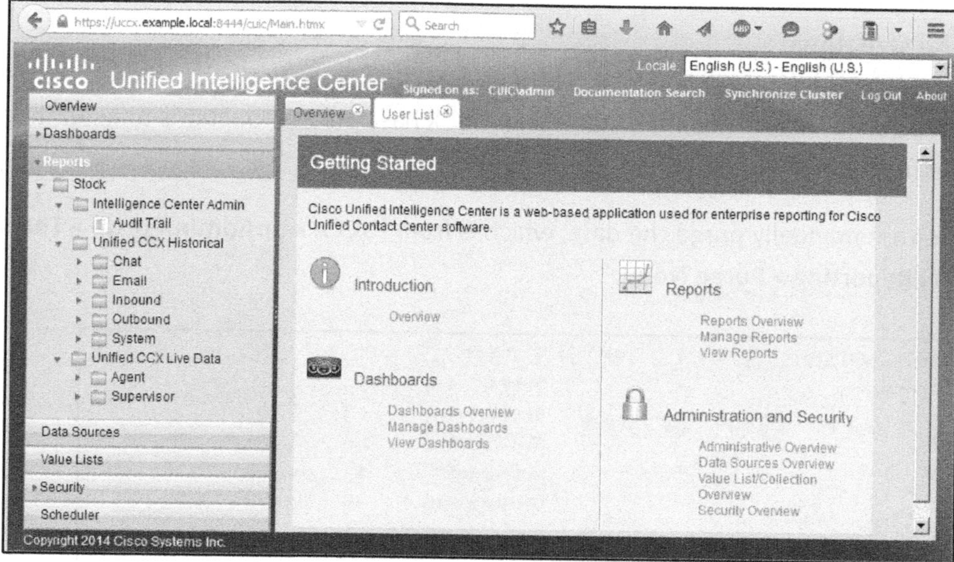

Figure 18-8 CUIC - Cisco Unified Intelligence Center

How to use CUIC is out of the scope of this book as CUIC itself alone deserves another book.

CUIC SMTP Configuration

CUIC can send scheduled reports by email if SMTP was configured under [**UCCX AppAdmin Portal > Tools > Historical Reporting > SMTP Configuration**].

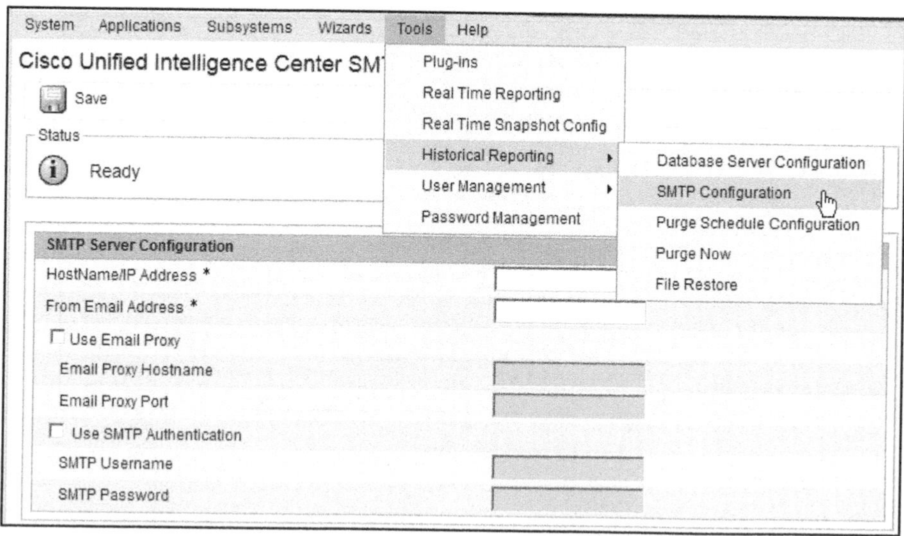

Figure 18-9 Historical Report (CUIC) SMTP Settings

Keep the size down

UCCX uses internal database to store historical data. UCCX cannot use external database to store historical data. That is why UCCX has "purge" functions to keep the database from overflow.

We can either manually purge the data, which is from [**UCCX AppAdmin Portal > Tools > Historical Reporting > Purge Now**]:

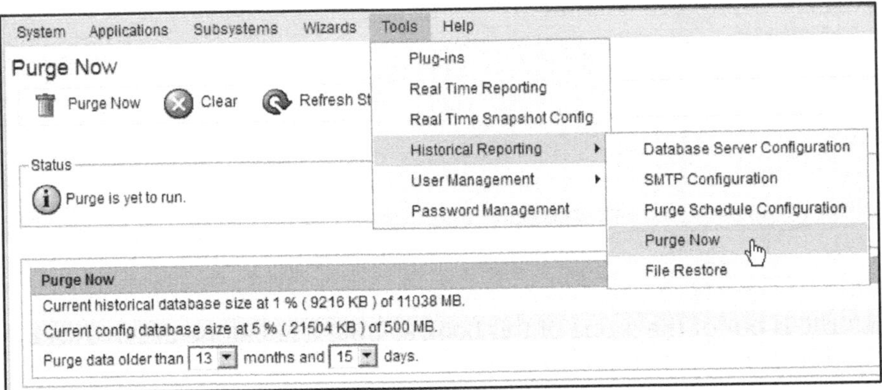

Figure 18-10 Manual Purge

Or we can set up auto purge through [**UCCX AppAdmin Portal > Tools > Historical Reporting > Purge Schedule Configuration**]

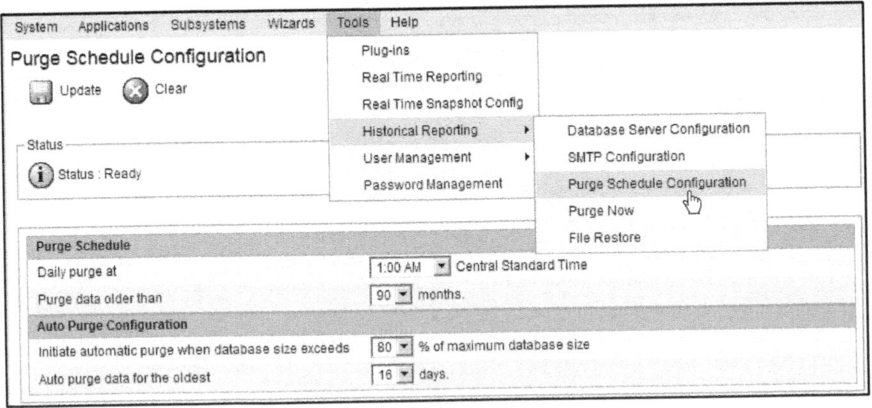

Figure 18-11 Purge Schedule Configuration

3rd-Party Reporting Tool

If you should use a 3rd-party reporting tool (such as Crystal Report) you may do it over ODBC. Same procedure as mentioned before:

1. UCCX is the server. Reporting tool is the client.
2. Informix ODBC driver is needed on client side as UCCX internal database is Informix.
3. DSN (Data Source Name) password is set on [**UCCX AppAdmin Portal > Tools > Password Management**]. Change the password for "Historical Reporting User". Again, the username is hardcoded to "uccxhruser". You cannot change the username.

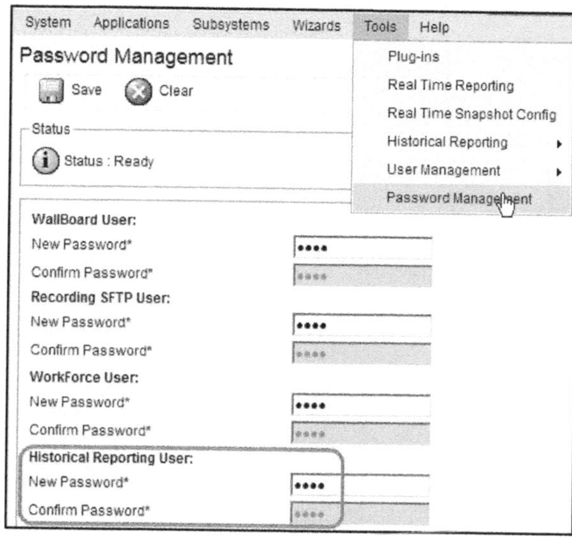

Figure 18-12 Historical Reporting User

Chapter 19 Troubleshooting

Troubleshooting Overview

UCCX has many components. Those components interact with different systems such as CUCM, phones, voice gateways, etc. In order to solve a problem quickly and effectively, we need to have some troubleshooting methodology.

1. Have a good problem description

   Instead of "call center down" or "agent didn't work" we should have a more specific symptom description. A good problem description usually consists of the following:

   - What happened? For example, "We have a customer hotline 800-555-1212 that is handled by UCCX system. Today at about 9AM, we noticed that all calls to that number got a busy signal."
   - What was supposed to happen? For example, "When call into 800-555-1212, the caller is supposed to hear a greeting of 'Welcome to contact ABC bank...'."
2. Have a good system diagram and/or description

   For example, how does the phone number 800-555-1212 associate with the CUCM CTI Route Point? If 800-555-1212 is not the DN of the Route Point, where the digit manipulation was done? Was it on the voice gateway or on the CUCM?

3. Use the symptom to isolate the problem

   For example:

   - If the caller got busy signal the call is most likely not hitting the UCCX yet. We should look at CUCM first.
   - If the caller got the announcement like "I am sorry but we are experiencing technical difficulty..." that is from UCCX and most likely a script problem.

- If the call was dropped when the caller was talking to the agent, it is unlikely the UCCX problem because UCCX is out of the picture at that point of time.

4. Use the easiest and quickest method to isolate the problem

   Instead of asking for tons of logs, packet captures, we should perform some quick/easy test to isolate the problem. For example:

   - Do we have the same problem (symptom) when calling from external and internal? Say, 800-555-1212 is the external number, 1212 is the corresponding internal DN. Try to call 800-555-1212 from a cell phone and call 1212 from an internal phone. If the problem only happens on external calls, it is unlikely the UCCX issue.
   - If UCCX is handling multiple hotline numbers, are they all having the same issue? If yes, the problem is system wide like out of memory, hard drive failure, etc. If not, the problem is probably related to misconfiguration.

Configuration Repository

Configurations control software behavior. Understand where and how configuration are stored helps us troubleshoot problems. Ideally, all configurations should be stored in a single place. For example, Windows registry is a configuration repository. However, due to historical reasons, UCCX has three different configuration repositories:

UCCX Database (Informix)

Most Cisco appliances (such as CUCM, CER, CUPS, Unity, etc.) use Informix database as configuration repository. UCCX uses database to store call routing related configurations, such as CSQs, Agent Skills, etc.

XML Files

UCCX uses XML files to store system related configurations, such as cluster setup, JTAPI provider, etc.

Spanlink Directory

Remember Desktop Suite was developed by Spanlink (now Calabrio). Spanlink decided to store Desktop Suite related configuration in a directory service called "Spanlink Directory". Directory Service is a way to store centralized configurations, such as Microsoft Active Directory, OpenLDAP, etc.

Tools

Some of the tools are provided by Cisco and safe to use, for example "Real Time Monitoring Tool" (RTMT). Some of the tools are provided by Cisco but should be used with caution such as CET Tool. Some of the tools are from third party such as Wireshark, LDAP Browser and WinGrep.

Cisco Unified CCX Serviceability Portal

UCCX Serviceability can be accessed via URL https://*ip-of-uccx*/uccxservice. It is a web portal allows you start/stop UCCX services, configure trace levels, etc. You may log into serviceability portal with the same credential you used to log into UCCX AppAdmin portal.

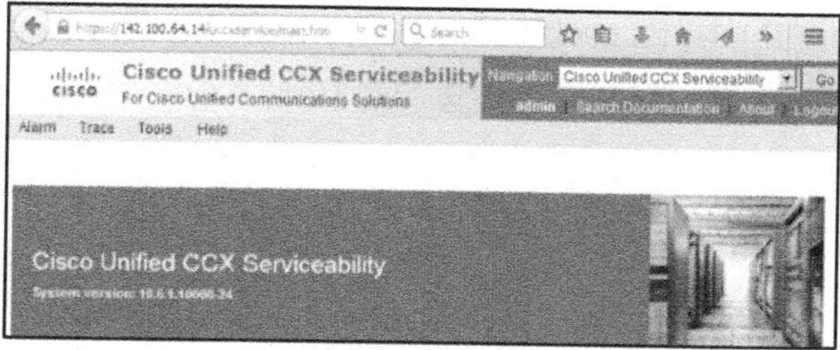

Figure 19-1 UCCX Serviceability

Tools > Control Center – Network Services

One the most important functions of serviceability is to start/stop services (or see the state of services). To do that, you go to [**UCCX Serviceability Portal > Tools > Control Center – Network Services**]. Services are grouped into categories and sub-categories. You may click on the triangle icon to expand/collapse groups.

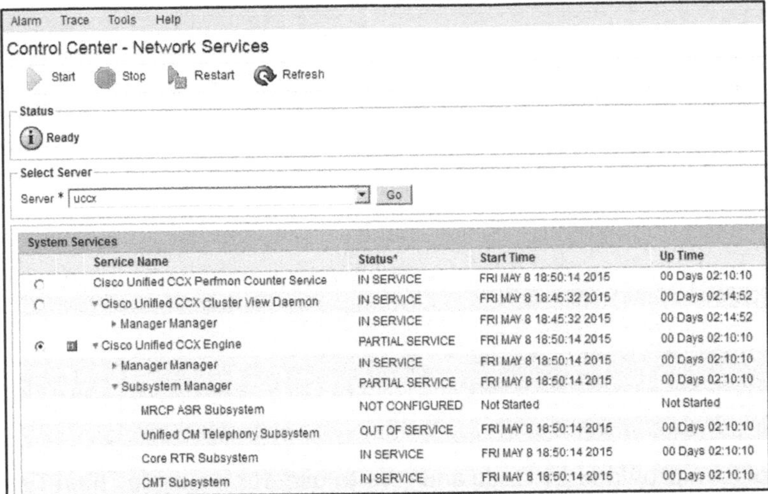

Figure 19-2 Control Center

To Start/Stop/Restart a service, select the radio button next to the service, then click the desired action button at the top of the screen. Please note that you can only select top tier services. You cannot select sub-services. For example, you may restart "Cisco Unified CCX Engine" service. However, you cannot restart "CMT Subsystem" alone, which is a sub-service of "Cisco Unified CCX Engine".

"Status" column indicates the service running state:

- IN SERVICE = Running without problem
- OUT OF SERVICE = Not able to run (error)
- NOT CONFIGURED = Not a problem at all. You just haven't configured it yet
- PARTIAL SERVICE = Running with error. Or at least one of the sub-services is having problem

In the example screenshot above,

- "CMT Subsystem" is running without problem.
- "Unified CM Telephony Subsystem" is having severe problem and not running
- "MRCP ASR Subsystem" is not running because it is not configured, which is OK
- "Subsystem Manager" is in partial service because some of its sub-services are having problem

The "Refresh" button on the top is to refresh the service status. Please do not use the web browser's fresh button (F5 key on Windows). Web browser's refresh button means "repeat the last action". For example, you restarted the "Cisco Unified CCX

Engine" service. It will take a couple minute to restart all sub-services. You want to refresh the service status and see if all sub-services are up. If you use the web browser's fresh button, it will repeat the last action, which is to restart the "Cisco Unified CCX Engine" again!

Trace > Configuration

To save system resource, most of the trace options are turned off by default. If you are troubleshooting a problem, you might want to turn on some of the trace options. This is done from [**UCCX Serviceability Portal > Trace > Configuration**].

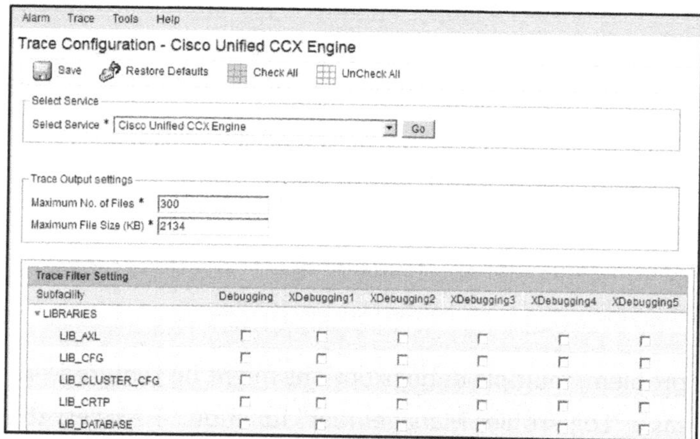

Figure 19-3 Trace > Configuration

Follow the procedures below to turn on trace options:

1. Select the service you want to trace from "Select Service" drop-down menu. For example, if you are troubleshooting call routing issues, you want to select "Cisco Unified CCX Engine" because it is the component that controls contact center call routing.
2. Enable debug options for corresponding sub-components. For example, "CCX Engine" has many sub-components such as CTI, Chat, Email, etc. For each component, you may enable different debug levels. "Debugging" is general debug. "XDebugging1" to "XDebugging5" are more in-depth debug from least verbose to most verbose level.

"Maximum No. of Files" and "Maximum File Size (KB)" control the total log size for this particular service. For example, if the "Maximum No. of Files=300" and "Maximum File

Size (KB)=2134", the maximum log size for "CCX Engine" is 300x2134 = 640,200KB. That is about 640MB.

UCCX writes log files in a circular style. If the log reaches the maximum size, UCCX will start overwriting the log files from the oldest one.

How much you should set those numbers really depends on the situation. If you are troubleshooting a problem that happens at random time, you might want a larger log buffer so valuable information didn't get overwritten quickly.

As a best practice, do not set the file size bigger than 2134KB. Bigger files degrade system performance. If you want a larger log buffer, you should increase the number of files instead of the size of the file. For example, Instead of increasing the file size from 2MB to 4MB, you should increase the number of files from 300 to 600.

Trace > Profile

The most frequently asked question on trace debug is "How do I know which debug to turn on and at what level?"

To troubleshoot a problem, multiple debugs options might be required. To make this task easier, UCCX has a "Log Profiles Management" function. To access this function, go to [**UCCX Serviceability Portal > Trace > Profile**].

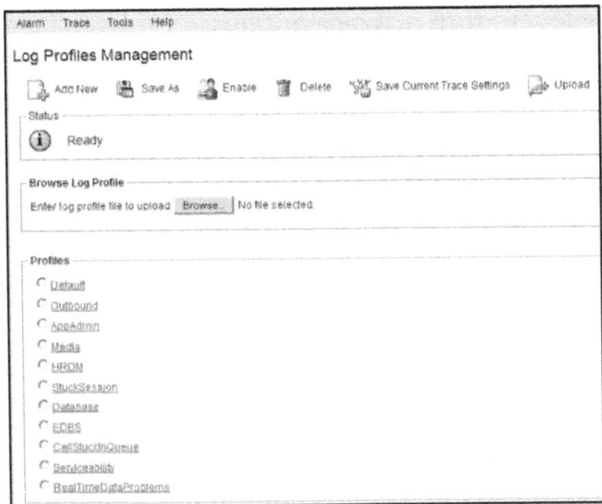

Figure 19-4 Log Profile Management

A Log profile is a set of pre-defined debug options that are related to a specific feature or function. For example, there is a pre-defined profile called "Outbound". If you are troubleshooting outbound dialer problems, you may enable this profile by select the radio button next to it, then click the "Enable" button. What it does is to enable the debug options that are needed to troubleshoot outbound functions.

If you are curious, you may click on the "Outbound" profile to see what debug options are included. It includes the following:

- SS_CM: Debugging
- SS_OB: Debugging, XDebugging1, XDebugging2, XDebugging3, XDebugging4, XDebugging5
- SS_RM: Debugging, XDebugging1, XDebugging2

Besides the pre-defined profiles, you may create your own profiles. You may also modify the pre-defined profiles to meet your needs.

Real Time Monitoring Tool (RTMT)

Real Time Monitoring Tool (RTMT) is a Cisco-built Java-based tool to monitor system statistics (such as memory, CPU, number of calls, etc.) and collect log files.

RTMT can be downloaded from [**UCCX AppAdmin Portal > Tools > Plug-ins**]. RTMT can be used on Windows or Linux.

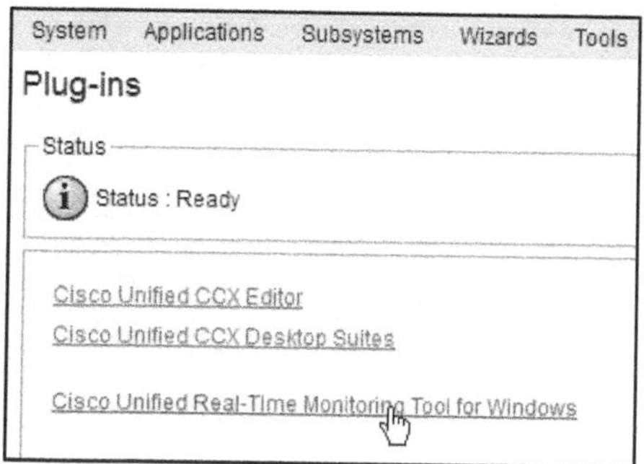

Figure 19-5 Download RTMT Plug-in

The first time launching RTMT, you will be prompted to enter the IP address of the UCCX server.

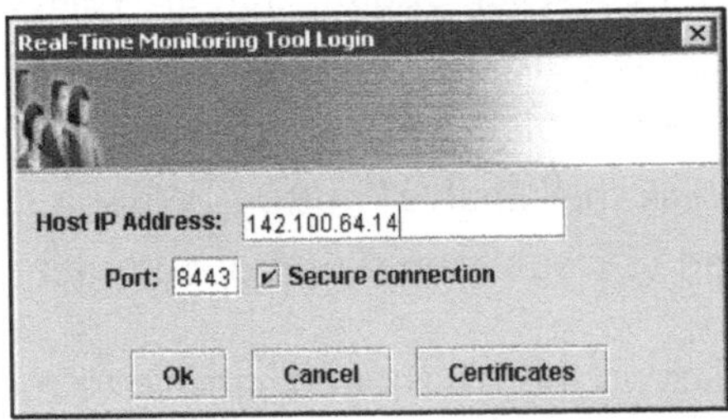

Figure 19-6 RTMT - Host IP

If you never connected to this host before, you will get a certificate warning. Just click "Accept" button.

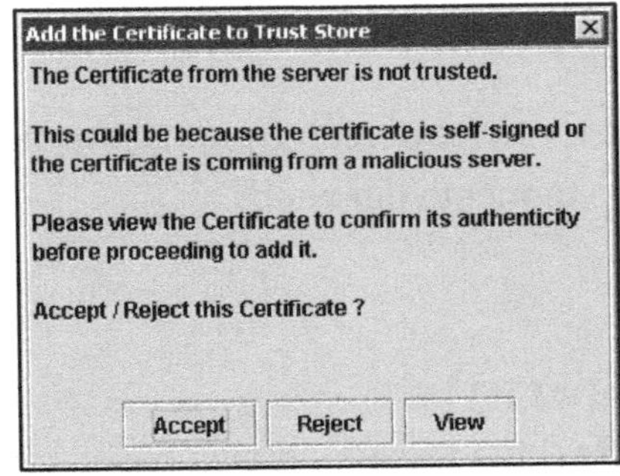

Figure 19-7 RTMT - Certificate Warning

Next you will see the logon screen. Enter the same credential you use on UCCX AppAdmin portal.

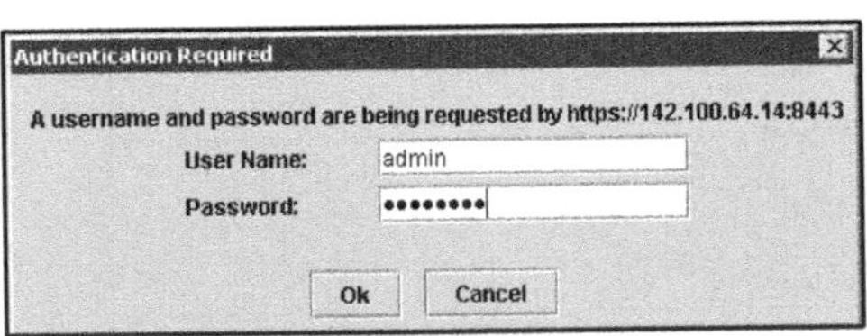

Figure 19-8 RTMT - Logon Screen

After logon, the main screen is as below.

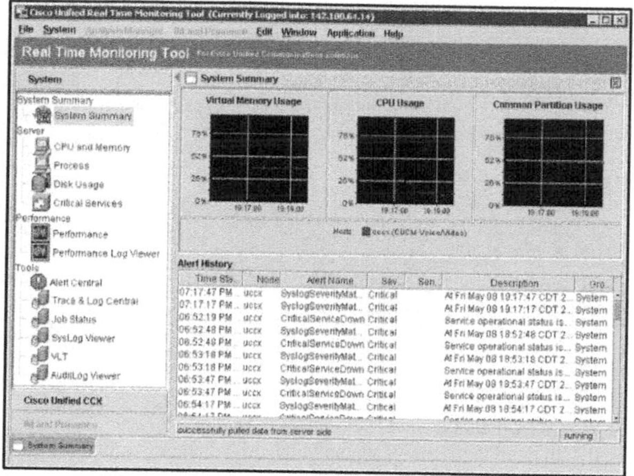

Figure 19-9 RTMT - Main Screen

RTMT has many functions. What we are most interested here is the log collecting function. From the navigation panel on the left, click “Trace & Log Center”. From the middle panel, double-click “Collect Files”.

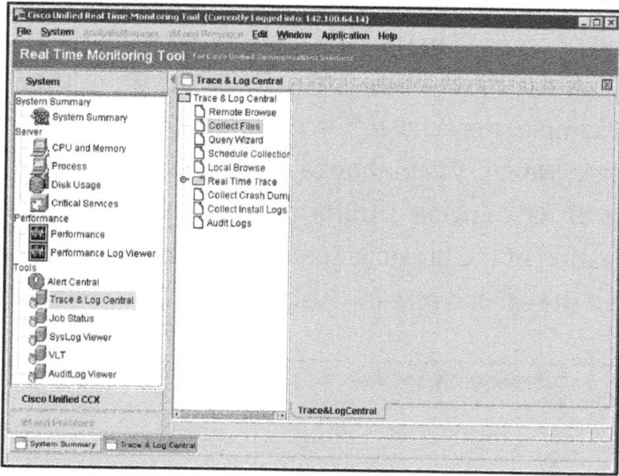

Figure 19-10 RTMT - Collect Files

You will be presented a list of different traces. You may select specific server by enabling the checkboxes in corresponding column. Or enable the checkboxes in “All Servers” column to select all servers in the cluster. Click “Next” button to go to the next screen.

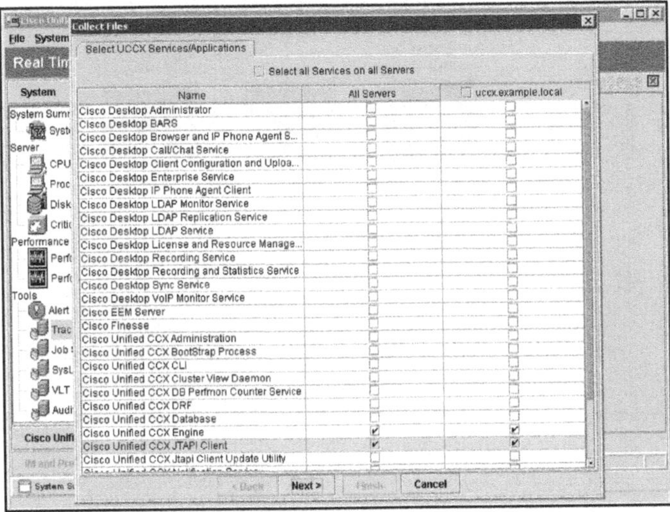

Figure 19-11 Traces List

Here comes the confusing part of RTMT. The next screen is another list of traces. From UI (User Interface) design perspective, the "Next" button usually means "Next Step" or "Next Function" instead of "second part of the previous screen". So most of the users would think the next screen is a list of sub-categories of the items they chose in the previous screen. For example, they chose "Cisco Unified CCX Engine" from the previous screen and click "Next". When they saw a screen of traces list, they thought it was the sub-categories of "CCX Engine". Unfortunately, that is not true. The next screen is just a continuation of the previous screen. In most cases, you may leave the checkbox unchecked on the second screen. Just click "Next" to skip the second screen.

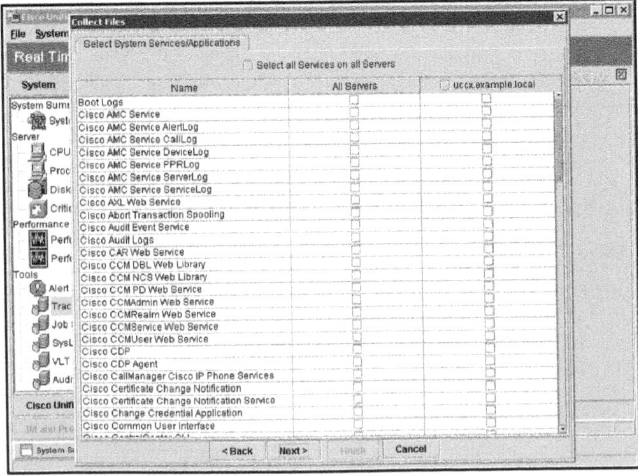

Figure 19-12 RTMT - Trace List (2nd Screen)

The next screen (the third screen) is to choose the time range of traces and download location of the trace files. For "Download File Directory" you may use the "Browse" button to select a desired location. Default location is your "home directory". On Windows platform, it is your user profile directory. Don't know where that is? Go to Windows "Start" menu > Run. Type %userprofile% (including the percentage sign). Then click "OK" button.

For "Collection Time", you may choose relative range (relative to the current time) or absolute range.

Below is a screen of absolute range. If you are troubleshooting an unexpected problem that happened a while ago and you know the exact time of the problem, you may specify the absolute range.

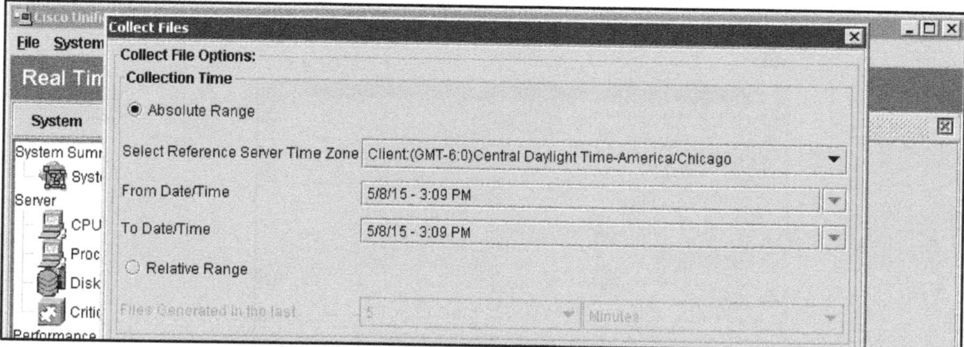

Figure 19-13 RTMT - Collect Files - Absolute Range

Below is a screen of relative range. If you just ran a test, say 2 minutes ago, you choose a range of "Past 5 minutes". This will cover the time frame of the test.

Figure 19-14 RTMT - Collect Files - Relative Range

Depending on the trace and range selected, it may take a while to download all files. When it is done, you will see a message says "Completed downloading".

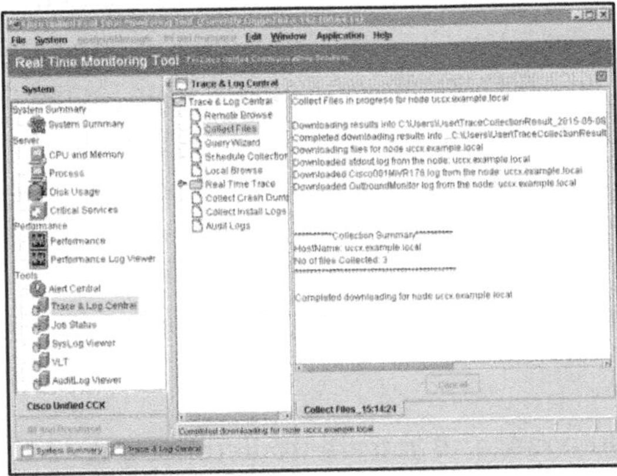

Figure 19-15 RTMT - Completed Downloading

RTMT will create a folder within your home folder with the server's FQDN (fully qualified domain name), for example, "uccx.example.com".

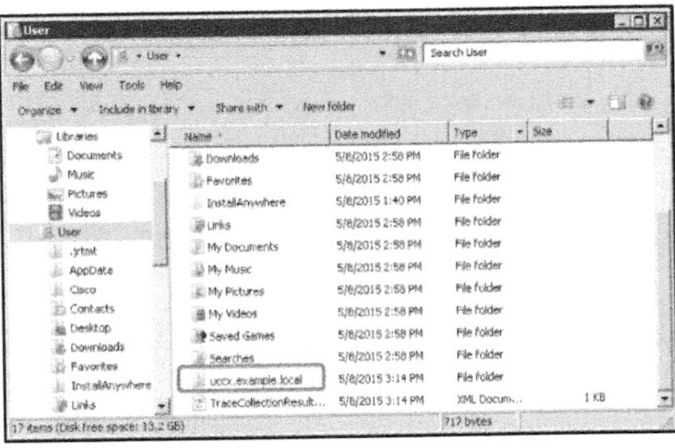

Figure 19-16 RTMT - Download Location

Within the server name folder, there will be one or more folders named with the download time. For example, if you collected some files at 3:14:30PM May 8, 2015, the folder name will be "2015-05-08_15-14-30". If you collected files multiple times, there will be multiple folders.

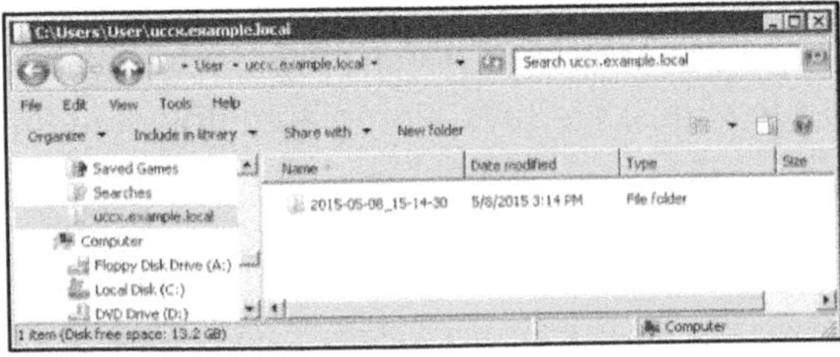

Figure 19-17 RTMT - Folder named with download time

CET (Configuration Editing Tool)

UCCX store its configuration in XML files. Normally, all configurations should be made via UCCX AppAdmin Portal. You should not have to touch those XML files. In rare occasions, there might be a need to change configurations that are not exposed to AppAdmin Portal.

Cisco provides a tool called CET (Configuration Editing Tool) to edit those configurations. The tool is supposed to be used by Cisco TAC or used with Cisco TAC's guidance.

For Windows-based UCCX (7.x and before), you may find the CET tool on UCCX server C:\program files\wfavvid\cet.bat. Just the the cet.bat file.

For Linux-based UCCX (8.0 and above), you may find the CET installer on the UCCX installation DVD (\Installer\CetTool\CetTool.exe). Or download from an already-installed UCCX server for example, http://address-of-uccx/uccxinstalls/CetTool.exe (case-sensitive). CET can be installed on Windows platform only.

After installation, a shortcut will be created in Windows "Start" menu. DO NOT use the shortcut. Instead you should go to the installation folder (for example "C:\Program Files (x86)\wfavvid_1051cet"). There is a "CetTool.bat" in the folder.

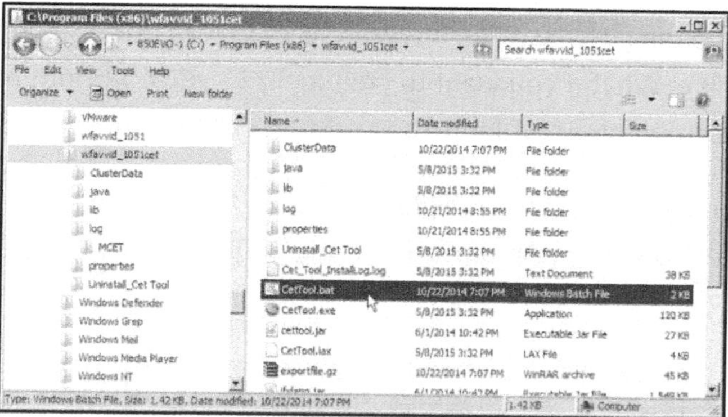

Figure 19-18 CetTool.bat

Double-click the "CetTool.bat" to start the program. The program will pop up a warning screen asks if you want to exit. You should click "No" if you decided to use CET.

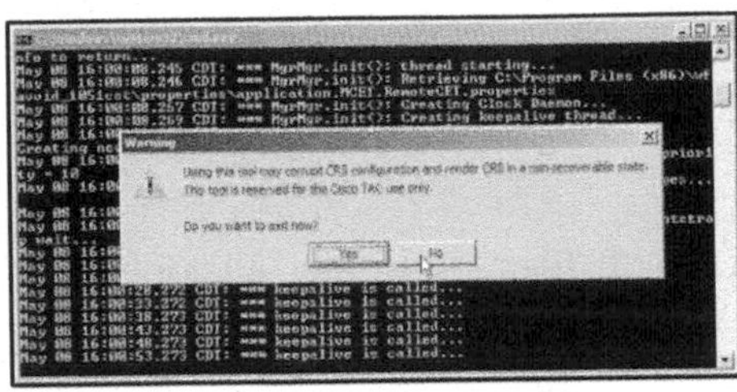

Figure 19-19 Starting CET

Here is the main screen of CET.

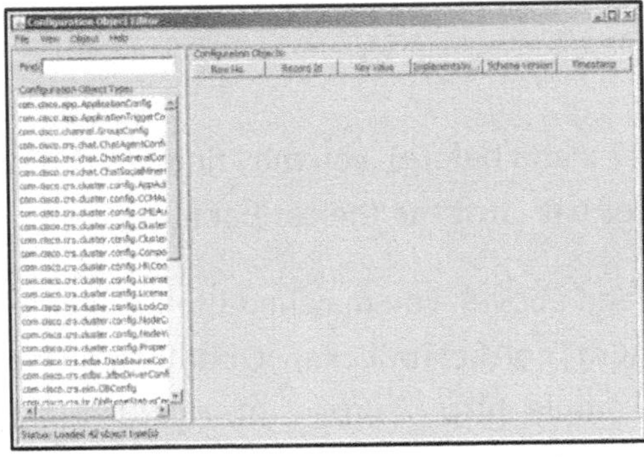

Figure 19-20 CET Main Screen

To make use of CET, you need to know what each entry does in the configuration XML tree.

For example, after a fresh install of UCCX, you have to go through an "initialization process", such as uploading License file, integrate with CUCM, etc. (See [**Initialization**] on page 27 for details). What if you want to "reinitialize" UCCX without reinstalling it? There is no such an option on AppAdmin Portal. But it can be done via CET.

In the "Configuration Object Type" list, highlight "com.cisco.crs.cluster.config.AppAdminSetupConfig". On the right panel, double-click the only record.

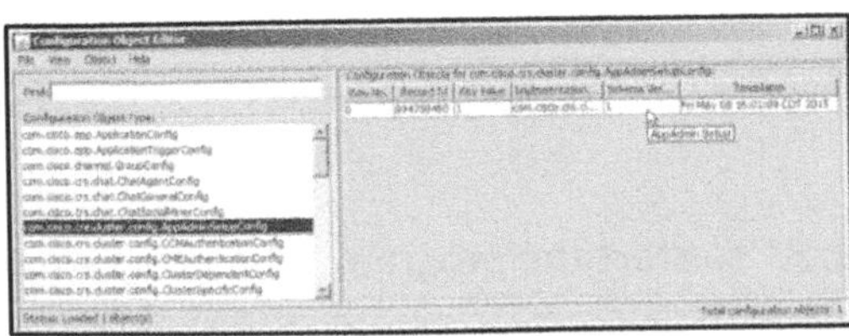

Figure 19-21 com.cisco.crs.cluster.config.AppAdminSetupConfig

A window will pop up with two tabs. Click on the second tab which says "com.cisco.crs.cluster.config.AppAdminSetupConfig".

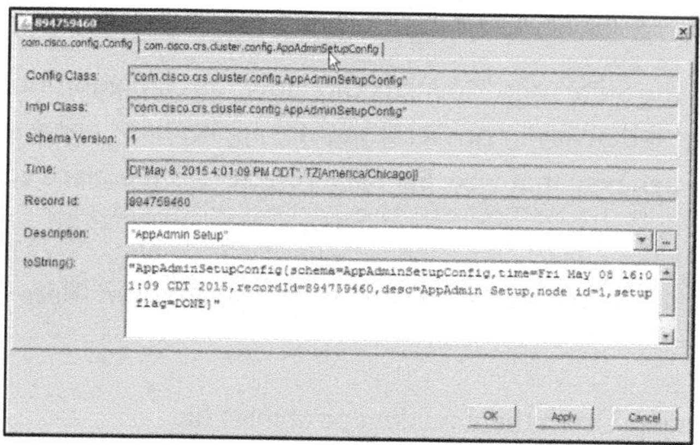

Figure 19-22 Record Editing Window

Click the "Setup State" drop-down menu, select "FRESH_INSTALL". Then click "OK".

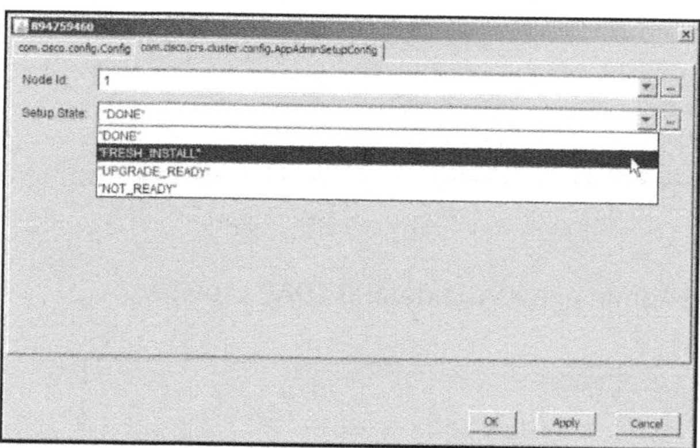

Figure 19-23 Reset to FRESH_INSTALL

If you try to log into UCCX AppAdmin Portal now, you will be presented the initialization screen. The system thinks it just finishes a fresh install.

Above just one of the examples how CET can do something that AppAdmin cannot do. However, if you don't know what you are doing, CET could be a dangerous tool. Always use CET tool under Cisco TAC's guidance.

LDAP Browser

"LDAP Browser" here is a general term versus a specific name. It refers to the software that can read and write a directory service. If you search Internet for "LDAP Browser", you will find many freeware or commercial ware. We will use software called "LDAP Admin" as an example. "LDAP Admin" is a freeware and can be downloaded from http://www.ldapadmin.org.

Remember that Desktop Suite uses "Spanlink Directory" as configuration repository. If you observed unexpected behavior on Desktop Suite applications and want to investigate why they behaved that way, Spanlink Directory is the place you want to look at.

To "look at" the Spanlink Directory, you will need a LDAP browser. Here is what we do with "LDAP Admin".

Launch "LdapAadmin.exe" from the downloaded archive file.

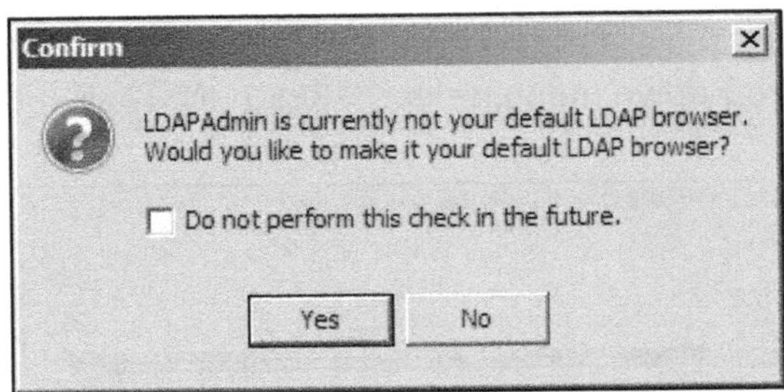

Figure 19-24 Default LDAP browser

Click "Yes" to use LdapAdmin.exe as the default LDAP browser.

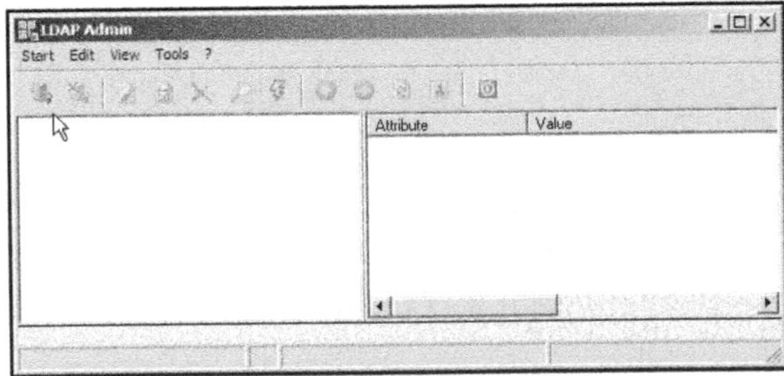

Figure 19-25 LDAP Admin - Main Window

On the main window, click the first button on the toolbar, which is the "Connect" button.

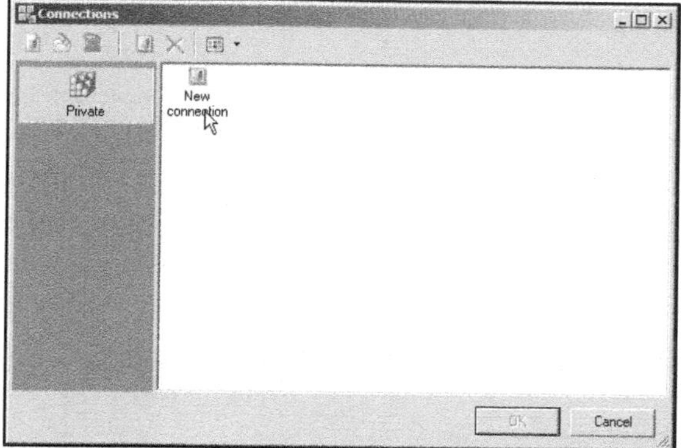

Figure 19-26 LDAP Admin - Connections

The "Connection" screen comes up. We want to double-click the "New Connection" icon to create a connection to Spanlink Directory.

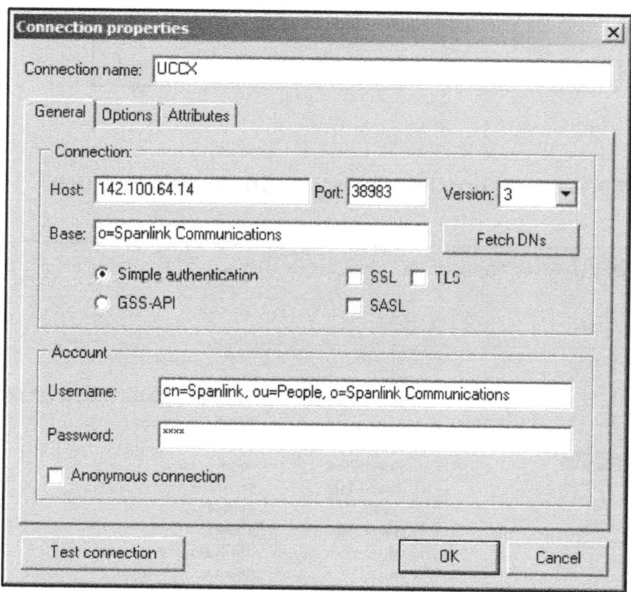

Figure 19-27 LDA Admin - Spanlink Directory Configuration

Uncheck the "Anonymous connection" option and enter the following values:

- Connection Name: whatever name you like, such as "UCCX" or "Spanlink Directory", etc.
- Host: IP address of the UCCX server
- Port: 38983
- Base: o=Spanlink Communications
- Username: cn=Spanlink, ou=People, o=Spanlink Communications

- Password: 5385

You may click the "Test connection" button to test the configuration. If connection is successfully, you may click OK to save the configuration. You will return to the "Connections" screen like below. Now you can see the newly created "UCCX" connection.

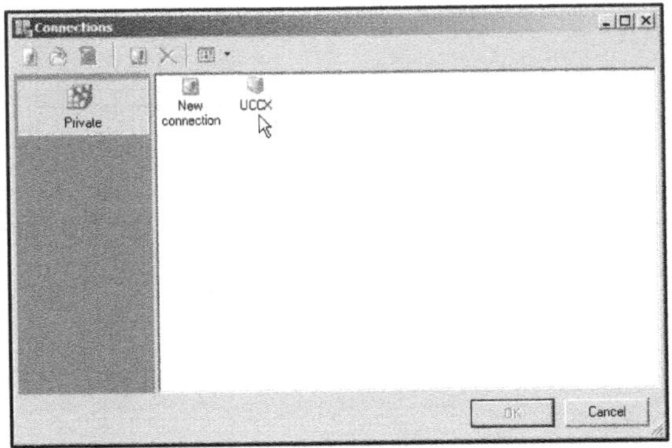

Figure 19-28 LDAP Admin - Newly Created Connection

Double-click the "UCCX" connection to connect to Spanlink Directory.

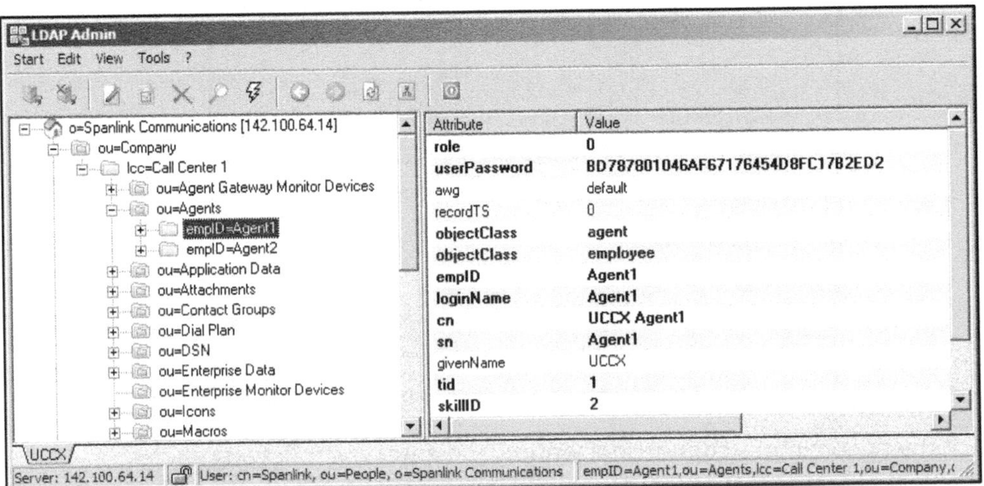

Figure 19-29 LDAP Admin - Spanlink Directory

Now you may expand the directory tree to review the configurations stored in Spanlink Directory. Desktop Suite applications use the configurations here to perform their functions.

What if the configuration in the Spanlink Directory doesn't make sense? For example, you made some changes from UCCX AppAdmin Portal. But the change was not reflected in Spanlink Directory. Why was that?

Remember that UCCX has multiple configuration repositories. The changes you made updates the Informix database directly. But for Spanlink Directory to pick up the change, a UCCX service called "Cisco Desktop Sync" has to do the job.

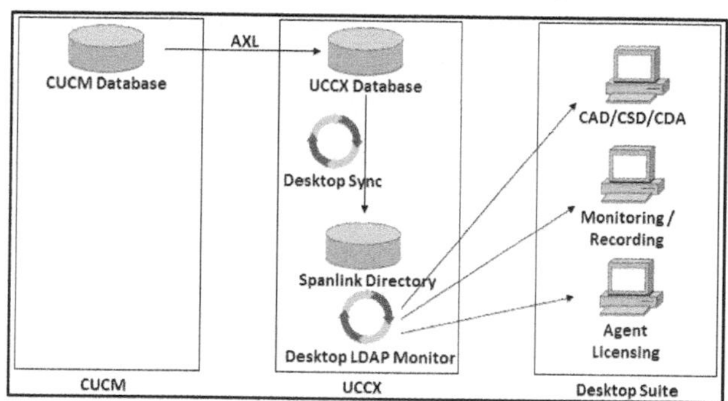

Figure 19-30 Configuration Data Flow for Desktop Suite

As shown in the diagram above, there are two services that are critical to Spanlink Directory.

- **Cisco Desktop Sync Service**: This service synchronizes the data from UCCX database (Informix) to Spanlink Directory (LDAP).
- **Cisco Desktop LDAP Monitor Service**: This service provide the LDAP interface to Desktop Suite applications.

You may find these services in [**UCCX Serviceability > Tools > Control Center Network Services**].

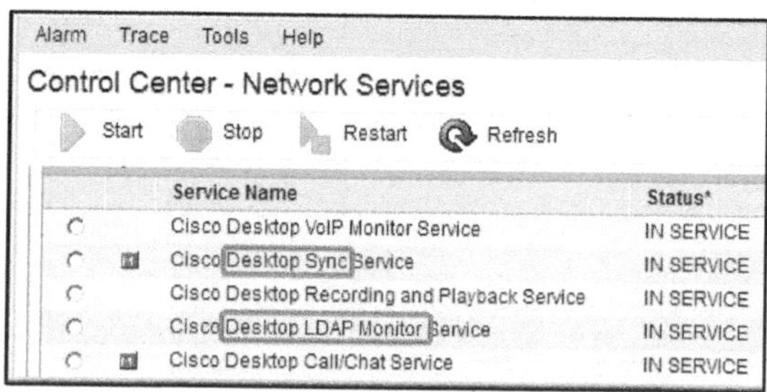

Figure 19-31 Services related to Spanlink LDAP

Make sure both services are up and running ("IN SERVICE"). Synchronization between UCCX database and Spanlink Directory should happen in real time. If you noticed they are out-of-sync, you may manually synchronize them.

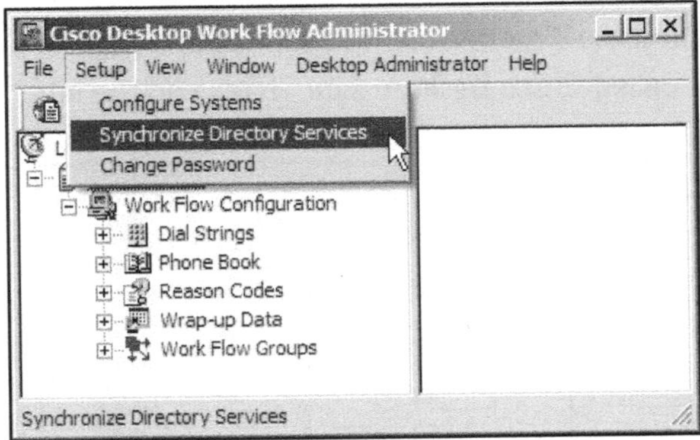

Figure 19-32 CDA - Manual Synchronization

Launch "Cisco Desktop Work Flow Administrator" (CDA). Highlight "Call Center 1". Go to menu "Setup > Synchronize Directory Services". This will force Spanlink Directory resynchronize with UCCX database.

NotePad++

NotePad++ is my favorite text editor to review log files. It is a freeware and can be downloaded from http://notepad-plus-plus.org/. NotePad++ can handle large text files which will be helpful when reviewing log files.

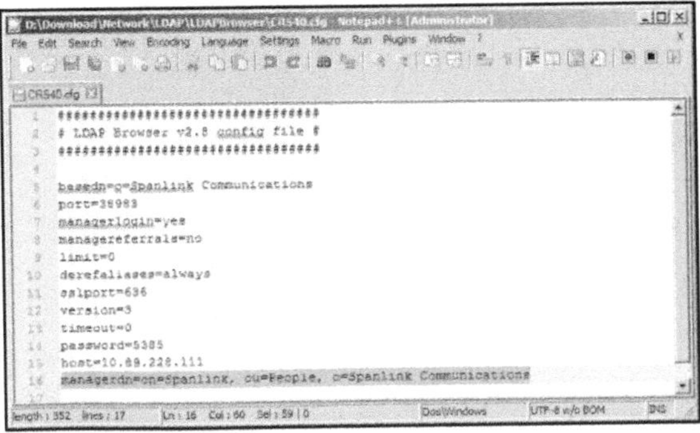

Figure 19-33 Notepad++

WinGrep

WinGrep is a powerful keyword searcher. The name comes from "Windows Grep". Grep is a command line text search utility originally written for Unix. The program's name derives from the Unix ed command, g/re/p which performs a similar operation. WinGrep can be downloaded from http://www.wingrep.com.

After Wingrep was installed, you have a "Windows Grep" context menu when you right-click a folder.

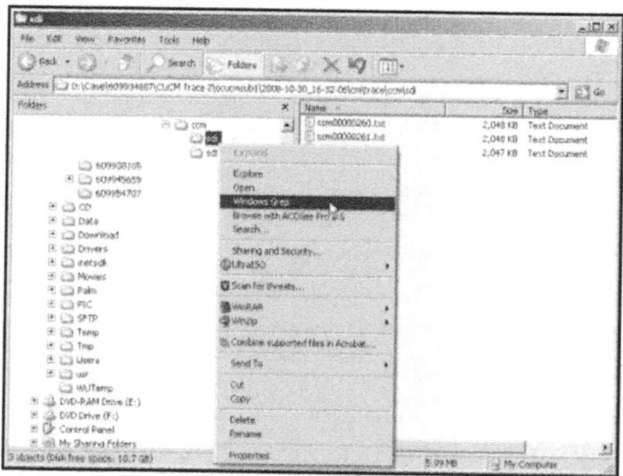

Figure 19-34 Windows Grep Conext Menu

When you click "Windows Grep", it'll come up with a search option Window like below.

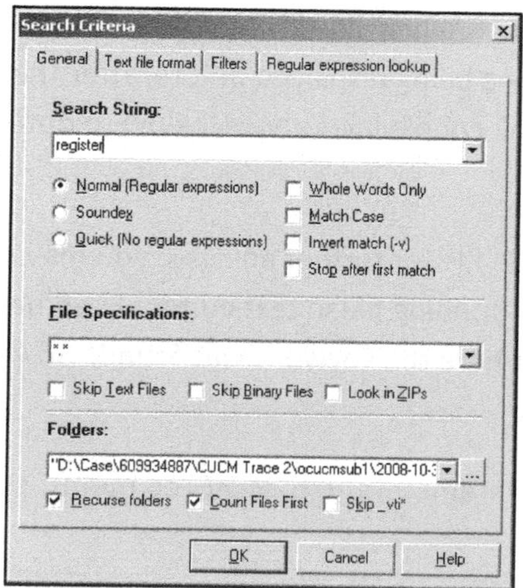

Figure 19-35 Windows Grep Search Criteria

We're not going to explain every option (it deserves another book). You put the keyword(s) in "Search String" box. For example put "register" to search for keyword "register". You put file name wildcards in "File Specifications". For example, put *.* to search all files. Put *.log to search files with extension .log. You may either choose "Normal (Regular expressions)" or "Quick (No regular expressions)". If you don't know what "Regular express" is, I recommend you choose "Quick (No regular expressions)". Below is a sample of search result.

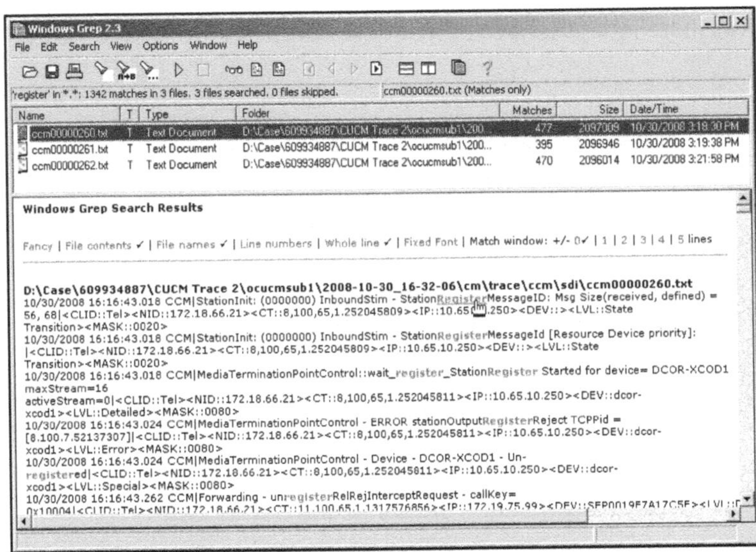

Figure 19-36 Windows Grep Search Results

As you can see, WinGrep listed the files that contain the keyword. When you highlight that file, WinGrep will display matching lines with keyword highlighted. The "+/-" option controls how many lines being displayed before/after the matching line. Sometimes, you'll have to look couple lines above/below to determine if it's really the one you interested.

If you'd like to open the whole file for further analysis, you may click on the keyword. WinGrep will open the corresponding file in text editor. Even better, it will position the cursor at the exact location where the keyword was found. So you can start looking at the logs at the right spot.

To configure the text editor parameters go to WinGrep menu "Options > Preferences > Editor".

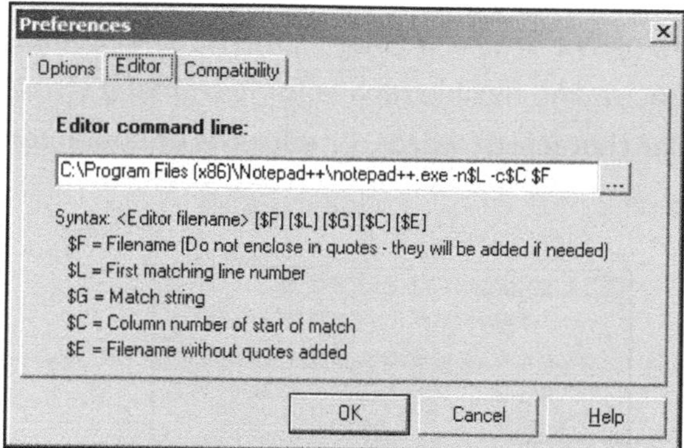

Figure 19-37 WinGrep Editor Command

If you have NotePad++, put in "`C:\Program Files (x86)\Notepad++\notepad++.exe -n$L -c$C $F`" (without the quotation marks).

First part of the command is the text editor's location. In this example, that's "C:\Program Files (x86)\Notepad++\notepad++.exe".

The first parameter is -n, which is a NotePad++ parameter that indicates the value followed is the line number. The $L variable is a WinGrep variable, which passes the actual line number where the keyword was found.

The second parameter is -c, which is a NotePad++ parameter that indicates the value followed is the column number. The $C variable is a WinGrep variable, which passes the actual column number where the keyword was found.

The third $F parameter is a WinGrep variable, which passes the actual file name where the keyword was found.

For example, WinGrep found the keyword "register" in a file "C:\Logs\ccm0000001.txt". The keyword is at line 12, column 34 in the file. When you click the highlighted keyword in WinGrep search results, WinGrep will run the following command:

```
C:\Program Files (x86)\Notepad++\notepad++.exe -n12 -c34
C:\Logs\ccm0000001.txt
```

Notepad++.exe will open the file and position the cursor at line 12 and column 34.

Please note that different editor has different parameters. Please check the user manual to put in the right parameter.

Another powerful feature of WinGrep is regular expression. In computing, regular expressions provide a concise and flexible means for identifying strings of text of interest, such as particular characters, words, or patterns of characters. See screenshot below for examples.

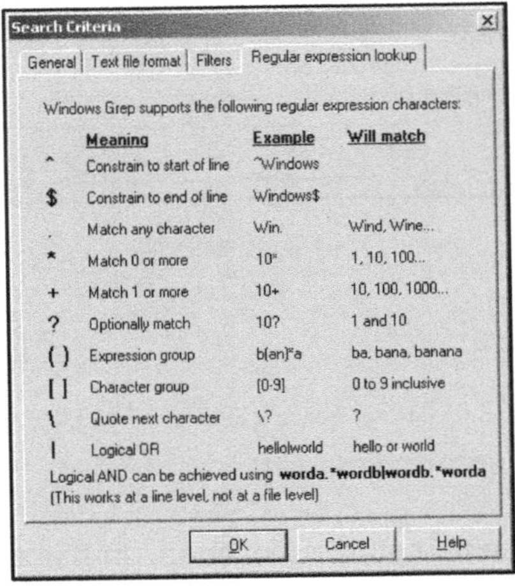

Figure 19-38 WinGrep Regular Expression

What keyword to search depends on the nature of the problem, the logs files you are searching and the debug optioned turned on. It also comes from experience. However, if you really have no idea, you may search for the following keywords:

- error
- fail
- exception
- unable

These keywords usually indicate problems. You want to use regular expression and separate the keywords with pipe sign "|". The search strip will be like "error|fail|exception|unable" (without the quotation marks).

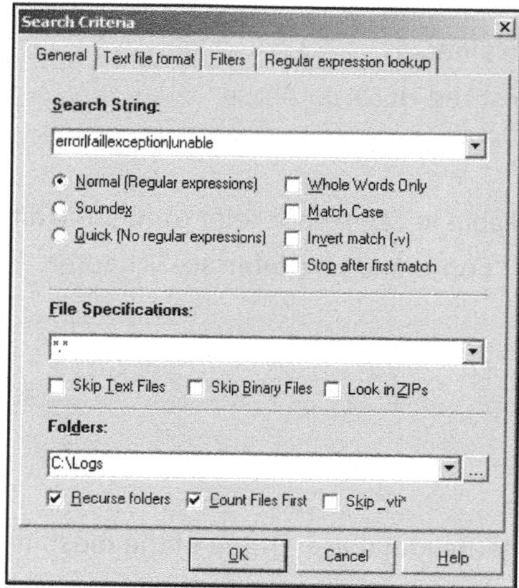

Figure 19-39 WinGrep - Search String

CLI Commands

We normally manage UCCX server via web portal (AppAdmin Portal or Serviceability Portal). However some of the tasks can only be done from Command Line Interface (CLI).

To access the CLI, you SSH to the UCCX server with "Platform Administrator" credential. See [**Platform username/password**] on page 8 for details.

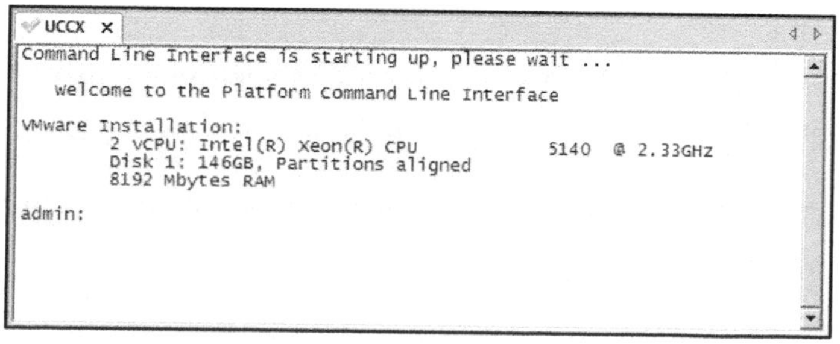

```
UCCX
Command Line Interface is starting up, please wait ...

   Welcome to the Platform Command Line Interface

VMware Installation:
        2 vCPU: Intel(R) Xeon(R) CPU           5140  @ 2.33GHz
        Disk 1: 146GB, Partitions aligned
        8192 Mbytes RAM

admin:
```

Figure 19-40 UCCX CLI

Many tasks can be done in CLI and CLI only such as:

- Reset the AppAdmin password
- Troubleshoot High Availability issues (such as database replication)

- Activate/De-Activate Finesse
- Run SQL query against the UCCX database
- Etc.

For commands that are available in CLI, please refer to [**Cisco Unified Contact Enter Express Operations Guide**], "Command Line Interface" chapter.

Database Schema

UCCX uses Informix as its internal database. Three of the most important databases are:

- **db_cra** – Used to store Unified CCX configuration information, stored procedures, and call statistics.
- **db_cra_repository** - Used to store information related to prompts, grammars, scripts, and documents
- **dh_hist** – Used to store information for historical and real-time reports

If you need to create customized reports or troubleshoot bizarre problems, you might want to know the database schema.

UCCX database schema can be found in [**Cisco Unified CCX Database Schema Guide**].

To query the database, you may use the CLI command `run uccx sql <database_name> <sql_query>`

Substitute *<database_name>* with db_cra or db_cra_repository. Substitute *<sql_query>* with a valid SQL statement.

For example, to pull the Resource IDs and Resource Names from Resource table, use the CLI command below:

```
run uccx sql db_cra select resourceid,resourcename from resource
```

```
admin:run uccx sql db_cra select resourceid,resourcename from resource
RESOURCEID       RESOURCENAME
----------------------
2          UCCX Agent1
3          UCCX Agent1
4          Agent2 UCCX
5          UCCX Agent2
6          UCCX Agent2
7          UCCX Agent1
8          UCCX Agent1
9          UCCX Agent2
10         UCCX Agent1
11         UCCX Agent1

 Command successful.
admin:█
```

Figure 19-41 Run SQL Query from CLI

Here are some more examples of database related CLI commands.

To show the database files on file system, use **`show uccx dbserver disk`** command.

```
admin:show uccx dbserver disk
SNO. DATABASE NAME       TOTAL SIZE (MB) USED SIZE (MB) FREE SIZE (MB) PERCENT FREE
---- ------------------ --------------- -------------- -------------- ------------
 1    rootdbs                      358.4           60.8          297.6          83%
 2    log_dbs                      317.4          307.3           10.1           3%
 3    db_cra                       512.0           21.6          490.4          95%
 4    db_hist                    34508.6         6843.7        27664.9          80%
 5    db_cra_repository             41.0            3.5           37.5          91%
 6    db_frascal                   512.0            3.4          508.6          99%
 7    temp_uccx                   1572.9            0.1         1572.7          99%
 8    uccx_sbspace                3145.7         2988.1          157.6           5%
 9    uccx_er                      204.8            0.1          204.7          99%
 10   uccx_ersb                   1572.9         1494.1           78.8           5%
 11   sadmin                       102.4            5.3           97.1          94%

CHUNK NO. OFFSET TOTAL SIZE (MB) FREE SIZE (MB) FILENAME
--------- ------ --------------- -------------- ---------------------------------------------
 1         0              358.4          297.6  /var/opt/cisco/uccx/db/root_uccx_dbs
 2         0              317.4           10.1  /var/opt/cisco/uccx/db/log_dbs
 3         0              512.0          490.4  /var/opt/cisco/uccx/db/db_cra_dbs
 4         0            34508.6        27664.9  /common/var-uccx/dbc/db_hist_dbs
 5         0               10.2            6.8  /var/opt/cisco/uccx/db/db_cra_repository_dbs
 6         0              512.0          508.6  /var/opt/cisco/uccx/db/db_frascal_dbs
 7         0             1572.9         1572.7  /common/var-uccx/dbc/temp_uccx_dbs
 8         0             3145.7          157.6  /var/opt/cisco/uccx/db/uccx_sbspace_dbs
 9         0              204.8          204.7  /common/var-uccx/dbc/uccx_er_dbs
 10        0             1572.9           78.8  /common/var-uccx/dbc/uccx_ersb_dbs
 11        0              102.4           97.1  /var/opt/cisco/uccx/db/sadmin_dbs
 12        100             30.7           30.7  /var/opt/cisco/uccx/db/db_cra_repository2_dbs

 Command successful.
admin:█
```

Figure 19-42 How Database Files

To get a schema report for a specific database, use **`show uccx dbschema`** **`<database_name>`** command.

```
admin:show uccx dbschema db_cra
 This operation may take a few minutes to complete. Please wait...

 Output is in file: uccx/cli/db_cra_Schema_1431292886037.txt

 Command successful.
admin:█
```

Figure 19-43 Show Database Schema

Because of the length of the report, UCCX put the database schema report into a TXT file instead of displaying it on screen. To view the content of the file, use **`file view active log <output_file>`** command, where *<output_file>* is the filename created by the "show uccx dbschema" command above.

```
admin:file view activelog uccx/cli/db_cra_Schema_1431292886037.txt

DBSCHEMA Schema Utility       INFORMIX-SQL Version 11.70.UC7XA
grant dba to "informix";
grant dba to "uccxuser";
grant resource to "uccxhruser";
grant connect to "uccxhrc";
grant connect to "uccxcliuser";
grant connect to "uccxwallboard";
grant connect to "uccxworkforce";
grant connect to "uccxsct";
grant connect to "uccxcaduser";


create role "uccxHrUserRole" ;
create role "uccxCliUserRole" ;
create role "uccxwallboardRole" ;
create role "uccxWfoUserRole" ;
create role "uccxCadUserRole" ;

grant "uccxHrUserRole" to "uccxhruser" ;
grant "uccxHrUserRole" to "uccxhrc" ;

options: q=quit, n=next, p=prev, b=begin, e=end (lines 1 - 20 of 22527) :
```

Figure 19-44 Content of the DB Schema Output File

To show the table names in a specific database, use `show uccx dbtable list <database_name>` command.

```
admin:show uccx dbtable list db_cra_repository
List of tables in database 'db_cra_repository'  is -
 crsproperties
 documentsfiletbl
 documentsfoldertbl
 grammarsfiletbl
 grammarsfoldertbl
 latestsynchedtime
 promptsfiletbl
 promptsfoldertbl
 scriptsfiletbl
 scriptsfoldertbl
 sysgrammarsfiletbl
 sysgrammarsfoldertbl
 versiontbl

 Command successful.
admin:
```

Figure 19-45 Show Tables in a Database

General Troubleshooting Procedure

Troubleshooting is a sequence of deductive reasoning. Each step we performed should further narrow down the problem (thus closer to the root cause).

The general procedure of troubleshooting is:

1. Get a problem statement.
2. Ask questions to clarify the problem statement.
3. Define problem domain based on problem description and product knowledge.

4. With deductive reasoning, use the quickest and easiest way to narrow the problem domain as much as possible. In some cases, root cause can be identified at this step.
5. Review logs files for the time frame when the problem happened. If log files provide sufficient information, root cause can be identified.
6. If log files didn't provide sufficient information, enable appropriate trace/debug options. Recreate the problem or wait for the problem happens again. Repeat step 5 above.
7. Propose solution based on the root cause of the problem.

We will use an example to go through the procedure above.

Get a Problem Statement

8 AM in the morning, you got a report from the contact center supervisor that "the call center is down"!

This is not a good problem statement as it didn't help us define a problem domain. You want to know the exact symptom of the problem.

Ask Questions to Clarify Problem Statement

You talked to the contact center supervisor to clarify what it meant by "call center down". You were told that no call was coming in.

What does it mean "no call was coming in"? How are the calls supposed to come into contact center? You were told that the customer service hotline was 1-800-555-1212. That is where customer calls come into the contact center.

What happened when customers call 1-800-555-1212? You use your cell phone to dial that number and hear a busy tone.

What was supposed to happen in a normal situation? You were told that customer was supposed to hear a greeting saying "Thank you for calling ABC Bank customer service..."

Now we have a good problem statement:

"When customers dial customer service hotline 1-800-555-1212 they hear busy tone versus greetings."

Define Problem Domain

"Define Problem Domain" means define what could be in the scope of the problem.

On the path of the call flow, there are following components:

- Customer phones
- Service providers
- Voice Gateways
- CUCM (Call Manager)
- UCCX (Contact Center Express)

Obviously, this problem domain is too large to troubleshoot. We need to narrow it down further.

Narrow the Problem Domain

Most of the problems can be narrowed down by common sense.

For example, does the problem happen to all users globally or the users in specific geographic location?

If the problem happens globally, it is most likely a system-wide problem. If the problem happens to the users in a specific geographic location, it could be caused by component that is dedicated to that location, such as a local router, switch, server, application, etc.

Back to our case, we may test different phones, service providers, voice gateways, etc. to eliminate the possible causes. But if you were suspecting UCCX the quickest way to tell is to make an internal test call. This way we can eliminate customer phone, service provider, and voice gateway in one shot.

The diagram below shows different paths when calling from external phone and internal phone.

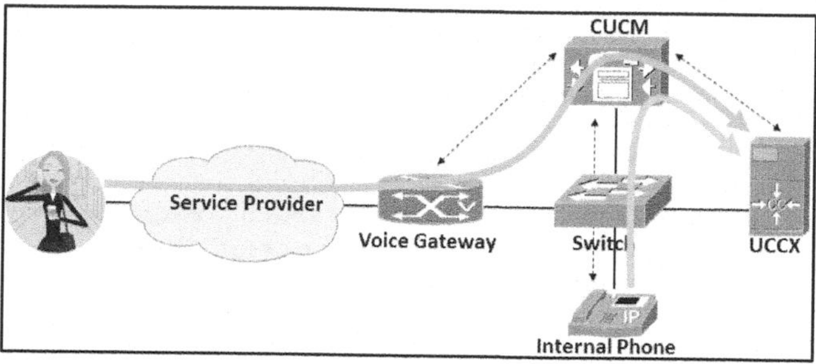

Figure 19-46 Different Call Paths

To make internal test call, we need to find out the internal DN (Directory Number) for the "Customer Service Hotline". Let's say the internal DN is 6000. We dial 6000 from an internal phone and hear busy tone as well. The problem can be reproduced with only CUCM and UCCX in the picture. Thus we can narrow the problem domain to CUCM and UCCX.

Can we further narrow down the problem before collecting logs? Sure we can. And we should.

With UCCX knowledge, we know 6000 is the DN associated with the CUCM Route Point. Let's take a look at the Route Point on the CUCM Admin Portal. We go to [**CUCM Admin Portal > Device > CTI Route Point**]. We noticed that all CTI Route Points' status is "Rejected".

CTI Route Point (1 - 3 of 3) Rows per Page 50

Find CTI Route Point where Device Name begins with Find Clear Filter
Select item or enter search text

Device Name	Description	Device Pool	Calling Search Space	Partition	Extension	Status	IPv4 Address	Copy
RP_6000	My First UCCX Application	Default			6000	Rejected	142.100.64.14	
RP_6001	Remote Monitor	Default			6001	Rejected	142.100.64.14	
RP_6002	OB_IVR_Progressive	Default			6002	Rejected	142.100.64.14	

Figure 19-47 CTI Route Points

With UCCX knowledge, we know the CTI Route Points on CUCM are corresponding to "Unified CM Telephony Triggers" on UCCX, which are handled by the "Unified CM Telephony" subsystem. We should verify if this subsystem is running.

We go to [**UCCX Serviceability Portal > Tools > Control Center Network Services**], expand "Cisco Unified CCX Engine > Subsystem Manager". We notice the "Unified CM Telephony Subsystem" is "OUT OF SERVICE".

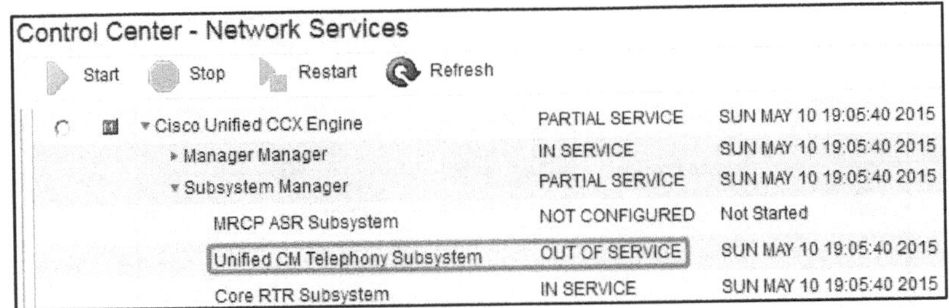

Figure 19-48 UCCX - Control Center

Of course no CTI Route Point will register if the UCCX "CM Telephony Subsystem" is out of service. We just need to figure out why.

On CUCM side, the CTI Route Point registration is handled by a service called "Cisco CTIManager". We want to verify the "Cisco CTIManager" service is running.

CM Services

Service Name	Status:	Activation Status	Start Time
Cisco CallManager	Started	Activated	Sun May 10 10:27:39 2015
Cisco Unified Mobile Voice Access Service	Not Running	Deactivated	
Cisco IP Voice Media Streaming App	Started	Activated	Sun May 10 10:27:40 2015
Cisco CTIManager	Started	Activated	Sun May 10 10:27:43 2015
Cisco Extension Mobility	Not Running	Deactivated	

Figure 19-49 CUCM - Control Center - Feature Services

The "Cisco CTIManager" service is up and running. It looks like we need to look at the log files.

Now we have the problem domain narrowed down to:

- UCCX – Cisco Unified CM Telephony Subsystem
- CUCM – CTIManager Service

We will collect the following logs to investigate:

- UCCX – Unified CM Telephony Client Logs (a.k.a. JTAPI Client Logs)
- CUCM – CTIManager Logs

We don't know exactly when the problem start happening. Thus we don't have a specific time frame of logs files to download. We could download all the logs, which could be thousands of files, may or may not contain the information we need (if it was overwritten already). We need to narrow the time frame and download as few files as possible.

Since all UCCX controlled route points are down, it wouldn't hurt if we restart the CCX Engine, which will restart the route point registration process. It should take no more than 5 minutes to restart CCX Engine. We should only have to download the logs for the past 5 minutes.

Collect and Review Log Files

Turn on Unified CM Telephony client debug options on UCCX.

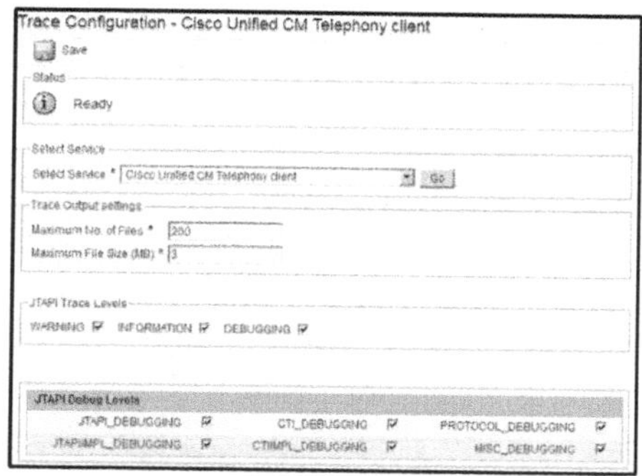

Figure 19-50 UCCX - Turn on JTAPI Client Debug

Set CTIManager debug level to "Detailed" on CUCM.

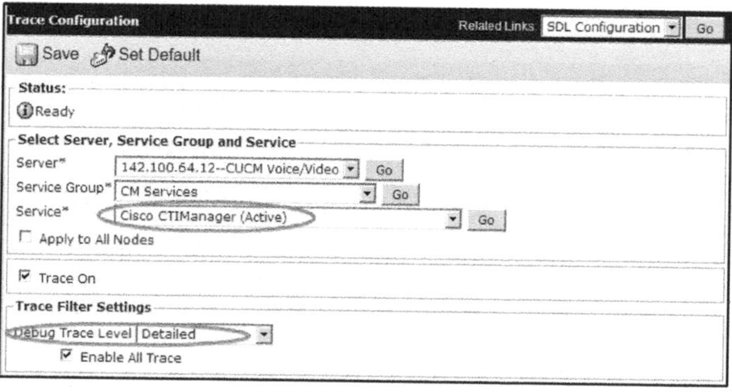

Figure 19-51 CUCM - CTIManager Debug Level

We should get RTMT (Real Time Monitoring Tool) ready before restarting the CCX Engine.

From [UCCX RTMT > Trace & Log Central > Collect Files] choose "Cisco Unified CCX JTAPI Client".

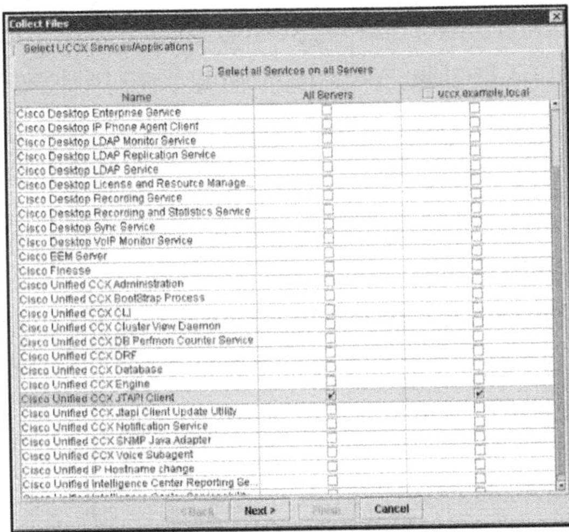

Figure 19-52 UCCX RTMT JTAPI Client

Click "Next" twice to go to "Collect File Options" window.

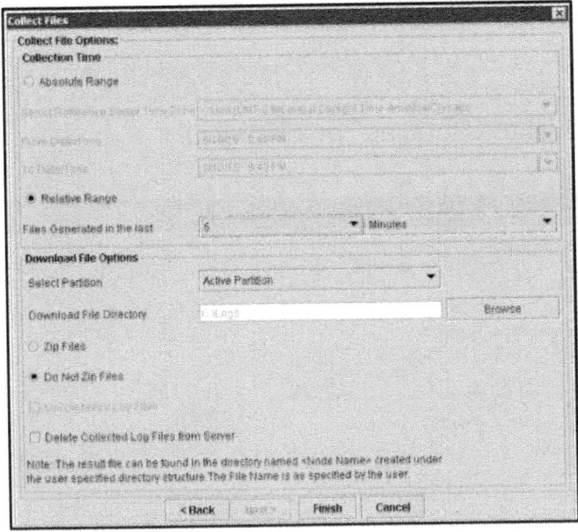

Figure 19-53 Collect Files Options

Select "Relative Range" and select "5 minutes". Select a download location for logs files ("C:\Logs" in our example). Leave the window open. Don't click "Finish" yet.

Launch CUCM RTMT. Follow same procedures except that we choose "Cisco CTIManager" from the service list.

Now go to [**UCCX Serviceability > Tools > Control Center – Network Services**]. Select "Cisco Unified CCX Engine". Take a note of the current time. Then click the "Restart" button.

Move you mouse over the "Refresh" icon on the top of the web page (not the "Refresh" button of your web browser, but the one below the "Control Center – Network Services".

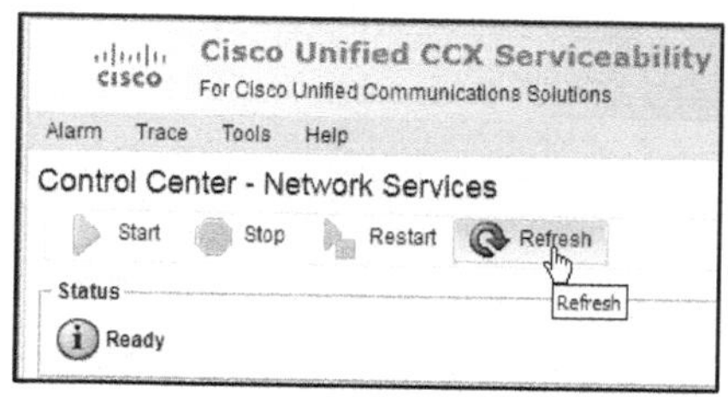

Figure 19-54 Refresh

The icon should be available within a minute or two. Click on this "Refresh" icon until you see the subsystem status change from "SHUTDOWN" to "IN SERVICE" or "OUT OF SERVICE". The "Unified CM Telephony Subsystem" will still be "OUT OF SERVICE", which is expected.

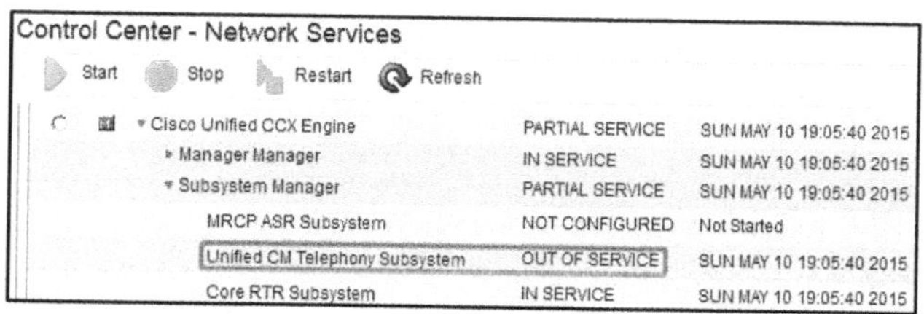

Figure 19-55 UCCX - Control Center

When the subsystems come back to "IN SERVICE" it means the restart has completed. Go to UCCX RTMT and CUCM RTMT and click the "Finish" button to collect log files.

When finish downloading logs, you should have folder structures created in your download location, similar to the screen below:

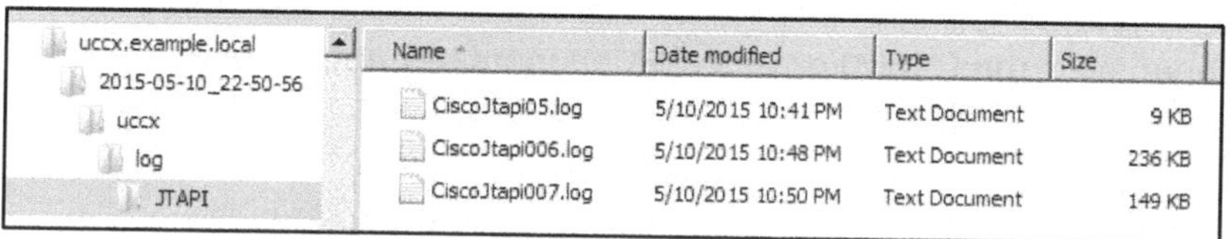

Figure 19-56 JTAPI Client Logs Downloaded

If you don't know what to look for, just do a WinGrep on "error|fail|unable|exception".

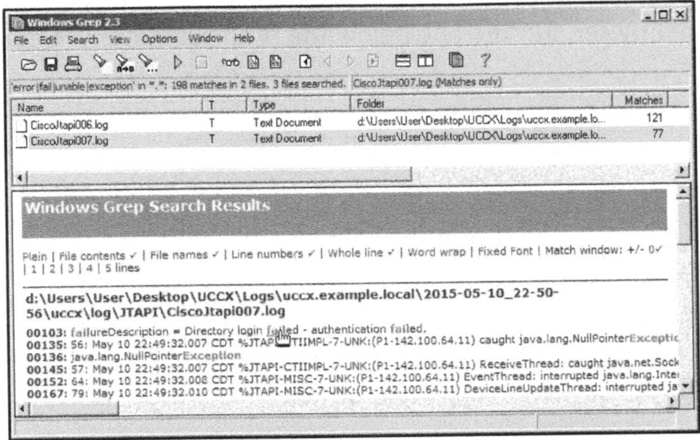

Figure 19-57 JTAPI Logs - Search Results

The first match says "failureDescription = Directory login failed - authentication failed". This seems interesting. Click on the keyword to open up the log in text editor.

```
42: May 10 22:49:31.483 CDT %JTAPI-MISC-7-UNK:(P1-142.100.64.11) DeviceLineUpdateThread starting up...
43: May 10 22:49:32.002 CDT %JTAPI-PROTOCOL-7-UNK:(P1-142.100.64.11) received Event: com.cisco.cti.protocol.ProviderOpenCompletedEvent
  eventSequence          = 0
  reason                 = -1932787616
  sequenceNumber         = 1
  providerInfoString     = 10.5.1.11900-13.i386
  clientHeartbeat        = 0
  serverHeartbeat        = 0
  failureDescription     = Directory login failed - authentication failed.
  bMonitorCallParkDNs    = false
  providerId             = 16778516
  precedenceValue        = 0
  canSupportIPv6         = false
  loginUserName          = com.cisco.cti.protocol.UnicodeString {
  unicodedisplayName =
  count          = 0
```

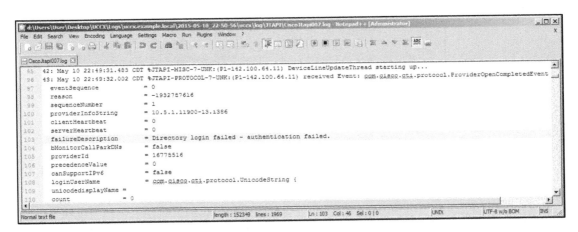

Figure 19-58 JTAPI Logs

By looking at a couple lines above, we realize this is a message received from 142.10.64.11 (which is the CUCM) on a "ProviderOpenCompletedEvent" on JTAPI protocol.

Cross reference with CTIManager logs on CUCM, we got the following:

```
00117498.003 |22:49:32.000 |AppInfo  |[CTI-APP]
[CTIHandler::OutputCtiMessage      ]     CTI
ProviderOpenCompletedEvent   (seq#=1) provider id=16778516 CM
Version=10.5.1.11900-13.i386 error code=2362179680 description=Directory
login failed - authentication failed. enableIpv6=0
NoOfDaysPwdToExp=4294967295
```

```
00117498.004 |22:49:32.000 |AppInfo  |CtiProviderOpenFailure - CTI
application failed to open provider; application startup failed
CTIconnectionId:1300  Login User Id:jtapi_1 Reason code.:-1932787616
UNKNOWN_PARAMNAME:IPAddress:142.100.64.14 UNKNOWN_PARAMNAME:IPv6Address:
App ID:Cisco CTIManager Cluster ID:StandAloneCluster Node ID:cm-pub
```

The problem was:

1. JTAPI Client on UCCX (CM Telephony Subsystem) tried to register the CTI devices (CTI Ports, CTI Route Points) with CTIManager on CUCM.
2. JTAPI Client on UCCX tried to authenticate with CTIManager on CUCM with user id "jtapi_1"
3. Authentication failed thus no CTI device was registered

Propose Solution

Knowing the problem is related to user authentication on "jtapi_1", which is the user ID for UCCX/CUCM CTI Integration, we suspect the credential on UCCX side and CUCM side was out of sync. The solution would be set the password on both sides to the same.

Go to [**UCCX AppAdmin Portal > System > Cisco Unified CM Configuration**]

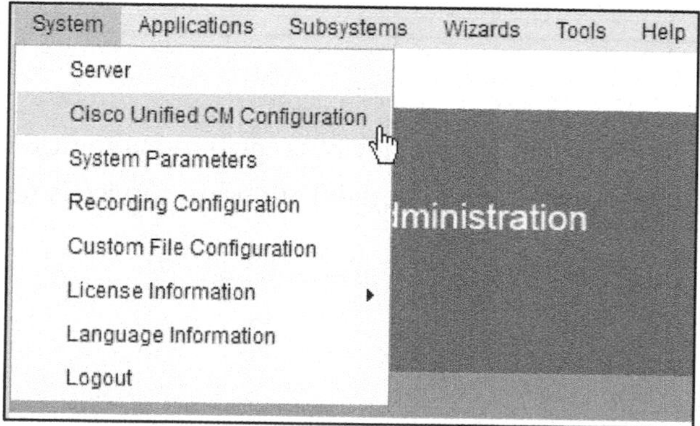

Figure 19-59 UCCX - CM Configuration

Reset the password.

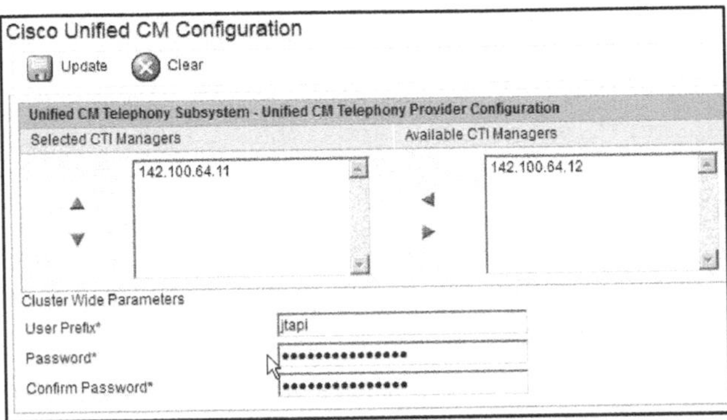

Figure 19-60 Reset JTAPI Password

Go to [**CUCM Admin Portal > User Management > Application User**], find the "jtapi_1" user. Set the password to the same as on UCCX side.

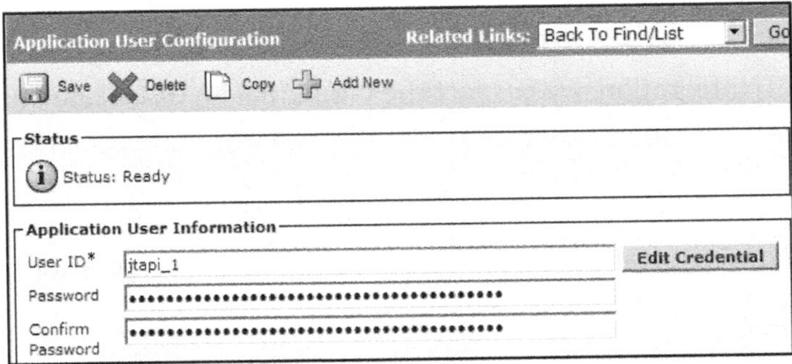

Figure 19-61 CUCM – Reset JTAPI Password

Restart CCX Engine one more time. All CTI devices registered with CUCM. Make test calls to the route point (customer service hotline). Confirm service is restored.

UCCX Logs

Two of the most important types of UCCX logs are MIVR logs and JTAPI logs.

MIVR logs

MIVR logs are the main logs for UCCX Engine. With appropriate debugs turned on, you can find almost everything in MIVR logs. Thus MIVR logs are "must-have" logs in troubleshooting.

Please note that MIVR logs are referred to as "Cisco Unified CCX Engine" in RTMT.

Cisco Unified CCX Engine	☑
Cisco Unified CCX JTAPI Client	☑

Figure 19-62 MIVR Logs in RTMT

Naming convention for MIVR logs is "Cisco*xxx*MIVR*yyy*.log", where xxx indicates the UCCX node number and yyy indicates the sequence number of the file. For example, "Cisco001MIVR213.log" means the 213th MIVR log from the first UCCX node. The sequence number will increase by one when the size of the log file reaches the "Maximum File Size" configured on UCCX Serviceability page. The sequential number will be reset to 001 when it reaches "Maximum No. of Files" configured on UCCX Serviceability page (when the original 001 file will be overwritten).

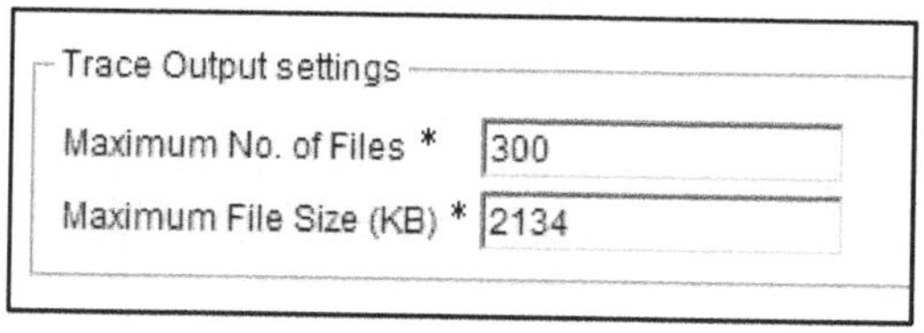

Trace Output settings

Maximum No. of Files *	300
Maximum File Size (KB) *	2134

Figure 19-63 Trace File Settings

Each line in MIVR log follows the same format, which makes it easy to filter out the information we want.

```
1248: May 21 21:48:56.307 CDT %MIVR-SS_OB-7-UNK:GatewayImpl: init, version=1.0(0); based on Cisco Caffeine S
Local: Address=142.100.64.14:5065, userAgent=Cisco-UCCX/8.5, pTime=20, T1=-1, retryCount=-1, rnaTimeout=120
Remote: Address=142.100.64.100:5060, controlTransport=udp
CPA Configuration: events=[FT,Asm,AsmT,Sit], minSilencePeriod=375, analysisPeriod=2500, maxTimeAnalysis=3000
use local Address 142.100.64.14:5065
1249: May 21 21:48:56.607 CDT %MIVR-CLUSTER_MGR-7-UNK:send: Cmd[ServiceStateChangedCmdImpl[1]={0:ServiceStat
1250: May 21 21:48:56.612 CDT %MIVR-CLUSTER_MGR-7-UNK:try to process NodeIncrementalUpdateCmdImpl, nodeId=1,
1251: May 21 21:48:56.642 CDT %MIVR-SS_OB-7-UNK:GatewayImpl: set T1=-1
1252: May 21 21:48:56.642 CDT %MIVR-SS_OB-7-UNK:GatewayImpl: set retryCount=-1
1253: May 21 21:48:56.642 CDT %MIVR-SS_OB-7-UNK:GatewayImpl: udp control transport listen on 142.100.64.14:5
1254: May 21 21:48:56.653 CDT %MIVR-LOG_MGR-6-CATALOG_LOADED:Log catalog loaded: Catalog=MIVR_STEPS_USER
1255: May 21 21:48:56.653 CDT %MIVR-STEPS_USER-4-ON:Enabling WARNING messages
```

Figure 19-64 MIVR Log Content

The first part is the line number, which is a chronological sequence number. Such as 1248, 1249, 1250, etc. in the example above.

The second part is the date and time when the event happened, for example "May 21 21:48:56.307 CDT".

The third part is the component identifier. For example,

- MIVR-SS-OB means "Subsystems, Outbound"

- MIVR-CLUSTER_MGR means "Cluster Manager"
- MIVR-STEP means "Script Steps"

Say, if you are troubleshooting a script related issue. You want to see how UCCX performs each step in the script. You may use WinGrep to filter keyword "MIVR-STEP". You will see different step types. For example:

- MIVR-STEP_ICD is about resource (agent) selection
- MIVR-STEP_CALL_CONTROL is about call transfer

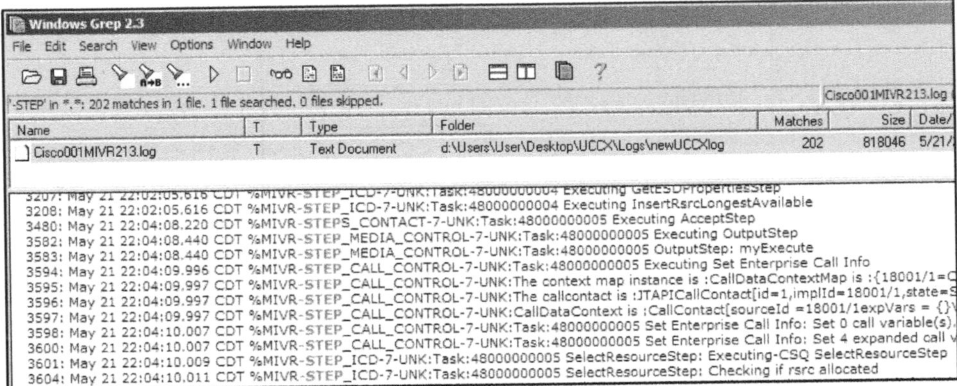

Figure 19-65 WinGrep

Instead of filter by component, we may also filter by "Contact ID". A "Contact ID" uniquely identifies a specific call to the UCCX system. If you want to trace that call, you may filter by that Contact ID. "Contact ID" is sometimes referred to as "Call ID" or "CID".

How do we find the "Contact ID"? We may use regular expression "accept.*contact" on WinGrep to search the log file.

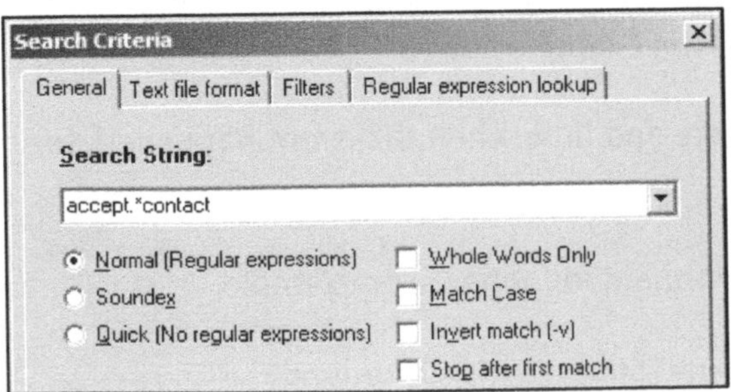

This tells WinGrep search for any lines that has the word "accept" followed by any characters then followed by the word "contact". This is because whenever the contact lands on UCCX, there will be a "ContactAccepted" message with the Contact ID.

```
Cisco001MIVR213.log
actAdapter 0 : ContactAccepted received for App FW contact 0, iefSourceContact is 16795217 [18001/1] (0)
```

Figure 19-66 Contact ID

In the example above, we see the Contact ID is 16795217.

Now we may search 16795217 in the log files with WinGrep.

```
22:04:19.015 CDT %MIVR-SS_CM-7-UNK:ContactMgr.getRmCmContact(18001/1) returns 16795217 [18001/1]
22:04:19.016 CDT %MIVR-SS_CM-7-UNK:ContactMgr.getRmCmContact(18001/1) returns 16795217 [18001/1]
22:04:19.016 CDT %MIVR-SS_CM-7-UNK:RmCm contact 16795217[18001/1] (0) .removeConnectedResource(8001)
22:04:19.016 CDT %MIVR-SS_CM-7-UNK: IEF Contact ID: [18001/1] 16795217 ContactEventsGenerator: Posting the ContactRsrcDisconne
22:04:19.016 CDT %MIVR-SS_CM-7-UNK: IEF Contact ID: [18001/1] 16795217 ContactEventsGenerator: Posting the ContactRsrcDisconne
22:04:19.016 CDT %MIVR-SS_CM-7-UNK:RmCm contact 16795217[18001/1] (0) .dequeueAll(CALLER_DROPPED)
22:04:19.017 CDT %MIVR-SS_CM-7-UNK:RmCm contact 16795217[18001/1] (0) .setAllocatedResource(null)
22:04:19.017 CDT %MIVR-SS_CM-7-UNK:rsrc is:Agent1 in CTIPort 0 .processSessionTerminatedMsg() for App FW contact 1, iefSourceConta
22:04:19.017 CDT %MIVR-SS_CM-7-UNK: IEF Contact ID: [18001/1] 16795217 ContactEventsGenerator: Posting the ContactDisconnected
22:04:19.018 CDT %MIVR-SS_CM-7-UNK:rsrc is null in ICDContactAdapter 0 .cancelSessionForContact(16795217 [18001/1])
22:04:19.019 CDT %MIVR-SS_CM-7-UNK:RmCm contact 16795217[18001/1] (0) .setIaqState(NOT_IN_QUEUE) from QUEUED_ALLOCATED
22:04:19.019 CDT %MIVR-SS_CM-7-UNK:RmCm contact 16795217[18001/1] (0) .setIaqState(NOT_IN_QUEUE) from NOT_IN_QUEUE
```

Figure 19-67 Filtered by Contact ID

When search (filter) with Contact ID, we can see all chronological events related to a specific call. This helps us trace the call from beginning to end.

JTAPI Logs

Remember UCCX uses JTAPI protocol to communicate with phone system (CUCM). UCCX uses JTAPI to answer, transfer, conference, hold and terminate calls. UCCX also use JTAPI to query phone status (busy or idle). The debug messages are so verbose that UCCX put them in a separate category called "JTAPI logs".

Please note that JTAPI logs are referred to as "Cisco Unified CCX JTAPI Client" in RTMT.

Cisco Unified CCX Engine	☑
Cisco Unified CCX JTAPI Client	☑

Figure 19-68 JTAPI Logs in RTMT

If you are troubleshooting a call issue (such as call was disconnected unexpectedly), you want to review JTAPI logs.

Naming convention for JTAPI logs is "CiscoJtapi*xxx*.log" where xxx is the sequence number.

While MIVR logs are self-autonomous, JTAPI logs are usually cross referenced with CUCM CTIManager logs. That is because UCCX is a JTAPI client and CUCM is a JTAPI server. When UCCX JTAPI logs indicate abnormality, we always want to review CUCM CTIManager logs to see why the abnormality happened. Having the time synchronized between UCCX and CUCM will help on correlating the events.

Appendix

Appendix A. Frequently Used URLs

UCCX Application Administration Portal

URL: https://<address-of-uccx>/appadmin
(Log in with admin credential)
Usage: UCCX Configuration and Administration

UCCX Supervisor Portal

URL: https://<address-of-uccx>/appadmin
(Log in with supervisor credential)
Usage: UCCX supervisor tools such as real time reporting, etc.

UCCX User Portal

URL: https://<address-of-uccx>/appuser
Usage: UCCX user options

UCCX Serviceability

URL: https://<address-of-uccx>/uccxservice
Usage: UCCX Service Control, Alarm, Trace, etc.

Cisco Desktop Administrator Web Portal

URL: https://<address-of-uccx>/teamadmin
Usage: Desktop Suite related configuration, such as Enterprise Data, Monitoring & Recording, CAD configuration, etc.

UCCX Web Chat Agent Desktop

https://<address-of-uccx>/agentdesktop
Usage: Used by agents to handle Web Chat CSQs

UCCX Web Chat Supervisor Desktop

https://<address-of-uccx>/agentdesktop/supervisor
Usage: Used by supervisors to monitor Web Chat CSQs

Cisco Finesse Administrator

URL: https://<address-of-uccx>:8445/cfadmin
Usage: Finesse related configuration

Cisco Finesse Agent and Supervisor Desktop

URL: https://<address-of-uccx>:8445/desktop
Usage: Finesse Agent and Supervisor desktop features (based on login credentials)

CUIC (Cisco Unified Intelligent Center) Reporting

URL: https://<address-of-uccx>:8444/cuic
Usage: Contact Center Historical Report

416
1—5

Lightning Source UK Ltd.
Milton Keynes UK
UKOW05f2145110816

280417UK00001B/56/P